THE WORK

OF THE

LONDON SCHOOL BOARD.

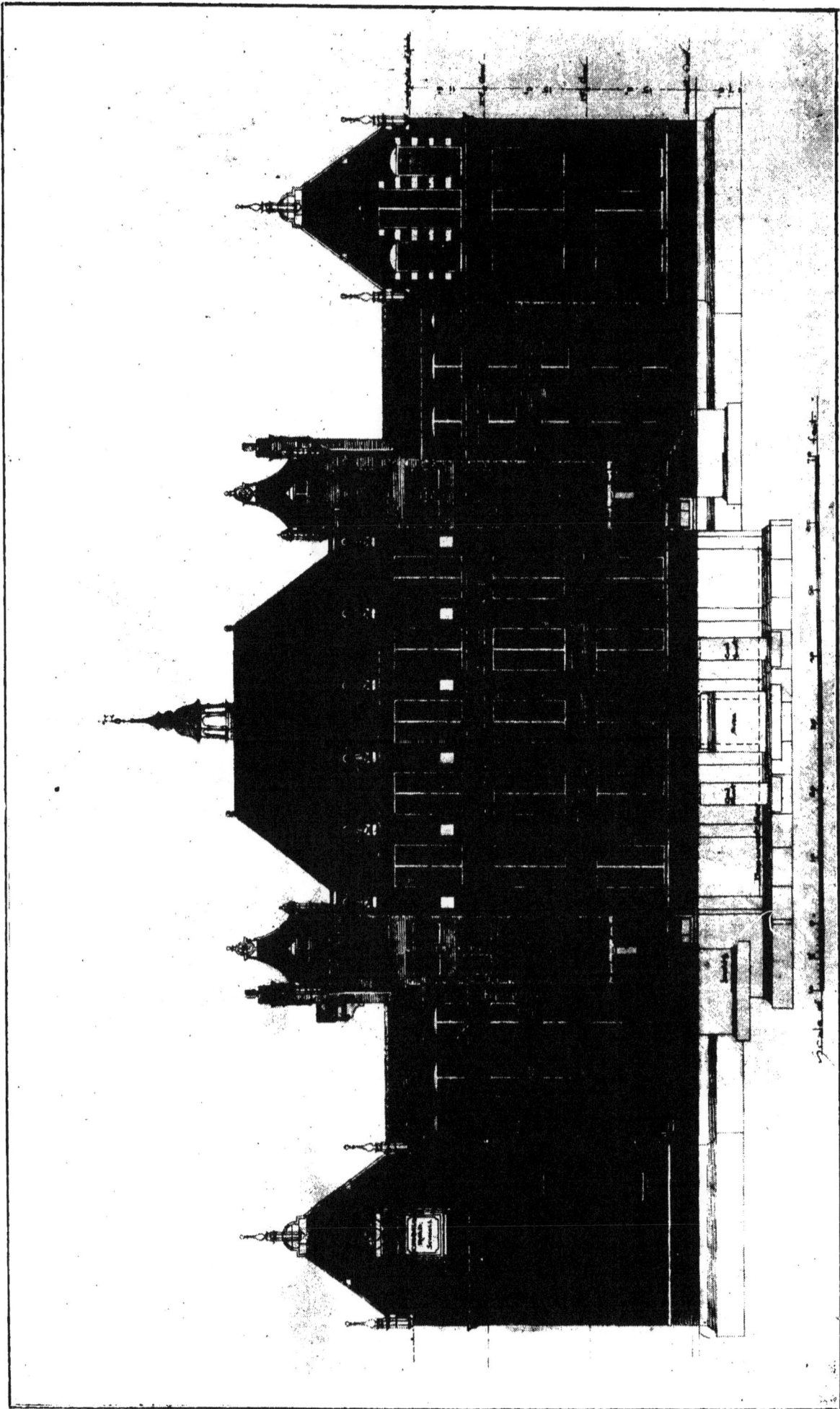

FRONT ELEVATION OF COBBOLD ROAD BOARD SCHOOL.

ARCHITECT : T. J. BAILEY, F.R.I.B.A.

THE WORK

OF THE

LONDON SCHOOL BOARD.

BY

THOMAS ALFRED SPALDING LL.B.,

BARRISTER-AT-LAW, PRIVATE SECRETARY TO THE CHAIRMAN OF THE SCHOOL BOARD FOR LONDON.

ASSISTED BY

THOMAS STANLEY ALFRED CANNEY, B.A.

WITH CONTRIBUTIONS BY MEMBERS OF THE STAFF.

AND A PREFACE BY

LORD REAY, G.C.S.I., G.C.I.E.,

CHAIRMAN OF THE BOARD.

PRESENTED AT THE PARIS EXHIBITION, 1900.

London:
P. S. KING & SON,
2 AND 4, GREAT SMITH STREET, VICTORIA STREET,
WESTMINSTER, S.W.

PREFACE.

THIS volume has been prepared for presentation at the Paris Exhibition by my direction. It is a record of the work achieved by the School Board for London from its foundation, in 1870, to the present time. Although the School Board has only been in existence for thirty years, it has wrought so great a revolution in the educational condition of London that people are apt to forget the calamitous state of affairs which existed before it was established, and the difficult nature of the problems that it was called upon to solve. An attempt has been made in the following pages, first, to describe the condition of education in London prior to 1870, then to set forth the policy of the first School Board in laying the foundations of the new educational system, and, lastly, to trace the various extensions and developments of elementary education which have been effected by subsequent Boards.

It has been the aim of the compilers to record facts rather than opinions. All reference to divergent views which separate parties upon the Board has been, as far as possible, avoided. The object has been to give a broad and continuous view of the Board's labours, without reference to minor differences on questions of detail, which, after all, have had but little influence upon the larger issues of policy. Where opinions are expressed, they are those of the individual writers, and they in no way bind the Board.

It is hoped that this volume may be found useful, not only to foreigners who are interested in the history of education, but also to many of our own countrymen, who find it impossible, owing to the voluminous character of the Board's official publications, to obtain in a convenient form an account of the Board's work.

A

My thanks are due to all the contributors to this volume, who have so willingly responded to my request that they would write upon the subjects which are dealt with under their names; also to those members of the Head Office Staff who have facilitated the somewhat laborious work involved in the compilation of this volume by their valuable assistance and advice.

REAY,

Chairman of the London School Board.

May 31st, 1900.

CONTENTS.

PART I.

HISTORICAL.

	PAGE
Introduction	3
(i.) The Influence of the Reformation	5
(ii.) Education in the Seventeenth and Eighteenth Centuries	10
(iii.) The Education Societies	13
(iv.) Government Aid to Education	16
(v.) The Period of Legislation	20

PART II.

THE FOUNDATIONS.

CHAPTER

	PAGE
I.—The First School Board for London	27
II.—Statistics	33
III.—School Buildings.	
(i.) Before 1870	51
(ii.) 1870 and after	59
IV.—School Management.	
Section I. Before 1870.	
(i.) Curriculum	73
(ii.) The Teacher	84
(iii.) School Book and Apparatus	88
Section II. After 1870.	
(i.) Curriculum	91
(ii.) The Teaching Staff	105
(iii.) The Management of the School	109
(iv.) School Books and Apparatus	113
(v.) Evening Schools	116
V.—Compulsion	120
VI.—Industrial Schools	187
VII.—Finance	148

PART III.

CURRICULUM AND SCHOOL LIFE.

CHAPTER	PAGE
I.—Educational Progress	159
II.—The Ordinary Day School. By S. E. Bray, M.A., Barrister-at-Law	177
III.—Method in Infant Schools. By Miss Phillips, Superintendent of Method ...	189
IV.—Higher Grade Schools. By F. G. Landon, M.A., Inspector to the Board ...	193
V.—The Training of Teachers.	
(i.) The Pupil Teachers' School. By J. Nickal, Inspector to the Board	200
(ii.) Training Classes for Teachers. By W. T. Goode, M.A., Organising Superintendent	207
VI.—Special Subjects of Instruction.	
(i.) Science. By W. H. Grieve, F.C.S., Science Demonstrator	209
(ii.) Drawing. By A. W. F. Langman, Drawing Instructor	213
(iii.) Singing. By A. L. Cowley, Singing Instructor	217
(iv.) Manual Training. By S. Barter, Organiser in Manual Training ...	222
(v.) Cookery. By Miss E. Briggs, Superintendent of Cookery	226
(vi.) Domestic Economy. By Mrs. Lord, Superintendent of Domestic Economy	227
(vii.) Needlework. By Miss S. Loch, Examiner in Needlework	233
(viii.) Physical Education.	
(1) For Boys. By T. Chesterton, Organising Teacher ...	237
(2) For Girls and Infants. By Miss E. Kingston, Organising Teacher	242
VII.—The Abnormal Child.	
(i.) The Blind. By Miss Greene, Superintendent	248
(ii.) The Deaf. By W. Nelson, Superintendent	251
(iii.) The Physically and Mentally Defective. By Mrs. Burgwin, Superintendent	254
VIII.—The Evening Continuation School. By S. E. Bray, M.A., Inspector of Evening Schools	257

NOTE.—The "Report of the Committee of Council on Education" and the "Minutes of the Proceedings of the School Board for London" are, for the sake of brevity, referred to in the following pages as "Education Department Report" and "Board Minutes" respectively.

PART I.

—

HISTORICAL.

PART I.

HISTORICAL.

INTRODUCTION.

THE object of this volume is to illustrate the Educational work of the School Board for London; to elucidate the problems which were submitted to it when it was created in 1870 and the methods by which it has endeavoured to solve them. In order to form an adequate conception of the magnitude of the question which is about to be discussed, it must be remembered that London, for density of population, and for wealth, if not in area, may be compared to a State rather than to a city. Its total population is more than double that of Denmark or of Greece, is larger than that of Scotland, and is only slightly exceeded by that of Bavaria and of Holland. The child population of London standing in need of elementary education is larger than the total population of any European city, except Paris, Berlin, St. Petersburg, Moscow, and Vienna, and is more than double that of Bristol, Dresden, or Prague.

The total sum raised within the administrative area of London for municipal purposes (including education) is equal to the total revenue of Saxony, or Portugal, or Chili; while the sum expended in London upon elementary education alone is equal to the total national expenditure of Denmark, Norway, or Switzerland.

These comparisons convey some idea of the vastness of the administrative burden which was laid upon the School Board for London. It must not be forgotten, however, that they represent the present facts, not the condition of affairs in 1870. During the thirty years that have elapsed since that date, the population and the rateable value of London have increased with great rapidity. One test of this increase may be found in the number of children requiring public elementary school accommodation, which has nearly doubled since 1872. In that year the estimated number was about 455,000; in the present year it approaches 785,000. In the same years the rateable value of London was about £20,000,000 and £36,000,000 respectively. A rate of a penny in the pound produced £85,000 in 1872; at the present time it produces about £150,000.

The vastness of the population with which the School Board for London had to deal was not the only factor which differentiated its work from that which was imposed upon other School Boards. London, in 1870, with all its concentrated wealth, was more in arrear in the matter of school provision than any other part of the kingdom. It was estimated in 1872 that there were no less than 176,000 children within the metropolitan area for whom, if they had desired to go to school, no efficient school places were provided. These waifs and strays of the vast city received only such education as they could pick up in its streets and alleys, or at best in establishments which were schools only in name. The Voluntary system had not been able to cope with the evil either by its own unaided effort, or by help of the subvention afforded to it by Government during the period immediately preceding the establishment of School Boards. Lord Brougham, speaking in 1837, had said, in regard to the whole of the country, that the voluntary school system was able to supply the needs of the annual increase of child population, but that it was incapable of overtaking the accumulated deficiency in school accommodation. And this gloomy view of the question was true as regarded London. Between 1837 and 1868 there was apparently but little improvement in the proportion between the number of school places and of school children.

The main cause of this paralysis was the cost of obtaining sites for the erection of schools. In the heart of a crowded city the price of land runs up to a figure which is prohibitive to the charitably inclined, and it is precisely where population is densest that school buildings are most required. The task had become impossible save by a State or municipal effort, coupled with the power of acquiring sites compulsorily in districts where school accommodation was needed. The problem of London education was so complex and presented such apparently insuperable difficulties, that the first educational scheme of the Government in 1870 excluded London entirely from the operation of the Bill which ultimately became the Education Act of 1870. It was the intention of the Government to deal with the question in London at a later date and by different methods. It was only after much hesitation that they finally decided to apply to London similar machinery to that which they had devised for the rest of the country.

The foregoing attempt to estimate the magnitude of the work devolving upon the School Board for London has inevitably led to an excursion into the domain of history. An inquiry into the subject of elementary education as it exists to-day must of necessity lack lucidity unless some historical preface is afforded. Much of the administrative machinery by which the English system is carried on must, to an outside observer, appear chaotic, unwieldy, and unintelligible. The reason is that the English have no genius for logical symmetry in the creation of institutions. They are essentially opportunists; they build up no orderly edifice; they provide for the requirements of the moment, too often in haphazard fashion. As the need for expansion arises, they make additions to the old fabric without much regard to its original design. Hence it is that the study of English institutions must be made, at any rate at the outset, from the historical standpoint. Their germination and growth must be observed and traced before the apparent chaos can be reduced to any appearance of order.

These facts must justify the following sketch of the history of education in England. It will not always be possible to confine the attention to that aspect of the subject which is now termed "elementary," because at no period can a hard and fast line be drawn between elementary and secondary education. Even at the present time, as the sequel will show, when it is supposed that the cleavage, for good or ill, is more marked than at any previous date, education, nominally elementary, invades the recognised sphere of secondary education.

(i.) The Influence of the Reformation.

Until quite recently it has been almost universally assumed that national education in England was the offspring of the Reformation, and that before that event the land lay shrouded in heathen darkness, unprovided with any means for the training of youth. To the sickly boy who is known to history as Edward VI. has been attributed the glory of having founded the English system of secondary education.

The fallaciousness of this doctrine has been sufficiently exposed by Mr. A. F. Leach in a work of great learning and research, entitled " English Schools at the Reformation." Mr. Leach has conclusively proved that a great number of schools, which have hitherto been classed as post-Reformation foundations, existed long before that great event : that England was, under the Catholic domination, not ill-supplied with schools, both elementary and secondary ; and that the so-called " foundations " of Edward VI. were merely re-endowments ; while many endowments which had previously existed disappeared into the coffers of the State.

As the pre-Reformation schools were mainly if not entirely the creation of the Church or of devout Catholics, and the endowments which supported them were often portions of funds devoted to purposes which were subsequently deemed " superstitious," it was inevitable that they should be severely dealt with by reforming zeal. It is evident that the intention both of Henry VIII. and of the Protectors, Somerset and Northumberland, in the reign of Edward VI., was to preserve the educational endowment while they abolished the " superstitious use," but a combination of adverse circumstances too often resulted in the destruction of both.

The pre-Reformation schools were mainly intended for the children of the poor. They were almost invariably free, and most of the trusts under which they obtained their revenues declared that the benefit was intended for " poor scholars." The reason for this was that training in letters and the humanities formed but a small part of the education of the well-born child. He was brought up to the duties of chivalry, and in contempt for clerkly learning. The duties of the tutor of young aristocrats have been defined thus : " To lerne them to ryde clenely and surely : to drawe them also to justes : to lerne were their harneys : to have all curtesy in wordes dedes and degrees ; diligently to kepe them in rules of goyinges and sittinges after they be of honour. Moreover to teche them sondry languages and other lernyings vertuous, to harpe, to pype, sing, dance," &c.[1]

Even after the Renaissance the gentle-born youth received but a limited education. The tutor of Gregory Cromwell, the son of Thomas Cromwell, Earl of Essex, has thus described the education which he imparted to his pupil : " After he hath herde Masse, he taketh a lecture of a Diologe of Erasmus' Colloquium, called ' Pietas Puerilis,'

---

[1] Furnivall : " Education in Early England," p. ii.

whereinne is described a veray picture of oone that sholde be vertuouslie brought upp, and forcause it is so necessary for hime, I do not onlie cause him to rede it over, but also to practise the preceptes of the same. . . . After that he exerciseth his hande in writing one or two houres and redith uppon Fabian's Chronicle as longe : the residue of the day he doth spende uppon the lute and virginalls. When he rideth (as he doth very ofte) I tell hime by the way some historie of the Romanes or Greekes, which I cause him to reherse agayn in a tale. For his recreation he useth to hawke and hunte and shote in his long bowe."[1]

Such was the curriculum designed for a youth at the time when the love of learning had begun to permeate the upper classes. That it had not penetrated very deep is proved by the fact that an Act of Edward VI., amending the criminal law, provided that a Lord of Parliament, convicted of any felony except murder, should be allowed his benefit of clergy for the first offence, *even though he were unable to read.*[2] The school of the young aristocrat being a school of arms and of manners, the schools, properly so called, were left to the classes below the order of chivalry. Being almost entirely under the control of the Church, their tendency was to educate youth for the priesthood. They were for boys only, the girls finding their education in the still-room and the kitchen. The curriculum was usually confined to reading and writing, Latin, and singing, the subjects that were necessary for the priesthood.

The schools were almost invariably dependent upon a religious foundation. Some were connected with the cathedrals, and of these, which were untouched by the Reformation, many exist as choir schools to the present day. Others were attached to the collegiate churches. Most of these disappeard at the dissolution of the monasteries. The endowments of the collegiate church at Southwell are described as being in part " for the relieving of poor scholars thither resorting for their erudition either in grammar or song."[3] The churchwardens of Southwell petitioned the Chantry Commissioners, appointed by Edward VI., for the preservation of the endowment. " We, the poor inhabitants and parishioners," they pleaded, " the King's Majesty's tenants there, do not only make our request that our parish church may stand, and to have therein such preachers apt and meet to instruct us in our duties towards God and our king as his Majesty shall appoint, but also that our Grammar School may also stand, with such stipend which appertaineth [to] the like, wherein our poor youth may be instructed ; and that also, by the resort of their parents, we, his Grace's poor tenants and inhabitants there, may have some relief, whereby we shall be the better able to serve his Grace at time appointed."[4] The last reason shows that the collegiate school of Southwell had obtained more than a local reputation. Most monasteries supported schools, but these, as was inevitable, were nearly all swept away at the Reformation. Only a few were spared. Thus the Chantry Commissioners of Edward VI. found at Evesham that " since the reign of the noble Prince of famous memory, King Edward III., there hath

---

[1] Ellis : " Historical Letters " ; 3rd Series, I. 344, 345.
[2] 1 Ed. IV. c. 12 s. 13.
[3] Leach, part ii. p. 162.
[4] *Ibid.* part ii. p. 169.

been paid by the Abbots of the late Monastery of Evesham for the time being yearly the sum of ten pounds, with meat and drink freely within the said monastery, to one schoolmaster for the keeping of a Free Grammar School in the said town of Evesham, until the surrender of the said late monastery. Since which time the King's Majesty's receiver of his Highness's revenues there for the time being hath likewise paid yearly to the said schoolmaster ten pounds for his teaching of the said Free School, until the Feast of the Annunciation of our Lady last past. And the said town of Evesham is a great market town, and a great thoroughfare from the Marches of Wales to London. And that there is no school within twelve miles of the said town of Evesham."[1] The school was eventually continued, but this forbearance may have been due to the fact that it was not supported out of the general funds of the monastery, but by a special endowment, of which the Abbot was merely a trustee. The endowment was confirmed by James I., who re-christened the school "The Free Grammar School of Prince Henry." At the commencement of the present century the endowment was appropriated to the Evesham National School.[2]

There were schools also attached to hospitals, which were in those days foundations established for the maintenance of the poor. These schools remained untouched by the Reformation. They probably provided for the poorer class of children, and most of them supplied food as well as education.

More important historically were the schools maintained by Guilds. The Guilds were associations or corporations for regulating trade or for other purposes. Among the benefits which a Guild conferred upon its members was frequently to be found the free education of their children. These Guild schools, like the Hospital schools, escaped, as a rule, the ravages of the Reformation, and many of them survive at the present time as seminaries for secondary education.

The most prolific source of small country schools was the Chantries. A Chantry was an endowment to support a priest to sing for the soul of some person deceased, usually the founder of the Chantry. Some of these were attached by the endowment to existing ecclesiastical edifices, some to chapels especially erected, while others had no local habitation. Most of the bequests for Chantries provided that the singing priest should also instruct youth, and where this was not the case the endowment was frequently applied for that, as well as for its original purpose. The following quotations illustrate the character of the Chantries. In the parish of Thornton, Bucks, the Commissioners of Henry VIII. found "Barton's Chantry, founded by one Robert Ingleton, to the intent to find a priest for ever. And that the said priest shall give yearly to six poor folks continually sixpence the week for every of them. And to give for the livery of six poor children every year to every of them, four shillings. And also the said priest to teach the children of the said town. The said Chantry is founded within the Parish Church of Thornton aforesaid, and is observed according to the foundation before declared, and so is very necessary."[3] The Commissioners of Edward VI. reported that " the incumbent of

[1] Leach, part ii. p. 272.
[2] Carlisle: "Endowed Grammar Schools," vol. ii. p. 754.
[3] Leach, part ii. p. 14.

the said Chantry of our Lady is called Sir[1] William Abbott, and is of the age of 60 years, having none other promotion but only that, who hath done heretofore and yet doth, teach a free school of grammar according to the foundation of the same." In the parish of Mattersey, Nottingham, the Commissioners of Henry VIII. found some difference of opinion as to the object of the endowment. "Robert Buttie, stipendiary priest there," they wrote, "deposeth upon his oath that the same is no Chantry, but certain lands given by diverse men, as appeareth by deeds of feoffment, to find a priest for helping of the vicar there and to teach children, being no foundation thereof, nor donative perpetual, but a priest to sing at the will of the parishioners."[2] The view of John Buttie was eventually adopted by the Commissioners of Edward VI.

Besides all these classes of schools which were connected with some religious or semi-religious foundation, a few schools were established before the Reformation without any such dependence upon the Church. Where no school of any kind existed, the function of schoolmaster devolved upon the priest as part of his parochial work. John Buttie, at Mattersey, doubtless relieved the vicar of this portion of his duties. In the Statute of Provisors, 3 Rich. II. c. 2, 3, which aimed at preventing benefices being farmed in the interests of aliens, it was declared that benefices were intended to be given to honest and meet persons of the realm, "to serve and honour God diligently, and also to keep hospitality and *to inform and teach the people,* and to do other worthy things pertaining to the cure of souls." If the work of a schoolmaster was not obligatory upon the priest, it was work which, in most cases, was voluntarily, if not cheerfully, performed. Parson Evans, in "The Merry Wives of Windsor," is a type that existed for centuries before the days of Shakespeare.

It cannot, therefore, be alleged that, before the Reformation, England was ill-provided with the means for affording education to its youth, or that the Catholic Church had shown itself indifferent to the subject. Nor must it be supposed that the benefits thus conferred were confined to the middle classes. Most of the schools, and more especially the Chantry schools and those conducted by the parish priest, were elementary in their character. No hindrance was placed by the State in the way of parents who desired to educate their children. The Statute of Labourers,[3] which declared (among other things) that persons with land or rent less than twenty shillings a year might not put their children to other trades than agriculture, contained this clause: "Provided always that every man or woman of what estate or condition so ever, shall be at liberty to send his son or daughter to learn letters at whatsoever school they please in the kingdom."[4] The clause is interesting as the first attempt in England to legislate on the subject of education. Four hundred and seventy years elapsed between the statutory declaration of the right of a parent to educate his children and the statutory declaration of his duty to do so.

Indeed, it appears incontrovertible that the effect of the Reformation was to inflict

[1] The accustomed title of a priest.
[2] Leach, part ii. p. 161.
[3] 7 Hen. IV. c. 17.
[4] "Purveux toutesfoitz q̃ chun hōme ou fēme de quele estate ou condicion qil soit, soit fᵃunc de mettre son fitz ou file dappñdre lettereure a quelconq̃ escole q̃ leur plest deinz le Roialme."

a check upon the progress of education, not only by the destruction of schools and the confiscation of endowments, but also by calling into existence the doctrine that education was not a gift to be distributed too lavishly. It was inevitable that the sturdy Protestant should look askance upon schools which were under the domination of the Catholic priesthood, and upon a curriculum which tended to an over-production of priests. The curse of theological controversy had descended upon education—a curse which has paralysed effort and has impeded progress from that time to the present. Even Mulcaster, the great Master of St. Paul's School, was in favour of some limitation being placed upon the numbers to be educated. He advocated the education of girls as well as of boys.[1] But he said that in the investigation of his subject "there be two great doubtes which crosse me. The first is whether all children be to be set to schoole, without restraint to diminish the number. The second is, how to work restraint of it if it be thought needfull. . . . I say this, that to many learned be to burdenous; that to few be too bare; that wittes well sorted be most civill; that the same misplaced be most unquiet and seditious. . . . To have so many gaping for preferment as no goulfe hath stoore enough to suffice, and to let them rome helpeles whom nothing else can helpe, how can it be but such shifters must needes shake the verie strongest piller in that State where they live, and loyter without living? . . . Sure, all children may not be set to schole, nay, not though private circumstance say 'Yea.' And therefore scholes may not be set up for all, though great good-will finde never so many founders."[2] Mulcaster was out of sympathy with the Education Clause of the Statute of Labourers. He by no means desired that every man should be permitted to send his child to any school he pleased. He advocated a legal restraint upon the numbers to be educated, and the distribution of children, according to the needs of the kingdom, to various branches of employment. "Be artificers fooles?" he asked; "and do not all trades occupie wit?"[3]

The position which Mulcaster took up is unintelligible unless it be remembered that the Protestant could not look upon schools otherwise than as seminaries of religion. Later on Mulcaster explained the foundation of his views very clearly. "While the Church was an harbour for all men to ride in which knew any letter," he said, "there needed no restraint. The livinges there were infinite and capable of that number; the more drew that waye and found reliefe that waye, the better for that State. . . . The State is now altered, that book maintenance maimed; the preferment that waye hath turned a new lease. And will ye let the fry increase where the feeding failes? Will ye have the multitude waxe where maintenance waines? Sure I conceive of it thus: that there is a great difference in ground between the suffring all to booke it in these dayes, and the like libertie to the same number in the ruffe of the Papacy amongst us, as there

---

[1] But "the bringing up of young maidens in any kynd of learning is but an accessory by the waye."—"Positions," p. 133. The edition referred to is that of 1581.

[2] "Positions," pp. 133, 138. Mulcaster, however, would have allowed all to learn reading and writing. "And yet by the way of writing and reading, *so they rest there*, what if everyone had them for religion sake and their necessary affairs? . . . Every parish has a minister, if none else in the parish, which can help reading and writing."—*Ibid.* p. 138.

[3] *Ibid.* p. 146.

is betwene the two religions; the one expelled and the other retained." Mulcaster concluded, therefore, that universal education would be a political evil. Catholicism would attract the scholar because it could offer him a better chance of livelihood. "And is it not mere folly," he concluded, "by sufferance to encrease your enemies' force which you might by ordinance supplant at ease? It is the booke which bredes us enemies and causeth corruption to creepe where cunning never came."[1]

Mulcaster's opinion has been quoted at some length because it appears to throw light upon the mental attitude of the Protestant reformer towards education. Mulcaster was a man of considerable ability and breadth of view. He had high ideals in regard to educational curricula, and in his day he was a noted schoolmaster. Yet such a man was found advocating the limitation of education to the few, and publicly avowing his reason to be based upon a fear that education would lead the young to join the Catholic Church.

It is not necessary to trace in further detail the processes by which the Commissioners of Edward VI. succeeded in strangling most of the schools of England, and more especially the elementary schools. It is enough for the present purpose to point out that their action crippled the progress of elementary education for nearly three centuries. The endowments devoted to education, considerable in themselves, consisted mainly in land. If they had been preserved for the purpose to which they had been originally devoted, they would, in the course of time, have increased greatly in value and would have formed a substantial, if not sufficient, income for the maintenance of elementary schools.

(ii.) Education in the Seventeenth and Eighteenth Centuries.

The fate of such elementary schools as were spared by the Reformation was hard. Some lost their endowments by pure peculation, others were gradually perverted into secondary schools; nearly all suffered from a vicious system of patronage which gave the schoolmaster a life interest in the emolument, regardless of his capacity for his office, or of his neglect to perform its duties. The political and religious quarrels of the seventeenth century did not forward the cause of education, and during the reigns of the first two Stuarts not a few schools sank into abeyance.

The Commonwealth period was fruitful in good intentions in respect to national education as well as other matters, but the political troubles of the time prevented their realisation.[2] The curse of religious controversy lay heavy upon the schools and the "scandalous"[3] schoolmaster suffered no less heavy penalties than the "scandalous" clergyman. The Act of 1654, which legalised a previous ordinance of Cromwell's for the ejection of scandalous ministers, included the schoolmaster within its provisions, and a sequestrated schoolmaster was forbidden to teach within the district from which he was ejected. The grounds upon which a schoolmaster might suffer sequestration were not, however, purely political. Although he might forfeit his post for refusing to take

---

[1] " Positions," pp. 147, 148.
[2] The University of Durham was, however, founded.
[3] This was frequently a synonym for "Royalist."

the oath of abjuration, or for open disaffection to the Government, he might lose it also for shortcomings which more nearly touched his fitness for his profession, such as "cursing and swearing," "common haunting of taverns and ale-houses," "frequent quarrelling or fighting," and it was particularly and significantly provided that "such schoolmasters shall be accounted negligent as absent themselves from their schools and do wilfully neglect their duties in teaching their scholars."[1]

The confiscatory legislation of the period, as a rule, made an exception in favour of schools. The Act of 1646 for the appropriation of the Archbishops' and Bishops' lands especially exempted revenues devoted to the maintenance of grammar schools or of scholars,[2] and a special Act was passed in 1650 to exempt similar revenues from the operation of the Act of 1649 for the sale of Free Farm Rents.[3]

The good intentions of the Long Parliament went further than this. There is an entry in the daybook of the Council of State for September 7th, 1650, to the effect that "when the propositions for reforming schools are presented, the Council will give them all possible furtherance."[4] The influence of Milton is, perhaps, apparent in this entry, but, with the news of the victory at Dunbar fresh in their ears, the Council were not in a favourable mood to consider the subject closely, nor does it appear that the propositions were ever presented.

The Parliament appointed Commissioners to regulate the charities existing in the County of Middlesex under an Act of Elizabeth's reign.[5] These Commissioners had to deal, among other matters, with the endowments of schools. In their endeavours after reform they found themselves constantly opposed by the existing governors or trustees. The Act under which they were appointed excepted from its provisions all colleges, hospitals or schools for which special governors had been appointed by the founders to administer the trust. These officials, therefore, relying upon this exception, resisted the attempts of the Commissioners to interfere with the educational endowments. The scandal was so great that the Commissioners appealed to Cromwell either for a special Act to amend the Statute of Elizabeth, or for an additional commission to regulate these charities, without interfering with those who held places of profit in them.[6]

The retaliatory legislation of the Restoration fell no less heavily upon the school-

---

[1] Scobell : "Acts of Parliament," II., p. 340.
[2] *Ibid.* I. 101.
[3] *Ibid.* II. 107, 128.
[4] Cal. State Papers (Domestic), 1650, p. 331.
[5] 43 Eliz. c. 4: "An Act to redresse the misemployment of landes, goodes, and stockes of money heretofore given to charitable uses."
[6] Cal. S. P. D. 1655, p. 265. The following summary of a petition upon the subject of education in 1656 is not without interest : "Petition of inhabitants of Grimstone, co. Norfolk, and parts adjoining, to the Protector. There are in and near Grimstone 100 families, half of them unable to read, and within 4 miles 30 other villages without a schoolmaster. Whereupon, 20 years ago some well-disposed persons erected a school and endowed it with 5 or 6 pounds a year, but through these distracted times no addition has been made, as was hoped for, so that the schoolhouse is fallen into decay, the schoolmaster gone, and error and malignancy like to flow in upon them. But that learning may not be altogether discountenanced, these persons have now provided *a well-affected* schoolmaster and intend to repair the school. Beg an augmentation for the school, which will oblige them to double their devotion." The Council of State thereupon made an order for £30 per annum to be paid to the schoolmaster.—*Ibid.* 1656, pp. 387-8. See also a declaration by Cromwell in 1658 appropriating £1,200 a year out of Church lands in Scotland, to be applied for the provision of schools in the Highlands of Scotland who, for want of such assistance "are but little different from the most savage heathens."—*Ibid.* 1658-9, p. 4.

master than upon the clergy. It was inevitable that the measure which the Commonwealth had meted to the Episcopalians should be measured again to the Presbyterians
and Independents who had succeeded them. All schoolmasters who refused to sign a
declaration abjuring the Solemn League and Covenant were ejected from their posts and
were disabled from becoming teachers of youth.[1] All persons in Holy Orders who had
not taken the declaration of Uniformity were rendered incapable of teaching either
publicly or privately.[2]

It was not until the period of comparative quiet and of limited toleration which
followed the Revolution of 1688 that education was afforded a chance of raising once
more its stricken head. Towards the close of the seventeenth century a movement was
inaugurated for the establishment of elementary schools which was remarkable, not only
for the enthusiasm with which it was commenced and the rapid decay with which it was
overtaken, but also for the manner in which it anticipated some of the more modern
educational ideals. In 1698 the Society for the Promotion of Christian Knowledge was
founded. One of its objects was to promote the erection of schools in each parish in and
about London. The Society and its schools were entirely under the control of the
Established Church. The schools were designed for the children of parents who, by
reason of poverty, were unable to pay for their education. The children were boarded,
clothed, and, in some cases, lodged. The curriculum included reading, writing, arithmetic, and the Catechism of the Church of England. Three such schools were erected
in London in 1698, and in 1714 there were already 117 schools, with accommodation for
nearly 5,000 children.

These schools underwent periodical examinations by the clergy. In 1700 the Society
appointed an Inspector of Charity Schools in London. The establishment of a Grammar
School for the further education of clever boys was contemplated, corresponding almost
exactly to the present Higher Grade school, for which the Parochial schools were to act as
feeders; but this part of the scheme was never carried into effect. Another ambition that
failed was the establishment of a Training School for masters and mistresses. Efficient
teachers were in those days hard to obtain, although the qualifications demanded were
not exacting. Beyond membership of the Church of England and certain moral
attributes, they were required to write a good hand and to have a knowledge of
arithmetic. In the cases of mistresses the two latter qualifications were not peremptorily
insisted upon. The cost of this scheme of education was necessarily heavy, but great
enthusiasm was shown in raising funds for it. In the course of time the benefactions
acquired were so great that the schools became practically endowed. But popular
interest in them was not maintained; inspection ceased, and the practice of regarding
the teacher as vested with a life interest in his emoluments, without regard to his ability
for the performance of his duties—a practice which had ruined the older endowed
schools—became almost universal. By the middle of the eighteenth century the
system was no longer expansive, and an educational movement which had commenced with great promise of success died out. Many of the better endowed

[1] Act of Uniformity, 14 Car. II. c. 4.   [2] The "Five Mile" Act, 17 Car. II. c. 2.

charity schools exist at the present day; the poorer ones gradually came under the control of the National Society during the earlier part of the present century.[1]

At the close of the seventeenth century a movement commenced which hardly deserves to be treated as educational, but cannot be ignored in any review of the progress of education in England because, for a time, a wholly unreasonable amount of importance was attached to it. In 1783, Robert Raikes, a printer of Gloucester, established, with the assistance of a clergyman of the Church of England, a free Sunday school, in which religious and secular instruction were combined. Similar schools soon sprang up in every part of the country. It was part of the scheme that the teachers in these schools should be paid, and, as far as possible, qualified for the work of instruction; but before long the Sunday schools fell entirely into the hands of voluntary helpers, the greater proportion of whom mistook their zeal to serve for the ability to serve effectually. In 1785, a Society was formed for the support of Sunday schools, and the Sunday School Union, which still exists, was founded in 1803.

Whatever may have been the value of the religious instruction imparted in these schools, a question which it is not within the scope of this inquiry to discuss, the value of the secular training afforded was infinitesimal. Three or four hours a week, even if they had been devoted exclusively to elementary education, was too short a time to produce satisfactory results; but in all cases the secular was subordinated to the religious teaching.

The Sunday school continued as an offshoot of the system of elementary education until 1870. At the present time it confines its energies to its proper province. In 1858, in the small district in South London which was subjected to the investigations of the Assistant Commissioner to the Newcastle Commission, there were 144 Sunday schools with a roll of more than 27,500 scholars. The character and value of the teaching given in them are thus appraised by the Assistant Commissioner: " The instruction in all Sunday schools, whether of the Established or of Dissenting Churches, or even non-denominational, is certainly not secular, but as purely as possible religious, that is, theological. In no one instance have I found writing taught, and reading is taught only incidentally and by means of Bible lessons. In one school I found a class of infants being taught their letters, but even here every letter was made a peg on which to hang a Scripture narrative—' A ' standing for Abraham or Abel, instead of Archer or Apple-pie of the ancient primers."[2]

(iii.) THE EDUCATION SOCIETIES.

While Robert Raikes and his supporters were engaged in extending the Sunday school system, more important educational developments were pending. In 1798 Dr. Bell published his " Experiment in Education," made at Madras, and at about the same time Joseph Lancaster opened his school at his father's house in St. George's Fields.

The system of teaching advocated by these two pioneers of education was practically

---

[1] *See* Bartley : " Schools for the People,"
pp. 325 *et seq.*

[2] Newcastle Commission Report, vol. iii. p. 495.

identical. Both proposed that the difficulty caused by the expense of a school staff should be overcome by adopting the system of "mutual instruction," or monitorial system. Dr. Bell defined it as "a school conducted by a single master or superintendent, through the agency of the scholars themselves." Joseph Lancaster defined it more courageously as "the division of a school into classes," whereby, with "the assistance of monitors, one master was able to conduct a school ot 1,000 children."

There was nothing so antagonistic in the two schemes as to suggest or even to countenance rivalry between them. But unfortunately each scheme was taken up and advocated by different religious bodies, and united action thenceforth became impossible. In 1808 the Royal Lancastrian Institution was founded, which in 1814 changed its name to "The British and Foreign School Society." In 1811 the National Society was founded for the purpose of putting into operation Dr. Bell's system. This Society laid down as its fundamental principle that "the national religion of the country should be made the foundation of national education, which should be the first and chief thing taught to the poor, according to the excellent liturgy and catechism provided by our Church for that purpose." The fundamental rule of the British and Foreign School Society, on the other hand, was "the introduction of the sacred Scriptures without note or comment, to the exclusion of the formularies of any particular Church." The National Society was supported entirely by members of the Church of England, the British and Foreign School Society was supported in the main by Dissenters. The National Society has always been the richest and most influential of all the educational societies, and has supported by far the greatest number of schools. It still remains one of the most important educational influences in England. The lack of distinctive religious teaching in the British schools differentiated them hardly at all from Board schools when the latter were established, and they have been, to a very great extent, absorbed into the Board school system. Comparatively few National schools, on the other hand, have been transferred to School Boards.

It will be convenient to conclude the account of the establishment of educational societies without regard to strict historical sequence of educational events. The first infant school was established in 1818, and in 1836 the Home and Colonial Infant School Society was founded for the extension of infant schools. This society did excellent work, more especially in training teachers in the Froebelian methods, and introducing those methods into English schools.

In 1837 the Educational Committee of the Wesleyan Conference was first elected to superintend all day, evening, and Sunday schools in connection with the Wesleyan body. At that time there were only about thirty Wesleyan day schools in existence, but the number subsequently increased rapidly.

In 1843 the Congregational Board of Education was formed. Children belonging to the Congregational body had, up to that date, been educated in the schools of the British and Foreign School Society. The cause of the secession of the Congregationalists from the parent society was disapproval of the acceptance of Government grants for the British schools. The seceders held that such acceptance was dangerous to religious liberty. They feared that Government inspection would be followed by interference with religious teaching. The fundamental principle of the new Congregational Board, therefore, was that schools under their control should be supported entirely by voluntary effort.

The Ragged School Union was founded in 1844 to promote the education of the waifs and strays of great cities. The Union was formed to support and extend the work among the semi-criminal classes which had already been begun by zealous but not too well educated persons in various parts of the country. The education provided was of an extremely elementary character, and was entirely gratuitous. Meals and clothing were also occasionally supplied to the scholars. In 1844 there were twenty such schools in London. In 1870 there were about 200, educating 23,000 pupils. The Ragged Schools endeavoured to deal with a class of children for whom the Industrial or Reformatory School system would have been better adapted.[1] Most of these schools disappeared after the establishment of School Boards.

In 1845 the " Catholic Institute " was founded to promote the education of poor Roman Catholics. It was superseded in 1847 by the Catholic Poor-School Committee, which still exercises its functions. Catholic schools received no help from Government until 1849. The Jewish community also, from so early a date as 1817, have maintained separate and highly efficient schools for the education of their co-religionists, in which especial attention is paid to instruction in Hebrew. The Jewish Voluntary Schools Association, founded in 1897, deals only with the allocation of the grant in aid of these schools, under the provisions of the Voluntary Schools Act, 1897.

It will be seen, therefore, that the work of elementary education, from the early part of the century until 1834, when the first Government assistance was granted, was carried on almost entirely by the two great bodies, the National Society and the British and Foreign School Society. Much will be said in subsequent pages, when it becomes necessary to advert to the educational condition of the earlier schools, which may appear to depreciate the noble work which was done by these Societies. This result will ensue solely because the earlier efforts will have to be compared with more recent educational development. The immense service which was rendered to the cause of education by the enthusiasm and self-sacrifice of those who, when Governments were apathetic, determined, at all costs, to grapple with an ever-growing national disgrace by increasing the supply of public elementary schools, ought never to be forgotten. If there were any danger that their work in the earlier part of the century should fall into oblivion, the following account, by one of the first Inspectors, of the results of the establishment of a Voluntary school in one of the worst districts of London, should save it from that fate :—

" As an example of what may be effected in a short time by good management, I would instance the school in the Potteries at Kensington. This quarter, almost unknown to the neighbourhood, was but lately in a deplorable condition. The manners of the people were coarse and brutal, and the children grew up neglected and without the means of education." Then a school was established. " I visited it a month after it

---

See Report of Newcastle Commission, vol. iii. p. 381.

was built," the Inspector continues, "and a second time nine months later. The change which had taken place was most extraordinary. . . . The most pleasing and promising symptom was the improvement which had manifestly taken place in the habits and character of the children. Their countenances had undergone a change, the light of intelligence was kindled in their eyes, and discipline, which at first could hardly be maintained with severity and unrelaxing attention, was this time evidently preserved by the influence of the master and of those children who had been long enough in the school to feel both deference and affection for him."[1]

(iv.) GOVERNMENT AID TO EDUCATION.

The work of the two Societies attracted public attention to the condition of education in England. In 1816 the question was taken up by Mr. Brougham (afterwards Lord Brougham), who for many years remained the foremost advocate of State responsibility for National Education. In that year he obtained the appointment of a Select Committee of the House of Commons, to inquire into the state of education in London Westminster and Southwark. This Committee reported that there were 130,000 children living in those districts for whom no school accommodation was provided. The chief recommendation of the Committee was that Government should make a grant in aid of school building.[2] In 1818 Brougham obtained the appointment of a second Select Committee, with a more general instruction " to inquire into the education of the lower orders." The great lack of all means of educating the masses which these reports disclosed afforded Brougham the material upon which he based his first appeal to Parliament to legislate upon the subject. In 1820 he introduced into the House of Commons " a Bill for the better promoting the means of education for His Majesty's subjects in England and Wales." It was proposed by the Bill to levy, as an addition to the Poor Rate, a rate of not more than fourpence in the pound to form a fund for the remuneration of schoolmasters, and the Treasury was to be empowered to make building grants when a deficiency of school accommodation was reported to Quarter Sessions. The Bill was violently opposed by Dissenters, who saw in it a malign endeavour to extend the influence of the Church of England over all elementary schools, and it was in consequence withdrawn.

Brougham did not repeat his attempt to obtain legislation upon the question until 1835 ; but before that date one portion of his proposals had been adopted by the Government. In 1834 commenced the new era of Government Aid to Elementary Education. The House of Commons voted a sum of £20,000 a year for building-grants to schools. The grant was administered by the Treasury. The actual amount so dispensed was insignificant, but the grant was important, in that it marked a change of policy towards education. Applications for a share of the grant were referred to the two great educational Societies, who inquired into them and reported to the Treasury whether the applicants were deserving of help. No application was entertained unless one-half of the

---

[1] Education Department Report, 1844, vol. ii. p. 149, 150.   [2] Report, vol. iii. p. 57.

proposed expenditure was raised by private contribution. This system prevailed until 1839.

In the meantime Brougham had made two more unsuccessful efforts to pass a Bill for the organisation of education—in 1835 and again in 1837. By the latter Bill he proposed to create a Board of Education to distribute the Parliamentary grant, and to confer with local authorities as to the provision of schools. These local authorities were to be the Municipal Councils in corporate boroughs, and in rural districts, Education Committees elected by such parishes as desired to establish them. They were empowered to draft schemes for the provision of education in their districts, and to submit them to the Board of Education. If the schemes were approved by the Board, they were to be carried into effect by means of a rate levied by the local authority. Religious teaching was to be given in every school, subject to a conscience clause in favour of Jews and Catholics. The Bill never reached a second reading,[1] but as in the case of the abortive Bill of 1820, it bore fruit. Another Select Committee of the House of Commons, to inquire into the state of education in large towns, was appointed in 1837. This Committee, in 1838, stated the result of their inquiries with commendable terseness. They said "(1) That the kind of education given to the children of the working classes is lamentably deficient; (2) that it extends (bad as it is) to but a small proportion of those who ought to receive it; (3) that without (*sic*) some strenuous and persevering efforts be made on the part of the Government, the greatest evils to all classes may follow from this neglect."[2] These declarations were excellent for their definiteness. Unfortunately the recommendations of the Committee were not correspondingly definite. All they were prepared to advise was that the Treasury grants should be continued and extended.

The result of this recommendation was the partial adoption of Brougham's scheme for the establishment of a Board of Education. Lord Melbourne's Government, in 1839, proposed that the grant for erecting schools should be increased to £30,000 a year, and that it should be administered by a Committee of the Privy Council, which should be empowered to assist all elementary schools, and not merely those connected with the two educational Societies. The new Committee was to appoint inspectors of schools, to report upon the efficiency of schools, and a Normal School for the training of teachers was to be established. This scheme pleased nobody. Brougham derisively called attention to the fact that, while Parliament was proposing to spend £30,000 on National Education, it had voted more than double that amount for the Queen's stables. Churchmen feared that their control over National Education would slip away from them and be concentrated in the hands of politicians. Neither Churchmen nor Dissenters relished the prospect of Catholics sharing in the benefits of the grant. After an acrimonious debate and the abandonment of the proposal for a Normal School, the resolution was only carried by a majority of two. In the House of Lords a hostile resolution was carried on the motion of the then Archbishop of Canterbury by 229 to 118, and an address to the Crown

---

[1] Brougham introduced similar measures in 1839 and 1841.

[2] Report, 13th July, 1838, No. 589, p. vii.

against the scheme was adopted.[1]   The Government, in spite of these rebuffs, carried their proposal into effect, and the Committee of the Council on Education administered the grant for school building until 1846.   In that year the grant was extended to the maintenance of schools.

After the establishment of the Committee of the Council on Education the prospects of legislation appeared brighter.   In 1843 the late Lord Shaftesbury, then Lord Ashley, moved an address to the Crown praying that "the best means of diffusing the benefits and blessings of a moral and religious education among the working classes" might be taken into consideration.[2]   It is not necessary to dwell upon the terrible picture that he drew of the depravity which then existed amongst children of school age in manufacturing districts.   The House of Commons agreed to the address without a division, and the reply of the Government was the educational clauses of the Factory Act which was introduced in the same year.   But the House of Commons, which had been unanimous that something ought to be done, fell into hopeless conflict upon the methods of doing it.   The education clauses had to be abandoned, and the debate upon a Bill brought in by Mr. Hume for dealing with the question somewhat upon the lines of Lord Brougham's proposals was counted out.[3]

The failure of these efforts, upon which so many hopes had been based, was followed by a period of inaction.   In 1847 Lord Lansdowne, the President of the Council, regretfully said that the difficulties caused by the unformed state of public opinion upon the subject prevented the Government from bringing forward a general plan of education.[4]   In 1850 Mr. W. J. Fox brought in a Bill in which he proposed that education should be compulsory and gratuitous.[5]   It was defeated by a majority of 229.   It was not until 1853 that Government attempted to deal with the subject.   In that year Lord John Russell brought forward a very small measure, which aimed at aiding existing schools by means of a local rate.[6]   But even this minute proposal had no force of public opinion behind it.   The Bill was read a first time, and was then dropped. In the following year, speaking on the Education Estimates, Lord John Russell echoed the opinion which had been expressed in 1847 by Lord Lansdowne.   "I must confess," he said, "that unless there is a prospect of a greater concurrence of opinion upon the subject of education . . . I think it will be useless attempting to bring forward in this House any general plan of national education."[7]

Before any further attempt at legislation was made, the Department of Science and Art was established in 1853.   Since 1836 Parliament had voted increasing sums, which were administered by the Board of Trade, for the encouragement of a School of Design. In 1853 a Science Division was added, and the Department was re-named the "Department of Science and Art."   When, in 1856, the Committee of the Council on Education (thenceforth called the Education Department) was re-organised, and a Vice-President of the Council was appointed, the Science and Art Department was

---

[1] Walpole : "History of England," vol. iii. pp. 486-487.
[2] Hansard, vol. lxvii. p. 47.
[3] *Ibid.* vol. lxx. p. 1350.

[4] *Ibid.* vol. lxxxix. p. 858.
[5] *Ibid.* vol. cix. p. 27.
[6] *Ibid.* vol. cxxv. p. 522.
[7] *Ibid.* vol. cxxxiv. p. 959.

transferred from the Board of Trade, and was placed under the same executive with the Education Department. From 1855 until 1898 the grant for drawing was made to elementary schools by the Science and Art Department, and on the establishment of School Boards, grants for other branches of science and art were made to schools under their control.

The confusion into which the Legislature was cast by attempts to deal with the question of education by methods for which the public mind was not as yet prepared, is illustrated by the Parliamentary proceedings of the years 1855-58 It is usual in this country to approach legislation upon any difficult subject by three stages. First, a Royal Commission to investigate the question ; second, resolutions to test the opinion of Parliament upon it ; and, lastly, a Bill. During the years in question this course of procedure was reversed. In 1855 there were no less than three Bills dealing with education before the House of Commons. One was introduced by Lord John Russell ;[1] a second was brought in from the other side of the House by Sir John Pakington ;[2] and a third, representing the views of an advanced party, was introduced by Mr. Milner Gibson. These signs of unanimity were as deceptive as they were, for the time, encouraging. It was hoped that when all parties were agreed upon the need for legislation, it would not be difficult to effect a compromise on questions of detail. But the hope was soon dashed, and after considerable discussion all the three Bills were withdrawn.

In the following year Lord John Russell tried to induce the House of Commons to accept a series of resolutions which declared in favour of rate aid to meet school deficiency, of the election of local bodies to manage the schools, and of religious teaching subject to a conscience clause. The apathy of the public reflected itself in the apathy of the House, and the resolutions were shelved upon a side issue by a majority of 102.[3] In consequence of this division, a Bill which had been introduced by Lord Granville in the House of Lords was withdrawn.

These two forms of procedure—by Bill and by resolution—having thus conspicuously failed, resort was at last had to a Royal Commission. In 1858 Sir John Pakington, who had reproduced and abandoned his Bill in the previous year, obtained the appointment of a Royal Commission " to inquire into the present state of popular education in England, and to consider and report what measures, if any, are required " for its improvement.[4]

Such was the origin of the " Newcastle Commission," which sat for nearly three years. After a most elaborate and exhaustive inquiry, it issued a report in which it recommended that the Government Grant should be apportioned upon the result of the individual examination of children ; and that county boards should be formed, with power to provide funds out of the county or borough rate for the assistance of existing schools. The former recommendation was accepted by the Government, and resulted in

---

[1] Hansard, vol. cxxxvi. p. 1378.
[2] *Ibid.* vol cxxxvii. p. 640.
[3] *Ibid.* vol. cxl. p. 1955.
[4] *Ibid.* vol. cxlviii. p. 1184. 1372.

the Revised Code of 1862. The latter was rejected, being deemed insufficient, because it did not propose any machinery for the provision of new schools.

Thus the Revised Code, which provided a grant for school maintenance based partly on capitation and partly upon results of examination, was the only practical outcome of the movement which, in 1855, appeared so full of promise. Well might the friends of education despair of seeing any satisfactory result from their prolonged labours. That despair was reflected in a Bill which was introduced in 1860 by Mr. Adderley, now Lord Norton, who had been Vice-President of the Council in 1858. He proposed to enact that no child under 12 years of age should be employed in any continuous labour unless he produced the certificate of a competent master that he was able to read and write ; or, in the alternative, unless an undertaking was given by the employer that the child should receive instruction for at least twenty hours in every month. The Bill had no chance of success. The objection that it was unjust to impose a general disability without providing the means of escaping it was deemed unanswerable by the Government, and the Bill was defeated on the second reading.

The failure of the Newcastle Commission to produce an acceptable scheme was followed by a cessation of legislative effort for some years, during which the effect of the Revised Code was tested. It was not until 1867 that any further attempt was made to deal with the question. In that year the late Lord Aberdare, then Mr. Bruce, introduced an Education Bill in the House of Commons,[1] and Earl Russell brought forward a series of resolutions in the House of Lords.[2] Both Bill and resolutions were opposed by the Government, and negatived without a division ; but in the Queen's Speech, delivered only a month before, legislation upon the question had been promised.[3]

The Government endeavoured to redeem that promise during the session of 1868. The Duke of Marlborough, Lord President of the Council, introduced an Education Bill in the House of Lords.[4] The aims of the Bill were to bring a greater number of schools under inspection by rendering more elastic the method of distributing the grant and to encourage the building of new schools by increasing the building-grant. These proposals were favourably received by both sides of the House. But soon after the second reading, the Irish Church resolutions were carried in the House of Commons ; preparations were made for winding up the session with a view to an early dissolution, and the Bill was consequently abandoned.

(v.) The Period of Legislation.

In 1869 two Education Bills were introduced in the House of Lords, but they were withdrawn upon a promise being given by the Government to deal exhaustively with the subject in the following year, and the result was the Education Bill of 1870. The Bill, as it was first brought in by Mr. Forster, was by no means the measure which ultimately passed into law. In several vital respects it was metamorphosed during its passage through the House of Commons. The measure proposed by the Government

---

[1] Hansard, vol. clxxxviii. p. 1317.
[2] *Ibid.* vol. cxc. p. 478.
[3] *Ibid.* vol. cxc. p. 5.
[4] *Ibid.* vol. cxci. p. 105.

went further than the Duke of Marlborough's Bill, which merely aimed at increasing accommodation and efficiency by means of Imperial funds administered by existing agencies. But, although it authorised expenditure out of the rates for educational purposes, it did not go so far in the direction of placing education under popular control as the proposals of Lord Brougham, Earl Russell, and others to which reference has already been made. School Boards, within the meaning of the Bill, were to be elected annually by the Town Councils of boroughs and by the vestries of rural parishes. There was no provision for any central body to control the educational interests of London. "With regard to the Metropolis," Mr. Forster said, "the difficulties of which, from its peculiar position, defy almost all attempts at legislation, we shall be guided very much by the counsel and advice of the Metropolitan members; but, after the greatest possible inquiry, we have come to the conclusion that the best districts that we can take in the Metropolis are, where they exist, the school districts already formed for workhouse schools, and, where they do not exist, the boundaries of the vestries. . . ." "In the case of the school districts of the Metropolis," he added, "we need have no provision for election, because we have already School Boards elected by the different Boards of Guardians within these school districts.[1]

The direct election of Boards for the control of elementary education was therefore no part of the Government's original scheme, and the administration of education in London was to be devolved upon a number of small Boards; not vested in a central body controlling the whole area of the Metropolis. It may be said, indeed, that the School Board for London was an afterthought which was the consequence of a parlimentary accident. When the question of the constitution of School Boards, as proposed by the Bill, was under discussion, an amendment was moved that they should be elected by the "ratepayers of the district for which such School Board was elected." Mr. Forster was personally opposed to this alteration of the principle of the original plan, but the Government did not resist the amendment, and it was carried in a very thin House by the small majority of five. The whole scheme of the Bill in regard to the constitution of local authorities was thus revolutionised. The proposed method of dealing with London became impracticable, and the Government were obliged to accept an amendment which placed education in the metropolis under the control of one Board directly elected by the ratepayers.[2] The electoral divisions of London were specified by the Act; but it was left to the Education Department to determine the boundaries of those divisions and the number of members which should be assigned to each.

The Government plan was also abandoned in another important respect. In the first draft of the Bill, School Boards were empowered not only to build and maintain new schools, but to grant pecuniary assistance to existing Voluntary schools, provided that, if such assistance were granted, it must be given on equal terms to all schools in their district. This provision, which aimed at giving much needed support to existing schools, disappeared from the Bill in Committee, and the operations of School Boards

[1] Hansard, vol. cxcix. p. 438 *et seq.*   [2] *Ibid.* vol. ccii. p. 1420.

were confined to building, and accepting transfers of, schools, and the maintenance of such schools.

The working details of the Education Act of 1870, and of the various subsequent Acts of Parliament which amended it, or enlarged the scope of the operations of School Boards, are sufficiently explained in the subsequent sections of this volume which deal with the methods of the Board's administration. It is not necessary in this historical introduction to allude to them further.[1] The chief recommendations of the important Royal Commission on the working of the Elementary Education Acts, which was appointed in 1886 and reported in 1888, are also referred to in the same manner.

In 1896 the Government introduced an Education Bill which, if it had passed, would have made great changes in educational administration. It was proposed by the Bill to empower County Councils to appoint Education Committees, a minority of the members being eligible from outside the Council. These committees were to hold office for three years, a third of the members retiring annually. They were to exercise the powers already vested in a County Council by the Technical Instruction Act, 1889, and to administer any moneys paid to the County Council under the Local Taxation Act, 1890. They were also to be empowered, by agreement with the Education Department, to undertake the administration within the county of any grant provided by Parliament for education or for science and art.

Provision was made for the limitation of the amount of grant which could be earned by a school, in accordance with a suggestion made by the Royal Commission of 1888.[2] The educational grant and fee grant per scholar in day schools was not to be greater than the amount per scholar paid for the year ending on July 31st, 1896, unless that amount was less than twenty-nine shillings per scholar; in which case the latter sum might be paid. A special grant for Voluntary schools and poor Board schools was, however, authorised, for the improvement of the staff, fittings and apparatus of the schools.

In school districts in which a School Board was required under the provisions of the Act of 1870, and none had as yet been formed, the duty of supplying the deficiency of school accommodation might be imposed by the Education Department upon the Education Committee for the county, or, in boroughs, upon the Borough Council. Powers were introduced to enable School Boards to transfer their schools and duties to

---

[1] These Acts are:—The Elementary Education Act Amendment Act, 1873, 36 & 37 Vict. c. 86. The Elementary Education Act, 1876, 39 & 40 Vict. c. 79. An Act to make further provisions as to bye-laws respecting the attendance of children at school under the Elementary Education Act, 1880, 43 & 44 Vict. c. 23. An Act for making operative certain Articles of the Education Code, 1890, 53 & 54 Vict. c. 22. (This Act provided that elementary education need not be the principal part of the instruction given in an evening school.) The Elementary Education Act, 1891, 54 & 55 Vict. c. 56, authorising the Fee Grant. The Elementary Education (Blind and Deaf Children) Act, 1893, 56 & 57 Vict. c. 42. Elementary Education (School Attendance) Act, 1893, 56 & 57 Vict. c. 51. The Voluntary Schools Act, 1897, 60 Vict. c. 5. (This Act authorised a special grant for Voluntary schools, and freed the buildings from local rates.) The Elementary Education Act, 1897, 60 Vict. c. 16. (which gave an increased grant to poor School Boards). The Elementary Education (School Attendance Act, 1893), Amendment Act, 1899, 62 & 63 Vict. c. 13. Elementary Education (Defective and Epileptic Children) Act, 1899, 62 & 63 Vict. c. 32.

[2] *See* Final Report, p. 222, para. 178.

the new education authority. That authority was also to be entrusted with the duty of controlling secondary education.

The Bill contained various other proposals, but the only provision which claims particular notice is that which attempted to place a limit upon the amount which a School Board might levy by rate. It was provided that no School Board should receive from the rating authority in any year, for the maintenance of day schools, a sum greater than the existing cost of maintenance per scholar, multiplied by the total number of scholars in its schools during the previous year,[1] or a sum equal to twenty shillings per scholar, whichever might be the greater, without the consent of the local authority of the district.[2]

The evident design of the Bill was to decentralise the Education Department and to limit the activity of School Boards; to create an alternative body which might eventually supersede School Boards, and to promote the efficiency of Voluntary schools. The second reading was debated for five nights, and was carried by the astounding majority of 267.[3] But the opposition which the Bill aroused in the country was intense, and consequently the opposition to it in Parliament, when it reached the Committee stage, was prolonged. A hopeless confusion was created by an amendment accepted by the Government on the first section, which dealt with the constitution of the new education authority, and after six nights of discussion in Committee, the Bill was withdrawn. The minor proposals contained in the Bill for aiding Voluntary schools and poor School Boards were carried into effect in 1897, but the more serious changes which were contemplated have not been heard of in Parliament again.

The only other Statute which requires notice is the Board of Education Act of 1899.[4] The main objects of the Act are to vest the government control of education in a single Board, and to provide means for the organisation of secondary education. The powers of the Education Department and the Science and Art Department are vested in the Board of Education, and the educational powers of the Charity Commissioners and the Board of Agriculture may be transferred to it by an Order in Council. The office of Vice-President of the Council is abolished upon the occurrence of the next vacancy, and the President of the Board and one of its secretaries are rendered eligible to sit in the House of Commons. Provision is made for the inspection of any secondary schools that shall desire inspection. Power is given to appoint a Consultative Committee to frame a register of teachers, and to advise the Board of Education upon any questions which may be referred to them by it.

This act is a specimen of the "Skeleton Statute" so common in the present day, when all legislation is effected in a hurry, in which the bare outline of a proposed reform is indicated, and the duty is cast upon a Government Department of breathing into the dry bones the breath of life. The Act only came into operation on April 1st in

---

[1] But it was to be legal to add any sum due to an automatic rise of salaries of teachers under any scale already in existence.

[2] Borough, District, or County Council, as the case might be.

[3] Owing to the fact that the Irish Nationalist party voted for the second reading.

[4] 62 & 63 Vict. c. 33.

the present year. It is too soon, therefore, to make any estimate of the probable effect of the change upon the future of education.

In this introductory chapter an attempt has been made to sketch the history of Elementary Education in its relation to the State. In the following section an acccunt is given of the condition of Elementary Education during the period immediately preceding the establishment of School Boards, and of the manner in which the first School Board for London laid the foundations of the new system. The story of those branches of the Board's work which do not relate directly to school life and curriculum is carried down to the present day. The latter topics are dealt with in the third part of this volume by specialists who are peculiarly qualified to expound the various subjects upon which they write.

PART II.

—

THE FOUNDATIONS.

PART II.
THE FOUNDATIONS.

———

CHAPTER I.

THE FIRST SCHOOL BOARD FOR LONDON.

ON October 7th, 1870, the Education Department, acting under the powers conferred upon it by the Elementary Education Act, issued an order defining the boundaries of the ten divisions into which the Metropolis was to be divided,[1] and the number of members which each division was to return to the Board.[2] These divisions were formed upon the basis of the then existing Parliamentary divisions, and they were not equal either in respect of area, population, or rateable value. The consequence was that the number of members assigned to each varied. Four divisions—namely, the City, Southwark, Chelsea,[3] and Greenwich—were to elect four members each; five seats were assigned to four other divisions—Lambeth,[4] Tower Hamlets, Hackney, and Westminster. Finsbury received six seats, and Marylebone seven.

The impending election of members of the first School Board for London, which was fixed for November 29th, 1870, stirred the interest of the community profoundly. Never before had any municipal contest called forth so much excitement. Many of those who had heartily supported the policy of the Education Act deemed that policy to be a grand experiment which would have to justify itself by its success. Not a few ardent advocates of elementary education for the people doubted whether the machinery created for the provision of that education was the best that could be devised. No less than 135 candidates appeared to contend for the 49 seats upon the Board, and as the contest proceeded, those who most sincerely desired the success of the new policy noted with regret, and almost with despair, that the battle raged, as it had raged in Parliament, round the narrow question of the nature of the religious instruction which should be given in the schools of the Board, ignoring the broader educational problem which was submitted to the ratepayers of London. A perusal of the addresses of candidates shows that this question of religious instruction was looked upon as the vital issue.[5] Casual allusions are to be found, here and there, in vague terms, to " efficiency," " economy," the question of compulsion and other subjects, but it

---

[1] 33 & 34 Vict. c. 75, s. 37, and 5th Schedule.
[2] Education Department Report, 1871, p. lix.
[3] A fifth seat was given to Chelsea in 1882 by an order of the Education Department.
[4] Lambeth was made into two divisions by

48 & 49 Vict. c. 38, s. 2. Four seats were assigned to East Lambeth and six to West Lambeth.
[5] See p. 1 (Advertisements) of the *Times*, September, October, and November, 1870.

would appear that very few candidates had any definite policy to place before the electors apart from their views upon the question of religious instruction.

There was another element of interest in the approaching election besides the question of education. The Act, and the powers exercised by the Education Department under the Act, had imported into English municipal life two changes which were foreign to all its traditions. The London School Board Election of 1870 was the first election of any importance which was conducted by ballot,[1] and with a cumulative vote. It would be foreign to the purposes of this inquiry to deal at large with the prophecies of accident, mistake and fraud which, it was declared, would result from the abolition of the system of open voting which was at one time deemed a bulwark of the Constitution. It is enough to say that in the result the working of the election proved these prophecies to be groundless. The cumulative vote, devised especially for School Board elections, to meet a particular political exigency, needs more consideration. This mode of voting, which gives to each elector a number of votes equal to the number of candidates to be elected, which he may give to one candidate, or divide as he pleases among a number of candidates, was the outcome of the religious controversy. It was designed to assuage the fears of the smaller religious sects that their views would obtain no representation upon the Board. Even the permissive application of compulsory bye-laws contemplated by the Act would have been impossible if the Board had been composed of members of one dominant creed, and the Government hoped that, by adopting the cumulative vote, the representation of minorities would be secured. In this respect it is to a certain extent effectual, more especially in periods of apathy, which result in a small poll. On such occasions the pastor of a strong and energetic church, or the favourite orator of a political club, can, by a concentration of all the votes of a following comparatively small in relation to the whole constituency, secure his own return. But on occasions when the feeling of the electorate is deeply moved, as was the case at the first election of the London School Board, the minority candidate has far less chance of success. The fact that the most diverse opinions were represented upon the Board was due rather to the formation in many divisions of influential committees to promote the return of suitable candidates, irrespective of their religious and political views, rather than to the operation of the cumulative vote. But the general opinion was that the working of the new system of election would result in the return of faddists and of persons who had some ulterior political or social object in seeking election, and that the true educationist would find little popular support in seeking the suffrages of the electorate. On the day of election, the *Times,* after pointing out the dangers of the position, adjured the electors to avoid them. "What is wanted," the *Times* said, "is a set of candidates with the capacity to understand the problem before them, the independence of mind to deal with it in the spirit of the Act and regardless of preconceived notions, and the influence to carry their constituents with them."[2]

---

[1] Except in the City of London. Education Department Report, 1871, pp. lxii. lxiii.

[2] The *Times,* November 29th, 1870.

It cannot be said that the electors failed to act upon the sound advice thus tendered to them.

On the 29th of November, 1870, when Paris, held bound in the death-grip of the German armies, was preparing one of the most terrible sorties of that most terrible siege, and while all Europe was awaiting restlessly the political results of Russia's repudiation of the Treaty of Paris, the London ratepayers were engaged in the inauguration of a new era in the history of education. "The great event of to-day for this country," the *Times* said on that morning, "whatever may be passing on the Continent of Europe, will be the election of the first London School Board. No equally powerful body will exist in England outside Parliament, if power be measured by influence for good or evil over masses of human beings."

The result of the poll was the election of a Board remarkably representative of the varied schools of thought. Upon it were to be found politicians, two of whom subsequently attained to Cabinet rank; clergymen, two of whom afterwards rose to the Episcopal bench; and representatives of various dissenting bodies. Science and literature were represented; men well known for philanthropic work found seats on the Board, together with many who had earned a reputation as educationists. Ladies succeeded in gaining seats in two divisions.

The first meeting of the Board was held at the Guildhall on Thursday, December 15th, 1870, at the invitation of the City Corporation. The first business before the Board was the election of a chairman. Before the election took place a preliminary question had to be settled. The Act of 1870 conferred upon the School Board for London the power to pay its Chairman such salary as the Board should fix, subject to the consent of the Education Department[1] —a power which was not granted to any other School Board. A motion was at once moved "that no salary be awarded to the chairman," and this, after some discussion, was carried by a large majority. This decision practically settled in the negative the question whether the chairman of the Board should receive a salary. Although two attempts have been made to reverse it, neither was successful. In 1879, soon after the fourth triennial election, a memorial was presented to the Board praying that a salary might be paid to the chairman on the ground that "the growing work of the Board renders it desirable in the interest of the ratepayers that the Board should have the full advantage of the entire services of its chairman, who would thus be enabled to exercise a more efficient control over the expenditure and general work of the Board."[2] A very heated debate ensued, acrimonious out ot all proportion to the importance of the question which had been raised by the memorialists. The Board eventually resolved "That the memorial be respectfully received, and that an answer be returned stating that it is inexpedient at the present time to entertain the prayer of the memorial."[3] The "inexpediency" of "the present time" was alleged to be due to the fact that the Board had only just been elected and that new

---

[1] 33 & 34 Vict. c. 75, s. 38.
[2] Board Minutes, vol. xii. p. 184.
[3] *Ibid.* p. 185.

members were, on that account, unable to judge of the wisdom of the proposal; but the terms of the answer were merely the courteous cloaking of a refusal to consider the memorial. Rather more than a year afterwards, when members had enjoyed a full opportunity of measuring the merits of the proposal, the question was again raised in the form of a motion to pay the Chairman of the Board an annual salary of £1,500. Only three members voted for the motion, while thirty voted against it.[1] Since that time the question has never again been raised. The Chairmen of the Board have always discharged their onerous duties gratuitously, although there is a very prevalent opinion that they have been in receipt of a substantial salary. The Chairmanship of the Board is only one more instance of the fact that in English public life, men of position are frequently found who are willing, often at considerable personal sacrifice, to undertake onerous, and sometimes thankless, offices without reward.

Another peculiarity in regard to the Chairmanship of the London School Board may be mentioned here. The Education Act empowered the Board, if it saw fit, to elect a chairman who was not one of its members. An outside Chairman, if so elected, was created, by virtue of his office, a member of the Board in all respects, as if he had been elected by the ratepayers.[2] He could, therefore, exercise the right of voting as a member of the Board as well as give a casting vote in the event of an equality of votes. It does not appear that the suggestion was ever made that the first Board should seek a Chairman from outside its own ranks. Within the Board there were many men of ability who were capable of performing the duties of the office; but one of them, Lord Lawrence, who had filled the post of Viceroy of India, a man of rare business capacity and universally esteemed, was more particularly marked out for the post. Three other candidates were nominated, and the selection was conducted by two ballots,[3] after each of which the lowest candidate retired. Lord Lawrence headed the poll in each ballot, and was eventually elected Chairman by an unanimous vote. The practice of electing a member of the Board as Chairman was continued until 1894. After the election in that year, which resulted in a somewhat equal balance of parties, an outside Chairman was elected. Since that date this precedent has been followed.

After appointing the necessary committees and officers, and drawing up rules of debate, the Board devoted itself to the discharge of the duties which had been imposed upon it. These duties were novel in character, and experience afforded but little guidance in the performance of them. The Board was compelled, as it were, to grope its way in unexplored regions in order to lay the foundation of the new system of education. The Act itself was in a large measure a compromise between keenly contending parties,

---

[1] Board Minutes, vol. xiv. p. 725.

[2] 33 & 34 Vict. c. 75, s. 37, sub-s. 9.

[3] It is doubtful whether the election was legally conducted. The Education Act provided (Schedule III. *f*) that "the names of members present, as well as those voting upon each question, shall be recorded." This provision was not complied with.

The record shows that forty-six members voted; two, mentioned by name, did not vote; and one, mentioned by name, was absent. All the forty-nine members were, therefore, accounted for; but the names of members "voting" were not "recorded." The clear intention of the Act was that the voting on all questions should be *vivâ voce.*

and the form which the compromise took was the relegation to School Boards of questions which Parliament had found it inconvenient or impossible to determine. School Boards were left to decide whether, within their districts, religious instruction should be given; whether children should be compelled to attend the schools which were provided for them. They had to obtain statistical information—which was then non-existent—regarding the number of children requiring accommodation and the number of available school places. They had to consider and adopt suitable plans for school buildings at a time when the school-house was at a most rudimentary stage of development. They had to decide upon a curriculum for the children who were to attend the schools which they were about to erect or acquire. They had to organise a novel and intricate system of finance.

Upon the School Board for London the duty of deciding so many and such complicated questions pressed with especial gravity. Its decisions affected not only the vast population under its immediate administrative control, but also, indirectly, all those areas in which School Boards were about to be established. The School Boards in the country, to a large extent, took guidance from the decisions of the School Board for London. In the matter of religious instruction, it may be said that the compromise devised by the London School Board was adopted by the great majority of the School Boards in England and Wales.

The first London School Board laid the foundations of a policy upon which the present educational edifice has been built up by its successors. Subsequent Boards, with the sanction and approval of Government, have enlarged and beautified the super-structure so that it would hardly be recognised by its original founders. But these developments have been the natural sequence of, and not departures from, the liberal and prudent policy adopted by the first Board.

It would be impossible to explain this policy intelligibly by following the proceedings of the Board from week to week. Most questions were in process of simultaneous settlement, and any attempt to illustrate their development by such a method would lead to confusion. To ensure clearness of view it will be necessary to set out the questions of policy which the Board had to decide in what may be deemed a natural order, and to explain the solutions which the Board applied to them.

The problem was presented to the Board in six main sections.

I. *Statistical.*—This included the methods of ascertaining the number of children of school age who required accommodation and the number of school places already in existence. Until these figures could be ascertained the Board could not know precisely for how many children, or in what localities, it would be necessary to build schools, although it was notorious that a large amount of school provision was immediately necessary.

II. *School Buildings*—Having thus ascertained the amount of school provision that was needed, the next questions which arose were the acquisition of sites for new schools and the character of the buildings which should be erected upon those sites. In regard to school buildings the Board inaugurated a policy of improvement upon the old type of school which was almost revolutionary. In the light of modern construction, the older schools of the Board are now deemed ill-designed and inconvenient, but when they are thus criticised it is necessary to bear in mind the type of school which they supplanted.

III. *School Management.*—Having examined the character of the school buildings which the Board designed to erect, the next subjects of investigation are the scope of the instruction which was to be given to the scholars; the nature of the school apparatus; and the organisation of the teaching staff. The first branch of this subject must include the vexed question of religious instruction. When it is remembered that under the new Code of 1871 the only subjects of instruction which earned Government Grant were reading, writing and arithmetic, and not more than two specific subjects in Standards IV.-VI., and that the cost of teaching any other subjects must of necessity fall upon the rates, it will be seen that the temptation, from the point of financial economy, to place a narrow limit upon the curriculum was great. Fortunately the Board took a broad view of its duties in this respect. Indeed, it may be said that in regard to school curricula the locally elected educational bodies have as a rule led the Education Department. They have introduced subjects of instruction into their schools without the financial aid, and often without the encouragement, of the permanent Governmental organisation. When the experiment has proved a success the Education Department has tardily admitted the subject into the Code, and allowed it to earn a grant. The result of such a policy has been the piling up in the Code of an aggregation of subjects of instruction which, viewed as a curriculum, seems designed rather to confuse than to guide the teacher. Nothing is more remarkable in the history of English education than the lack of initiative which has until recently been characteristic of the Education Department. It has limited itself to the duties of dispensing the Government Grant and of criticising the results obtained in the schools; but for any initiative, any well-ordered schemes for the improvement of educational efficiency, it was necessary, until within the last few years, to look, not to the Department, but to the School Boards and to independent enthusiasts for educational progress. The evil arising from the lack of co-ordination in subjects of instruction has been to a great extent remedied by the Code for 1900, which has for the first time introduced a " course of instruction " for elementary schools.

IV. *Compulsion.*—The schools having thus been established and staffed, the next question for consideration was whether the children who failed to make use of them should be compelled to attend, and, if so, by what machinery. This, with the exception of the question of religious instruction, was the most delicate point which the Board was called upon to decide. Many ardent educationists doubted the wisdom of enforcing education by compulsion, and more feared that parents would resent its application as a new and intolerable limitation of their liberty.

V. *Industrial Schools.*—The Education Acts[1] conferred upon School Board powers to deal with the class of children who are vagrants, and are in danger of falling into criminal

---

[1] 33 & 34 Vict. c. 75, ss. 27, 28, and 29 & 30 Vict. c. 118.

courses. The education of these children had been provided for by Statute some four years previous to the passing of the Education Act, and certain powers under the Industrial Schools Act of 1866 were conferred upon the Board. It was manifestly convenient that the Education Authority of any district should have control over the education of the waifs and strays of that district, although it had to be conducted in institutions other than the public elementary school. Subsequent developments of the law and of administrative practice have made Industrial Schools ancillary to the work of compulsion; the habitual truant is committed to a school conducted under the Industrial Schools Act, called a "Truant School." After a short period of detention, he is licensed out, on the condition that he attends school with regularity. A breach of the condition involves re-commitment to the Truant School.

VI. *Finance.*—The last branch of the Board's work which will remain for consideration is the sources from which its income is derived, the methods by which such income is raised, and the control which is imposed upon its expenditure.

CHAPTER II.

STATISTICS.

The first duty which the School Board had to perform was to ascertain the number of children resident within its jurisdiction who required elementary education, and the number of efficient school places which were already provided. Until these figures had been ascertained it was impossible that the main object for which the Board had been created could be efficiently performed. The Board, in making this attempt, was breaking new ground. Never before had any effective endeavour been made to obtain these statistics. Returns upon the subject had been made to the Newcastle Commission on Education in respect to certain portions of the Metropolitan area, and published in 1861, but these returns the compilers themselves admitted to be inaccurate. They included all schools, whether efficient or not. They included also as elementary schools institutions which charged fees as high as a guinea a term. These statistics, therefore, were incomplete, unreliable, and, moreover, out of date.

The clause in the Act of 1870 which required these returns to be made provided that the London School Board, before the expiration of four months from the date of the election of its chairman, should send to the Education Department a return containing such particulars with respect to the elementary schools and children requiring elementary education as the Education Department might require.[1]

The burden of deciding the character of the returns to be made devolved, therefore, upon the Education Department. When the terms of the Education Department's

---

[1] 33 & 34 Vict. c. 75 s. 67. These returns, except in the case of London, were made in boroughs by the Town Council, and in parishes by the Overseers.—*Ibid.* sec. 69.

circular come to be considered it will be seen that a period of four months was but a scanty time in which to comply with the demands which were made. The Chairman of the Board was elected on December 15th, 1870. The Education Department's circular was not received by the Board until February 2nd, 1871.[1] A "Committee on Returns" had then been at work for some weeks, and had already commenced to make arrangements for the conduct of the necessary statistical inquiries. But it was not possible to complete and put these arrangements into operation until the actual form in which the Department would require its returns to be made was communicated to the Board.

The Department's letter was known as "Circular No. 86.' Its importance justifies a somewhat full quotation.

". . . The election of a School Board" . . . does "not supersede the necessity for the issue of a requisition from this Department setting forth the amount and description of the public school accommodation required for the district.

"In order that they may make such requisition it is essential that My Lords should receive precise information as to :—

"(1.) The requirements of the borough in respect of public school accommodation :

"(2.) The amount and character of public school accommodation :

"(3.) The manner in which those locally interested in the question wish that any ascertained deficiency should be met.

"The object of the present communication, therefore, is to request that the Board will furnish this Department with full and accurate information upon each of these points. The local knowledge possessed by the members of the Board, and the fact that they have been chosen to represent the views and interests of the borough in reference to elementary education, naturally point to their being asked to undertake this duty, and My Lords have reason to hope that, in inviting the co-operation of the Board, they are not only taking the best means in their power for obtaining the information that is required, but are also entrusting to the Board a task which they are both prepared and competent to discharge satisfactorily. . . .

"My Lords would be glad to receive from the Board . . . a report showing :—

"1. The number of children within the municipal limits for whom means of elementary education should be provided (a) between the ages of 3 and 5, and (b) between the ages of 5 and 13.

"2. The provision to meet the requirements of these children which the Board considers to be (a) already supplied by efficient schools or (b) likely to be supplied by schools either contemplated or in the course of erection.

"3. The deficiency (if any) in the supply of efficient elementary education for the borough, as shown by comparing 1 and 2.

"4. By means of what schools the Board would propose to supply this deficiency.

"5 The precise localities in which such schools will be needed.

"This report should be supplemented by detailed information respecting the

[1] Board Minutes, vol. i. p. 45

individual schools which the Board take into account, either as efficient or otherwise. Separate schedules should therefore be carefully prepared and appended to the report setting forth the name, description (whether for boys, girls mixed, or infants), situation, superficial and cubical area (in schools and class-rooms), and average attendance of each of the schools from which returns have been received which the Board propose to classify as—

"I. Supplying efficient elementary education.   The schools should be arranged under the following heads :—

(*a.*) Schools now in receipt of annual grants from this Department.

(*b.*) Schools not receiving such grants, but which will be conducted as public elementary schools, and will seek annual aid.

(*c.*) Schools which will not seek annual aid.

(*d.*) Private adventure schools (to which no annual grant can be made).

"II. *Not* supplying efficient education.   Under this head the Board should point out the schools or buildings which, with improvements, might be recognised as efficient and the steps recommended to be taken for making them so.

"III. Required to complete the school supply of the borough.

"It will necessarily take some time to obtain the information required for these returns, which, when sent to this Department, should be accompanied by a map of the borough, showing the positions of each of the schools referred to in the schedules.   The local knowledge, however, the number, and the constitution of the Board will enable them, with the aid of such assistants as they may employ for the purpose, to complete the inquiry now committed to them at a much earlier date than if it were undertaken by the Education Department."

This circular, as will be seen from the terms used in it, which in many respects were inapplicable to London, was drawn up to meet the case of municipal boroughs. The demand thus made could be complied with without much difficulty by all municipalities except, perhaps, the largest ; but the assumption that the London School Board, within any reasonable time, would be able, not only to ascertain the number of children in need of education, to classify the existing school accommodation with the minuteness directed by the circular, but also to indicate "the precise localities in which schools would be needed," shows that the authorities at the Education Department had by no means grasped the magnitude of the burden which had been laid upon the School Board for London.   In the event, it will be seen that the circular was only partially complied with ; complete compliance was impossible.   If completeness had been attempted, years must have elapsed before a new school could have been built in London. The Board, while it laboured in its almost superhuman task, discovered a more excellent method of procedure, which admitted of the immediate provision of a certain amount of school accommodation.

The inefficiency as well as the insufficiency of the school provision for London was admitted on all hands, but the estimates of the number of children and the amount of accommodation provided varied considerably.   It will be convenient first to consider the number of children requiring school accommodation; reserving the question of the accommodation provided for subsequent investigation.

With a view to ascertaining the need for a building-grant for the erection of school-houses, the Education Department had, previous to 1870, adopted a rule, based upon the Census figures, for estimating the number of children requiring school provision in any given district. This rule was that one-sixth of the population required school provision, and it was arrived at by the following reasoning. In every thousand of the population 23·4 per cent. are between the ages of 3 and 13. From these 234 children must be deducted one-seventh—that is, 33—as representing children who do not require elementary school accommodation. From the remaining 201 must be deducted 17·5 per cent.—that is, 35—for all causes of absence, such as illness or permanent physical disability. The residue, 166 children, will represent the number of persons in every thousand of the population who require elementary education; in round numbers, one-sixth of the population. This rule has been found by experience to be practically as well as theoretically correct. As the estimated population of London in 1871, based upon the Census of 1861, was about 3,258,000,[1] the number of elementary school places required would be, upon the above basis of calculation, about 543,000.

The Board on January 5th, 1871, appointed a special committee, called the "Committee on Returns," to prepare the statistics which the Board was bound to furnish to the Education Department.[2] This Committee was, within three months' time, amalgamated with a standing committee called the "Statistical Enquiries Committee."

This Committee was evidently frightened of adopting the "practically" as well as "theoretically correct" method of calculating the number of school places required, probably because of the enormous deficiency of school places that it would have disclosed. The rejection of the Education Department's theory is nowhere recorded in the Minutes of the Board; but in a statement upon the work of the Board, published by its authority in October, 1873, a justification for not adopting it was presented to the public. After stating the Education Department's theory, the Board declared: "On this supposition, and taking the figures of the Registrar General, corrected to the present time, the number of school places in London should be about 560,000.[3] As the school places have been shown to amount to 308,000, a comparison of the two leads to the conclusion that the Board would have to provide about 252,000 school places. It is obvious, however, that, in a city like London, no general theory will hold good alike for St. George's, Hanover Square, and for Ratcliff Highway. The Board therefore determined to set aside theory and to ascertain the facts for themselves."[4]

The inconclusiveness of this reason for rejecting the Education Department's

---

[1] The Census figures for 1871 were not published when the Board first considered this question. They showed the population of London to be 3,266,987.

[2] Board Minutes, vol. i. p. 15.

[3] Calculated upon the Census of 1871.

[4] Board Minutes, vol. iii. p. 1072.

rule of calculation points to the fact that the Board was staggered by its results. That rule was devised to ascertain the total number of children requiring accommodation, not to fix the localities in which school accommodation was required. It is manifest that if this method of calculation had been applied to a rich district like St. George's, Hanover Square, or to a poor district like Ratcliff Highway, the figures arrived at would have been misleading in both cases. It was only by aggregating the population of the poor and the rich districts that the resultant could by any possibility prove correct. The Education Department's method was, nevertheless, rejected in favour of a plan of enumeration which resulted in demonstrating a far smaller deficiency of school places.

The Census figures were not rejected on account of the Department's "Circular No. 86," which demanded information as to the precise localities in which schools were needed. Long before the returns to that circular were complete the Board resolved that it would proceed to build at least ten schools in various parts of London where the deficiency of accommodation was notorious.[1] The Education Department accepted this decision, and allowed sites to be selected. Thus one of the chief hindrances to practical work contained in Circular 86 was surmounted.

On April 5th, 1871, the Statistical Enquiries Committee laid before the Board a return of the number and accommodation of existing schools. At the same time, the Committee reported the estimated population of the ten divisions into which London was divided, based upon the Census of 1861, showing a total population of 3,258,469. The Committee then expressed their regret that they were not in possession of data sufficiently trustworthy to enable them to advise the Board as to the proportion of the population in each division of the class whose children would attend public elementary schools. They therefore recommended that this fact should be stated in the letter covering the returns. This report was the result of an application by the Board to the Registrar General to be furnished with a statement of the number of children between the ages of 3 and 13 as ascertained by the 1871 Census, which had just been taken. The Registrar General had replied that it would be impossible to furnish these statistics within two years from that time, and that the social condition of the children could not be specified.[2] The Board therefore resolved to send the returns on school accommodation to the Education Department, together with a covering letter stating its inability to ascertain the number of children between 3 and 13. It then proceeded to discuss the further methods to be adopted for taking an Educational census. It resolved " that with a view to obtaining satisfactory information as to the number of children in London requiring elementary education between the ages of 3 and 5 and 5 and 13, and of the social and religious condition of the districts in which they live, a committee be appointed for each division, and that they be recommended to avail themselves of the assistance of residents in the division, with the understanding that the responsibility for the inquiry rests with the committee."

---

[1] Board Minutes, vol. i. p. 117. [2] *School Board Chronicle*, vol. i. p. 235.

[3] Board Minutes, vol. i. p. 105.

A deputation from the Board waited upon the Home Secretary and requested that the Registrar General might be allowed to furnish to the Board, at its own cost, copies of the Householders' Schedules taken in the recent Census, so far as they related to children between the ages of 3 and 13. The request was granted The Board then prepared Census books, with the necessary headings. The authorities at the Census Office copied into these Census books from the Householders' Schedules the names and ages of all children between 3 and 13, together with the names and addresses of the parents. If a child was registered as a "scholar" in the Census returns, the letter " S " was placed after its name.

By these means the Board obtained the information that on the night of April 2nd, 1871, there were 681,101 children in London between the ages of 3 and 13. Having secured this basis of fact, the Board proceeded to complete its inquiries. A staff of enumerators, under a superintendent, was appointed to act under each of the ten divisional committees. The enumerators were mostly paid officials; but some enthusiastic educationists gave their services gratuitously. The duty of these enumerators was to ascertain, under the guidance afforded by the Census books, the number of children who required elementary education and also the number of those who did not require it. In the case of the former class, they were to ascertain the name of the school (if any) that the child attended, and if no school was attended, the cause of absence. These inquiries were made and answered verbally; but in the case of the absence of the head of the household, a printed form was left to be filled up, and it was called for in about three days.

This method was probably the best which could be adopted, but several circumstances combined to affect the accuracy of the results obtained by it. The scheduling was not, like the Census, simultaneous. It occupied a period of about eight weeks. The answers of heads of households were not given, as in the Census, under a legal penalty for making inaccurate returns. The scheduling was unpopular, and it was taken by untrained and inexperienced agents. All these facts combined to increase the possibilities of error. It was easy for an unwilling parent to return his child as attending one of the many inefficient private adventure schools at which a fee greater than ninepence a week was charged, or as attending an elementary school where the attendance was of the most nominal and perfunctory character.

As the Census books were completed they were sent up to the Head Office of the Board for analysis and tabulation. Working upon the basis that there were 681,101 children between the ages of 3 and 13, the Board deducted 97,307 children who had been returned as educated at home or in schools at which the weekly fee exceeded ninepence. It was further found that 9,101 children were inmates of institutions such as asylums, reformatories, and boarding-schools. When these two classes of children were deducted, there remained 574,693 children who might be considered as belonging to the class requiring elementary education.

Of this total, 139,095 children were between the ages of 3 and 5, and were not, therefore, subject to the compulsory bye-laws which the Board had decided to adopt, although they were at liberty to attend school if they were sent by their parents. The remainder, 435,598 children, were between the ages of 5 and 13.

The Board then proceeded to consider the number which ought to be deducted on account of children who were able to offer reasonable excuses for non-attendance at school. It estimated that 17,502, because of illness or disablement, and that 55,760, being the number of children between 3 and 5 whose parents had claimed that they were too young to attend school, might be excluded from the calculation. It also allowed a liberal deduction for children necessarily employed and for children claiming exemption under the bye-laws, and it estimated that for all these causes of absence a deduction might be made of 95,975 children, leaving 478,718 children for whom elementary education ought to be provided.

The discrepancy between this result and that which was arrived at by adopting the Education Department's method of calculation does not seem to have startled the Board. One-sixth of the ascertained population of London in 1871 was 544,000. The result of the Board's scheduling was to reduce this estimate by more than 65,000. But even the reduced figure thus arrived at was subjected to a further diminution. " A further and final deduction," the Board explained, " must now be made, in order to determine the school accommodation which will be necessary for the above number of children. This deduction is on account of merely temporary causes of absence. The Board procured a return from thirty of the largest schools in London giving the absence, day by day, for a whole week, and assigning to each absence its proper cause. The result shows that on the average about 5·09 per cent. of the number on the rolls were absent day by day owing to these temporary causes. No doubt the absence is greater in many schools; but this percentage is no more than needs to be the case in a well-conducted school. The Board entertains the hope that, with the bye-laws in force, the percentage may be considerably reduced in the best schools, and that on the whole it will be sufficient to deduct five per cent. from the number of children who could attend school in order to ascertain the number of places which will be necessary to receive them. On this basis of calculation the schools for 478,718 children should have accommodation for 454,783 children in average attendance."[1] Thus a further reduction of nearly 24,000 school places was effected.

By the above process of reasoning the Board convinced itself, and, in the event, the Education Department, that the number of children actually requiring accommodation was nearly 90,000 less than the estimated number according to the method of calculation hitherto adopted by the Education Department, based upon a theory which had always been found to work out correctly in practice. It seems surprising that so considerable a difference in the results of the two methods of calculation did not cause the Board to hesitate in accepting as indubitably accurate the result of it scheduling. But it does not appear to have occurred to it for a moment that it was possibly accepting a serious under-estimate. So far from this being the case, in the year 1873 the Board accepted as accurate an estimate based upon the figures

---

[1] Report of School Board to Education Department March, 1872, p. xi.

of the previous year, with a deduction of about 2,000 for children who had passed the school age.

Subsequent events proved to demonstration that the first School Board for London grievously miscalculated the amount of work which needed to be done before the education of the children of London could be fully provided for. When the Board's officers became, by experience, more skilful in the work of enumeration, the number of children scheduled leapt rapidly up until, in 1887, sixteen years after the first scheduling, the numbers practically agreed with those shown by the Education Department's rule of calculation. Since 1887 the scheduling has, on the whole, shown a slightly larger number of children requiring elementary education than the estimate based upon the Census figures.

The actual difference between the two methods of calculation in each year between 1872 and 1900 is shown in Diagram I. on the opposite page. The result of the Board's scheduling is shown by the straight line; the result of the Education Department's method of estimating is shown approximately by the dotted line. The dotted line, in fact, represents the figures more accurately than the Department's estimate. It is obtained by taking the increase in the number of children between 3 and 13 as shown by one Census as compared with its predecessor, and, after making the necessary deductions for reasonable excuses, attributing one-tenth of the total to each year as the average yearly increase. It seems to have been admitted that the Education Department formula gave a slight over-estimate of the child population of London on account of the migration of adults to the metropolis in search of work. The diagram shows, therefore, that the Board's scheduling has in later years demonstrated the practical correctness of the Department's calculation. The conclusion, therefore, is inevitable that in 1871 the Board very seriously under-estimated the number of children requiring accommodation.

In order to assist in ascertaining the amount of existing and contemplated school provision, the Education Department issued a form to be filled up by managers, teachers, and proprietors. This form was known as " No. 74L 1871." It required the classification of all schools into three categories:—(1) Public schools—*i.e*, those which were conducted in buildings secured to educational objects by a deed of trust; (2) private schools—*i.e.*, conducted by private managers or committees, not under any deed; and (3) private adventure schools—*i.e.*, schools conducted by the teacher at his own risk and on his own responsibility. The form had also to be filled up by persons responsible for the erection of any (1) new school buildings, or (2) enlargements. Minute inquiries were made into the character and dimensions of the school buildings, and the uses, if any, to which they were put for non-educational purposes. Another section required information as to the age and qualifications of teachers and the days and hours when the school was open. The schools were further required to set out the number of their scholars, classified according to age, the fees charged, the subjects taught, and the number of children taught in each subject.[1] On January 25th, 1871, the Committee on

---

[1] The schedule of subjects as set out in the return was probably considered exhaustive in 1871. It included Reading, Writing, Arithmetic, Dictation, Religious Instruction, History, Grammar, Geography, Needlework, Music, Drawing, and Drill. A small space was left blank for "other subjects, if any."

Returns reported to the Board that they had appointed agents in each division for the collection of these statistics. Each agent was provided with a supply of copies of the Form 74L, with instructions that it was to be filled up by each school in duplicate. One copy was for the information of the Education Department, the other was to be retained

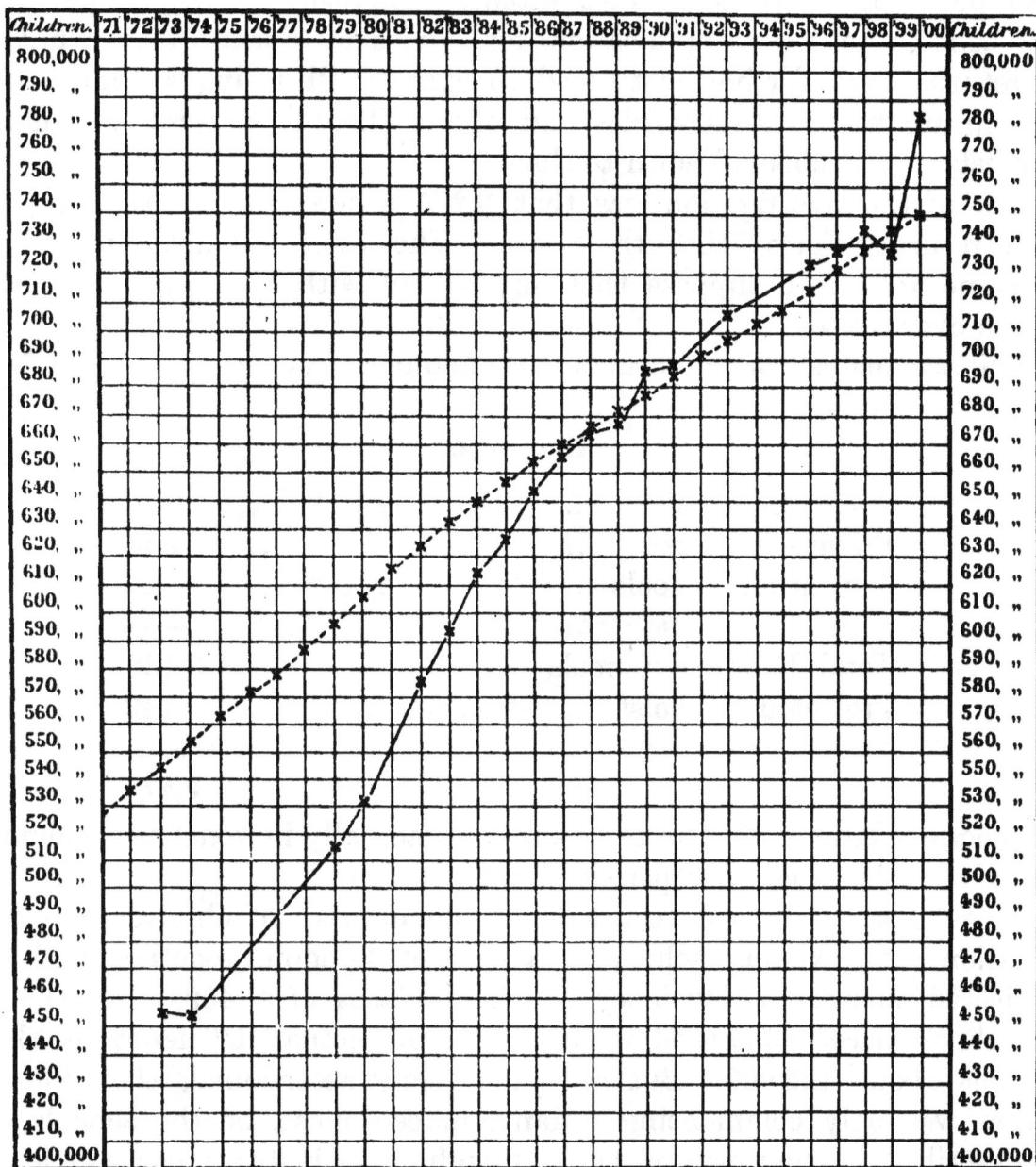

Diagram I. *showing the actual increase of the child population of London requiring Elementary Education (dotted line) as compared with the numbers scheduled by the Board (continuous line) from 1872 to 1899. In 1899 the Board first scheduled children over 13 years of age who were actually attending school.*

by the Board. The agents were also furnished with lists of the Public Elementary Schools under the control of the great Voluntary Societies.[1] All these schools were

[1] *I.e.,* The National Society, the British and Foreign School Society, the Wesleyan Educational Committee, the Roman Catholic Poor-School Society, the Congregational Board of Education, and the Ragged School Union. See *ante*, pp. 13-16.

easy of identification; the difficulty arose in regard to schools conducted by committees not in connection with these Societies, and to the large and uncertain number of private adventure schools. To discover these the Board inserted advertisements in local papers, and posted notices at the doors of churches, chapels, and in other conspicuous positions likely to attract attention, inviting managers and teachers of elementary schools to make application for copies of Form 74L. The agents for collecting returns were further instructed to consult all rating authorities, ministers, teachers, Scripture readers, missionaries, and others likely to possess information on the subject, for lists of all schools known to them.[1]

The result of the investigation was that 3,275 schools, good, bad, and indifferent, filled up and returned Form 74L to the Board.[2] The return was not absolutely complete; but there is no reason to suppose that any school with the slightest pretensions to efficiency was overlooked.

A preliminary analysis of the forms in the manner directed by Circular No. 86 gave the following results :—

SCHOOLS.

Public Schools[3]	866
Private Schools	343
Adventure Schools	1,923
	———
Total Existing Schools	3,132
Projected Schools[4]	143
	———
	3,275

The total accommodation afforded by the schools actually in existence, calculated upon an allowance of eight square feet per child, was 373,314.

Taking the Board's reduced estimate of the number of children requiring school accommodation, the existing school provision of London, together with the school places projected, showed a deficiency of school places of 81,469. But the number of projected school places amounted to 41,000. The actual deficiency at the moment, therefore, was about 122,000. But so much being ascertained, the difficulty of the investigation was only commencing. Many, indeed most, of the schools enumerated might be described, in the words of Lord Brougham, as institutions "which by courtesy, and courtesy only, had the name of school applied to them and to the operations pursued in which the application of the term 'teaching' was also by courtesy applied."[5] A large number were conducted in buildings utterly unsuited for educational purposes,[6] and a larger number were conducted by persons destitute of any qualifications

---

[1] Board Minutes, vol. i. p. 40.
[2] This total included 86 projected new schools and 57 proposed enlargements.
[3] This included schools coming under the definition of "private" in the circular, but which were in receipt of Government Grant.
[4] Including 57 projected enlargements.
[5] Hansard, vol. xxx. p. 437.
[6] See *post*, p. 51 *et seq*

for the office of teacher. It was necessary, therefore, to winnow out the inefficient schools, and the question at once arose as to how this task was to be performed. To inquire into the structural and educational efficiency of more than 3,000 schools would require an army of expert inspectors, and the Board had as yet appointed no such officers. The Education Department, on the other hand, had a staff at its disposal well versed in such inquiries, which could be safely trusted to undertake the work. The Statistical Committee came to the conclusion that an appeal for such aid ought to be made to the Education Department, and they proposed " that the inquiry into the ' suitability ' and ' sufficiency ' of the existing schools, points which must be determined largely by a reference to the social and religious condition of a district, be undertaken by the Board, but that the inquiry into the ' efficiency ' of the schools be left in the hands of the Education Department." [1]

This proposal was not accepted by the Board without vehement opposition. It was asserted that the Board, in making such a proposal, would be deliberately shirking the duty which had been imposed upon it by Parliament and by the ratepayers, and would, at the commencement of its career, be voluntarily making the Education Department the autocrat of its proceedings. An amendment was moved proposing that the inquiry into efficiency should be carried out by Inspectors to be appointed by the Board.[2] The mover of this amendment[3] said that " the Board existed because it had been thought that the ratepayers of London ought, by their representatives, to take heed of the want of education amongst them, to take some care as to what the better education should be, and to take notice and thought how the great want, when discovered, should be provided for. He believed that the thinking men in both Houses of Parliament had this in their minds in passing the measure—viz., that in teaching the people to take thought for the teaching of their children, they were teaching the country a lesson, the right executing and conning of which would be better than most political things amongst us. This was the first lesson the country was set to learn. At the first step would the Board go whining to the master and say it could not do the lesson ? If so, what sort of a figure would they cut when they came to the end of their task ? It was proposed they should shirk the first page of their duty. Why ? Because it was troublesome ? Of course it was troublesome. That was the explanation of the long cumbrous Act itself, and of its long delay. But why had they called on the people of London to elect them to the Board if they were going to run away from the performance of their duty ? " [4]

The argument, thus strenuously asserted, was not without weight. The Education Department exercised a control over certain well-defined spheres of the Board's action ; in others the Board was supreme. When duties are thus divided between two organised

---

[1] Board Minutes, vol. i. p. 90.

[2] " That the Statistical Committee be instructed to inquire into the best means of ascertaining, by Inspectors or other persons to be appointed by this Board, the efficiency, adequacy, and condition of existing schools, and to report thereon without delay, in order that the Board may ' proceed at once to supply their district with sufficient public school accommodation,' as prescribed by law."— Board's Minutes, vol. i. p. 91.

[3] Mr. McCullagh Torrens, M.P.

[4] *School Board Chronicle,* vol. i. p. 168.

bodies there will always be a tendency to encroachment by the more energetic upon
the territory of the more supine. It might well be a question whether it were wise
at the outset to cede to the Education Department any portion of that domain which
had been allocated to the Board. But this reasoning did not weigh with the majority.
They took the view which was thus expressed by one of the supporters of the Statistical
Committee's proposal : " It appeared to him that they were in the position of having a
very heavy load at the bottom of a hill, whilst there was a team of oxen ready to
help them in the next field, the owner of which said, ' If you want me to help you,
you must tell me exactly how to do it.' "[1] The metaphor was hardly complimentary
to the officials of the Education Department, but it helped to allay the doubts of
those members who were alarmed at the prospect of the immediate creation of an
expensive inspectorate. It was inevitable that such an inspectorate would eventually
have to be called into existence, but for the present, by asking the Education Department to undertake the inquiry into " efficiency," the expenditure could be postponed.
Expenditure was a subject upon which the Board was properly, but, perhaps, exces-
sively, timid. When the Board first proposed to levy a rate of ½d. in the £, one member
suggested that the rate should be reduced to ¼d. in the £, " as it would not be
desirable to create an impression in the public mind that the Board was going to
spend £40,000 a year unless it was really necessary." [2]

Influenced by these considerations the Board decided to ask the Education Department to undertake the inquiry. The Department proved somewhat coy in its
reception of the Board's advances. Its staff was overworked by the additional duties
imposed upon it by the Education Act, and it was unwilling to lay a further burden
upon its servants ; but under pressure, it finally consented. Nine of Her Majesty's
Inspectors were told off, with extra assistance, to conduct the investigation, which
commenced on May 1st, 1871.[3]

When the Inspectors had completed their examination in their several districts they
communicated the results to the Board. The outcome of the inquiry was a fearful
separating of wheat from tares, followed, so far as the private adventure schools were
concerned, by the garnering of marvellous little wheat. The schools were classed in
three categories : (1) Efficient ; (2) Efficient in buildings or in instruction only (semi-
efficient) ; (3) Condemned. The efficient schools of all classes (public, private, and
adventure) numbered 1,019 ; the semi-efficient, 237 ; and the condemned, 1,876. But
condemnation fell upon the three classes of schools in very unequal proportions. Of the
public schools, no less than 84·5 per cent. were efficient, 7·0 per cent. were semi-efficient,
and 8·5 were condemned. Of the private schools, 36·4 per cent. were efficient, 28·0 were
semi-efficient, and 35·6 per cent. were condemned. But of the private adventure schools,
only 8·4 per cent. were efficient, 4·2 per cent. were semi-efficient, and no less than 87·4
per cent. were condemned.

[1] Professor Huxley, *School Board Chronicle,*
vol. i. p. 170.

[2] Mr. W. H. Smith, M.P., *School Board Chronicle,*
vol. i. p. 235.
[3] Board Minutes, vol. i. p. 122.

These figures prove that Government inspection was synonymous with efficiency, and that inspection for the period before the Education Act is a practical criterion of efficient schools. It must be remembered, however, that the schools classed as "semi-efficient" were essentially, according to any more recent standard, "inefficient."

The foregoing figures deal with the school as the unit, and therefore present the question in its worst aspect. It was necessary thus to present it in order to bring into prominence the desperate condition of the private adventure schools. But these schools, though forming the most numerous class, were fortunately of very limited accommodation, while the public schools, mainly the creation of the great Educational Societies, were, as a rule, large. If, therefore, the efficiency of education is tested by the efficient, semi-efficient, and condemned accommodation of 1871, the prospect is far more cheering. Of the total number of school places in existence—namely, 373,314—no less than 275,136, or 73·7 per cent, were in efficient schools, while only 34,271, or 9·2 per cent., were in semi-efficient schools, and 63,907, or 17·1 per cent., were in schools that were doomed to condemnation.

In estimating the number of available school places the Board did not take the condemned schools into account. The intermediate, or semi-efficient class were allowed a period of grace. They were provisionally recognised as public elementary schools with the consent of the Education Department. A circular was addressed to the managers of the schools informing them of this provisional recognition, and inviting them, within three months, to bring their schools up to the necessary standard of efficiency.

The inquiry, therefore, showed the following results:—

School places in existing efficient schools	275,136
School places in existing semi-efficient schools...	34,271
	———309,407
Efficient projected new schools and enlargements	37,789
Semi-efficient projected new schools and enlargements ...	3,724
	——— 41,513
Total	350,920

It has already been stated that the Board had come to the conclusion that 454,783 school places would be a sufficient provision for the children of London who required elementary education. Having ascertained that the existing and projected accommodation amounted to 350,920 school places, it reported to the Education Department that schools would have to be provided for 103,863 children. But it did not propose to provide this accommodation at once. "The Board submit the above statistics to the Department," it reported, "with the conviction that the conclusions arrived at are as accurate as can reasonably be expected. They do not, however, propose that the whole of this accommodation should be provided at once. Taking the whole area of the metropolis, they would ask the Department to authorise the immediate provision of schools for 100,600 children. . . .   The reasons for this modified proposal may be briefly stated as follow :—

"To provide schools for even 100,000 children will be a task which will not easily be accomplished in eighteen months or two years.   During that time the Board will have the opportunity of watching the operation of many causes, the effect of which is, at present, wholly undetermined.   How will the bye-laws work ?—the second, which enforces attendance at school, and the fourth, which exempts from attendance under certain conditions ?   Will the half-time Acts, which at present are almost a dead letter, come into more general operation ?   To what extent will schools which have been condemned by Her Majesty's Inspectors transfer themselves to the Board and be made efficient ?   These and other causes may contribute to *reduce* the deficiency of school accommodation which now appears to exist.   Lastly, there is the growing difficulty of obtaining qualified teachers for elementary schools, the number of which is increasing day by day.

" All these considerations, too, are independent of any errors which may have crept into the figures.   The original schedules, on which the census of children was founded, having been collected from parents whose answers were given under a penalty for inaccurate returns, are as trustworthy as any which can be obtained, but the supplemental information concerning the children and the statistics concerning the schools had to be collected from persons who were not compelled to act under the same sense of responsibility, and may contain some elements of error.   The Board have, therefore, thought it wisest, on the whole, to leave a margin for possible miscalculations and to provide, in the first instance, for a number of children less than the absolute number which represents the total deficiency."[1]

The foregoing quotation shows that the Board was conscious of the possibility of error in its calculations ; but it shows also that it imagined that, if error existed at all, it arose from an under-estimate of existing accommodation and an over-estimate of the number of children requiring such accommodation.   In regard to the estimate of existing accommodation the conclusions of the Board were doubtless fairly accurate.   If a few schools did escape enumeration they must have been private adventure schools which had no desire to court public attention, and would in all probability have been condemned upon discovery.   The semi-efficient school was doubtless treated with great leniency ; but temporary leniency was, in the circumstances, politic.   Unnecessary opposition would have been aroused if the generous but ineffective efforts of charitable persons to provide elementary education had been ruthlessly condemned without allowance of any period of grace for reformation.

It was in the estimate of the number of children requiring accommodation that the Board failed to grasp the magnitude of the question with which it had to deal.   The deductions on account of reasonable causes of absence from school were made on far too liberal a scale.   The deduction of 24,000 children from the estimated number of children requiring school accommodation was not to be justified on any principle.[2]

---

[1] Report of the School Board for London to the Education Department, March, 1872, p. xi.

[2] See *ante*, p. 39.

The figures of "average attendance"[1] are useful statistically for the purpose of ascertaining the regularity of the children in presenting themselves at school, but for the calculation of accommodation needed they are misleading. The average attendance at school must of necessity be frequently exceeded in practice. In that event, if the average attendance only is provided for, the school becomes unduly crowded and the work of education is dislocated. A further deduction of 3,263 children was made for no other reason apparently than that it would take a long time to provide schools for a smaller number. Thus more than 27,000 places were deducted from the estimate of the number required on grounds which it is difficult to justify.

It must be noted also that the Board failed to take into consideration two factors which should have increased the estimate of the number of school places required. Although the Board had no power to compel a child over 13 years of age to attend school, it also had no power to exclude any such child who desired to attend. The returns from the schools showed that a not inconsiderable number of children over 13 were in attendance at school, and yet no addition upon this account was made to the estimated number of school places required. Again, the Board admitted that no school provision could be made by it for "eighteen months or two years." The population of London requiring elementary school accommodation was increasing at the rate of about 9,000 annually. Before the Board could open a school there would be another 18,000 children requiring school places and finding none.

It becomes clear, therefore, that the Board in the first instance very seriously underestimated the number of school places which would have to be provided. The adoption of the Education Department's method of estimate would have shown that about 193,000 school places were required. The Board declared that 100,600 would suffice. Public attention should at least have been called to this discrepancy. There is no reason for doubting that the Education Department's method told the truer tale. The Board doubtless deemed it unwise to frighten the public by even hinting at such large requirements, and preferred to present in the first instance a most attenuated demand, hoping that time would educate or inure the ratepayer into a recognition of the more extended need. This course may have been judicious in respect to the reputation of the then existing Board, but it was hardly generous towards its successors, who at some time would be compelled to admit and to reveal the facts. If the actual needs of London had been disclosed from the first, there might have been some preliminary outcry, but the ratepayers would have known the facts and time would have induced acquiescence in the inevitable. The odium of revealing the actual deficiency fell upon succeeding Boards, upon whom a more accurate method of scheduling enforced the truth. It is a curious coincidence, if it is merely a coincidence, that at the very period (1885—1886) when the Board's scheduling was approximating most closely to the figures based upon the Education Department's formula, and the true needs of London in regard to accommoda-

---

[1] The average attendance of a school is the total number of attendances registered during the school year, divided by the number of times that the school was open.

tion were fully disclosed, the ratepayers elected a Board more definitely pledged to economy in expenditure than those which had preceded it.[1]

Most of the errors of calculation into which the first Board fell were exposed by the Statistical Committee of the third Board in 1879. "These calculations" (*i.e.*, in the report of March, 1872), they reported, "were made without any reference to the growth of population, although, as experience has shown, it requires two years at the least, on the average, to secure a site and to erect school buildings upon it. The calculations were also made upon the supposition that all schools at that time projected by voluntary bodies would be actually built, and that a large number of schools condemned by the Government would, if a period of grace were given, succeed in making themselves efficient. With reference to the growth of population, the Board have found that a very slight proportion of the necessary school accommodation is provided by voluntary agency. They have also found that a great number of schools projected, as a consequence of the passing of the Education Act of 1870, have fallen through, or have only taken the place of schools which have been closed. And, finally, they have found that a very considerable proportion of the inefficient schools which were temporarily taken into account have failed to make themselves efficient."[2]

This was a statement of a discovery which had been made some years previously. The estimated decrease in the number of children in 1873, in spite of the fact that the number must have actually increased by about 9,000, proved the imperfection of the methods which had been adopted. In November, 1873, the first School Board for London ceased to exist, and the second did not attempt an enumeration of the children. In the second year of the third Board, the scheduling was made upon a different basis. It was agreed between the Board and the Education Department that 10 per cent. should be added to the total of the children enumerated on account of those who escaped scheduling, and that 23 per cent. should be deducted from the augmented total on account of all causes of absence."[3]

Under this method of enumeration the estimate of the number of children for whom school places were required rose rapidly. The officials engaged in the work had gained experience, and as time went on fewer and fewer children slipped through their fingers. In 1881 it was thought that it was no longer necessary to make any allowance

---

[1] This is not the place to discuss the question of parties at the Board, or their relations to educational questions. But many points in this account of the Board's work will be rendered clearer if the position is shortly explained. Until the end of 1885, the Board was controlled by a majority which was in favour of a forward policy in educational matters, although in the first Board this policy was carried out with greater timidity than it was by its successors. But during this period, neither party was "organised" in the political sense of the term. In 1886 and onwards until 1894, power was in the hands of the party which became known as the "Moderate" party, as opposed to the "Progressives,"

who laid greater stress upon economy in expenditure. From this date more attention was given to party organisation and party "whips" were appointed to secure the attendance and, so far as possible, the votes of members. In the Board of 1894—1897 parties were practically balanced, although there was a slight preponderance in favour of the Moderates. In 1897 the Progressives were restored to power with a substantial majority. In the contests of 1894 and 1897 the election turned almost exclusively upon the vexed "religious question."

[2] Statistical Committee's Report, 1879, p. 3.
[3] Statistical Committee's Report, 1878, p. 2.

A DIAGRAM

Showing (1) The Number of Children requiring School Accommodation, and (2) the amount of School Accommodation provided in every year from 1838 to 1870 (approximately), and from 1871 to 1899 (actually). The accommodation provided by Voluntary Schools is coloured green; that provided by Board Schools is coloured red; the slate-colour represents the deficiency of efficient School Accommodation. The reduction in the accommodation of Voluntary Schools in 1899 is due to the fact that in that year the accommodation of the Senior Departments of those Schools was calculated for the first time at the rate of 10 square feet per child, instead of 8 square feet.

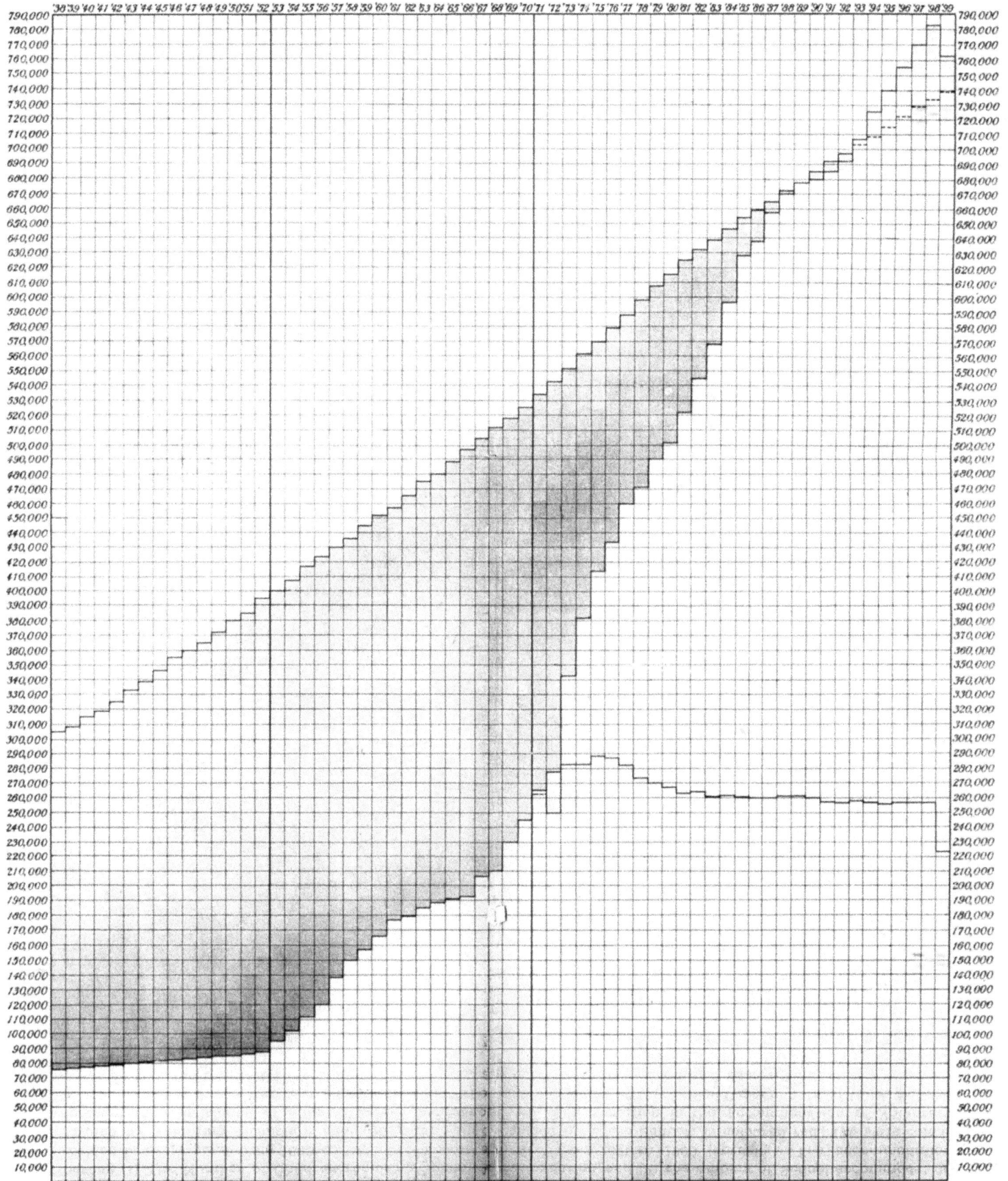

for faulty scheduling, and a gross deduction of 12½ per cent. from the number of children enumerated was deemed to account for all causes of absence.[1]

The growth of school accommodation since 1870 as compared with the increase in the number of children requiring school places is represented in the third section of the accompanying diagram. The number of children requiring accommodation is estimated in the manner previously described.[2] The total for each year is represented by the top of the column coloured slate, until 1893. In that year and onwards the accommodation provided was greater than the number of children requiring it, and the total of child population is therefore represented by a dotted line. The total accommodation existing in any one year is represented in green and red. The accommodation provided by Voluntary schools is green; that provided by Board schools is red. When the enormous number of children for whom in 1870 no efficient education was provided is considered, the rapidity with which the deficiency has been overtaken is not a little remarkable. The actual deficiency of 1871 was, it will be observed, overtaken in 1881; but the annual increase of child population created further deficiencies, which were not overtaken until 1893.

The above statement must not be taken as implying that, because the number of school places equalled the number of children requiring them, there was in existence an available place for each child. In a huge area such as that of London, the vacant places and the unaccommodated child may be miles apart, and no child can be compelled to travel more than two miles to school. Vacant places in Roman Catholic and Jewish schools are not necessarily available for Protestants, nor, since the passing of the Free Education Act, 1891, are places in schools where fees are charged available for children whose parents demand free education. During the thirty years which have elapsed since 1870, great migrations of population have taken place within the Metropolitan area. People whose children require elementary education have been driven out of many parts of Central London towards the suburbs, and their former habitations have given place to buildings of a totally different character. Thus there are in these districts schools which are by no means full, and yet their vacant places are not available for any scholars, while the emigrants have had to be provided with accommodation elsewhere.

An apt illustration of the difficulties caused by this migration was given by Lord Reay in his Annual Statement[3] to the Board in 1899. Speaking of the difficulties to be

---

[1] Board Minutes, vol. xiv. p. 571. In 1888 the Board endeavoured to increase the rate of deduction to 20 per cent., but the Education Department declined to sanction the provision of accommodation based upon such a calculation.

[2] See *ante*, p. 40.

[3] It has become the custom for the Chairman to address the Board upon the work of the Board at the commencement of the Autumn Session. This custom did not prevail during the existence of the first Board, but at the end of its triennial period it issued a statement, officially, which was at once an apology and a justification. The first Annual Statement was made in 1874, but this was not officially printed. Subsequent Annual Statements were officially printed and circulated until 1895. In tnat year the Chairman of the Board, Lord George Hamilton, resigned, having accepted office in Lord Salisbury's Cabinet. The Board met in October without a Chairman, and consequently there was no Annual Statement. Since that date the former practice has been adhered to.

E

encountered in estimating the number of new school places which ought to be provided, he said:—

"The disturbing factor in all these calculations is the rapid growth of Outer London, consequent to a large extent upon the depletion of the population of the central portions. Thus we find a considerable excess of school places in Southwark as a result of the gradual substitution of factories for houses. On the other hand, some rural districts, such as Catford and Ladywell in Greenwich, are being rapidly covered with small houses. The deserted school places in Central London are manifestly useless for the accommodation of the immigrants, and the Board is compelled to provide not only for the children now existing in these remoter districts, but also by anticipation for the future population. In illustration of this point the case of the Division of Greenwich may be cited. That division shows a net excess of upwards of 2,000 school places, but these school places are not available for the accommodation of the growing southern districts. Thus in Deptford there is an excess of nearly 400 school places; but these are useless for children in Lower Sydenham, where there is a deficiency of nearly 600."

The Chapter which is now drawing to a close has dealt with statistical questions of a somewhat dry and unattractive character. Before passing to topics of greater educational interest, it is perhaps permissible to speculate upon what the present social condition of London would have been if the Education Act of 1870 had not been passed, and the provision of education had been left entirely to voluntary effort. The second section of the diagram just alluded to, although it is founded upon statistics which are only approximately accurate, shows the rate of progress which voluntary effort had been able to make from 1853 to 1870. It practically substantiates Lord Brougham's assertion that the voluntary system was able to supply the needs of the annual increase of child population, but that it was not equal to the task of overtaking the accumulated deficiency in school accommodation. The average yearly increase of efficient school places during the eighteen years preceding 1871 was apparently about 9,000. The average yearly increase of children requiring accommodation was very nearly the same. It is true that the increase of school places in the years 1869 and 1870 was larger than this average, but this abnormal energy was caused by fear of Government interference. If that fear had never existed, the energy would not, in all probability, have been exerted; had the Education Bill failed to pass into law, it would quickly have subsided. To assume that, apart from legislation, school provision would have continued to increase at the rate of 9,000 places a year is to assume much. The great cost of land prevented voluntary agencies from placing schools in those localities in which they were most needed. So early as 1851 Mr. Cook, H. M. Inspector, reported that "one cause of deficient accommodation [in London] has scarcely received sufficient attention in discussions upon the subject—viz., the enormous expense of purchasing a site tolerably well situate in any part of the Metropolis, and the extreme difficulty, amounting, it would appear, almost to an impossibility, of procuring one, at any rate, in many of our parishes. For instance, in St. Pancras and Marylebone, and St. George's, Hanover Square, the funds for erecting buildings and maintaining schools could be raised with comparative ease; but a tenure can scarcely be purchased which would satisfy" the Education Department. "The difficulty might be obviated in some instances if large houses in second-rate situations were taken upon lease and arranged as well as possible for schools."[1]

The value of sites has increased enormously since 1851, and this hindrance to voluntary effort in providing additional school accommodation would have been correspondingly formidable. But assuming that the great Societies had been able to continue to increase school accommodation at the rate of 9,000 places per annum since 1870, the total number of school places in efficient schools would have numbered about 514,000 in 1899. The number of children requiring school accommodation in March, 1899, was more than 784,000. There would therefore have existed a deficiency of at least 270,000 school places. Assuming, moreover, that without the operation of compulsion these places would have been fully occupied, a child population equal to about half the total population of Brussels, concentrated chiefly in the most densely populous portions of London, would be growing up without the means of obtaining any efficient education. What the social condition of London would have been in such circumstances is, perhaps, worth some reflection.

CHAPTER III.

SCHOOL BUILDINGS.

(i.) BEFORE 1870.

When the first School Board began to consider the best type of school building to be adopted, it was breaking new ground. The construction of a building adapted to the work of a public elementary school, although it had been much considered on the Continent, had received but little study in England, for the very sufficient reason that perfect adaptation meant large expenditure, and hitherto the necessary funds for such experiments had not been forthcoming. To understand the value of the work done by the first School Board in this direction it is necessary to form some estimate of the style and condition of school buildings in the period previous to 1870.

It would give but an incomplete picture of the buildings in which education was conducted if no description were afforded of those schools which were not under Government inspection. Before, therefore, proceeding to describe the public school of the period, a brief sketch of the condition of that almost extinct phenomenon, the private adventure school, must be interpolated.

The investigators for the Newcastle Commission classified private adventure schools under three heads :—(1) Superior, when the terms exceeded one guinea per quarter;

---

[1] Education Department Report, 1851, p. 382.

(2) Middling, terms from 6d. a week to a guinea a quarter; and (3) Schools in which the terms did not exceed 6d. a week.[1] It is evident that the whole of class (1), and a great proportion of class (2) could not reasonably be included in an estimate of elementary school provision. It is only the lower class of these adventure schools which could come under that category.

It was calculated that at least two-thirds of the then existing schools were adventure schools, and that at least a quarter were Dames' Schools.[2] If this statement of the case be correct, as it doubtless is, the percentages of the different classes of schools would stand thus :—

Public Elementary Schools	...	...	34·0
Private Adventure Schools	...	...	41·0
Dames' Schools	... ...	...	... 25·0

To avoid the possibility of a charge of exaggeration in the description of the buildings in which the Dames' Schools were conducted, the following estimate, made by an acute observer, may be quoted :—

"Two things were remarkable : the recent date of many of these schools, and the brevity of their duration. These two things are, indeed, but different phases of the same thing. When other occupations fail, even temporarily, it is an ever ready resource to open a school. No capital is required; no outlay beyond the cost of a ticket to hang in the window. The smallest room that suffices for the combined parlour, kitchen, and bedroom of a single person suffices for the largest number of children likely to be drawn together; the floor serves instead of benches; desks are not needed, even if there were space for them; the children bring what books they please, and the establishment is complete, unless, indeed, a cane be added as a not always idle emblem of authority. The closeness of the room makes animal heat save artificial fuel; and though foul air may for a time make the children restless, it soon acts as a narcotic, and, in keeping them quiet, is as effective as Daffy's Elixir, and much cheaper. Should the income not suffice to pay the rent, an emigration ere long takes place. The children are dispersed, or received by the next tenant, and the ticket adorns another window; perhaps in the same or an adjoining street, unless recourse be had to quite a fresh field."[3]

Such was the housing of a large number of school children in London forty years ago. In 1858 the Dames' Schools were growing less numerous on account of the competition of the State-aided Voluntary Schools, but, nevertheless, a great number existed in 1870. The private adventure schools of a higher grade, although less meanly housed, were all conducted in houses unsuited for school work. It is almost certain that none of these occupied buildings designed for school purposes. The higher class private adventure school appears to have offered more sturdy resistance than the Dames' School to the encroachments of the State-aided Schools. This power of resistance seems to have been reinforced by the current opinion of the parents of the children frequenting them, that they offered a greater guarantee of

---

[1] Newcastle Commission, vol. iii. p. 343.
[2] *Ibid.* p. 481.
[3] Dr. Hodgson, Newcastle Commission, vol. iii. p. 482.

exclusiveness and respectability. The parent of 1860-70 preferred the private "Academy" to the new-fangled "College,"[1] and was inclined to reject the comparative commodiousness and efficiency of the latter, in favour of the social distinction which was conferred by attendance at the former.

If the percentages of the three classes of schools given in the report of the Newcastle Commission represent with approximate accuracy the percentages for the whole of London, 66 per cent. of the schools were carried on in buildings such as those which have just been described. The remaining 34 per cent. was represented by schools which were conducted without any view to profit, many of which were in receipt of Government Grant. The character of the buildings occupied by such schools requires more particular consideration, for these—or rather, such of them as had been erected for school purposes—were the types which would present themselves to the Board for their guidance in deciding upon the designs for new schools.

It is not possible to ascertain the exact number of school buildings, existing in 1870, which had been erected for school purposes; but it is certain that a large proportion of them were mere adaptations. "In London," said one of the Assistant Commissioners to the Newcastle Commission, "it can hardly be expected that the generality of school buildings should be quite equal to what could be desired. The necessity of economising space by putting one school [*i.e.*, department] over another, using the basements of chapels, and converting railway-arches and ill-adapted buildings to the exigencies of education, are all sad obstacles, and I have found reason to lament that some well-contrived ground plan was not put forward by authority. Many instances came under my notice where buildings recently and expressly erected were ill-adapted to the purpose. The prevailing defect throughout my district is want of ventilation. I have found this to exist to such a degree as to be prejudicial to the health of teachers and children too: very often it was occasioned by the substitution of close stoves for open fire-places. The internal arrangements of the schools are generally very similar; parallel desks with spaces in front to form squares for reading lessons, and occasionally a gallery. I did not find the low curtains,[2] recommended by the Government, much used, indeed in several cases they were removed. . . . A very ingenious contrivance is sold, adapted to a building used both as a chapel and a school: a seat with a back, which is converted by opening it into a form with a desk before it."[3] The opinion thus expressed confirmed that of Mr. Matthew Arnold, who reported in 1855: "In no school premises anywhere, so far as my observation goes, is want of space, want of cleanliness, want of ventilation, want of playgrounds, so much felt as in the school premises of London."[4] In 1857, another Inspector gave the following description of an Infants' School in the wealthy locality of St. George's, Hanover Square: "It was dark, and could not be properly lighted; so dark, in fact, that not one-half of the children could see to read even on a fine day. Good ventilation was quite impossible, every contrivance had been tried and found ineffectual. The room was thoroughly unfit for

[1] Newcastle Commission, vol. iii. p. 376.
[2] To separate classes.
[3] Newcastle Commission, vol. iii. p. 395.
[4] Education Department Report, 1855. p. 571.

a school, and would not have been tolerated in the most destitute and impoverished districts."[1]

The actual condition of school buildings may be forcibly illustrated by the descriptions of schools offered to the School Board for transfer in 1871 and succeeding years. The following are a few specimens of schools conducted in adapted buildings. :—

1. " The Tanners' Hill Day School, near New Cross, is a substantial detached building, consisting of one lofty room, with a gallery across the end. It was originally intended for a chapel, and will accommodate 145 children."[2]

2. " The Bermondsey Ragged School . . . is held under two railway-arches, under parallel lines belonging respectively to the Brighton and South Coast, and South-Eastern Railway Companies, and is capable of accommodating 241 children. The average attendance last year was 388."[3]

3. " Newington Green Day School . . . The building was originally a six-roomed dwelling-house. The upper floors are at present used by the caretaker, and the first and ground floors are used as a school, and are not capable of accommodating more than 85 children."[4]

4. " The Wilmington District Mission School, Ann Street, Clerkenwell . . . The School-house consists of one large room under a carver and gilder's shop, and is capable of division into two by a framed partition. The lighting and ventilation are sufficient; an expenditure of £25, however, will be necessary to put the premises into thorough sanitary condition and to provide an additional stove."[5]

5. " The British School (Girls), Hill Street, Peckham. . . . The premises consist of two small one-storey wooden buildings of one and two rooms respectively, which are in a very old and dilapidated condition."[6]

The foregoing examples of the shifts to which earnest educationists were put to find accommodation for school children are merely average specimens. Many worse types could be found in reports of earlier date. The quotations which follow, taken from the same source, are to illustrate the condition of school buildings which had been expressly erected for school purposes.

1. " The Orchard-street, Hackney, Boys', Girls', and Infants' Schools consist of two separate buildings, with a playground between, common to both Schools. The girls' and infants' school is a new structure of one room only. The boys' schoolroom and classroom are two long and narrow buildings, erected about twenty years ago. The schools will accommodate 319 children."[7]

2. " The Gray's Yard, Oxford Street, Ragged School . . . is a new building of three storeys, having also one room in the basement. It will accommodate 317 children without the basement, which is too dark for school purposes." [8]

3. " St. Paul's National Schools, Goswell Road . . . The schoolhouse is a large,

---

[1] Education Department Report, 1857, pp. 242, 243.
[2] Board Minutes, vol. ii. p. 508.
[3] *Ibid.* vol. ii. p. 764.
[4] *Ibid.* vol. iii. p. 124.
[5] *Ibid.* p. 153.
[6] *Ibid.* p. 1016.
[7] *Ibid.* vol ii. p. 508.
[8] *Ibid.* p. 788.

detached brick building of two storeys, substantially built and having a playground beneath. The ground floor consists of one large room with a classroom on either side of the entrance. The first floor is of the same shape, has also two classrooms, and is approached by a separate entrance up a wide and well-lighted stone staircase. The whole of the rooms are well-lighted and ventilated, and together will accommodate 679 children   The sanitary arrangements are very good." [1]

4. "The Wesleyan School, Dartmouth Road, Sydenham . . . The premises consist of a one-storey building at the rear of the chapel, capable of accommodating 115 children, with a gallery across one end of the room, and of an infant classroom with accommodation for 29 children." [2]

5. "The British School, Compton Mews, Upper Street, Islington . . . The schoolhouse is an old building of one storey, with an open roof, and consists of one room divided across the centre by a movable partition." [3]

These examples have been selected to illustrate the diverse classes of school buildings prior to 1870. There are types of the best and of the worst. No. 5 illustrates the original idea of the schoolhouse, which was nothing but a large hall. The partition was a more recent introduction in the interests of efficiency. No. 3 is a specimen of the most advanced type of building. In order to explain how the change in design arose it is necessary to consider the influence exerted by the Committee of Council on Education upon the question of school design.

It was the custom, when the Committee of Council first made grants for the advancement of education, to allow promoters of schools to present their own plans and specifications; but in February, 1840, the Committee, to save promoters of schools needless expense, and to ensure efficiency of construction, decided to prepare typical plans and specifications, distinguishing in the estimate (1) the schoolrooms; (2) the dwelling of the schoolmaster; (3), the desks and apparatus of the school. The document containing this information is known as the Minute of February 20th, 1840. Before the issue of that document the ideas of the great Societies upon school planning had been elementary in the extreme. The National Society's schoolrooms were remarkable for their simplicity and economy. In the "General Observations on the Construction of Schoolrooms, &c.," published by the National Society, it was laid down " that the form of the schoolroom should be oblong—*a barn furnishes no bad model, and a good one may be easily converted into a schoolroom.* If one large room is built to accommodate boys and girls together, arrangements should be made for dividing it into two parts when needful. A framed partition may be put up for this purpose, either removable altogether or else with a large portion of the middle framework made to slide upon rollers in an iron groove, so that it may be moved easily to the sides of the room. As regards size, 7 square feet should be allowed for each child, so a sufficient allowance for 50 children is 350 feet, and for 100 children, 700 feet; but if absentees are to be taken into account, 6 square feet is sufficient to allow on the total number on the register."

---

[1] Board Minutes, vol. iii. p. 124. [3] *Ibid.* p. 603.
[2] *Ibid.* p. 165.

If the number of children in attendance, or the funds, did not admit of two school-rooms, the length of the room was to be increased and the breadth diminished. Thus the girls whilst at needlework, &c., might be separated by a curtain or light partition, or by folding doors. This last suggestion was very valuable when the school was to be used for infants during the week and for boys and girls as a Sunday-school. As to the construction of British schools, the Manual of the British and Foreign School Society of 1839 laid down " that the form of a room best adapted to the working of the British System is that of a parallelogram. The centre of the room should be occupied by desks and forms, a clear passage of from 6 to 8 feet being reserved for the reading stations. At the upper end of the room a raised platform should be erected, surmounted by a master's desk and drawers. The windows should be either in the roof or elevated at least six feet from the ground. The ground space between the desks and the walls ought to have curved lines traced on it of nearly a semi-circular form, to make the station of each reading or spelling draft."

In promulgating a series of plans the Committee of the Council did not enforce one style of architecture, or favour any particular school system. They wished to bring more clearly to the notice of promoters of schools such designs as would fulfil the conditions necessary for a school which had adopted the newer and less widely practised system known as " the mixed method," which was a combination of the system of *mutual* instruction, in which monitors were employed, with the "simultaneous method," in which all the pupils were taught collectively by the master or one of his assistants. According to this method, 100 or 120 might be taught at once in a well-arranged schoolroom, or better, in a schoolroom to which one or two classrooms were attached. When the number of children increased beyond that which the master could conveniently instruct in successive classes, the *mixed method* was adopted, in order to save the expense of providing teachers to take charge of the classes which the master could not himself superintend.

With this object, the Minute of February 20th, 1840, gave plans in which small classrooms were attached to the main schoolroom, and a gallery for thirty or forty was provided in the latter. The Inspector reporting on Middlesex for 1853 said that few schools erected in this district before 1850, and not many after, had galleries, but that they were very advantageous for the efficient conduct of the school. Mr. Cook, in his report for Middlesex in 1857[1] said that they should not be larger than to contain sixty or eighty children, and should consist of six or seven rows with steps of varied height, with from seven to eleven inches rise.

Recognising the impossibility of providing in every case a building designed and erected for a school-house, the authors of the Minute advised the adoption of the plan then common in Holland of adapting for educational purposes buildings which had been erected for some other purpose. They suggested that for towns, double houses which had been deserted should be purchased, and altered according to the design which was given. This advice was very generally followed in London, as the descriptions of school buildings offered to the Board for transfer have shown. Mr. Cook,

---

[1] Education Department Report, 1857-8, p. 258.

in his report on Middlesex for 1851, referred to the difficulty in London of procuring sites, because the wealthy proprietors were either unwilling to alienate land, or demanded such enormous prices for the freehold. In one or two cases it was reported the promoters of schools who had collected funds for the erection of schools were unable to apply them for some years on account of the difficulty in securing a site. H.M. Inspector in 1853 said that the difficulty could only be overcome by hiring workshops, imperfectly adapted for schools, or by purchasing the lease of a large house. He suggested that if a grant could not be made for that purpose, assistance should be given towards the rent, rates, and taxes.

The expense of sites was as great in the poorer districts of London as it was in the more wealthy localities. To illustrate how efficient educational accommodation could be provided by an able man in such a district, the case of the parish of St. Thomas's, Charterhouse, may be cited. The rector of this parish, which then had a population of 10,000, was the late Rev. W. Rogers, a member of the first School Board. In 1845 the parish was destitute of any kind of school whatsoever. He at once built two for 600 children, which filled immediately. In 1853, as a result of the success which followed his efforts, he erected a new set of buildings at a cost of £6,212. There were then 900 children in attendance. In 1856 the accommodation consisted of (*a*) Upper School, for sons of tradesmen, paying £1 per quarter—80 in attendance; (*b*) National School for boys, with 260 in attendance: fees, 3d., 4d., and 6d. per week; (*c*) Free School for boys, 90 in attendance; (*d*) Girls' School, 160 in attendance paying from 3d. to 1s. weekly; (*e*) Infant School in two divisions, the upper having 70 boys and girls, the lower 200. In 1858 H.M. Inspector reported that no less than £19,031 had been spent on the building of these schools in the last few years.

Such highly-developed schools were rare in London in 1845, and, indeed, for many years afterwards. The object of the Minute of February, 1840, had been to encourage the addition of one or two classrooms to the schoolroom which had been the type of the National and British School Societies, thus tending to convert the main schoolroom into a central hall, which, however, continued to be used for the accommodation of classes. The Minute gradually effected its object.

"It is not customary at the present time," wrote one of H.M. Inspectors in 1844, "to build such enormous schoolrooms as those which were erected at the time when it was believed that one well-trained and able master could conduct the instruction of a thousand children not less efficiently than that of a hundred. And I believe that there is a general and increasing opinion that no school ought to contain more than 200 children. Indeed, unless the room be capable of division into compartments, I have no doubt that this is far too large for one master."

This quotation shows that the adoption of classrooms was a very slow process. The reason for this was that the new system was not adapted to the employment of monitors, and few schools were so affluent as to be in a position to engage paid assistants. This difficulty was partially overcome in 1846 by the introduction of the pupil teacher system, which, by securing the assistance of the elder and more efficient pupils and providing a grant for their support, made the adoption of the classroom more possible.

The accompanying plans exhibit the change which was thus effected. The first plan

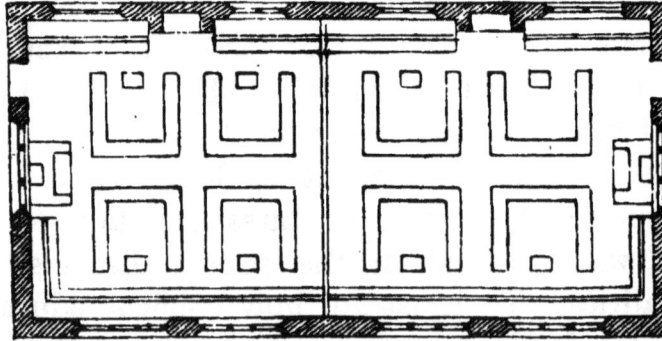

NATIONAL SCHOOL PLAN

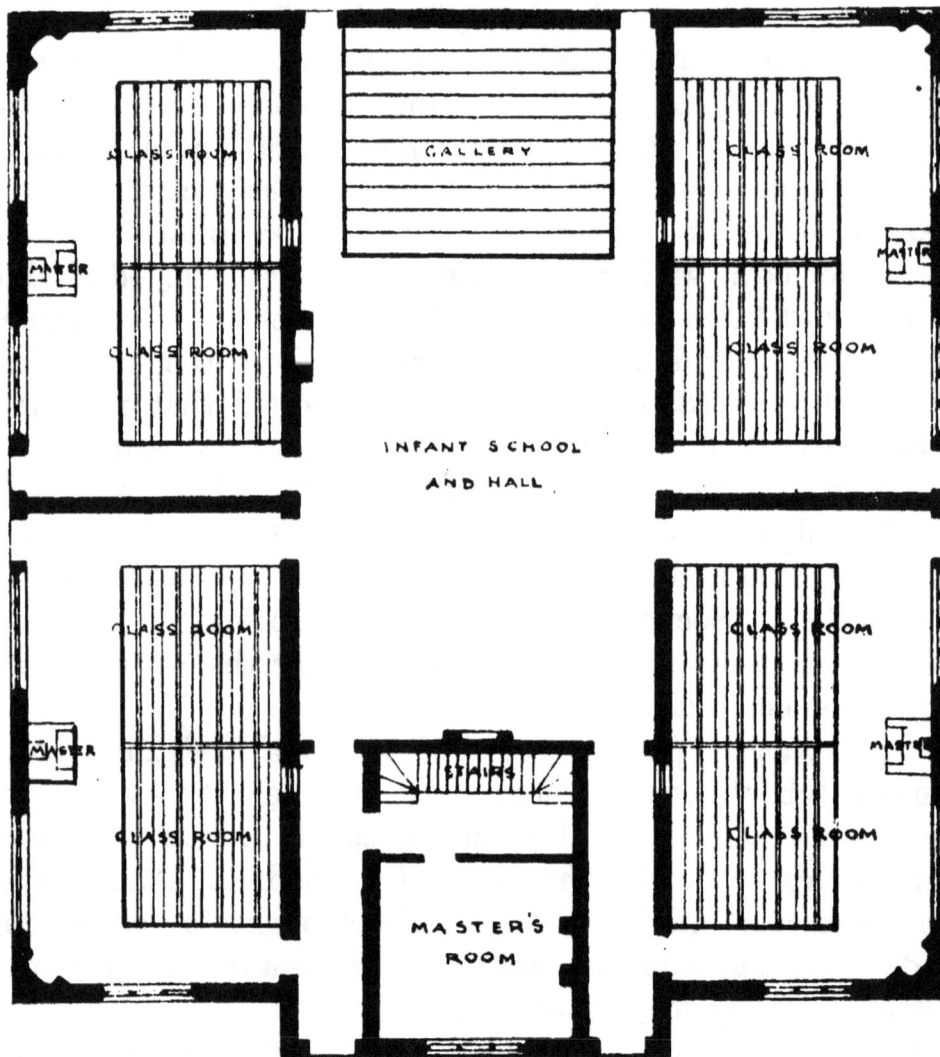

PLAN

shows the oldest type of school, designed to meet the requirements of the National Society. The benches forming three sides of a square were for the accommodation of classes taught by monitors. A later development was a similar structure divided into classrooms by means of curtains or movable partitions. The second plan shows the evolution of the classroom out of the main schoolroom.

(ii.) 1870 AND AFTER.

One of the earliest questions which the Works and General Purposes Committee had to consider was that of proposed transfers of existing schools to the Board, under the powers for that purpose contained in the Act.[1] The managers of many schools, especially of the poorest and least efficient, were eager to transfer to the Board the heavy responsibility entailed by their enterprise. Offers of all sorts and conditions of buildings were made to the Board. Descriptions of certain of these have already been quoted to illustrate the character of school buildings prior to 1870. The first offer, that of the Harp Alley British Schools, Farringdon Street, built in 1820, was made in January, 1871. The Board had then to determine what action it would take in respect of proposed transfers. It was not desirable that the Board should accept transfers blindly, without regard to the suitability of the school or the educational needs of the district in which it was situated. These facts could not be elicited until the statistical inquiry into the educational condition of the Metropolis had been completed. The Board, therefore, decided to send a reply to all applicants to the effect that it " is not prepared to deal with such applications until the returns of elementary schools throughout the Metropolis shall have been received and duly considered, and that in the meantime, and until the Board is in a position to come to a definite decision, every effort should be made[2] to maintain the school in operation."[3]

On May 3rd, 1871, the Works Committee brought up a recommendation to the Board in regard to transfers. This report, which was accepted by the Board, made it clear that the Board was by no means willing to undertake responsibility for inefficient and ill-found school buildings. It proposed that every school offered should be subjected to a preliminary inquiry as to the need for such a school in the locality; whether the situation and buildings were suitable for school purposes; whether the buildings were in good repair; whether any buildings more suitable could be obtained in the locality; and as to the nature of the tenure. It was further proposed that, as a rule, no transfer should be accepted in perpetuity unless the site was eligible, the title good, the existing buildings capable of extension and improvement, and land could be obtained close adjoining, on which the Board could erect additional classrooms, or provide playgrounds.[4] These conditions having been adopted, the Board notified that it would be ready, after June 1st, 1871, to receive applications for transfers.

The applications received placed the Board in a considerable difficulty. Most of the schools offered to it failed to come up to the standard which the Board had

[1] 33 & 34 vict. c. 75 s. 23. The Board has no power to compel the transfer of a school, but it has the right to decline it. The Education Department's consent is necessary before a transfer can be completed in cases where there is an educational trust. The Department has laid down certain rules in regard to transfers. *See* Owen's Education Acts Manual, Ed. 1897, pp. 48-58, and letter of Education Department to School Board, Jan. 1st, 1872, Board Minutes, vol. ii. p. 84.

[2] *i.e.* by the Managers.
[3] Board Minutes, vol. i. p. 54. *See also* p. 61.
[4] *Ibid.* p. 120.

established. But the application for transfer was frequently accompanied by a hint that, unless the school were accepted, the managers, much against their will, would be compelled to close it. The most usual plan was to take over the school for a year, or a term of years, pending the provision of more efficient accommodation. But this was manifestly a cumbrous and expensive method of procedure. The Board asked its solicitor whether it had power to subsidise a school for one year instead of taking a transfer. Unfortunately, the solicitor was compelled to advise that this prudent and economical proposal was illegal.[1] Nevertheless, the Board proceeded cautiously in accepting transfers, and at the end of 1871 there were only 1,101 school places in schools so acquired.

Transfers became more frequent during 1872 and 1873. In October, 1873, the Board had accepted transfer of 75 schools, accommodating 21,828 children. Of these the Board believed that no less than 40, accommodating 14,828 children, might be looked upon as permanent, and be included in an estimate of efficient accommodation.[2]

Even at the present time transfers are occasionally made. The efficiency of the school buildings thus acquired by the Board may be measured by the following figures. From June, 1871, until March, 1899, 155 schools,[3] accommodating 53,082 children, have been transferred to the Board. Of these schools no less than 145, accommodating 46,109 children, have been closed, giving place to schools of more modern design. Only ten transferred schools, with an accommodation of 6,973 children, now remain in existence.

In order to provide further accommodation while permanent school buildings were being erected, the Board, on November 15th, 1871, decided to hire temporarily buildings in which schools could be carried on in those districts which were most lacking in school accommodation.[4] The object was to collect the children together so as to form the nucleus of future permanent schools. It was a task of some difficulty to secure suitable buildings. In one case an old hospital was used; in another, assembly rooms; while some schools were carried on in mission-halls. The Board admitted that the use of such buildings "could only be justified by the urgent necessities of the case."[5] The experiment of conducting schools in these unsuitable buildings does not appear to have been attended with any very conspicuous success. In May, 1872, the Board instructed the Works Committee to make no further recommendation for the hire of buildings, except in special cases, but to give their attention mainly to the provision of sites and the erection of schools.[6] In October, 1873, the Board had 105 such schools, with an accommodation of 21,203 school places. Thus about 43,000 places out of the 58,581 places provided by the Board in 1873 were either in transferred schools or hired buildings.

Subsequent Boards adopted a more efficient method of providing temporary accommodation pending the erection of a permanent school. They caused iron

[1] Board Minutes, vol. i. p. 266.
[2] Ibid. vol. iii. p. 1,074.
[3] Of these schools 61 were Church of England, 41 British, 23 Ragged, 15 Miscellaneous, 8 Wesleyan, and 7 Congregational.
[4] Board Minutes, vol. i. p. 330.
[5] Ibid. vol. iii. p. 1,074.
[6] Ibid. vol. ii. p. 357.

buildings to be constructed suitable for school purposes, which could be shifted from site to site as occasion demanded. In March, 1899, the Board was carrying on 23 schools in 62 such iron buildings, affording accommodation for 8,000 children.[1]

The foregoing interpolation respecting the transfer and hiring of schools has been necessary in order to afford a complete view of the Board's work. It is possible now to return to the consideration of the more important question of school designs.

Under a strict interpretation of the Education Act, and of the rules laid down by the Education Department, the Board would not have been at liberty to consider the question of building new schools until its statistical returns had been completed, and the precise localities in which deficiencies in school accommodation existed had been ascertained. But the actual deficiency in many parts of London was so notorious that it needed no figures to prove it, and, before the returns had been received and analysed, the Board resolved that it would forthwith provide " a limited number of schools in various divisions of London where the deficiency is already ascertained to be great, and where there is no doubt that a large provision for public elementary education must hereafter be made." The Statistical Committee was, therefore, asked to recommend " ten or more " localities suitable for such immediate action, and an application was ordered to be made to the Education Department to send the necessary requisition to the Board to establish schools in the localities thus recommended.[2] The Statistical Committee eventually recommended the immediate erection of twenty schools,[3] and the Education Department was asked to requisition for the same. This the Department declined to do, but they approved the Board's proposal.[4]

If this action had not been taken the provision of new school accommodation would have been unduly delayed. The necessary steps for securing a site for a school are long and complicated. First, a notice must be published during three consecutive weeks in October and November, or either of them, stating: (1) The quantity of land required; (2) The purpose for which it is required; and (3) The place where a plan of the land can be seen. Then, after such publication, a notice must be served upon every person having an interest in the land, asking whether he assents to, dissents from, or remains neuter as to the acquisition of the property by the Board. The next step is for the Board to present a petition to the Department praying for a

---

[1] The Board still, in rare emergencies, hires temporary premises. In March, 1899, temporary accommodation was provided for 770 children in hired rooms. *See* 13th Annual Report, pp. 28-9.

[2] Board Minutes, vol. i. p. 117. This application to the Education Department seems to have been superfluous. The Department can only " requisition " a School Board to provide a school in two cases : (1) if they " are satisfied that a School Board have failed to perform their duty. . . . by not providing a sufficient amount of school accommodation in their district " (33 & 34 Vict. c. 75 s. 19). That condition of affairs had certainly not arisen in May, 1871, when the Board had only been in existence for six months. (2) Where there is a deficiency of school accommodation in any district, and no School Board has been constituted, the Department may then order the formation of a School Board and requisition the Board to supply the deficiency (sec. 10). It does not appear that this section could apply to the London School Board, which was formed compulsorily under the Act. The Board may have thought that a requisition, if issued, might cover any technical irregularity that it might have committed in commencing to establish new schools before the deficiencies were ascertained.

[3] *Ibid.* vol. i. pp. 184, 190.

[4] *Ibid.* p. 199.

Provisional Order, authorising the Board to acquire such lands. The Education Department may assent to or refuse the prayer of the petition; or they may interpose further delay by ordering a public inquiry in the locality as to the propriety of the Board's proposal. If the order is made, the Board acquires the right to purchase by compulsion; but no such order is valid unless it is confirmed by Act of Parliament at the instance of the Department.[1]

Such methods, admirable as they are for the prevention of injustice or error, do not conduce to expedition. If, in addition to all these delays, the Board had been compelled to wait until it could satisfy the Department of the existence of a deficiency in any given locality, and to obtain its sanction to the acquisition of a site for a school to supply that deficiency, most certainly a year, if not two years, would have elapsed before the Board could have signed contracts for the erection of schools and have commenced the actual process of building.

Some time before the date on which the erection of twenty schools had been sanctioned, the Board had been invited to consider the question of the improvement of the design of school buildings. The motion by which this question was brought before the Board was void of immediate practical effect, because it was withdrawn after discussion. At the time it was condemned as Utopian, but it is not a little remarkable that nearly all the proposals contained in it have, sooner or later, been adopted. As representing a not altogether unattainable ideal, the motion is worth quoting in full. The following were the terms of the resolution:—

"That it be an instruction to the Works and General Purposes Committee to invite, consider, and report upon suggestions, designs, and apparatus by which schools provided by the Board, especially those for the poorest children, may be made—

"1. *Healthful*, by playgrounds and facilities for exercises and for bathing.[2]
"2. *Pleasant*, by children's games and music.[3]
"3. *Attractive*, by comfortable school furniture, simple, tasteful decoration, wall-pictures, diagrams, and flowers.
"4. *Stimulative* to good conduct, attention, and progress by prizes, holiday excursions, visits to exhibitions and museums, &c.
"5. *Instructive*, by illustrated lectures and by periodicals and publications suitable for the children.
"6. *Useful* to children of parents at work, by arrangements for dinners brought by the children, or provided by voluntary contributions.
"7. *Influential* in after life, by a system of communication with scholars after they

---

[1] 33 & 34 Vict. c. 75 s. 20.
[2] Up to 1860 scarcely any London school possessed a playground; in 1870, very few. The Education Department would not now sanction a school without a playground. The first bath in connection with a Board School was opened in February, 1899. In June, 1872, a proposal was made to build a bath attached to one of the schools, but the solicitor advised that such a course would be illegal. When in 1891 the Education Department authorised expenditure upon the teaching of swimming, the illegality disappeared.
[3] Games, both indoor and outdoor, are excellently organised in many schools by the teaching staff, and also by the Children's Happy Evenings Association.

leave school and of certificates and rewards (from voluntary contributions) to those who retain situations and give satisfaction to employers."[1]

Having dismissed idealism from its purview, the Board proceeded to consider the type of school which it would erect. The development of the school building up to 1870 must be distinctly borne in mind. The first stage was the single room or hall, in which all classes were taught together. The second was the attempt to create, within the hall, embryonic classrooms by means of curtains or low partitions. The third and most advanced stage was the central school, flanked by one or two separate classrooms.[2] In 1870 school planning had not passed this point.

But on the Continent, and more especially in Germany, greater strides had been taken. In October, 1871, the Board passed the following resolution:—"That it be an instruction to the School Management Committee to obtain information concerning the Prussian system of class division, with a separate room and a special teacher to each class, and to report to the Board how far it would be desirable, in determining the plans of new school buildings, to keep in view the possibility of the adoption of a similar system in London."[3] This reference was a fortnight later transferred from the School Management Committee to a special committee which was sitting to consider and bring forward a scheme of education.[4]

At the end of November the Committee brought up a recommendation that the "Prussian System" should be tried as an experiment in one of the new schools that the Board was about to build. The recommendation was not adopted without considerable searchings of heart. Some members dreaded the expense of staffing such a school. Another feared that the supplanting of the "schoolroom" by a series of classrooms would create a congeries of little schools that would have no effective educational co-ordination. Another thought that classrooms might "cause invidious distinctions among the pupils."[5] There was an ambiguity in the Committee's suggestion which was cleared up by the discussion. It was not stated whether the "schoolroom" was to disappear entirely, or to remain as an adjunct to the classrooms. Some members presciently desired that the "schoolroom" should be retained as a hall, where all the classes could assemble; others wished that it should be reduced to the position of a simple classroom. Ultimately an amendment was accepted which effected a compromise between these divergent views, and the resolution, as adopted by the Board, ran thus: "That in one of the new schools about to be built the children of the junior and senior schools be divided into classes of not more eighty each, with a special teacher

---

[1] This condition has been but slightly realised. The idea of the Board converting itself into an unofficial Labour Bureau is not perhaps desirable. Many schools have excellent old scholars' clubs, but the success of these is due to the energy and initiative of the teachers, not to any action of the Board. It is, perhaps, to be regretted that the initial idea of the schoolhouse did not include some design for keeping the past scholars in touch with the school. A library and reading-room attached to each building and reserved for the use of old scholars would probably have proved more regenerative socially than much other more costly outlay. The resolutions quoted were moved by the late Mr. MacGregor ("Rob Roy").

[2] See *Ante.* p. 58.
[3] Board Minutes, vol. i. p. 268.
[4] *Ibid.* p. 298.
[5] *School Board Chronicle*, vol. iv. p. 70.

for each class, and that a separate room be provided for every class, the general schoolroom being available for one class."[1]

The site finally selected for the experiment was the Johnson Street Site, Stepney. The school is now known as " The Ben Jonson." It will be seen that the plan adopted marked one more step in the evolution of the schoolhouse. Hitherto the " schoolroom " had been the main portion of the building, the classroom the accessory. In the proposed new type the sets of classrooms are the main features, and the " schoolroom " becomes a mere adjunct—a larger classroom.

The original plan was to build the school for 1,000 children, but this number was afterwards increased to 1,500.[2] Before this change was made twelve architects had been asked to send in designs for the school building.[3] The particulars given to the competing architects were as follows :—

1. The three departments for boys, girls, and infants to be for equal numbers.

2. The infant school to have no other sub-division than separate classrooms respectively for the youngest and most advanced infants. The area of the schoolroom and classrooms together to be not less than eight feet superficial for each infant.

3. The boys' and girls' departments to be arranged in classrooms, accommodating not more than eighty children in each room. The area not to be less than nine feet superficial per child. A general room to be provided for the assemblage of the whole of the boys and girls at one time, calculated at not less than four feet superficial for each child, and to be available for one of the classes.

4. One of the classrooms to have a toplight, suitable for a drawing class.

5. Each of the three departments to have separate offices (approached, if practicable, by covered ways), cap and bonnet rooms, playgrounds, entrances, and stone staircases.

6. Provision to be made for a master's (or mistress's) room for each department, &c.

7. Also for a caretaker's residence of two rooms.

8. The building to be of not less than two nor more than three storeys.

Such was the scheme for the erection of a school upon the Prussian system. The question of plans for the other schools to be erected by the Board was referred to a sub-committee of the School Management Committee. This Committee brought up its report in January, 1872. The Committee recommended two types of school, one to afford accommodation for under 1,000 children; the other to afford accommodation for a larger number than 1,000. The former were to be planned in three departments, infants', boys', and girls'; the latter in four departments, infants', junior mixed (Standards I.—III.), boys' and girls'. They advised that 30 was the best numerical unit for a class, but that it should in no case exceed 40. In order to provide effectively for varying totals of accommodation, they adopted three units, 30, 35, and 40. They proposed that a school to accommodate 540 children should be based upon the 30 unit, viz. :—

Infants.	Boys.	Girls.
180	180	180

[1] Board Minutes, vol. i. p. 355. [2] *Ibid.* vol. ii. p. 350. [3] *Ibid.* p. 98.

That a school for 630 children should be based upon the 35 unit, viz. :—

Infants.	Boys.	Girls.
210	210	210

And that a school for 720 children should be based upon the 40 unit, viz. :—

Infants.	Boys.	Girls.
240	240	240

Each department in each class being composed of six units.

Passing to schools for 1,000 children and over, which were to be planned in four departments, the Committee doubled the three totals given for the smaller schools. This resulted in the following groupings :—

Unit.	Total.	Infants.	Mixed.	Boys.	Girls.
30	1080	360	360	180	180
35	1260	420	420	210	210
40	1440	480	480	240	240

The accommodation which was to be given to each grade was as follows :—

Accommodation.	Infants' Schools.	ccom.	Mixed Schools.	Accom.	Boys' Schools.	Accom.	Girls' Schools.	Accom.
540 (say 550)	1	180	...	...	1	180	1	180
630 („ 650)	1	210	...	...	1	210	1	210
720 („ 750)	1	240	...	...	1	240	1	240
1080 („ 1100)	2	180	2	180	1	180	1	180
1260 („ 1300)	2	210	2	210	1	210	1	210
1440 („ 1500)	2	240	2	240	1	240	1	240

Having thus decided the method of distributing accommodation in the six proposed grades of schools, the question arose as to what proportion of classrooms should be allotted to each department. It was proposed that as regarded infants, schools of 180 should be provided with two classrooms each for 30 children; schools of 210 should have three classrooms, two for 25 to 30 and a third "of a somewhat larger size"; and schools of 240 should have also two classrooms from 35 to 40 each, and a third somewhat larger. In all graded schools (*i.e.*, junior mixed, boys' and girls') there were to be, for every separate school department, a general schoolroom, the area of which was to be calculated on the scale of four square feet for every child, and four classrooms in two pairs, each pair being capable of being thrown into one room. The area of each classroom was to be calculated upon the scale of nine square feet for each scholar in the class and the number in each class was to be calculated according to the numerical unit (30, 35, or 40) adopted for the department.

The following table shows the distribution of accommodation in graded schools between the schoolroom and the classrooms :—

Accom.		Infants.		Graded.	Schoolrooms.	Accom.	Classrooms.	Accom.
540	—	180	=	360	2	120	8	240
630	—	210	=	420	2	140	8	280
720	—	240	=	480	2	160	8	320
1080	—	360	=	720	4	240	16	480
1260	—	420	=	840	4	280	16	560
1440	—	480	=	960	4	320	16	640

The classrooms for each department were, therefore, to afford double the accommodation of the schoolroom. Each pair of classrooms was to be made capable of being thrown into one room, and each schoolroom was to be provided with a movable partition to cut it into two classrooms, if required. It may be said, therefore, that each department was provided with either three schoolrooms or six classrooms at the pleasure of the teacher. There were, therefore, six possible classrooms for each 180, 210, or 240 children, according to the unit adopted for the school. Thus a classroom was provided for 30, 35, or 40 children as the case might be. At first sight it may appear that there was not very much to choose between the experimental school, designed upon the "Prussian system," and those which were to be erected according to the Board's design. The classes in the experimental school were not to exceed 80, while those in other schools could in no case exceed 40. On the other hand, only one class could be taught in the "schoolroom" of the experimental school, while two classes would have to be taught in the "schoolrooms" of the others. The vital difference was in the proposed method of staffing. In the experimental school it was intended that each class should be under the control of a certificated teacher; but this would not necessarily be the case in the other schools of the Board. It was supposed that in some of these schools the grading would not rise beyond Standard III. In that case each standard was to be under a "responsible" teacher, assisted by a pupil teacher. The "responsible" teacher might be a certificated teacher, an ex-pupil teacher, or a pupil teacher of not less than three years' standing. If the school was graded for all the standards the teacher was to be responsible for two standards, with the assistance of a pupil teacher. The idea was that in a three-standard department the partitions of the classrooms would be removed and the children taught in three schools. In a six standard department the "schoolroom" would be divided and the children taught in six classes. It will be seen, therefore, that for schools of six standards there was far more chance of efficiency in the Prussian type, in which the standards, although large, were under one teacher, than in the Board's type, which allowed only one teacher to two standards.[1] The plan on the next page, of one floor of Old Castle Street Board School, the first school opened by the Board, shows the arrangement of the convertible schoolroom and classrooms according to the Board's design.

Neither the experimental plan, as carried out at the Ben Jonson School, nor the Board's scheme, appears to have proved a practical success. "Johnson Street,"[2] says one of the first living authorities on school architecture, "cannot, when critically considered, be regarded in the light of a success which invites general imitation. One noticeable defect is the smallness of the accommodation for infants as compared with other departments. Another lies in the enormous aggregation in one building, rendering necessary the covering of too great an area of population and the bringing of children every day from great distances, a principle condemned in its application to elementary

---

[1] *See* **Board Minutes,** vol. ii. pp. 110, 390, and 482.   [2] The earlier name of the school.

CAPS &
COATS

JUNIOR BOYS

SCHOOL-ROOM

CLASS
ROOM

LANDING

CLASS
ROOM

PASSAGE

COALS

SCHOOL
APPARATUS
ROOM

MANAGERS
COMMITTEE
ROOM

CLASS
ROOM

JUNIOR GIRLS

SCHOOL ROOM

CLASS
ROOM

CLASS
ROOM

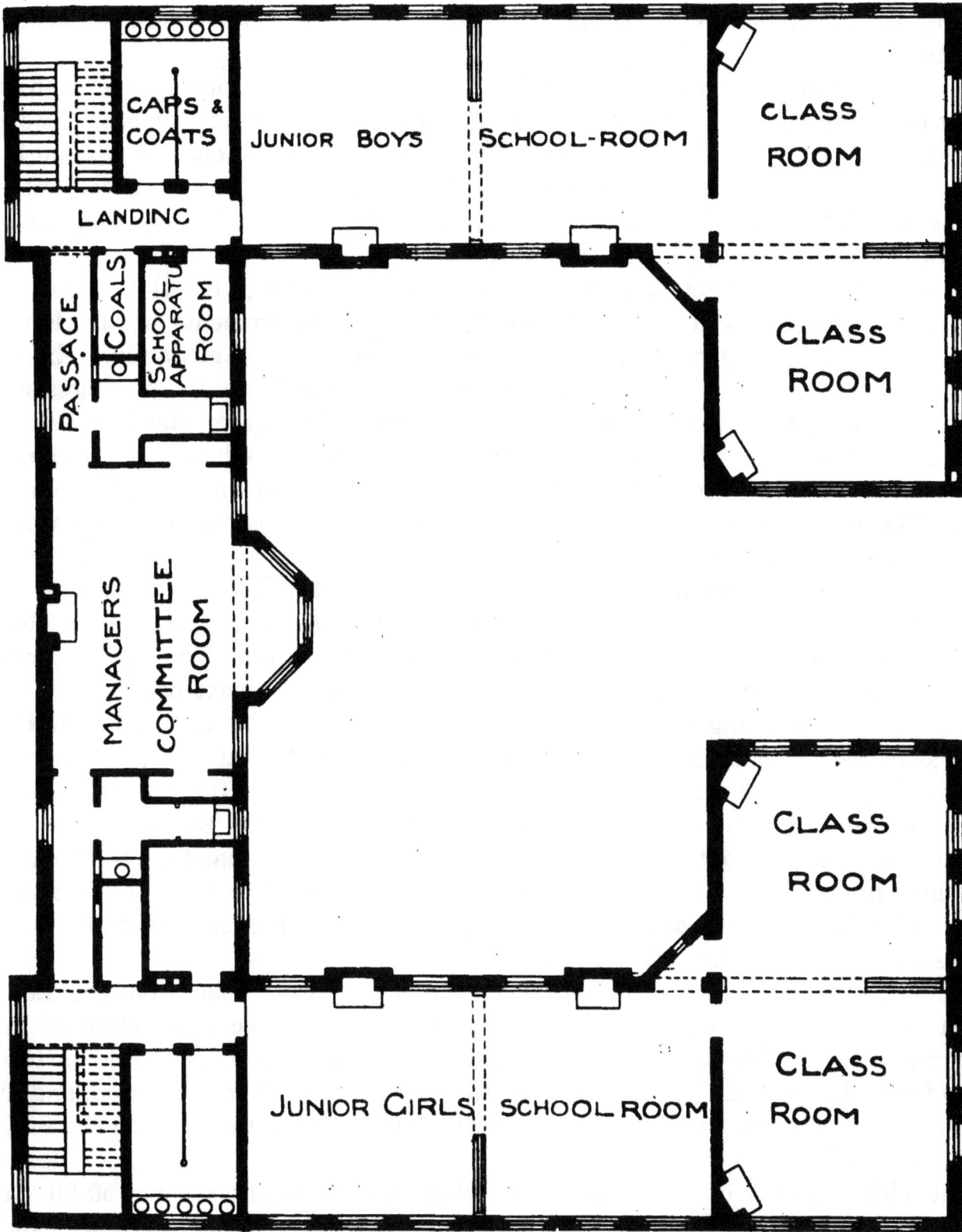

FIRST FLOOR PLAN

OLD CASTLE STREET BOARD SCHOOL.

F 2

schools by the experience of all Europe.[1]   A third consists in the comparative uselessness of the Hall."[2]

The Board's scheme was highly ingenious so long as it remained a scheme on paper. When it came to be put in practice it was found to have disadvantages.   The main defect was that the area allowed did not permit sufficient desk accommodation for the classes.   About thirty schools were designed by outside architects in accordance with the Board's scheme, and then, in July, 1872, the Board decided to employ an architect of its own.[3]   Thenceforth, neither the " Prussian System " nor the Board's scheme was rigidly adhered to.   Each school was planned according to the needs of the neighbourhood in which it was to be built and the requirements of the Education Department, without regard to any artificial rules as to accommodation.   Experience added knowledge, and each school plan was an improvement on its predecessor.   The outcome was a type of school which blended the main features of the Prussian system and of the Board's design.   The plan of separate classrooms for each class was retained, but the classroom was not built for so large a number as eighty, or for so small a number as thirty.   The mean number adopted was about sixty.   The partition disappeared from the schoolroom, which ultimately became a classroom.   It was proposed in 1873 that each school should in future be provided with a central hall, or room sufficiently large for the assembling of all the scholars; but the proposal was negatived.   The next type of school, therefore, consisted of corridors flanked on each side by classrooms, as shown in the plan of the Compton Street Board School on the next page.

The defect in planning which allowed insufficient superficial area to each child in the class, was overcome somewhat slowly.   It will be remembered that 9 square feet per child was allowed in the graded schools and 8 square feet per child in the infants' department. No change was made in this allowance until 1878, when the Education Department permitted the accommodation of graded schools planned from that time to be calculated upon the number of seats which the classrooms were planned to hold, and not upon the superficial area.   This concession practically increased the area per child in graded schools to rather more than ten square feet.

Infant schools did not fare so well.   It was not until 1896 that the Education Department agreed to allow the Board to calculate the accommodation of Infants' departments thereafter to be built at the rate of 9 square feet per child instead of 8 square feet.   In 1899 the Education Department made a further concession, and allowed the Board to calculate the accommodation of infants' departments upon the seat, or 10 square feet basis.

The older schools of the Board show classrooms accommodating 60-80 children, sometimes even more.   The early attempt to limit classes to 30-40 was soon abandoned;

[1] This was written in 1874. The school has since been enlarged, and yet has a larger roll than its accommodation.

[2] E. R. Robson, " School Architecture," p. 304.

[3] Board Minutes, vol. ii. p. 540. Mr. E. R. Robson, whose work on school architecture has been quoted above, was appointed.   Mr. Robson is now Consulting Architect to the Education Department.   His labours in connection with school architecture are too well known to need recapitulation.

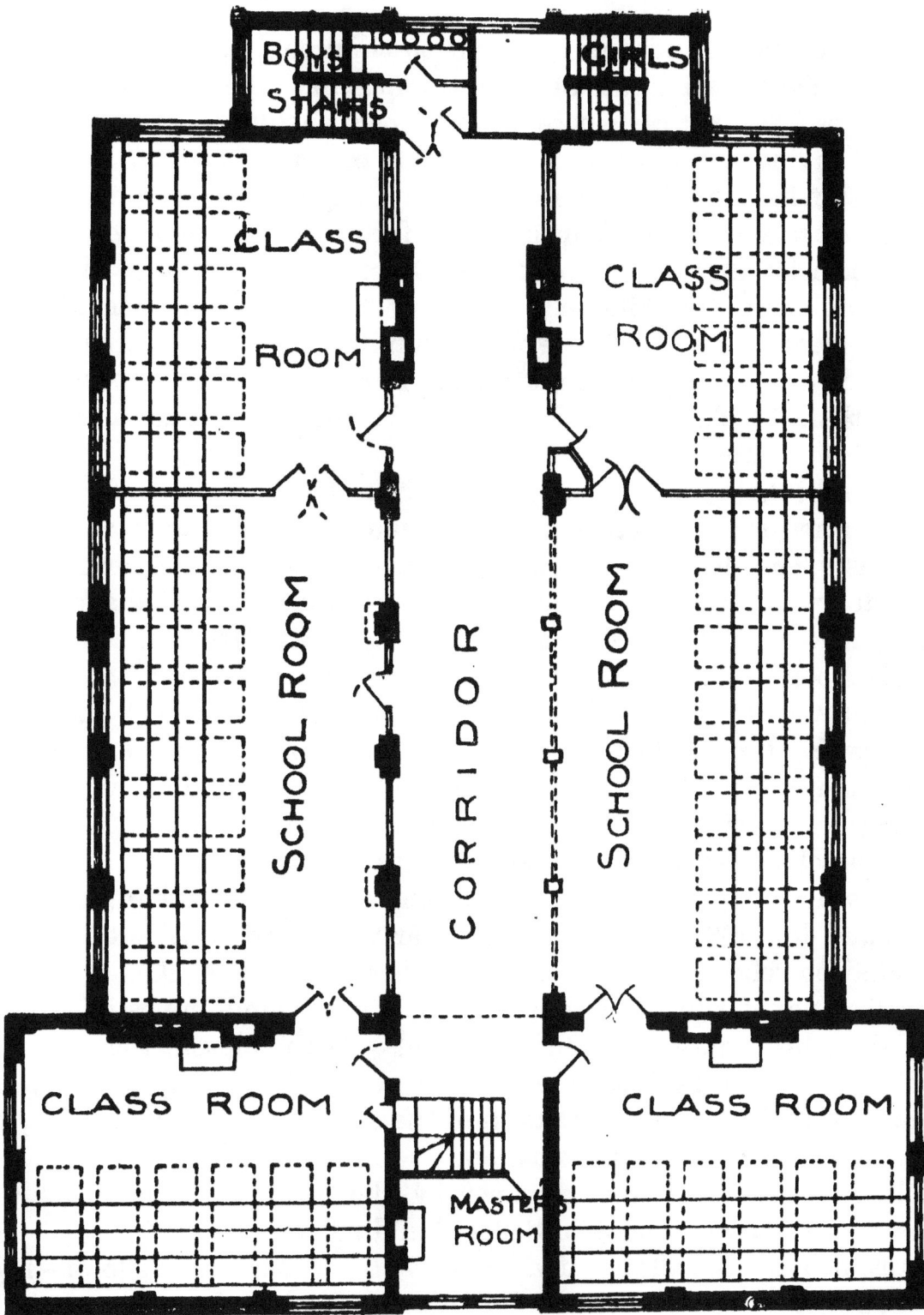

Boys Stairs

GIRLS

CLASS ROOM

CLASS ROOM

School Room

CORRIDOR

School Room

CLASS ROOM

MASTERS ROOM

CLASS ROOM

1ST FLOOR PLAN
Boys.

COMPTON STREET BOARD SCHOOL.

schools built later contain classrooms for about 60 children. This number is unwieldy in any case, and for higher standards, an almost impossible one to teach efficiently. In 1891, the Board resolved that certain selected schools should be provided with at least two classrooms, having a seat accommodation for not more than 50 children, in order that the higher standards might be more efficiently taught.[1] In March, 1898, the Board resolved that in all schools to be planned in the future, there should be, in every senior department, a room for 40 and one for 48 or 50 children, and that no room should be planned for more than 60 children.[2] Recently this rule has been laid down in a somewhat more definite form. The Works Committee has been instructed, in planning schools, to provide classrooms for not more than 40 children in and above Standard VI., for not more than 50 children in Standards IV. and V., and for not more than 60 children in the lower standards.

The provision of halls, which was negatived in 1873, was not further attempted until 1881, but some schools were built with wide corridors, which almost served the purposes of halls. The plan of the Bath Street Board School on the next page illustrates this transitional type. In 1881, several schools were planned with halls for the girls' and infants' departments. These halls counted in the accommodation of the department for one or two classrooms. The first school which was provided with three halls, one for each department, was the Carlton Road School, commenced in 1882, and completed in the following year. From 1883 onward, all schools have been erected with three halls. The plan, on page 72, of the recently erected school in Cobbold Road, Shepherd's Bush, shows the latest development of the Board School. The front elevation of this school forms the frontispiece to this volume.

These later schools proved much more efficient, educationally, than the earlier schools of the Board, and in 1898 and the following year the Board considered the question of providing halls for schools which had not hitherto possessed them. In some cases, owing to peculiarities of site or of construction, it was found impossible to add halls; but many of the schools have been thus improved. At the present time about 225 of the 447 permanent schools of the Board are provided with halls. The greater number of these do not count as part of the accommodation of the school, but in about thirty-three cases this is done, either temporarily or permanently.

The following quotation from a paper by the Board's present architect lucidly explains the Board's present policy in School-building :—

"Public elementary schools are divided into departments as follow :—boys' schools, girls' schools, senior mixed schools, junior mixed schools, infants' schools. Where the sites are sufficiently large and level, schools of all one storey are generally built; as a rule, a senior mixed school, consisting of classrooms grouped round a central hall, with an infants' department as a separate building. Another type is to put the boys' and girls' as a two-storey building, again with separate infants' schools. This type is suitable for a large site, where the levels are inconvenient for a one-storey school. The majority of sites will only allow for three-storey schools, and where additional accommodation is

---

[1] Board Minutes, vol. xl. p. 677.   [2] *Ibid.* vol. xlviii. p. 1000.

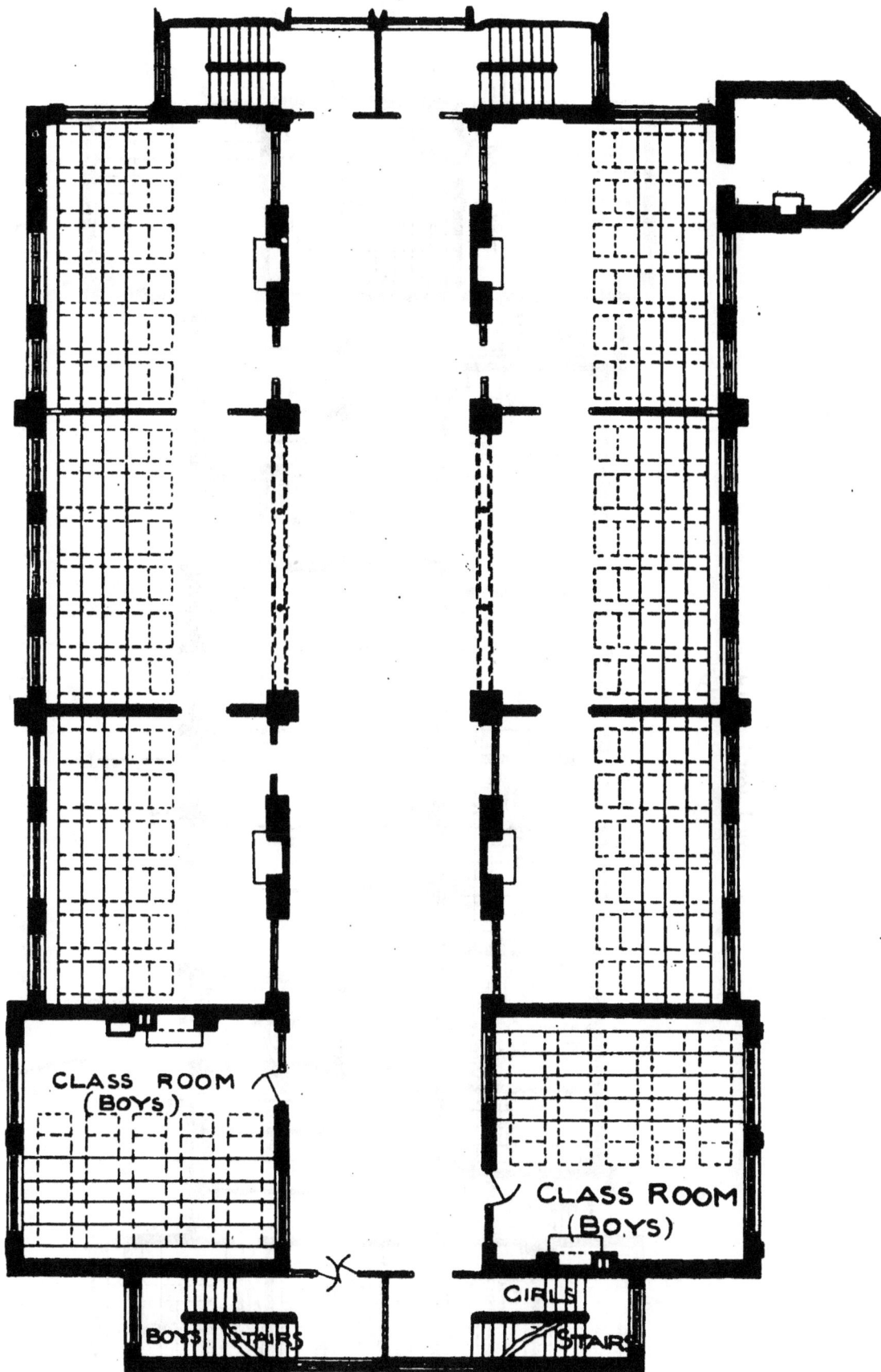

CLASS ROOM
(BOYS)

CLASS ROOM
(BOYS)

GIRLS
STAIRS

BOYS STAIRS

1ST FLOOR PLAN

BATH STREET BOARD SCHOOL.

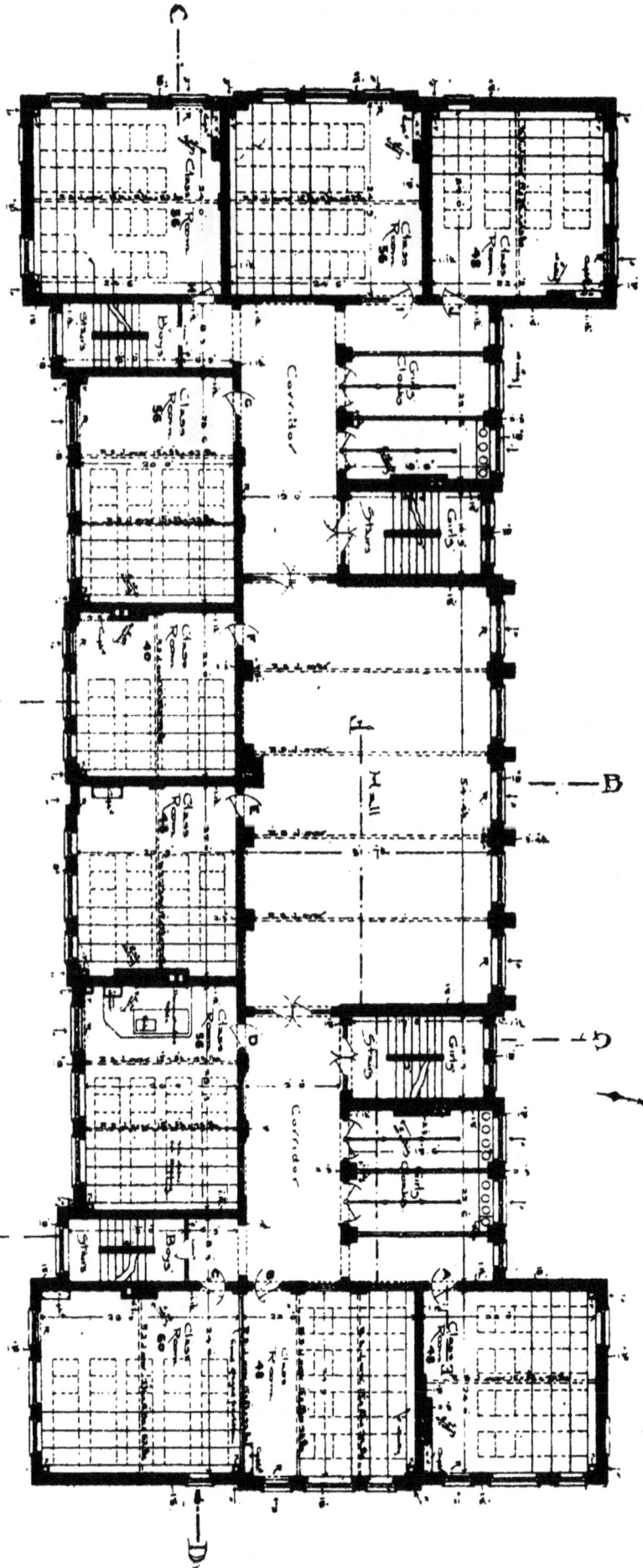

COBBOLD ROAD.

First Floor Plan
(Girls)

required in a neighbourhood where there is already a complete school, or group of boys', girls', and infants' departments, it is usually provided by acquiring another site and erecting a separate junior mixed or senior mixed department, according to the needs of the district; the junior mixed providing for children between the infant and fully graded, and generally suited to a poor neighbourhood; the senior mixed usually providing for the higher grades, and requiring rooms and facilities for teaching more advanced subjects. . . . The infants are naturally on the ground floor, on a level with their playground, the girls on the first floor, and the boys above. The London School Board considers a hall indispensable to every department of a school. Experience has shown that nearly every school built in London has required enlargement. There must naturally, however, be a limit to the size of a school, so that the departments do not become unwieldy. The maximum size or accommodation of a group should not exceed 1,548, in departments of boys 516, girls 516, infants 516; and if further accommodation is required it should be provided by a separate mixed department (either senior or junior), as already described. On the other hand, if a smaller school is needed to begin with, it is convenient to take the figures named as a maximum, and build a portion first, leaving it to be added to as needs arise. Of course, a one and two-storey school can be treated similarly. The hall for this type of school is a very good size at 54 by 30 feet, the classrooms 10 in number to each department, graduated from 60 to 40 in accommodation, thereby providing the necessary elasticity, as the lower standards, requiring the largest classrooms, are periodically reinforced by drafts from the infants' or junior mixed departments. As the numbers decrease as the higher standards are reached, the Board builds accordingly one room for 40, two for 48 or 50, and the remaining rooms for 56 or 60 will be found convenient. The Board has abandoned the use of sliding partitions, as each class is self-contained with its own teacher."[1]

CHAPTER IV.

SCHOOL MANAGEMENT.

Section I.—Before 1870.

(i.) Curriculum.

It would be almost impossible to describe with any lucidity the policy which the first School Board for London adopted in relation to this most important aspect of its work, without offering a prefatory sketch of the conditions of education during the period which immediately preceded the commencement of its labours. Without such knowledge it would be difficult to appreciate either the obstacles which the Board had to encounter, or the boldness of the changes which it sought to introduce.

---

[1] "The Planning and Construction of Board Schools." By T. J. Bailey, F.R.I.B.A. *Journal of* the *Royal Institute of British Architects,* vol. vi. p. 409.

That period may be divided into two portions, which may be designated roughly as the period of inspection, from 1839 to 1861 ; and the period of inspection with examination, from 1862 to 1870. Grants were not made for school maintenance until 1846. From that date until 1861 they were made upon the results of the reports of H.M. Inspectors. The curriculum to be adopted was decided upon by the managers, and the amount of the grant in no way depended upon any success or failure in examination. During the second period the grant depended to a large extent upon the success of the children (other than infants) in passing an individual examination in reading, writing, and arithmetic. It will be seen in the sequel that the result of the earlier period was to foster a system of education which, although it presented all the appearances of breadth and liberality, was based on no foundation of excellence, and was on that account sterile in results ; while the severe limitations of the second period, although they may have been necessary to counteract previous error, tended to reduce education to a low level of mechanical routine in mere rudiments, which, if they had been persisted in, might have proved equally disastrous.

The following account of the curriculum and its results is based, to a great extent, upon reports on elementary schools in England. It is impossible to extract from the earlier reports, which cover very large areas, the facts which related to London alone.

Previous to the promulgation of the Minutes of the Committee of the Council in 1839, and indeed for some years afterwards, in the great majority of schools, certainly in the uninspected, which were, as a rule, always inferior to those which sought Government aid, reading, and in many cases arithmetic, were taught, while writing was regarded as an extra subject in much the same way as at a later date was the case with drawing. The curriculum in girls' schools consisted of sewing and, if time allowed, a little reading was added. In both schools a certain amount of religious teaching was also given. Mr. Tremenheere said of the boys' departments of British schools in London, which he inspected in 1840, that "the great majority of the children are very imperfectly prepared to encounter the business, duties and trials of life, plunged into which they are at so early an age." [1] But some schools made an attempt at an extensive curriculum, for he reported that at Harp Alley Street, Farringdon Street, " drawing, the elements of mechanics, and singing by note were taught." [2]

In a report by the Hon. Baptist Noel, made in 1840, it is stated that the great majority of National and Lancasterian Schools only profess to teach reading, writing, and arithmetic, and that a knowledge of the English language, natural history, geography, physiology, and history of their country, are all excluded subjects. [3] Many in the highest classes were unable to read the New Testament fluently; words were mistaken, stops were misplaced, and short words were mis-spelt. In the girls' schools very few could write, and the writing was often very bad, and very few boys attained to a good running hand. In many girls' schools no arithmetic was taught : the boys, when taught, were deficient in the simplest rules. In one school, only six boys were

[1] Education Department Report, 1842, p. 48.   [2] *Ibid.* p. 457.   [3] *Ibid.* 1840, p. 173.

capable of doing a short sum, and five out of the six brought a wrong answer. In another, out of 167 boys only twelve professed to understand compound addition.

In order to obtain some idea of the actual progress in elementary subjects, and of the character of the curriculum in inspected public elementary schools five years after inspection by the Committee of the Council for Education was established, the following statistics, quoted by Mr. Cook in his report for 1844 on the Eastern District (which included London), are of value. He gave results as to 3,022 boys and 1,872 girls who attended inspected Metropolitan National Schools:—

As to reading—

    1244 boys and 732 girls were learning letters, and only able to read monosyllables.

    1168 „   „ 728 „ could read very simple narratives.

    610 „   „ 412 „   „   „ with ease Acts of the Apostles.

As to writing—

    1028 boys and 596 girls could form letters and simple words on slates.

    835 „   „ 304 „   „ write the Lord's Prayer and the Ten Commandments.

    272 „   „ 120 „   „ write the Catechism, texts, passages from reading books, neatly and correctly.

As to arithmetic—

    1561 boys were learning elementary rules.

    449 „   „   reduction and compound rules.

    148 „   „   the rule of three.[1]

From these figures it appears that while all boys and girls were learning reading, 887 boys and 852 girls were not learning writing, and 864 boys were not learning arithmetic. From the Inspector's silence on the subject of the girls' attainments in the last-mentioned subject, it would appear that they were not taught it at all.

Passing to other subjects, Mr. Cook said that geography was taught "in most schools." As to grammar, he remarked, " Very few of the elder children are able to tell the parts of speech or parse a common sentence." This general deficiency in teaching and its results he ascribed to two causes. The proportion of teachers to pupils was absurdly small. One master, often without any training, and assisted only by young monitors of 11 years of age, who themselves "read imperfectly and make gross errors in writing," naturally found it impossible to teach 100 or 150 children. It was thus not surprising therefore, that the proportion of " good " or " fair " readers did not exceed one-third.

But a second reason—in fact, the one which retarded all progress until compulsion was permitted by Statute in 1870—was the early age at which the children were withdrawn from school. In 1845 the same Inspector, reporting on the same district, recorded some improvement in the style of reading, the attention to English composition, and the introduction or extension of geography, grammar, and history.[2]

The time allotted to the different subjects of instruction in 112 London schools, containing 12,098 children, in 1846, was as follows:—Religious instruction (including

Education Department Report, 1844, vol. ii. p. 137, 138.   [2] *Ibid.* 1845, p. 143.

Catechism, reading and questioning on the Bible, and a collective lesson) occupied one-and-a-half hours; arithmetic, one hour; writing from dictation, grammar, geography, etymology, and lineal drawing took about one-and-a-half hours; while an hour was devoted to books on practical morality and general information. The time allotted to higher subjects in the upper classes was employed by the lower classes in reading, spelling, and writing.

H.M. Inspector, reporting on British schools in 1846, said that only one boy in ten read with ease, and only one in 200 read with expression. Of the girls, who read better than the boys, one in twenty read with expression, and four-fifths with ease. In reading, therefore, the British Schools compared favourably with National Schools; but the comparison was far less favourable in arithmetic, for the Inspector said: "Arithmetic is not far advanced, only one-half are learning it at all, and less than that number in the case of girls." The explanation of the poor results in girls' schools was that the time was generally occupied with needlework in place of arithmetic. The higher subjects were apparently less taught in British than in National schools, except "drawing, which has long been practised in the majority of schools." Geography was taught to one-fourth of the boys and to one-fifth of the girls; grammar to one-sixth of the boys and to one-tenth of the girls. History and science were taught to a slight extent in the upper classes.[1]

The foregoing quotations throw light upon the character and scope of education in the first of the two decades between the formation of the Committee of the Council on Education and the revised Code of 1862. It will be observed that the success in teaching the rudiments was not very great, and that, although some show of instruction in higher subjects was made, the teaching was superficial in character and unsatisfactory in result. The tendency to give a showy rather than a sound education was beginning to manifest itself, a tendency which developed more rapidly during the next decade, until it received a sharp and possibly too violent a check by the operation of the Revised Code.

In the following decade, 1851—1860, there was considerable apparent progress, so far as statistics and reports reveal the condition of education. The following figures are preserved in regard to the reading of children in the County of Middlesex. The percentages are those who were able to read letters and monosyllables, but were unable to read easy narratives :—

1850	...	...	...	39·72
1851	...	...	...	39·64
1852	...	...	...	33·11
1853	...	...	...	27·93

There was real progress in 1851, although it is not apparent; for, in that year, the infants were first taken into account. The percentage in 1853 was said to be practically identical with the percentage of children under 8 years of age.

But in regard to the children who were in advance of this class in reading, **a**

---

[1] Education Department Report, 1846, pp. 87, 88, 101.

considerable deduction must be made in estimating the reality of their attainments. From the prevalent custom of using the Scriptures as the sole reading book, the children grew to know passages by heart, and reading from the Bible served as no proper test. When the children were confronted with the same words differently arranged, in books of corresponding difficulty, they were completely puzzled. In 1847 H.M. Inspector said that of 12,786 children, 2,891 could read the Scriptures with ease; but only 651 could read books of general information. And he added that many who could read the Bible with great fluency could not read three lines together from the latter books.[1]

In regard to writing, whereas in 1844 only 26 per cent. wrote on paper, in 1850, 31·73, in 1851, 38·5, and in 1852, 43·32 wrote fairly from dictation. In 1851 it was reported that " our children write more correctly, neatly and easily than those of the same age in countries celebrated for educational progress, France and Germany."

The teaching of arithmetic was reported to have improved, but no figures were given in regard to it.

In the higher subjects, one of H.M. Inspectors, in his report for 1850-1,[2] with special reference to London, said that half the children learnt geography, and one-third learnt English grammar. A smaller number were taught history, but the teaching of this subject was not calculated to inspire an interest in it. The Inspector said that the only knowledge he had found was a matter of pedigree, and the succession of kings. In 1852 and the following years the increase in the teaching of the higher subjects seems to have been rapid, English history, geography, grammar being more frequently taught. Speaking generally of the effect of the curriculum on the pupils at this time the Inspector said, somewhat triumphantly, that, comparing with Germany, where he had inspected, and from conferring with Inspectors from France, Germany, and Ireland who had seen our schools, " boys of the same age are more advanced in reading, writing, and arithmetic, and in general knowledge, than in any of these countries— *i.e.*, comparing with schools which have taken benefit under the Minutes of 1846." [3]

It is impossible to feel convinced, having regard to the findings of the Newcastle Commission, that there was any valid basis for such boastfulness, and suspicion of its accuracy is confirmed by a passage in the report of the same Inspector in 1854 on education in Middlesex. In that report he thus sketched the supposed attainments of a typical boy at the age of 12, beyond which age few of the children of the working classes remained in London schools[4] :—

1. Reads fluently and with intelligence.
2. Writes very neatly and correctly from dictation and memory.
3. Works all the elementary rules of arithmetic with accuracy and rapidity, including decimals and vulgar fractions.
4. Parses sentences and explains their construction.
5. Knows elements of English history and geography.

---

[1] Education Department Report, 1847-8, p. 187.   [3] *Ibid.* 1852-3, p. 387.
[2] *Ibid.* 1850-1, p. 35.   [4] *Ibid.* 1854-5, p. 393.

6. Knows elements of physical science.

7. Knows the principles of political economy with reference to the question ot labour taxation, use of capital, effect of strikes on wages.

8. Draws with skill.

If such paragons had really existed, the labours of the Newcastle Commission would have been in vain and the Education Act a superfluity. If such a curriculum had prevailed to any considerable extent, while the vast majority of children were ill-grounded even in the rudiments, no further proof would be necessary that those who were responsible for it needed the wholesome check which was administered by the Revised Code.

An instance of the superficiality of the teaching is afforded by the report of an Inspector of Roman Catholic Schools for 1853-4. The Inspector asked: "What is the length of the Danube; the height of the Andes? How many million square miles there were in the Atlantic Ocean, and in the Pacific?" All these were answered correctly and quickly. He then inquired: "You say such an ocean contains 16,000,000 square miles. Can you compare this with any other, to show me you know how large it is?"—No answer. "Is it as large as Europe?"—No answer. "As England?"—No answer. "As that field?"—No reply. One of the boys then said, "It might be about as large." It may reasonably be doubted whether education in France and Germany ever sank to so low a level.

This ill-advised expansion of curriculum took place only in the more ambitious of the inspected schools in London, and it was not effected without opposition, although that opposition was based upon somewhat curious grounds. It was founded on the old complaint that the secular education was outstripping the religious. An Inspector in 1855-6 said that he lately heard that "in one of the Educational Societies some few years ago, when the limits of instruction were discussed, after determining that the first four rules of arithmetic should be taught in the schools, it was gravely maintained by some that it was *dangerous* to extend the course into reduction."

A further grave defect was noticed in the teaching of the higher subjects. Instead of being properly graduated throughout the school, the teaching of reading, writing, and arithmetic was generally confined to the lower classes of the school, while the upper were saturated with the higher subjects exclusively. Concerning this want of balance in teaching one of H.M. Inspectors said: "It is absurd that certain branches of knowledge should, by some arbitrary rule, be apportioned to certain sections of the school without noticing the complexity or simplicity of the subjects—*e.g.*, the lower sections are confined to reading and spelling, while the upper are loaded with geography and history as 'advanced' branches."[2]

At this time the Newcastle Commission on the State of Popular Education in England was concluding its labours. The evidence given before the Commissioners pointed conclusively to the fact that the efforts made in recent years to introduce higher

---

[1] Education Department Report, 1853-4, p. 839.   [2] *Ibid.* 1859-60, p. 174.

subjects of instruction into the schools had resulted in inefficient teaching, not only in those, but in the rudimentary subjects. The following were the conclusions of the Assistant Commissioner for South London :—

"The general impression left upon my mind by what I have witnessed is not very cheering, after every possible allowance for many excellent schools and for the progress which has been and is still being made." "Reading," he went on, " is by no means taught, in general, as it ought to be." "Writing in most schools is much more practised than taught. The pupil copies, with or without care, what is placed before him, but he gets too little guidance from the master, and even his errors in spelling, &c., are not regularly corrected." "Arithmetic is often well taught, and on the whole I should say that it was better taught than any other subject." Then passing to other branches, in which only about a third of the children received any instruction whatever, he said : "Geography and History are both taught with far too little discrimination of what is useful and what is useless." "In Grammar I have generally found great deficiency."

It was the proved failure to teach either the rudiments or the higher subjects successfully which induced the Commissioners to recommend that the grant should be apportioned upon the results of individual examination in the rudiments, a recommendation which brought forth the Revised Code of 1862.

It had been proved conclusively that sufficient attention had not been paid to the elementary subjects, reading, writing, and arithmetic, especially in the middle and lower classes of schools. It was therefore deemed advisable to endeavour to raise the standard in these subjects, and thus to encourage accuracy and soundness in those branches of instruction upon which alone a superstructure of higher teaching could be founded. The Revised Code, therefore, laid down that every scholar for whom grants dependent on examination were claimed must be examined according to one of six graduated standards in reading, writing, and arithmetic, and must not be presented for examination a second time in the same or a lower standard.

A grant, based upon average attendance, was given for every scholar, and a further grant for scholars over 6 years of age who had attended more than 200 morning or afternoon meetings of their schools, subject to deduction for every scholar who failed to pass the examination in reading, writing, or arithmetic.

The practical result of the Revised Code as regards curriculum, in the opinion of managers, who were bound to be guided by financial considerations, and of teachers, who naturally wished the results of their work to receive the Inspector's approval, was to limit instruction to those subjects for which alone grants would be paid. The more elaborate but ill-taught curriculum which had hitherto prevailed in the schools was narrowed down to the three elementary subjects. An Inspector reported in 1862 : "I have found a deliberate and systematic discontinuance of instruction in geography and other subsidiary subjects upon which no direct bonus is proposed by the Revised Code, nor has this been compensated for by improvement in the elementary subjects." [1] Another,

_____
[1] Education Department Report, 1862-3, p. 41.

two years later, said : " Grammar, geography, history have almost entirely dropped out of the course of instruction."

It is unnecessary to accumulate evidence upon this point. Nearly every educational report of this period confirmed the fact that, except in some few cases where enlightened teachers and far-seeing managers maintained the old wider curriculum in spite of obstacles, elementary teaching was confined to reading, writing, and arithmetic.

This result was not deliberately intended by the framers of the Revised Code. Their desire was to secure that the rudiments should be efficiently taught, trusting that the higher subjects of instruction would not be neglected. This distinction was well expressed by two of H.M. Inspectors in 1864 and 1865. " In promoting popular education," said one, " that which ought to be done must take precedence over that which ought not to be left undone, and this distinction in favour of reading, writing, and arithmetic will continue to be needed in the apportionment of public grants until those arts are acquired." [1] Another Inspector most concisely summed up the great difficulty felt at this time, namely, to construct " a type of education out of the double element of instruction which the State exacts and of instruction which it approves." [2]

The most significant point to notice in regard to this policy, which had the effect of narrowing down the instruction in most schools to reading, writing, and arithmetic, is that it did not very appreciably improve the teaching of these favoured subjects. From the imperfect statistics of this period it is possible to construct the following table of the percentage of failures in the three obligatory subjects :—

			1864.	1865.	1867.
Reading	...	...	11·87	11·23	9·29
Writing	...	...	13·98	13·39	12·41
Arithmetic	...	...	23·69	23·58	23·72

After five years the operation of the Revised Code had produced only an insignificant improvement in reading and writing, and a slight retrogression in arithmetic; a result which fully justified the opinion of those Inspectors who maintained that instruction in the rudiments could never be efficient if other subjects were entirely neglected.

In 1867, Mr. Alderson, after criticising the low standard of reading and writing, said : " In arithmetic the tendency to a mechanical and unintelligent type of instruction is even more apparent. Just what he expects to have to do, propounded in exactly the way in which he expects to have it propounded, a boy presented in Standard IV. generally does extremely well. But vary the forms of the proposition in the slightest degree, or state it in terms slightly different from those which his teacher has adopted, and he is altogether thrown out and puzzled. At the same time it appears to me clear that unless a vigorous effort is made to infuse more intelligence into its teaching, Government arithmetic will soon be known as a modification of the science peculiar to inspected schools, and noticeable chiefly for its meagreness and sterility."

Another remarkable circumstance is the wholesale manner in which the test

---

[1] Education Department Report, 1864-5, p. 114.　　　[2] *Ibid.* 1865-6, p. 246.

established by the new Code was avoided. The Department's Report for 1866 stated that out of 803,177 children qualified by age to present themselves for examination only 664,005 were qualified by attendance (200 times), and of these 161,773 only presented themselves for examination. The backward state of education is seen in the fact that out of these only 97,364 passed above Standard III., whereas 264,231 of the total were over ten years of age, and might reasonably have been expected to do so.

The main merit of the system introduced in 1862 was that it put an end to a great extent to the showy but valueless teaching of the previous period. It was also claimed for the new system that it prevented over-pressure upon the pupils; but some of the Inspectors attributed this slackening to the fact that the teacher, anxious to earn a grant at all hazards, intentionally kept back the pupils from passing into classes which they might well have entered. It was alleged also that the dull and backward children, who could not be squeezed through the examination except by special effort, were neglected in favour of those who were more certain to earn a grant.

The general opinion was that the Revised Code improved the condition of the lower standards in the schools, but that it had crushed the life and interest out of the upper classes. An attempt was made in 1867 to revive interest by allowing a grant for one specific subject in the upper standards. On the whole, the opinion of H.M. Inspectors who dealt with the London district was adverse from the Revised Code. The value of the new system was negative merely. Concerning it Mr. Alderson, after two years' experience of its working, said that it was "a very good test of a bad school, and a very indifferent one of a good school. It runs like a sword through a mass of half-acquired and ill-digested knowledge, and lays bare the shortcomings of an incompetent teacher with striking effect; but it is too mechanical, too monotonous and inelastic to be an adequate test of the school work of a conscientious teacher." Mr. Matthew Arnold reported upon his schools thus: "I find in them in general, if I compare them with their former selves, a deadness, a slackness and discouragement which are not the signs and accompaniments of progress." And again, in 1867-8, he reported: "The mode of teaching in the primary schools has certainly fallen off in intelligence, spirit, and inventiveness during the four or five years since my last report. It could not well be otherwise. In a country where everyone is prone to rely too much on mechanical processes, and too little on intelligence, a change in the Education Department's legislation which, by making two-thirds of the Government Grant depend upon a mechanical examination, inevitably gives a mechanical turn to the school teaching, a mechanical turn to the inspection, and must be trying to the intellectual life of a school. More than 14 per cent. of the children in average attendance are under 6 years of age, and so not examined; more than 27 per cent. did not appear upon the schedule at all, not having attended school often enough. Therefore, only 59 per cent. are left of the scholars as subjects of examination. The inspection, therefore, is not that stimulus to the whole school which it was when a proportion of each class, picked at random by the Inspector, were freely examined by him." [1]

---

[1] Education Department Report, 1867-8, p. 296.

It is evident that, notwithstanding the increase in the number of schools and scholars that was made in the decade 1861-70, and notwithstanding the attempt to introduce the teaching of a specific subject in 1867, elementary education, in its higher aspect, suffered a serious check.

The foregoing account of curriculum has been confined to an examination of the scope of teaching in inspected schools. There is but little material upon which to form an opinion of the teaching in those schools, not conducted for profit, which declined to submit themselves to the scrutiny of H.M. Inspectors. But all the evidence which is obtainable points to the conclusion that they were less efficient than the inspected schools, and, although they did not suffer from the deadening influence exerted by the Revised Code they were incapable of producing satisfactory educational results.

The private adventure schools, including the Dames' Schools, may be dismissed in a few sentences. It would be an abuse of language to speak of the " curriculum " of such schools. In the Census of 1851, more than 700 heads of such establishments authenticated their returns with their mark in place of a signature. Many were unable to write an intelligent answer to a simple question.[1] One, on being asked as to the terms on which she gave instruction, replied: " Not understanding the questing, I answer thus :—with a view of reading the Bibble." We have the authority of the late Lord Shaftesbury for the statement that one of these poor creatures, being asked if she gave moral instruction to her scholars, replied, " No, I can't afford it at 3d. a week." The whole case was summed up by another, who, answering a question as to the amount of remuneration she received and the amount of knowledge she imparted, said : " It's little they pays us, and it's little we teaches them."

It can hardly be said that the private adventure schools of a somewhat higher grade were much more efficient. Of them Lord Brougham said: " A great many of these day schools were conducted without any attempt at order or system, and nine-tenths of the children received no instruction whatever that was worthy of the name. A great number of the instructors were persons utterly unfit for the performance of the duty, and many of them had merely adopted the profession in despair of obtaining any other mode of livelihood." He went on to give specimens of the answers of some of these teachers to questions as to their acquirements. The replies showed that the masters rose but little above the dames in knowledge, and ranked far below them in honesty. One was asked whether he knew geography and the globes. His answer was that he knew geography and both the globes; and when asked for an explanation, he answered that he knew that one of the globes meant one part of the world, and the other the other. One " was asked whether he understood Greek?—Yes. Geography?—Yes. Latin?—Yes. Then one of the examiners observed : ' Aye, we have *multum in parvo*

---

[1] The following is an exact transcript of a letter addressed to one of the Assistant (Newcastle) Commissioners :— " 3rd March, 1859. Sir,—I regret that I am not able to attend to all the rules lade down in thee in closed, as my school is of to humbel a cast to meat eyes (of thee publick gaze) at thee same time Sir I shal be moust appay to refur you to my Children's Parents, as kindly favord me with thir children for some years. Any further information that you require Sir, I shall bee moust appey to give. Pardone defects ; I remain Your most humbel servant." Vol. iii. p. 485.

here!' upon which the teacher, seeing that notes of his answers were being taken, added: 'Yes, and you may put down *multum in parvo*, too'! In another place a teacher was asked whether proper attention was paid to the morals of the boys under his care. His answer was that they did not teach morals there, as they belonged to the girls' department." It was the opinion of the Newcastle Commission that not 5 per cent. of this class of teacher had received any regular training for the profession.

"None," said the Assistant Commissioner for South London, "are too old, too poor, too ignorant, too feeble, too sickly, too unqualified in any or every way, to regard themselves and to be regarded by others as unfit for school keeping. Nay, there are few, if any, occupations regarded as incompatible with school keeping, if not as simultaneous, at least as preparatory employments. Domestic servants out of place, discharged barmaids, vendors of toys and lollipops, keepers of small eating-houses, of mangles, or of small lodging-houses, needlewomen who take in plain or slop work, milliners, consumptive patients in an advanced stage, cripples almost bedridden, persons of at least doubtful temperance, outdoor paupers, men and women of 70 or 80 years of age, persons who spell badly, who can scarcely write, and who cannot cipher at all; such are some of the teachers, not in remote rural districts, but in the heart of London, the capital of the world, as it is said to be, whose schools go to make up two-thirds of English schools, and whose pupils swell the muster roll that some statistical philanthropists rejoice to contemplate and to inscribe with the cheering figures, 1 in 8."[1]

The reason why these schools were patronised, even in preference to the more efficient public elementary schools, has been already alluded to. By one class of parents they were considered more "genteel"; by another they were valued chiefly because there was no insuperable objection on the part of their proprietors to irregularity in attendance. The operation of these considerations was strikingly illustrated by a fact which was laid before the Newcastle Commission. "A poor cripple," it was reported, "without legs from infancy, was brought up in a National School. When about 14, possessing good abilities and teaching power, he was retained as a monitor until 18, when he was dismissed for misconduct. He then opened a school on his own account, and got twenty or thirty boys. This failed through his misconduct, and for some years he lived on alms, wheeling himself about the streets. Once more he tried a school, through the help of friends, who thought he had improved in character He then took two rooms in a small court close by a National School in high repute, under an excellent certificated master, an assistant, and five pupil teachers, where the fee is twopence a week and a penny extra for drawing. There are 150 boys and there is room for fifty more. The private school, under the cripple, is crowded to excess. The rooms being about twenty feet by ten, and eight feet high, the children have scarcely room to sit; fees 3d. and 6d. Boys are sometimes taken from the first, second, and third classes of the National School to be *finished* at this private school."[2]

---

[1] *i.e.* 1 in 8 of the population are attending school. [2] *Ibid.* p. 420.
Newcastle Commission Report, vol. iii. p. 483.

(ii.) THE TEACHER.

This section will be devoted to the consideration of the condition of the elementary school teacher in those schools which came under inspection in and after 1839. Enough has been said concerning the uninspected and adventure schools to prove that the acquirements and status of their teachers could of necessity be no better than those of teachers in the elementary schools, although the account which follows may render it difficult to conceive how in the earlier part of the century they could possibly have been worse.

It must be noted that before 1840 there was scarcely any organised system for training teachers. The first building grants to training colleges were made in 1841. Earlier in the century the two great Educational Societies had offered what was then dignified by the name of " training " to persons who sought employment as teachers. It consisted in a few weeks' attendance at on organised school, and the instruction was limited to the mere mechanism of the school, such as drilling children to sit down and rise up, and dismissing them in an orderly manner. Later on, both Societies endeavoured, under great difficulties, to give their teachers a more efficient training, and by their efforts they laid the foundations upon which have grown up some of the most efficient training colleges of the present day.

The remuneration of the teacher, dependent as it was upon voluntary contributions, was not sufficient to support him in decency. Hence the calling presented no attractions to persons of education and culture, but tended rather to offer an asylum to those who had failed to obtain a living in other avocations. Any broken-down tradesman who was able to write and cypher fairly, could, after undergoing the short training that was then deemed necessary, blossom forth into an elementary schoolmaster. The general condition of the elementary schoolmaster was very frankly described by one of H.M. Inspectors in 1840, who said that in his district the greater part of the schools were kept " by females and old men *unfit for anything else.*"

The consequence was that the teachers were too often feeble and worn-out persons who were quite as incapable of maintaining the discipline of a school as they were of imparting instruction. In some cases the master was crippled or deformed, or for some reason liable to seek relief from the rates, who had been placed in office from motives of economy. The following is a description, given by H.M. Inspector in 1846, of a type of teacher which was by no means uncommon: " The master has lost one arm and does not wear a coat; very seldom changes his shirt, and never combs his hair. He says he is allowed to take private pupils, teaching them, not as he does the rest, which he obviously neglects, but upon what he calls the 'Commercial plan.' "[1]   In another school, with an endowment of £25 per annum, the Inspector, when he paid his visit, found the school empty and locked at 11 o'clock in the morning. He reported that it was no uncommon thing for this teacher to be away for days together, and once, during a long

---

[1] Education Department Report, 1846, p. 170.

frost, he was absent for thirty consecutive days, because, having only one leg, he was afraid to go along the road from his house to the schoolroom until the ice thawed.

Even when the teacher, aided by climatic considerations and the wholeness of his limbs, was capable of regular attendance at his school, his time was too often occupied in the performance of duties unconnected with teaching. One of H.M. Inspectors reported in 1850 that in a large school, when he paid his visit of inspection, the master was engaged for two hours in receiving money for a clothing club, leaving it to be conjectured how much time might have been so absorbed on a day not devoted to inspection.

But it was not in occupations so nearly connected with the school organisation that the teacher was most often engaged. His inadequate remuneration too frequently forced him to eke out his slender pittance by other avocations. The establishment of inspection brought out the fact that teachers frequently added to their recognised functions some other pursuit, such as farming, shopkeeping, or even employment of a still lowlier character. In 1840 one of H.M. Inspectors found that one master had been in the habit of hiring himself out as a day labourer during harvest time, and his pupils were employed during the school hours of that period in gathering sticks for his winter store of firewood. In 1844, a school, with an endowment of £12 per annum, was inspected, which was "kept by a middle-aged female, who, at an hour when she should have been teaching, was busy at her wash-tub. She was imperfectly educated, and had been a domestic servant in the family of the acting trustee of the school, who, on her marriage, gave her the income of the endowment as a help to her maintenance."

If inspection had done nothing else for the cause of education it would have rendered it an inestimable service in bringing to light the fact that in a great number of cases the qualification for the office of teacher consisted too often in some form of disablement. Sometimes it was physical disability, such as a broken limb, but far more often it was a broken career and its attendant misfortunes. But inspection not only cast a fierce light on these imperfections, it brought help and encouragement to hundreds of teachers who, ill-qualified though they were for their work, were struggling to perform it against almost insuperable difficulties. Suffering from the hopeless discouragement of striving against the drag of poverty and the consequent result of inefficiency in the school, with the clergyman, or minister of religion, if he chanced to be interested in education, as the sole critic of his work, inspection brought to the teacher the conviction that he was no longer an isolated force, but a member of an organised service, working with the approval of the nation.

The Committee of the Council on Education very wisely dealt tenderly with the teachers upon the establishment of inspection. The office of Inspector was not to be extolled at their expense. Inspectors were instructed "not to interfere with the instruction or the management" of a school; they were "to give assistance, not to exercise control, and they were to be careful not to weaken the authority of the head of the school." The teachers were thereby encouraged to realise the importance of the office which they held, to put forth their best efforts in the performance of their duties, and in some measure to improve their qualifications for the fulfilment of them.

But a more important service rendered by inspection was that it proved the absolute and urgent necessity of some adequate provision for the training of teachers. In 1835 a grant of £10,000 had been made by Parliament for the erection of Normal Schools, but for some unascertainable reason the money remained unapplied until the Committee of the Council on Education was constituted. The Committee immediately decided that this money should be divided between the two great Societies. Difficulties arose as to the conditions under which this grant should be applied. Eventually the money was paid over to five training colleges. Between 1840 and 1870 a sum of about £446,000 was provided by Government for building grants to training colleges and £72,000 for maintenance.

Under the impulse of Government assistance, existing colleges were enlarged and improved and new colleges were founded. The Wesleyan Committee's College and the Roman Catholic Poor Schools Committee's College were opened in 1851, and in the same year certain members of the Congregational body, dissatisfied with the action of the British and Foreign Schools Society in accepting the Government Grant, established an independent college at Homerton, supported entirely by voluntary effort. In 1869, the total accommodation afforded by the training colleges was 3,261 places.

But this encouragement to improve the training of teachers was only half the task which lay before the Committee of the Council. It remained to offer some inducement to join a profession which was noted neither for its reputation nor its emoluments. The first step in this direction was to get rid of the monitorial system which had been introduced by Bell and Lancaster. The only efficient instructor in the school—if he, indeed, chanced to be efficient—was the head teacher. Under him were the monitors, children who did not average more than ten years of age. They imparted to the classes such scraps of knowledge as they possessed. As it was a rare occurrence for these monitors to retain their posts for more than a year, the result of their teaching was inevitably deplorable. The following is the outspoken report of one of the London Inspectors upon the system : " I have frequently remarked the inattention of the young monitors—their apparent dislike to their work, their negligence in passing over omissions and errors, their gross mistakes in putting questions and correcting the answers, their irreverent, familiar or passionate remarks upon the religious lessons . . . and I do but state what is now almost universally admitted, that their influence in many, if not the generality of cases is positively detrimental to the moral character, while it is assuredly of no great benefit to the intellectual improvement of the schools."

These baneful methods were abolished, and a great impetus to the work of the Training Colleges was at the same time given by the establishment of the Pupil Teacher System in 1846. The Committee of Council had noted the early age at which children acting as assistants to schoolmasters were withdrawn from school to manual labour, and the advantages which would arise if such scholars as might be distinguished by proficiency and good conduct were apprenticed to skilful masters, to be instructed and trained so as to be prepared to complete their education as teachers in a Normal School.[1] Such children were to be apprenticed to properly qualified teachers in suitable schools[2] for a period of five years. At the end of each year the child, who was bound to be at least thirteen years of age at the commencement of the apprenticeship, had to pass an examination conducted by H.M. Inspector, and to present certificates of good conduct from the managers of the school, and of punctuality, diligence, obedience, and attention to duty from the master or mistress. Having passed these examinations and presented the necessary certificates, the pupil teacher was entitled to a certificate that he had completed his apprenticeship. At the end of each year, if all conditions were satisfactorily complied with, the pupil teacher received a small stipend, graduated from £10 in the first year to £20 in the fifth. A grant was also made to the teacher to whom the pupil was apprenticed, in consideration of his devoting an hour-and-a-half for five days in the week to the instruction of his pupil.

The next step was to endeavour to attract the young person who had successfully completed his apprenticeship to the training college. For this purpose an annual examination of ex-pupil teachers was instituted, and the Committee awarded to as many candidates as they deemed fit an exhibition of £20 or £25, to enable them to enter a training college. The successful candidates were called " Queen's Scholars." To the college itself a grant was made, on account of each student, of £20 for the first year, £25 for the second, and £30 for the third, provided that H.M. Inspector reported, upon his annual examination, that " a certain standard of merit had been attained." For each year's course the student who passed the examination obtained a certificate, which became the evidence of his qualifications of a teacher. When he found employment, the Committee made a payment in augmentation of his salary, increasing in amount with the number of years of training which he had received.

The Minutes of 1846 formed the foundation upon which the superstructure for the training of teachers has been built. They were subsequently modified in many details, but the principle of the system remained unchanged. In 1858 the Assistant Commissioner to the Newcastle Commission for a part of South London reported that in 173 public schools there were 236 teachers. Only 122 had received any training, and of these only sixty-five were certificated.[3] It was inevitable that the new scheme should be slow in realisation. The promising pupil who would consent to enter into indentures was not frequently found. It was necessary that the teaching profession should offer greater attractions béfore he would be induced to enter it. So great was this difficulty that in 1858 it was found necessary to introduce another and less onerous method of obtaining qualification. This was established mainly to permit existing teachers who were unable to obtain the certificate, to secure a qualification which should be recognised by the Department. By passing a simple examination they were entitled to

---

[1] Education Department Report, 1846, p. 1.

[2] One of the tests of suitability exemplifies the condition of the elementary teacher at that time. It was " that there is *a fair prospect* that the salary of the master and mistress, and the ordinary expenses of the school, will be provided during the period of apprenticeship."

[3] Report of the Newcastle Commission, vol. iii. p. 516.

" registration," and the schools which employed registered teachers were enabled to receive the Government Grant.

Between 1860 and 1870 the number of certificated teachers increased more rapidly, and the improved financial condition of elementary schools, due to increased State support, rendered the prospects of the profession more tolerable. Legislation upon education had for long been under discussion, and it was evident at that time that the question would be dealt with by one or the other of the two political parties. But these inducements did not operate with sufficient force to produce an adequate supply of efficient teachers when the formation of School Boards created a largely increased demand for their services.

(iii.) SCHOOL BOOKS AND APPARATUS.

The Inspectors appointed by the Minute of February 20th, 1839, were, among other duties, to inquire into the funds at the disposal of schools for books. They ascertained the particular books used for reading, arithmetic, geography, history, grammar, etymology, vocal music, drawing, and land surveying; they also described the apparatus used in schools.

In the earliest accounts of the condition of schools which the Inspectors gave, the universal lack of school apparatus is described. In most schools there was no attempt to provide books, either by the parents or by the managers. If such were introduced at all, it was nearly always a few copies of the Bible, which were made to do service for instruction in reading. This practice was strongly criticised by Inspectors, because the pupils, in their initial mechanical efforts to master the art, associated their difficulties, errors, and punishments with religion itself, and this generated an illogical dislike and irreverence for the latter.

One of H.M. Inspectors, in 1840, said that only " fragments of books were to be found, and in many cases none to be seen." No money was available to buy them, so the books " were such as parents chose to send" In concluding his report he said that class books which were unobjectionable to all parties must be provided at a cheap rate.

Another Inspector, in his report for the same year, complained that " good school books cannot be bought," and that " generally only a fragment of a Testament and spelling-book are to be seen." And in his report on Greenwich Hospital Schools he said that the only books he found were " the Bible, Goldsmith's 'History of England,' and the 'Life of Nelson.'" In his report on British Schools in London for 1842 he noted as evidence of improvement in education that " books are employed," and that in two-thirds of the schools were to be found books " for general information," and " 18 out of 35 schools" possessed " school libraries." In the description of one school he stated how the general deficiency was met : " Nothing but lesson boards were used till one month ago, when some Bibles were lent." Concerning the school at New Pie Street, Westminster, in which 70 boys attended, it was reported that that the apparatus was scanty; there were twelve Bibles, six copy books, a few lesson boards and three slates.

The Committee of Council, in 1846, indirectly improved the apparatus by making it one of the conditions of the apprenticeship of pupil teachers that the schools in which they were to serve should be well furnished with books and apparatus. A more direct step was taken in 1847. The Committee of Council decided to make a grant in aid of school books and apparatus, provided the managers of the schools subscribed two-thirds of the total value. The grant was to be 2s. per pupil, or 2s. 6d. if a pupil teacher was apprenticed in the school. The Committee also undertook to issue schedules of the best text-books and maps, from which the managers might make a selection.

The explanatory circular which notified this grant said that : " While, by the aid of religious associations, the managers of schools have been enabled to procure a sufficient supply of Bibles, Testaments, and books of religious instruction, other lesson books and text-books are often either not found in elementary schools, or only to a very limited extent."

An Inspector, in 1847, referred to the great want of books in National schools, save the Bible, which seemed the only text-book supplied, and criticised adversely the utter " hopelessness of the task and the irreverence " which resulted from making the Bible the sole text-book for instruction in reading.

The beneficial results of the Minute of 1847 were immediately evident. An Inspector, in his report on the Metropolitan District for 1848-9, noted a great improvement in this respect. He said that a " copious supply of good reading books " was the greatest boon. But although much had been done under the Minute of 1847 for the improvement of books and apparatus, the supply was by no means perfect. In 1853 several Inspectors suggested that the Committee of Council should make grants to form lending libraries, and also that grants of books should be made to schools. The difficulty arose not so much from the lack of money to purchase suitable books and apparatus as from the lack of suitable books and apparatus to purchase.

In 1856 an educational museum was established under the Committee of Council. It was inaugurated to exhibit the importance of books, diagrams, and apparatus in connection with education, in the hope that it might stimulate the production of better material.

The Inspectors frequently laid stress upon the unsuitability of the books provided in the schools. In the report on Middlesex for 1858 it was stated that the books for elder pupils were instructive, but those provided for the younger ones were ill-adapted to their requirements. In a class of children aged between 10 and 13 it would be found that one-half of them had a dictionary, one-third a History of England, or a geography, or a grammar ; while nearly all had either " Robinson Crusoe," " Pilgrim's Progress," or some book of travel. The Inspector insisted that a series of books ought to be issued, adapted to the capacities of the different standards, in order that little children might not be discouraged by being compelled to use books beyond their comprehension.

It was the custom, mainly in British Schools, to make the children pay for their own books. In some cases this resulted in more care being taken of the books, but

H.M. Inspector did not encourage the practice, for he found that needy children, even in the higher classes, were entirely unprovided with them.

The special grant for books and apparatus was discontinued upon the introduction of the Revised Code of 1861. Instead of a grant in aid of efficiency, a penalty was imposed upon inefficiency. It was provided by article 52 of that Code that the grant might be reduced if the managers failed to remedy any defect in the school or to provide proper furniture, books, and maps. This step was taken in consequence of a suggestion made by the Newcastle Commission.[1] There was some divergency of opinion between H.M. Inspectors as to whether the result of this change was beneficial or not. The Inspector for Middlesex reported in 1862 that school fittings and apparatus had improved, and the broken blackboards, rickety easels, torn maps, and books without covers were very rarely found. Another Inspector, however, reporting on British schools in the same year, complained of the deficiency of slates and copybooks, the former being rarely perfect as regards frames, and the latter, being generally purchased by the parent, were insufficient. He said that this defect seriously impeded the progress of the lower standards of the schools, and that better progress would be made if necessary apparatus were more liberally supplied.

Mr. Matthew Arnold, in his report on British Schools for 1863, noted a distinct improvement in reading-books, which he attributed to the attention which had been drawn to that subject by the Revised Code. " At last," he said, " the compilers of these works seem beginning to understand that the right way of teaching a little boy to read is not by telling him to read such sentences as these (I quote from school books till lately much in vogue): 'The crocodile is viviparous,' ' Quicksilver, antimony, calamine, zinc, &c., are metals '; or the right way of teaching a big boy to read better, to set him to read : ' Some time after one meal is digested we feel again the sensation of hunger, which is gratified by again taking food.' Reading-books are now published which reject all such trash as the above, and contain nothing but what has really some fitness for reaching the end which such reading-books were meant to reach. Some of them even go a little too far in the effort to avoid dryness and pedantry, and to be natural and interesting ; they contain rather too many abbreviations, too many words meant to imitate the noises of animals, and too much of that part of human utterance which may be called the *interjectional.*"[2]

Between 1860 and 1870 the school text-book was in the course of development. The day was already long past when the Bible was practically the only book from which children were taught to read. But writers and publishers needed the spur of the increased demand caused by the establishment of Board schools to induce them to devote intelligence and capital to the production of really excellent primers.

The school furniture of the earlier National and British Schools was of a somewhat rudimentary description. The two Societies adopted different methods of seating the children. In the National Society's Schools the desks, which consisted merely of an inclined plane ten inches wide, with a horizontal ledge, two or three inches wide, at the

---

[1] *See* Report, vol. i. pp. 350, 351.   [2] Reports on Elementary Schools, pp. 104, 105.

upper part of it, were arranged along the sides of the wall, so that the children sat or stood with their faces towards it. The writing and ciphering classes were arranged at these desks, and the centre of the schoolroom was thus left free for the reading classes. For these, forms were frequently placed so as to form three sides of a square, thus grouping the class around the monitor.[1] In British schools the desks were arranged in parallel rows across the centre of the schoolroom so that each child faced the master. A passage of from six to eight feet was left on each side of the room to give space for the reading classes. Rails were fixed round the walls from which the lesson boards were suspended.[2] Although neither of the plans can have conduced very greatly to the efficient conduct of the school, it would appear that the latter was more favourable to the introduction of the system of simultaneous teaching, and was gradually adopted by the National Society.

The reports of Inspectors between 1840 and 1844 laid great stress upon the unsuitability and insufficiency of the desk accommodation in elementary schools. In consequence of these reports the Committee of the Council decided in 1844 to make a grant in aid of the provision of school desks. The plan adopted was the system of parallel desks in the centre of the schoolroom. Two-thirds of the cost of such desks was paid by the Committee, if the remaining third were raised by the managers of the school. In the case of any school which still retained the desks against the wall of the schoolroom, the Committee offered to pay two-thirds of the cost of removing them, and converting them into parallel desks.[3] Some time elapsed before the desks round the walls of the schools were finally abolished, but the system of parallel desks was almost universal in 1870.

SECTION II.—AFTER 1870.

(i.) CURRICULUM.

The foregoing account of the condition of education in London prior to 1870 shows that the Board had as little in the way of experience to guide it in framing a curriculum and organising a school as it had in the evolution of a plan for the school building. The Education Department, which had endeavoured to suggest designs for more efficient school buildings, never devoted its attention to the framing of a more efficient curriculum than was comprised in the meagre demand of the Code, which alone could secure the Government Grant. The reports of H.M. Inspectors form a new Book of Lamentations, coupled with suggestions for improvement, which the funds available for the Voluntary schools were insufficient to carry into practice. The Code of 1871 only gave a grant for reading, writing, and arithmetic for the school generally, and for any two specific subjects which might be successfully passed in by children in Standards IV., V., and VI.[4]

The Education Department did not then pretend, as it has subsequently done, that the subjects authorised by the Code to be taught in schools were the legal limit of the

[1] *See* first plan, *ante*, p. 58. [2] Education Department Report, 183?-40, p. 48-50.
[3] *Ibid.* 1844, p. 113. [4] *Ibid.* 1871, pp. 108, 124.

instruction which might be given. It took a broader view, recognising that Code subjects indicated the minimum, rather than the maximum of instruction that ought to be given, and it left the elected Boards to decide to what extent, after complying with the conditions of the Code, they would amplify their curriculum.

But it was quite possible that the School Board might have taken a less enlightened view of this important question. It might have been contended that a Board, created under Statute to provide elementary education, the scope of which was defined by a Departmental document having the force of a Statute, ought not to afford greater educational facilities than the law actually demanded. The Board might have declared that it would teach reading, writing, and arithmetic to every child; two other subjects to children in Standards IV.-VI., and nothing more. The temptation so to do cannot have been slight. Any subject beyond those which have been mentioned could earn no grant, and the total cost of teaching it would fall upon the rates. If so narrow a policy had been adopted by the London School Board it would have been difficult, if not impossible, for any subsequent Board to emancipate itself from it. A low standard of education would have been stereotyped, and any subsequent attempt to raise it would have been stigmatised as extravagant. The Education Department would never have been spurred to improve the Code by the persistent representations of the Board, and education at the present time would have been less adaptable to varying needs and less complete.

In February, 1871, the Board resolved to appoint a committee to consider the scheme of education to be adopted in public elementary schools, and to report thereon to the Board.[1] This Committee, presided over by the late Professor Huxley, rendered signal service to the cause of education in London, and through London, by example, to the country generally. Its report created a revolution in educational ideals, and if, as a matter of fact, those ideals were never absolutely realised, the ends achieved were none the less important.

The Committee held sixteen sittings, half of which were devoted to taking the evidence of experienced teachers, in order to ascertain the amount and quality of the instruction which it had, up to that time, been found practicable to give to children of the same age and condition as those with which the Board would have to deal. While the Committee was pursuing its labours the Board had resolved that at least three subjects should be included in the curriculum. The first was instruction in the principles of morality and religion—a question of such importance and involving so much debate that it must be dealt with separately. The second was physical training, the third singing. Physical training was encouraged by the Department by permitting attendance at drill, under a competent instructor, for not more than two hours a week for twenty weeks in the year, to count as attendance at school. Singing was not recognised until 1874, and then it was " encouraged " by the infliction of a fine of one shilling per scholar in average attendance, to be deducted from the grant to all schools in which vocal music was not taught. On February 1st, 1871, the Board passed a

---

[1] *Board Minutes*, vol. i. p. 60.

resolution to the effect that it was highly desirable that means should be provided for physical training, exercise, and drill in public elementary schools established by the Board.[1] An attempt was made to eliminate the word "drill" on the ground that such exercises might tend to foster the military spirit, but it met with no success. The resolution was subsequently referred as an instruction to Professor Huxley's Committee.[2] On March 22nd, 1871, the Board resolved "that the art and practice of singing be taught, so far as may be possible, in the Board schools as a branch of elementary education."[3]

These three subjects of instruction were therefore decided upon before the Committee on the Scheme of Education reported, and had merely to be included by the Committee in their proposed curriculum. Much of the Committee's report related to questions other than the proposed curriculum, such as the advantage of mixed or separate schools, the size of schools, the proportion of teachers to scholars, and evening schools, which are dealt with elsewhere. The particular recommendations as to curriculum were as follow :—

I.—*Infant schools.* After laying stress upon the importance of the infant department in the general school economy, for purposes not only of discipline but of instruction, and for enabling the elder children of poor parents to attend school with greater regularity, the Committee recommended that the instruction given in such schools should consist in :—

1. Morality and religion, on the principles already laid down by the Board.
2. Reading, writing, and arithmetic.
3. Object lessons of a simple character, with some exercises of the hands and eyes, as is given by the "Kindergarten" system.
4. Singing and physical exercises, adapted to infants.

The third recommendation was of paramount importance, and has led to striking developments in the education of infants. Up to 1870 no great attention had been paid to the Froebelian methods of education. The Froebel Society had struggled long and not altogether successfully for the recognition of Froebel's methods. Few teachers, except those trained by the Home and Colonial Society, understood the system. Where the infants' school was anything more than a crèche for the detention of infants during the school hours of the elder children, the instruction afforded was usually given by the same methods as those adopted in the graded schools. Not only were reading, writing, and arithmetic taught, but sometimes geography and history, in a manner well calculated to develop premature stupidity.

II.—*Graded schools.* In these the curriculum proposed was divided into "essential" and "discretionary" subjects. The essential subjects were to form part of the teaching of every elementary school; the others were to be added at the discretion of the managers of individual schools, or by the special direction of the Board.

---

[1] Board Minutes, vol. i. p. 47.   [2] *Ibid.* p. 77.
[3] *Ibid.* p. 93.

The essential subjects were :—

1. Morality and religion.
2. Reading, writing, and arithmetic; English grammar in senior schools, with mensuration in senior boys' schools.
3. Systematised object lessons, embracing in the six school years a course of elementary instruction in physical science and serving as an introduction to the Science Examinations conducted by the Science and Art Department.
4. The history of Britain.
5. Elementary geography.
6. Elementary social economy.
7. Elementary drawing, leading up to the examinations in mechanical drawing and to the art teaching of the Science and Art Department.
8. (In girls' schools.) Plain needlework and cutting out.

The discretionary subjects were :—

1. Algebra and geometry.
2. Latin, or a modern language.

The Committee then proceeded to deal with a question of prime importance; a question for which a satisfactory solution has not yet been found. "The Elementary Education Act," they said, "does not confer upon a School Board the power of providing secondary schools, and it is silent as to the mode by which a connection may be established between the elementary and secondary schools of the country. But it is of such importance to the efficacy of popular education that means should be provided by which scholars of more than average merit should be enabled to pass from elementary into secondary schools, that we feel it our duty to offer some suggestions upon the subject.

"The practical difficulty in the way of the passage of boys and girls from an elementary into a secondary school is the cost of their maintenance, and the best way of meeting that difficulty appears to be to establish exhibitions equivalent to the earnings of boys and girls from 13 to 16 years of age, tenable for the periods during which they remain under instruction in the secondary schools. The funds out of which such exhibitions may be created already exist, and the machinery for distributing them has been provided by the Legislature in the Endowed Schools Act.

"The Endowed Schools Commissioners have fully recognised the claims of scholars in public elementary schools to share the advantages of the endowed schools. We recommend, therefore, that the Board enter into official communication with the Endowed Schools Commissioners, and agree with them upon some scheme by which the children in public elementary schools shall be enabled to obtain their rightful share of the benefits of those endowments with which the Commissioners are empowered to deal."[1]

The discussion of these proposals occupied the greater part of four sittings of the Board. Attempts were made on the one hand to enlarge the proposed curriculum, and

---

[1] Board Minutes, vol. i. pp. 155-161.

on the other to restrict it. One member unsuccessfully endeavoured to add swimming, shorthand, navigation, telegraphy, and mechanics, to the list of discretionary subjects.[1] Perhaps the most important addition that was proposed was "household economy, inclusive of laundry work and cooking," as an essential subject for senior girls. The amendment was eventually whittled down to a resolution that domestic economy should be added to the discretionary subjects for senior girls. The remarks of one of the best-known lady members of the Board[2] upon the amendment sound strange at the present time. "She thought it would be impossible to teach cooking and washing in any valuable way to young children in the same way as they would do to persons of matured intelligence. Girls under 13 would be very difficult to teach how to market and how to cook in any really responsible way. Then she could see a difficulty on the score of expense, which would be really frightful at each school if the proposals were adopted."[3]

Unsuccessful attempts were made to limit the teaching of drawing to boys' senior departments and to remove algebra from the list of discretionary subjects.

The following changes were finally effected in the curriculum proposed by the Committee. English composition and the principles of book-keeping were added to the second section of essential subjects, and "The History of England" was substituted for the "History of Britain." The second section of the discretionary subjects, "Latin or a modern language," was rejected, and the words "any extra[4] subjects recognised by the New Code, 1871, in addition to algebra and geometry," were added.[5] The latter addition was somewhat comprehensive, and, to a certain extent, redundant. The fourth schedule of the Code of 1871 provided that "the specific subjects of secular instruction may be geography, history, grammar, algebra, geometry, the natural sciences, political economy, languages, *or any definite subject of instruction* . . . of which the Inspector can report that it is well adapted to the capacity of the children." Thus, at least, two subjects which had been included in the list of essentials re-appeared as discretionary, and "Latin, or a modern language," which had been rejected, was re-introduced inferentially.

The curriculum cannot be said to have failed for want of copiousness. It was a well-ordered, if somewhat one-sided, scheme of education, which honestly endeavoured to cover all the ground of instruction which could by any means be construed as elementary. But it aroused very serious opposition, not only among persons who were responsible for the management of voluntary schools, who dreaded that so liberal a curriculum would draw away children from their schools to those managed by the Board, but also from the Vestries, who conceived that, as they were by the Education Act constituted part of the machinery for the collection of the Board's rate, they were also constituted the authorised censors of the Board's proceedings. Towards the end of the year 1872 protests against the "extravagance" of the Board began to pour into the Board's offices. These protests were based upon many items of the Board's

---

[1] Board Minutes, p. 194.
[2] Mrs. Garrett Anderson.
[3] *School Board Chronicle,* vol. ii. p. 198. The expense on account of materials has proved to be less than nothing. The cooked products are sold at a profit.
[4] *i.e.,* Specific.
[5] Board Minutes, p. 195.

expenditure. One main charge was that the Board had built unnecessary schools, an accusation which has been already sufficiently refuted.[1] It was also alleged that the scheme of education was unnecessarily liberal, that it would tend to make fine ladies and gentlemen of the children in the Board schools, and that it involved the employment of teachers possessing far higher qualifications than would have been necessary had a more reasonable and restricted curriculum been adopted. These accusations became so numerous that, in order to avoid the necessity of sending a separate answer in each case, the Board, on December 18th, 1872, adopted a formal answer to all charges of extravagance, which was ordered to be printed and sent to all persons and bodies who sent protests against the Board's expenditure. In this answer the Board dealt with the criticisms on the scheme of education thus:—

"The third charge of extravagance is that the Board, instead of establishing 'special schools,'[2] has adopted an elaborate scheme of education, including a range of subjects so wide as to hinder the improvement of the scholars. It may be stated in reply that all the schools provided by the Board must necessarily, under section 14 of the Act, be 'Public Elementary Schools,' and that although the scheme of education may appear elaborate, the Board schools are not at present up to the average of other efficient schools, and that the instruction proposed to be given does not go beyond that sanctioned by the new Code. Many of the subjects enumerated are optional, and *the programme itself may be regarded as setting forth what is ultimately desirable, rather than what is at present attainable.*"[3]

A considerable amount of misunderstanding would have been avoided if the words italicised had been appended to the scheme of education in the first instance. There was some little ambiguity in the division of subjects to be taught into " essential " and " discretionary." The general public not unnaturally concluded that " essential " subjects were subjects which it was essential for every child to learn. The Board, it appears from its explanation, merely meant that they were subjects which it was very desirable, under favourable circumstances, that a child should learn. But unfortunately for this explanation, the Board had rejected an amendment which would have made this interpretation of its intention clear. This amendment proposed that teachers should be instructed to arrange that special attention should be given to the essential subjects mentioned in sections 1, 2, 3, and 8 of the report, and that no pupil should be advanced to a study of the subjects mentioned in the remaining sections until this object had been attained.[4] When, therefore, the Board rejected this proposal it could not have thought that the programme represented what was ultimately desirable, rather than what was at present attainable. The fact was that the Board, quailing, in December, 1872, before the violence of public criticism, and finding also, perhaps, that its scheme was incapable of immediate realisation, sought to minimise the importance of the decisions at which it had arrived in the first ardour of its enthusiasm.

One item of the educational curriculum demands particular attention. The only

---

[1] See *ante*, p. 45 et seq.
[2] *i e.* Schools for waifs and strays, or "gutter children."
[3] Board Minutes, vol. iii. p. 48.
[4] *Ibid.* vol. i. p. 170.

subject of instruction concerning which the Act of 1870 had laid down any definite conditions was religious instruction. These conditions, which were the result of prolonged and angry debates in Parliament, were in the nature of a compromise, and were negative in character. It was left to the School Boards to decide whether any religious instruction at all should be given in their schools; but if such instruction was given, it must be given subject to the following rules: (1) No religious catechism or religious formulary which is distinctive of any particular denomination was to be taught in the school.[1] (2) It was not to be required as a condition of any child attending a school that he should attend or abstain from attending any Sunday-school or place of religious worship, or that he should attend any religious observance or instruction in the school or elsewhere, from which he might have been withdrawn by his parent, or that he should attend school on any day exclusively set apart for religious observance by the religious body to which his parent belonged. (3) The times of religious instruction must be either at the beginning or the end of school, and must be inserted in the time-table. (4) Any scholar might be withdrawn from such observance or instruction without forfeiting any of the other benefits of the school.[2]

The London School Board, therefore, had to decide whether any religious instruction should be given in the schools under its control, and, if given, what should be the character of that instruction. The circumstances in which the Board approached this delicate question must not be forgotten if its decision is to be properly understood. The storm of controversy which had arisen during the passage of the Act of 1870 through Parliament had hardly subsided. A great number of Dissenters, dreading that any legislation upon the subject would give undue influence to the Established Church, had made common cause with the advocates of secularism in demanding that the teaching of religion should be altogether excluded from the State schools. Many Dissenters still looked upon the limited powers conferred upon School Boards with not a little apprehension, and very slight provocation would have driven them into open hostility. The Board, while it was considering the position which it should take up upon the religious question, was also making up its mind to adopt compulsory attendance at school and was framing bye-laws to carry its intentions into effect. Compulsion was an untried principle, and no one could foresee how it would be received by the class which it would most affect. If the Board had adopted resolutions respecting religious instruction that carried within them the slightest suspicion of an attempt to give an advantage to any particular form of religious opinion, the success of compulsion would have been seriously imperilled.

With a knowledge of these circumstances, and with a sense of their importance in relation to the problem which had to be solved, the School Board approached the discussion of the rules which it would adopt for the regulation of religious instruction in its schools. The Board was divided into three parties upon this question. The first, and undoubtedly the largest, desired that the Bible should be used as the text-book, and that the teacher should explain and enforce the lessons derived from

---

[1] 33 & 34 Vict. c. 75 s. 14.   [2] *Ibid.* sec. 7.

H

it by his own comments, while strictly adhering to the limitations imposed by the Act. The second desired that the Bible should be read in the schools without note or comment. The third wished to exclude religious teaching altogether from the schools of the Board. The first and last of these parties began the struggle. In February, 1871, the following motion was moved: "That in the schools of the Board the Bible shall be read, and '*instruction in religious subjects*' shall be given therefrom; provided always (1) That in such instruction the provisions of the Act in section 14 ('no religious catechism or religious formulary which is distinctive of any particular denomination shall be taught in the school') shall be strictly observed, both in letter and spirit, and that no attempt be made in any such schools to attach children to any particular denomination. (2) That in regard to any particular school, the Board shall consider and determine, upon any application by managers, parents or ratepayers of the district, who may show special cause for exception of the school from the operation of this resolution in whole or in part."[1]

To this resolution the following amendment was moved: "That this Board, whilst earnestly hoping means may be found, by voluntary zeal and effort, of providing a religious education for the children of Metropolitan schools, objects to the proposals for reading the Bible and giving instruction in religious subjects in rate-supported schools, as being opposed to the principle of religious equality, to the conscientious convictions of many ratepayers and parents, and as leading ultimately to a denominational system of religious teaching in the schools."

This amendment summed up in brief the arguments of the Free Churches against any interference of the State with matters of religion; arguments which had influenced the members of those churches so strongly as to lead them in some cases to reject the aid of the Government Grant for their schools. The fact that this amendment only found four supporters, one of whom was a clergyman of the Church of England,[2] shows that the great majority of the Board was convinced that a compromise might be found that would satisfy all parties.[3]

The second amendment, to the effect that "in schools under the Board the Bible should be read without religious note or comment," fared no better. Only three members voted for it, while forty-one voted against it.

The original proposal was evidently acceptable in its substance to the majority of the members, but many were dissatisfied with the wording of it, although that dissatisfaction did not carry them so far as to induce them to vote for either of the amendments which had been proposed. There could be no doubt that Mr. Smith, in framing his resolution, intended that the interests of every denomination should be safeguarded against attack. In the speech with which he introduced his motion, he declared that it did not represent his views as a private individual, but he considered it to be the only mode of effectually carrying out the provisions of the Education Act.[4] But the wording of

[1] Board Minutes, vol. i. p. 70. The resolution was moved by the late Rt. Hon. W. H. Smith.
[2] The Rev. W. Rogers.
[3] Board Minutes, vol. i. p. 71.
[4] *School Board Chronicle*, vol. i. p. 39.

the resolution was, nevertheless, open to insidious interpretation. The words " instruction in religious subjects " might be construed to mean all or any religious subjects, and might include, therefore, dogmatic teaching, although no dogmatic formulas were used. In order to meet this objection an amendment was framed, adopting Mr. W. H. Smith's proposal in substance, but making slight verbal alterations. This amendment was, after discussion, withdrawn, in order that Mr. Smith might re-draft his motion. Its final form was: " That in the schools provided by the Board the Bible shall be read, and there shall be given such explanations and such instructions therefrom *in the principles of morality and religion* as are suited to the capacities of the children, provided always (1) that in such explanations and instruction the provisions of the Act in sections 7 and 14 be strictly observed, both in letter and spirit, and that no attempt be made in any such schools to attach children to any particular denomination." [1] The second proviso remained unaltered. This resolution was carried by a majority of 38 against 3. There can be no doubt that the amended resolution expressed Mr. Smith's intention more clearly than did his original proposal. " Professor Huxley," he said, " had referred to the desirableness of giving to the children, amongst other instruction, reasons for those laws which regulate their conduct in this world, and which, passing under different names, are the primary notions of religion and morality. The learned Professor then went on to say that it is possible to instil into the child's mind very good reasons for all those great laws of conduct and principles of morality apart from any disputed matter. I entirely agree with those words." [2]

The " School Board Compromise," as this resolution was called, was an act of far-sighted statesmanship. It reconciled controversialists, it allayed apprehensions that were not altogether unreasonable, and it proved successful in its practical working. The number of withdrawals of children from religious instruction in Board schools has been insignificant. This has doubtless been due in part to the conciliatory spirit with which the Board approached the subject, in part also to the tact and discretion with which the teachers have given religious instruction under the Board's rules. Whether it may not be also due to the apathy of the majority of parents upon religious questions need not be discussed here. Whether the parent passively acquiesces, or actively approves, the result has been the same; the School Board compromise has proved an unqualified success as an administrative measure.

In July, 1871, a resolution was passed permitting the use of prayers and hymns during the period of religious instruction. The arrangements for these religious observances were left to the teachers and managers of each school, subject to a right of appeal to the Board, similar to that contained in the resolutions on religious instruction. [3]

For 21 years the compromise worked without friction. It stood the test of application, not only in the few schools which existed in 1871, but in the large numbers which the Board controlled in 1892. At the end of the latter year, out of an apparently

[1] *School Board Chronicle,* vol. i. p. 81. [2] *Ibid.* p. 39.
[3] Board Minutes, vol. i. p. 224.

clear sky, a storm arose, and the compromise was called in question. It is not an edifying episode in the Board's history, but it cannot be entirely passed over.

In the year 1892 a member of the Board, chancing to be present in one of the Board schools while a *vivâ voce* examination in Scripture knowledge was proceeding, heard the head teacher ask the children the question, " Who was the father of Jesus ? " The child called upon to answer replied " Joseph." The answer was passed by the teacher as correct, without any comment, and the member left the school greatly scandalised that not a word was added to point out to the children the Divine nature of Christ. However shocking the incident may have been, it was one which should have been brought privately before the School Management Committee; but this course did not recommend itself to the member in question. He communicated the story to the pages of a clerical newspaper.

Soon after the appearance of this letter a motion was placed on the Board's paper of business calling attention to the facts, and proposing that teachers in Board schools should be instructed that they must distinctly teach their children the Divinity of Christ and the doctrine of the Trinity.[1]

The debate upon this motion commenced in February, 1893, and after it had engaged the attention of the Board for a month it was superseded by the following amendment: " That the Board adheres to the scheme of Biblical and religious teaching which was settled by the first Board and has remained in force down to the present time," [2] and a further amendment was adopted which substituted the words " Christian religion and morality " for the words " morality and religion " in the resolutions of 1871.

While this question was being debated by the Board, deputation after deputation, representing the varying views of the various denominations, demanded audience. The Board-room became a cockpit for the exhibition of theological encounters; and of all the Christian virtues which might have illustrated the discussion, serpentine wisdom was far more in evidence than dove-like harmlessness. After four months of wearisome wrangle the whole question was referred to the School Management Committee for consideration and report.[3]

In the following November the School Management Committee reported in favour of amending the resolutions of March, 1871, by substituting the words " the Christian religion and morality," as stated above. They further recommended that a circular should be sent to each teacher giving specific instructions as to the doctrines which were to be inculcated in respect to the Divinity of Christ and the Trinity, and offering to release any teacher who could not conscientiously impart such instruction from the duty of giving the Bible lesson.[4] The resolution for altering the wording of the compromise was adopted in January, 1894, and the circular to teachers in the following March. More than 3,000 teachers requested to be relieved from the duty of giving the Bible lesson ; not because, in the majority of cases, they were unable to teach according to the terms of the circular, but because they resented the manner in which the Board had

---

[1] Board Minutes, vol. xxviii. p. 493.
[2] *Ibid.* p. 774.
[3] *Ibid.* vol. xxxix. p. 356.
[4] *Ibid.* p. 1564.

treated the subject. It is unnecessary to follow in detail the wrangle that ensued. In the event only a very few teachers were actually relieved, and these were conscientious objectors. The net result of the whole episode was a verbal change in the resolutions of 1871. It is not too much to say that the teaching in the Board schools was in no way altered in consequence of it. And for such a result the Board was engaged for more than a year in an altercation which certainly brought it little credit.

The attack upon the religious teaching in Board schools produced no effect because it was not supported by the people whose children received instruction in the schools. It was conducted by persons, of excellent intentions, doubtless, who were convinced that parents ought to want such docrines taught to their children as were set down in the circular. But there was no force of public opinion behind them, and turmoil was the only result of their enterprise.

One other point in connection with religious instruction may be mentioned here, in order to avoid future reference to the subject. In 1876, the late Mr. Francis Peek, then a member of the Board, paid a sum of £5,000 to the Religious Tract Society, who agreed to provide yearly, Bibles and Testaments to the value of £500, for prizes to be awarded to scholars under the London School Board who should excel in a voluntary examination in Biblical knowledge. These prizes are awarded by a preliminary and a final examination. In the year 1877 about 80,000 scholars sat at the preliminary, and 2,900 at the final examination. In 1899 the numbers were 292,000 and 9,000 respectively.[1]

When the Board had settled the character of the curriculum which was to be adopted in its schools, it became necessary to appoint officers whose duty it should be to see that the instruction was given efficiently. Before the end of 1871 the Board had resolved upon the appointment of an Inspector. The first Inspector was appointed in March, 1872,[2] and in the following month a second Inspector was added.[3] The duties of these officials were defined thus: "To assist in organising schools provided by the Board; to examine the scholars and pupil teachers in the subjects taught in each school; to ascertain whether the books and apparatus are in good condition and whether the log books and registers are duly kept; to make a report to the Board upon the efficiency of each school, and to carry out the general instructions of the Board."[4] The Board also appointed three officials to deal with special subjects, upon the teaching of which it laid considerable stress. Their duties were not merely to inspect and report upon the work done in the schools, but also to teach, or rather to show the permanent teachers how to teach, by giving specimen lessons.[5] In June, 1872, the Board appointed a drill master and a singing instructor.[6] A year later they appointed an examiner of needlework.[7]

[1] A syllabus of Bible instruction suitable for each of the standards and for candidates and pupil teachers is drawn up annually by the Sub-committee on Scripture and approved by the Board.

[2] Board Minutes, vol. ii. p. 172.

[3] Ibid. p. 278.

[4] Ibid. p. 74. In 1873 an attempt was made to include religious teaching among the subjects to be inspected. The solicitor expressed an opinion in favour of the legality of the proposal. The motion was defeated by an amendment which, while not directing the Inspectors to report on the religious instruction, left it open for them to do so. Board Minutes, vol. iii. pp. 83, 111, 146.

[5] Ibid. p. 438.

[6] Ibid. p. 464.

[7] Ibid. vol. iii. p. 836. A Kindergarten instructor was appointed in October, 1873. Ibid. p. 964.

The reports of these officials make it possible to obtain some estimate of the extent to which the " ideal " curriculum adopted by the Board was actually realised in practice. In 1873 both the Inspectors presented general reports to the Board upon the condition of education in Board schools. These reports throw a flood of light upon the progress which had been made during the period of office of the first School Board for London. This fact must justify somewhat copious quotations.

" It is quite a treat," said one of the Inspectors, speaking of infants' schools, " to go into some of these schools and observe to how great an extent it is possible to make instruction pleasant, and how easy it is to gain the affections of children by a kind and patient manner. I prefer to see infants, especially the younger ones, engaged, not so much in learning to read, and write, and count, as in singing, marching, and kindergarten work. The children eventually progress much more rapidly than when kept hard at their books and slates. I have examined 766 infants prepared to pass into junior schools, and always found the best results in such schools as I have here described. I should like to see kindergarten exercises become a more prominent feature in infants' schools than at present. With few exceptions, infants' teachers regard kindergarten rather as an ordinary subject, to be taught like reading and writing, than as a system which should underlie the whole fabric of infant education, and pervade, as far as possible, every lesson given to the children. There is a great want of suitable apparatus for this purpose, which I hope to see shortly supplied. The object lessons, as a rule, are too meagre, and the appliances totally inadequate. The small cabinets of specimens of out-of-the-way materials are little better than rubbish. Object lessons, to be useful and interesting, should be confined to articles in use in everyday life, such as children see at their homes and in the streets; and it would be easy for the teachers to collect specimens of these sufficiently large for all the children of a class to see and handle. This subject demands more attention than it at present receives from teachers."

Thus far as regards infants' schools. As to the graded schools the Inspector reported : " Owing to the very low state of the attainments of the children, it has been found impossible, in most of the schools, to attempt to teach any but the ordinary subjects of reading, writing, and arithmetic. Geography, grammar, and drawing come next in order as subjects in which the upper standards receive instruction. English history and book-keeping are too difficult for any but a few scholars in the best schools. Some teachers have introduced algebra, geometry, physical science, and physiology as extra subjects, and in three schools French is taught."

The foregoing paragraph must be read in the light of the educational results obtained by the teaching given. These can only be tested by the results of examinations by the Government Inspectors for grants. No complete return of these is in existence, but from the Government reports presented to the Board during the year 1873, it appears that 96 departments in graded schools were examined. Under the then existing Code each department was entitled to present children in two specific subjects. Only three subjects were selected in any of these departments, namely, geography, grammar, and history. Fifteen departments out of the 96 presented children in geography, seven in grammar, and four in history. It will be seen from these facts that the "ideal" curriculum was very far from realisation in 1873.

"The instruction in geography and grammar," continued the Board Inspector, "is, except in a few instances, very elementary, but the results are quite as good as could reasonably be expected. When we come, however, to the ordinary subjects, the results would be extremely discouraging if the circumstances of the schools were not taken into consideration. It would be altogether unjust to compare the Board schools with long-established Voluntary schools, for both in point of teaching staff and the educational status of the pupils the former are placed at immense disadvantage. . . . By far the larger proportion of pupils have either had no previous instruction whatever or have attended school so irregularly as not to have benefited at all by it. Of all the children over 7 years of age whose names are on the school register, no fewer than 53 per cent. are below Standard I. In some schools this percentage is considerably higher, reaching, in one instance, over 80 per cent. It is impossible that this fearful amount of ignorance can be eradicated for years to come. The education of such children has to be commenced at the very beginning."[1]

The second Inspector gave similar evidence. "Elementary geography is generally taught," he said, "and grammar and history occasionally, but the whole is in such an elementary stage that criticism would be out of place."[2] He examined the children in fifty departments in reading, writing, and arithmetic, and classified them according to the standards of the Code in which they were competent to pass. "I believe I am thus enabled," he said, "to give a fair picture of the state of education in the Board schools at the close of the first Board's existence." The table is so significant that it is worth reproduction.

TABLE.

No. of Children Competent to Pass in	BOYS.			GIRLS.		
	Reading.	Writing.	Arithmetic.	Reading.	Writing.	Arithmetic.
Standard VI.	3	...	2	1	1	1
„ V.	30	29	19	7	7	5
„ IV.	75	58	75	42	34	27
„ III.	247	241	200	225	184	140
„ II.	425	446	398	471	424	352
„ I.	753	1103	806	635	1014	744
Below any of the Standards .	1777	1433	1810	1667	1384	1779
Totals	3310	3310	3310	3048	3048	3048

---

[1] Board Minutes, vol. iii. p. 1249.   [2] Ibid. p. 1256.

Singing in the Board schools had, by the end of 1873, considerably improved. In most public elementary schools singing was taught by ear merely. The Board decided to adopt the Tonic Sol-fa method of notation.[1] But on October 3rd, 1872, the Music Instructor reported that out of 83 schools, only 5 were using that method. In the rest music was taught by ear only. "The singing generally," he said, "is fearfully coarse and noisy, the boys especially singing with all the force they can command. Certainly, in many schools, the material to be cultivated is very raw indeed, and much time and labour will be required to get anything like good singing."[2] A year later the Instructor was able to report a considerable improvement in the children's voices, especially in the boys' schools, and that noisy, coarse singing was fast disappearing.[3]

The Needlework Examiner reported in November, 1873, that: "The work generally is fairly clean, considering the time the children have been brought under school discipline. There is little or no system in the teaching, and, only in a few cases, any attempt at a proper classification. In some cases the teaching is left almost entirely to the care of very junior and inefficient teachers, while the head teacher is occupied in filling up registers and general supervision. As the needlework does not produce any revenue to the school it has to give way whenever any special cause produces extra pressure of work."[4]

The foregoing quotations illustrate not only the small measure of success which the Board achieved in translating its "ideal" curriculum into practice, but they reveal also the causes which prevented any more fruitful results. The Board was dealing with the very roughest material, the undisciplined child who had never attended school at all, or who had been trained, if training it can be called, in the inefficient schools which the Board was superseding. In such children the ideas of order, self-restraint, obedience were embryonic. The older children were as ignorant as the younger, and far more difficult to control. If the teacher's energies are mainly directed towards maintaining discipline instruction must inevitably suffer. While more than half the children in the schools were below Standard I. in reading, writing, and arithmetic, it was impossible to teach successfully even a tithe of the "essential" subjects which the Board had set down in its curriculum. Such an attempt would have been merely wasted energy.

The social status of the children was thus described by one of the Board's Inspectors. "The majority of these children," he said "are of a lower social grade than those attending Voluntary schools. In one school in an extremely low locality several of the scholars are well-known juvenile thieves, who have been forced into school by the action of the divisional committee. In many other instances a large proportion of the scholars are of the street arab class who are now for the first time brought under the influence of discipline and good example. It speaks volumes for the teachers in some of these schools that the children have been brought, not only in a measure to love their schools, but that they are able to be trusted with the charge of school books for their home

---

[1] Board Minutes, vol. ii. p. 185.
[2] *Ibid.* vol. ii. p. 744.
[3] *Ibid.* p. 1174.

[4] *Ibid.* p. 1175. In December, 1873, the Board petitioned the Education Department to make a grant for needlework. *Ibid.* p. 1195.

lessons, and in no instance that I am acquainted with have the books and slates been thus lost."[1]

The chief obstacles to the efficient conduct of schools containing such scholars were necessarily irregularity and unpunctuality. These, in the first years of the Board, were excessive. Irregularity and unpunctuality inflict injury not only upon the culprits, but upon the classes to which they belong, interfering with the progress of the more regular attendants. But regularity and punctuality are acquired habits. It was scarcely to be hoped that these could be cultivated with much success in the elder children, who had hitherto led so wild and undisciplined a life. The hope for the future lay in the infants' schools. In these the child was subjected to the wholesome school discipline before the evil training of the gutter had asserted an overpowering influence. It is remarkable how, in all the earlier reports presented to the Board, the condition of the infants' schools is contrasted favourably with that of the graded schools. When the infants began to replace the elder children who had filled the graded schools in the first instance, the teachers were provided with more promising pupils, from whom better results were obtained.

(ii.) The Teaching Staff.

Having described the curriculum which the Board proposed for its schools and the condition of the children who were to receive instruction, it now becomes necessary to deal with the question of the staff of teachers who were to give the education which the Board proposed to provide.

The methods of training teachers for public elementary schools have already been described, methods which have given the calling somewhat the character of a close profession. But in 1870 the greater number of teachers were untrained and uncertificated. The untrained teachers were too often persons of little education, who had drifted into their profession for want of a more lucrative calling. From the outset the Board was faced with the fact that, having regard to the sudden increase in the demand for trained teachers which would result from its operations, it was certain that the supply would prove inadequate. In April, 1872, the Board appointed a special committee to consider the question of the supply of trained teachers.[2] That Committee in the following June submitted an elaborate report. Taking as the basis of their calculations the facts that the Board had decided to provide school accommodation for 100,600 children, and that the Committee on the Scheme of Education had advised that nine trained teachers should be allowed to every 1,000 children, they concluded that 900 additional teachers would be required. Of this number 65 had already been provided; the remaining 835 would be needed during the next two years. But in that time the school population of London would have been increased by 20,000 children; therefore 180 additional teachers would be needed, bringing up the total to 1,015. This number would be required for Board schools alone. The total required for the whole of London was over 4,000. After the existing deficiency had been rectified it was

---

[1] Board Minutes, vol. iii. p. 1246.   [2] *Ibid.* vol. ii. p. 274.

calculated that the annual loss of teachers which would have to be replaced amounted to 377.

Passing to the consideration ot the supply of trained teachers for the whole of the country, they estimated the total school population to be between 3,200,000 and 3,500,000. Allowing a trained teacher for every 120 children, the number of teachers required would be 27,149. The number existing was about 18,750. Thus an addition of about 9,000 teachers was shown to be necessary during the next two or three years.

Turning then to a consideration of the sources from which this demand could be supplied, and basing their calculation upon the fact that the utmost accommodation of the existing training colleges was not more than 3,470, they concluded that in two years the colleges could not send out more than 3,402 teachers. To this they added 2,076 ex-pupil teachers, who had only been partially trained, giving a gross total of 5,478 teachers. These estimates showed, not only that the training colleges were incapable of supplying existing deficiencies, but that they would not be able to meet the annual loss on account of deaths and resignations.

A scheme was laid before the Committee for founding a great central day training college in London, supported by a Government Grant. The Board schools were to be used by the students as practising schools. This proposal was not adopted by the Committee. They contented themselves with suggesting the following alternatives: (1) The extension of accommodation in existing colleges; (2) granting increased facilities for instruction to persons anxious to prepare for the certificate examination; (3) admission of non-resident students to training colleges; (4) giving greater facilities to persons not able or wishing to enter training colleges in order to qualify for the profession.[1]

These were recommendations which the Board had no power to carry into effect They have been quoted in order to throw light upon a very practical difficulty which the Board had to overcome. If immediate success was to attend the endeavour to educate effectively the rough and ill-disciplined children who were thronging into the Board's schools, it was essential that the Board should be able to command the services of a competent staff of efficiently trained teachers. But precisely at this moment the supply of such teachers failed. Before the publication of the report to which reference has been made the Board had foreseen this difficulty. In March, 1872, the Board had approached the Education Department with a request that it would hold an examination at Midsummer to enable candidates to qualify themselves for acting as assistant teachers.[2] The Department replied that " My Lords " regretted that pressure of work made it impossible for them to hold such an examination, and they pointed out that 250 pupil teachers were completing their engagements in every month, and that these were eligible for employment under the Code.[3] In October, after the report of the Committee upon the Supply of Teachers, the Department tardily consented to hold such an examination.

---

[1] Board Minutes, vol. ii. p. 454. [2] *Ibid.* vol. ii. p. 207.
[3] *Ibid.* p. 260.

But this concession did not fully meet the needs of the case. The Board was compelled, whether it desired it or not, to rely very largely on ex-pupil teachers and certificated teachers with low qualifications for the staffing of its schools. Many inefficient persons crept into the service of the Board because none better qualified could be obtained; and this, coupled with the unruliness of the children placed under the care of such teachers, largely explains the very modified success which attended the earlier efforts of the Board.

The Board had to decide upon a scale of salaries for its teachers. In 1872 the teachers who were recognised by the Code as capable of being employed were :—

1. *Certificated teachers*, who had passed the Government Examination and had received the certificate of merit.

2. *Probationers*, who had passed the Government Examination, but who had not received the certificate of merit.

3. *Ex-pupil teachers*, who had completed their apprenticeship with credit, but who had passed no further examination.

4. *Pupil teachers*, who might not be less than thirteen years of age (completed) at the date of engagement.

The Code also required that one pupil teacher should be employed for every 40 children in average attendance after the first 20.

The first point that the Board had to decide was whether it would pay its teachers a fixed salary, or a salary partially fixed and partially dependent upon the Government Grant which was earned by the school. The advantage attendant upon the former course was that the teacher, not being dependent on results for the augmentation of his income, would devote his energies to the successful teaching of the subjects which did not earn grant, as well as of those which brought income from the Government. The advantage of the latter was that the teacher's devotion to grant-earning subjects would be assured. Having regard to the policy which the Board had adopted respecting the curriculum, a large portion of which was incapable of earning grant, it might be supposed that the Board would have adopted the former alternative. A special sub-committee appointed to consider the question unanimously recommended the latter, and it was adopted without opposition. It was agreed that the salary of teachers in graded schools should be made up of :—

(1) A fixed salary paid monthly.

(2) A share in the Government Grant, payable at the end of the school year.

It was estimated that the grant would vary between 6s. and 9s. per child. This grant was earned partly on average attendance, partly upon the results of examination. The examination grant was to be distributed amongst the teachers in the school, other than pupil teachers. The head teacher was to receive one-half of the grant, the remainder was to be distributed amongst the assistants according to the discretion of the managers, after consultation with the head teacher. If there was only one assistant he was to receive not more than a quarter of the grant.

Head teachers could augment their incomes by giving instruction to pupil teachers out of school hours for six hours a week. No teacher might instruct more than six pupil teachers without the consent of the Board, and the payment was dependent upon the successful passing by the pupil teacher of H.M. Inspector's examination.[1] He could also conduct an evening school under the Board, for which he received a small fixed annual salary[2] and half the Government Grant.

The salaries of teachers in infants' schools were placed on a somewhat different footing. These teachers were paid a fixed annual salary, and the head teacher received in addition 5s. for every child who was reported by the Board Inspector to be fit to pass into the junior school, and a further graduated grant if the infant had attended 80 times and had passed the Inspector's examination, according to the number of subjects passed.[3]

Pupil teachers received weekly payments varying from 6s. to 12s. for males and 4s. to 10s. for females, according to the year of service. Candidates for pupil teacherships received 3s. and 2s. respectively.[4]

The position of the pupil teacher was, therefore, as follows : He received a small salary for his services in the school, together with gratuitous instruction during six hours in the week out of school hours. The pupil teacher was not a very efficient assistant in the school, and the type of candidates which were offering themselves for the post did not promise any great improvement in the future. In 1873 one of the Board Inspectors examined nearly seven hundred candidates for pupil teacherships. "Unfortunately," he reported, "the demand for suitable boys and girls to serve as pupil teachers has in most parts of the Metropolis exceeded the supply, and for some considerable time there has been a notable falling off in the quality of the pupil candidates—children having been sent up for examination who could not pass the third standard with credit. In most of these cases teachers have had no choice between such material and nothing at all. But in some instances children were recommended as candidates who must have been known by their teachers to be utterly unfitted for the post. It should be remembered by teachers that such children will not only be a source of constant anxiety to them, but will tend to lower the status of the whole profession. To illustrate these remarks I give a few answers to questions set at a recent examination : 'Disaster' is defined as 'an afternoon sleep'; the Thames, the Nile, and the Amazon, are given as 'the three largest English rivers'; 'Plynlimmon' is 'the principal English river, and 'a river' is defined as 'a piece of water entirely surrounded by land, as Great Britain.' When I say that, so far from these being selected specimens, I could give a hundred equally ludicrous, it will be seen that the task of examining such utter rubbish is an infliction which ought to be spared an Inspector."[5]

It is no matter for surprise, considering the condition of elementary education before

---

[1] The payment was £5 for a male and £4 for a female pupil teacher.

[2] £20 ; altered subsequently to 15s. for every scholar up to 25, and 10s. for every scholar above that number who attends 60 times in the year and passes Government examination, and £10 per annum.—Board Minutes, vol. ii. pp. 373, 624.

[3] *Ibid.* p. 495. All teachers are now paid fixed inclusive salaries.

[4] *Ibid.* pp. 105-107.

[5] *Ibid.* vol. iii. p. 1248.

1870, that such should be the raw material which offered itself for conversion into public elementary teachers. It was the nemesis of the miserable makeshift called the "monitorial system," which degraded the status of the teacher, that a higher class of pupils was not attracted towards the profession. It was an ill augury that, even when a happier era seemed to have dawned for elementary education, no more promising candidates, who were to become the teachers of the future, should be obtainable. The Board had done its best, by framing a scale of salaries on somewhat more liberal terms than the rates of payment which had hitherto prevailed, to attract a better class of candidate into the profession. Towards the end of its term of office it asked the School Management Committee to consider whether the system of obtaining certificates was such as to hinder persons from seeking to become teachers in public elementary schools whose services, as teachers, would be desirable.[1] It does not appear that the subject was ever reported upon, nor is it probable that any resolutions of the Board could have effected the purpose. Until the profession itself offered brighter prospects than it offered in 1870, it was not to be expected that a better class of candidates would seek to enter it. The status of the public elementary school teacher has appreciably improved since that date and, although the candidates for the profession are still mainly drawn from children attending public elementary schools, it is from a distinctly higher and more intelligent class.

(iii.) THE MANAGEMENT OF THE SCHOOL.

Previous to 1870 all public elementary schools had been managed by committees which were called "committees of managers," which were the bodies responsible to the Education Department for the conduct of the schools. It was manifestly desirable that some similar body should exist in connection with Board schools, to act as an intermediary between the schools and the Board. There were innumerable petty details of school economy to which a central Board could give but inadequate attention, and it was not to be expected that the Board could exercise that intimate and sympathetic oversight of teachers and scholars which could be exercised by a small body of persons, interested in the work of education, who devoted their attention to one school, or a small group of schools. The Education Act provided, therefore, that a School Board might, if it thought fit, from time to time, delegate any of its powers under that Act, except the power of raising money, and in particular might delegate the control and management of any school provided by it, with or without conditions or restrictions, to a body of managers appointed by it, consisting of not less than three persons.[2]

It will be seen that in this short section lay an alternative scheme for the conduct of elementary education. A School Board might, if it saw fit, limit its own powers to those of a mere finance committee, and constitute smaller bodies, scattered over its area, which in effect would be School Boards. To these small bodies might have been delegated the powers of deciding the curriculum which should be adopted in the schools, the appointment of teachers, the methods of discipline to be employed, whether fees

---

[1] Board Minutes, vol. iii. p. 962.   [2] 33 & 34 Vict. c. 75 s. 16. *See also* Schedule iii.

should be charged—in fact, everything except the mere collection of the moneys to be contributed by the public towards the payment of school expenses.   On the other hand, it was within the power of School Boards to refrain from appointing local managers at all,[1] or, appointing them, to limit their office to that of a merely consultative body with no executive functions.   Between these two extreme policies lay the possibility of all manner of variations.   The London School Board does not appear to have deliberately passed any resolution in favour of the appointment of managers.   The question arose when schools began to be transferred to the Board.   These were necessarily under a committee of managers, and it was undesirable to break the continuity of their supervision.   The Board therefore resolved that eight managers should be appointed for each transferred school, of whom four should be nominated by the outgoing body of managers.[2]   Of those appointed by the Board one was always a member of the Board. The remainder were persons recommended by the divisional members.   In the case of new schools, the eight managers were all recommended by the divisional members.[3] Somewhat later arrangements were made for grouping several schools under one body of managers.[4]

Each body of managers appointed a " correspondent," usually one of their own number, as the official medium of communication between themselves and the Board. This office was at first honorary, but when the schools grew more numerous and the work more laborious, a paid officer was appointed for each division, with an adequate staff to perform the office of " correspondent " for all the bodies of managers within the division.

A sub-committee of the School Management Committee was appointed to give instructions to the managers of schools.   While the schools remained few in number, these instructions were given by the Committee in personal conference with the managers. Subsequently this became impossible, and the work was carried on by correspondence. In the earlier years of the Board's work no written instructions were provided for the guidance of managers in the performance of their duties; but it is evident that these conferences with the sub-committee ranged over all questions relating to the internal management of the schools, such as repairs to buildings, school apparatus, fees, and the appointment of teachers.[5]   Later on a " Code of Regulations " for the guidance of managers was prepared, which set out the powers and duties of managers.   This has been varied and amended from time to time in accordance with the changes which the Board has made in the powers confided to managers.   It would be useless to attempt to trace these changes in detail.   At the present time the rule of the Board is that a body of managers of a single school shall be eight persons.[6]   But, in most cases two or three schools are placed under one body of managers.   In the case of two schools

---

[1] In May, 1872, it was referred to the School Management Committee to consider the expediency of ceasing to appoint managers for the future. —Board Minutes, vol. ii. p. 309.

[2] Board Minutes, vol. i. p. 355.

[3] *Ibid.* vol. ii. p. 170.

[4] *Ibid.* pp. 374, 706.

[5] *Ibid.* vol. ii. p. 20.

[6] In July, 1873, the Board decided that ladies should be appointed to every, body of managers— Board Minutes, vol. iii. p. 686.

the maximum number of managers is twelve, in the case of three schools, fifteen. The same person may not serve on more than two groups of schools.

The chief duties of managers are in relation to the teachers of the school. For some time the Board confided to the managers the selection of all teachers, both head and assistant. It was found, however, that there was too great a tendency to select an assistant in the school in which a vacancy occurred for a head teacher, regardless of the claims of outside teachers, of whose merits the managers could have little or no cognisance. It was felt that this practice narrowed too rigidly the selection of the most capable candidate and operated unjustly towards meritorious assistants. In 1889, therefore, the Board took the appointment of head teachers into its own hands. In March, 1892, it was resolved that the sub-committee of the School Management Committee on the Teaching Staff should select the names of three candidates, and that the managers should select their head teacher from one of these and send up the name to the Board for appointment. Assistant teachers are selected and nominated by the local managers. An exception to the rule exists in respect to the staff of Higher Grade Schools. The heads and assistants in these schools are nominated to the Board by the School Management Committee without any reference to the managers.

Complaints against teachers lodged by persons other than the local managers themselves are investigated in the first instance by the local managers. Such complaints, emanating chiefly from the parents of scholars, are numerous, but in most cases entirely frivolous. The tact and discretion with which the teachers have dealt with the roughest class of parents and children are remarkable. This class of children cannot be disciplined entirely by the gloved hand, and the parent is prone to confuse discipline with cruelty. In investigating charges of alleged cruelty the managers have a most delicate task to perform. In ninety-nine cases out of a hundred justice compels them to bring in a verdict in favour of the teacher. It then becomes necessary to persuade the complainant that the verdict is just. The rarity of appeals against their decisions proves that they discharge their duties with conspicuous tact.[1]

It is also a part of the duty of managers to examine and check the registers of the children's attendance which are kept by the teachers. For this purpose they appoint two of their number. They also examine the log-book, kept by the teacher, in which is entered all matters of importance which affect the conduct of the school. They are also requested to give particular attention to the sanitary condition of the school building.

Managers have also important duties to perform in relation to the children in the

---

[1] The Chairman of the School Board for London is looked upon by the public as an autocrat, who can, by his ukase, remedy every wrong, even upon an *ex parte* statement of the facts. The compiler of these pages has, therefore, had considerable opportunities of judging of the nature of the complaints which parents make against teachers. Scarcely a day passes without producing a letter alleging some grievance. These letters are referred, as a matter of course, to the local managers of the school in which the outrage is said to have occurred. There is no better proof of the value of the unrecorded services which both managers and teachers render to the cause of education than the fact that it rarely happens that a complainant writes protesting against the decision at which the managers have arrived.

school. They are required to form a Health Sub-Committee, whose business it is to see that dull and delicate children are not unduly pressed. It is the duty of the teachers to furnish the managers with lists of such children. The Health Sub-Committee see these children, consider the condition of their homes, consult their parents as to their health, and take care that the instruction given to them is suitable. Some of the managers are expected to be present when H.M. Inspector visits the school.

Managers are also requested to draw up an annual report upon the work of the school in all its aspects—in relation to the teachers, the scholars, and the parents. They must report if there has been any abnormal amount of illness amongst teachers or children : if any special difficulties have occurred in the conduct of the school: upon the subjects that have been studied, and the condition and use made of school libraries. They also report on the efforts, which may be termed extra-scholastic, to interest and instruct the children; such as clubs for swimming, games, or natural history ; arrangements for country holidays, and for provident funds ; any special measures adopted to help cases of sickness or poverty among the children, or special plans for interesting the parents in the work of the school.

It is hardly necessary to state that in reporting upon these extra-scholastic efforts the managers are reporting upon services which they, in conjunction with the teachers and with other voluntary agencies, have combined to render, in order to make the life of the scholar easier and more pleasant. These efforts afford opportunities of influence over the scholars which could hardly be obtained if the work of managers were merely confined to a supervision of the necessary school routine. But they can only be obtained by a sacrifice of time and energy which meets with no public praise or recognition. More than three thousand ladies and gentlemen are daily labouring thus to promote the well-being of the elementary schools of London, and the public remain unaware of the services which are thus silently, ungrudgingly, and gratuitously rendered.

It will be seen from the foregoing statement that the most essential services which managers render to the cause of education are not capable of being expressed in written codes and regulations. They arise spontaneously from the possession of tact, discretion, and a lively sympathy with the teacher and the scholar. The Board has endeavoured to express in words the indefinable qualities which go to make an efficient manager. "It is the duty of managers to foster the school under their care by every means in their power, to see that the rules laid down for the guidance of teachers are adhered to, to smooth down the difficulties of teachers by constant encouragement and sympathy, to have at heart the mental, moral, and physical welfare of the scholars, and to see that they are brought up in habits of punctuality, of good manners and language, of cleanliness and neatness, and also that the teachers impress upon the children the importance of cheerful obedience to duty, of consideration and respect for others, and of honour and truthfulness in word and act."[1]

In 1882 the managers, of their own initiative, formed a representative committee for the discussion of questions which affect the work of the schools. Each body of managers

[1] Code of Regulations, Art. 44. ; adapted from the Code of Regulations of the Education Department.

is entitled, if it so desires, to send a representative to this Committee. The Committee meets once a month, during the sessions of the London School Board, at the Board's offices. This Committee has done much by conference and comparison of experience to improve the management of the schools,

(iv.) SCHOOL BOOKS AND APPARATUS.

The rudimentary character of the books and apparatus supplied to elementary schools before 1871 has already been described. Managers of schools, driven to hard straits to avoid insolvency, had little cash to expend on such objects. Commercial enterprise, therefore, received no encouragement to promote improvements in these directions.

The most important feature in the classroom is the desk. In Voluntary schools, after the grant made by the Education Department in 1844 in aid of the provision of school desks, the long form, capable of accommodating eight or ten children, faced by a slanting desk, was almost universally adopted.[1] These desks and forms were raised slightly in tiers, and were graduated in size to suit the varying stature of children. Such was the cheapest form of desk obtainable, but it was not constructed to promote efficiency in teaching. The teacher was unable to pass behind the scholars, and was out of reach of the farthest tier. It offered obstacles to the prompt and orderly entrance and dismissal of the children, and it rendered the clearing of the classroom difficult. In many Voluntary schools the desks were designed not merely for educational, but also for social, purposes; attempts were made to construct desks which, at short notice, could be transformed into tables for tea meetings and similar functions, and the effort to serve two masters, although it may have resulted satisfactorily for the tea drinkers, was by no means an advantage to the scholars.

The form desk had long been abandoned in the United States of America in favour of the dual desk, with most satisfactory results. The School Board had to consider whether it would continue to use the regulation English pattern, or adopt a more modern improvement. The School Management Committee, after testing the various designs of desks then in use, and after consultation with their architect and Inspectors, decided upon adopting the dual desk with a movable flap.[2] This design offered the following advantages: (1) The teacher could approach close to every child; (2) Each child could get to or from his seat without disturbing another; (3) The children could be drilled in their places; (4) The desks could be used at the inclinations most suitable for reading and for writing.

This kind of desk, although the details of the design have been improved from time to time, has nearly been provided in Board schools. The desks are graduated in size, the smaller being placed in the larger classrooms used by junior children. They are always arranged so that the light may fall from the left hand, and three or four back rows are stepped, the front rows being on the flat. In some of the more modern schools single desks are provided in Standards VII. and ex-VII., and occasionally a class-

---

[1] See *ante*, p. 90. [2] Board Minutes, vol. ii. p. 206.

room is so furnished for examination purposes.[1] Teachers' desks, blackboards, and slates completed the simple furniture of the earlier Board schools.

The first decisions respecting the books to be used in the schools were given by the Sub-Committee appointed to give instructions to managers. This arose from the fact that at the time only transferred schools had to be dealt with, and the continued use of school books already provided in the schools was a subject for conference with the managers of those schools.[2] Some books already in use had to be rejected as infringing the rules in relation to religious instruction. These duties continued to be discharged by this Sub-Committee until they were transferred to the Books and Apparatus Sub-Committee.

The question of school books suitable for adoption by the Board was the subject of long and anxious consideration. The meagre and unsatisfactory character of existing books was so great that the Committee debated whether it might not be wise for the Board to prepare and issue text-books of its own. The Sub-Committee ultimately reported that "without as yet giving any recommendation as to the ultimate action of the Board, they are of opinion that it is not at the present time desirable to publish, by authority, any books to be exclusively used in the schools under its control."[3] The Sub-Committee then gave a list of Readers, any of which might be selected for use in the schools, but managers were allowed to apply for leave to continue the use of any Reader which was not upon the selected list.

The selection of other text-books seems to have caused more difficulty. The Sub-Committee reported that the books on arithmetic, geography, and grammar were numerous and varied, and that many new text-books were continually being published. They therefore suggested, and the Board resolved, that no list of these should be recommended, but that the selection should be left to the managers; power being reserved to the Board to disallow any text-book that might be thought undesirable.[4] The same rule was applied to copybooks, and to reading-sheets, alphabet boxes and kindergarten toys for infant schools. It was ordered that these latter schools should be supplied with diagrams and pictures, especially pictures having reference to natural history. In regard to all other subjects in the curriculum adopted by the Board, no text-books were to be supplied, they were to be taught orally.[5]

The next point to be decided was the method of distributing the books and apparatus to the schools. It was proposed that the Board should organise a central depôt for storage and distribution; but eventually a sub-committee of the School Management Committee was formed to consider and allow the requisitions of the schools for books and apparatus,[6] and an agent was appointed to supply the articles requisitioned at a fixed rate of discount, and to deliver them to the schools.[7]

The Act of 1870 was silent on the question whether the School Board should make a

[1] "The Planning and Construction of Board Schools," by T. J. Bailey, Journal of the Royal Institute of British Architects, 3rd Series, vol. vi. p. 413.
[2] Board Minutes, vol. ii. p. 21.
[3] *Ibid.* vol. ii. p. 140.
[4] *Ibid.* p. 184.
[5] *Ibid.* vol. ii. pp. 228, 410.
[6] *Ibid.* p. 30.
[7] *Ibid.*, p. 564, vol. iii. p. 243.

charge for books and apparatus to the scholars. It provided that the scholar should be charged a weekly fee, and that remission of the fee might be granted for a period not exceeding six months to parents who, through poverty, were unable to pay.[1] It also provided that the Board might, with the consent of the Education Department, establish free schools in poor districts.[2] A very important question of principle arose for the Board to decide. Should books and apparatus be supplied free of charge or not? It was evident that in cases where the fees were remitted, or of free schools, it would be impossible to charge for books. There were three policies advocated upon the Board. The first was to supply books free of charge; the second to supply them free only to the poorest schools, and the third to fix the fee at a figure that should include a charge for books. The School Management Committee brought up a report which was a compromise between the first and second policies. They proposed that all reading-books used in the schools should be provided gratis, and also all books, stationery and apparatus in schools where the fee was less than threepence, leaving the children in schools with a fee of threepence and over to pay for everything but reading-books. The resolution respecting reading-books was carried; to the rest of the proposal an amendment was moved in favour of making the fee include a reasonable charge for books and apparatus.[3] Both the amendment and the original motion were withdrawn in order that the question might be reconsidered. The discussion had brought into prominence the great difficulties which the Board would have to encounter in making a charge for books. Such a charge must of necessity be a small one, in order to ensure a reasonable chance of its being paid. It followed that, if the cost were to be kept down, inferior material would have to be supplied. It was even a question whether such a charge would be legal. The Act bound the Board to keep the school in a state of efficiency, but it conferred no power to make any charge upon the parent except the school fee. Even if the charge were legal, the existence of thousands of small outstanding accounts, many of which it would be impossible to recover, would entail upon the Board an amount of labour and loss which must needs outweigh any advantage which could ensue from making the contemplated charge. The Board, therefore, when it reconsidered the question, rescinded its former resolution, and decided " that the use of all books, stationery and apparatus be allowed in Board schools without any additional charge."[4]

This resolution, although seemingly unimportant, was one of the decisions of the first School Board which permanently guided future policy. It undoubtedly made smoother the working of the Education Act in London. It was a prime necessity that the Board should be brought as little as possible into conflict with the parents of the children whom it desired to bring into the schools. If books and apparatus had

---

[1] 33 & 34 Vict. c. 75 s. 17. The maximum limit of the fee under the Education Act was 9d. a week. The Board has accepted the fee grant in lieu of fees under the provisions of the Elementary Education Act, 1891 (54 & 55 Vict. c. 56). The long and intricate story of the difficulties which the Board encountered in relation to the collection and recovery of fees has been omitted from these pages, it being now of no practical importance.

[2] This power was never acted upon.

[3] Board Minutes, vol. ii. p. 333.

[4] *Ibid.* p. 353.

been charged for, it would have been necessary to start a separate department of the Board's work for keeping accounts, with an army of collectors to enforce payment. Parents, in all probability, would have resented their visits far more than they resented the visits of school attendance officers. The attempt would have engendered an amount of friction which would not have been counterbalanced by any material educational gain.

In 1874 the Board reverted to the original proposal to establish a central store of its own, on the grounds that economy would be effected by dealing direct with manufacturers and publishers, and that goods could be delivered to the schools with greater expedition. The business of the store was for a short time conducted in a temporary depôt, and afterwards at the Head Office of the Board. In 1890 it was found impossible, owing to increasing business, to accommodate the store at the Head Office, and it was decided that a warehouse should be built. A site was secured in Clerkenwell. There was some delay in commencing building operations, and in 1893 the store was removed once more into temporary accommodation. The new warehouse was completed and occupied in 1896.

In order to afford some conception of the immense amount of business which this department transacts, the following figures may be quoted. In 1894 the total value of the goods issued to the schools was £63,000. The waste paper collected from the schools sold for £580. The goods issued to the schools weighed about 1,800 tons. This included about 685,000 printed books, 15,000 reams of paper, 320,000 copybooks, 7,600 gallons of ink, and 141,000 slates. These statistics have not been compiled for any year subsequent to 1894; but as the estimate of cost for the present year is nearly £100,000, it may be inferred that the above quantities have increased by at least 50 per cent.

Books and apparatus are supplied to the schools upon the requisition of the Head Teachers. For the convenience and guidance of teachers in making out their requisitions the Board issue a catalogue of approved books and apparatus which is called the "Requisition List." From this list the teachers are at liberty to select the material that they require. Before a book can appear on this list it is submitted by the publishers to the Books and Apparatus Sub-Committee. It is then referred to such of the members as have especial acquaintance with the subjects of which it treats. These members submit a written report to the Sub-Committee, and the book, if approved, is placed on the "Requisition List." A similar course is adopted with all articles of school apparatus which are submitted to the Committee. At the Head Office of the Board there is a sample room, where teachers can inspect all approved books and apparatus. Head Teachers requisition for ordinary books and apparatus half-yearly, and for other materials, such as kindergarden, needlework and science and art apparatus, annually.

(v.) Evening Schools.

It was the intention of the Board to establish evening schools concurrently with day schools. The evening school which had existed previously to 1870 was a school in which young persons who had passed school age, and were earning their living during the daytime, might obtain those rudiments of education during the evening which they had failed to acquire in their childhood. The instruction given was usually of the most elementary character, and the idea of the evening school as an institution in which well-instructed youth could continue and expand the education of their school days was not even conceived. The uneducated were too many and the half-educated too few for such a plan to be practicable. It could only be dreamt of as a future possibility when the day schools had raised a more educated generation.

The Education Department recognised evening schools, and assisted them with a grant,[1] but the only grant-earning subjects were reading, writing, and arithmetic. The Elementary Education Act of 1870 did not specifically empower School Boards to conduct evening schools; but it did not define the hours during which schools were to be open, and there was, therefore, nothing in the Act to prevent the establishment of evening classes. But a difficulty arose in regard to the question whether there was any limit of age beyond which it was illegal for the Board to provide a young person with educational facilities. The Act fixed no maximum age to limit the legality of the Board's expenditure upon a child's education; it merely fixed an age beyond which it was illegal to compel the child's attendance at school. The Education Department paid no grant for a child who had passed the highest standard of the Code for the time being in force, but there was no legal obligation upon the Board to refuse education to a child who had ceased to be a grant-earning pupil. Thus neither age nor attainments fixed a limit which, when reached, excluded the child from voluntary attendance at school. These questions so perplexed the first Board that it referred them to its solicitor for advice. He arrived, with great hesitation, at the conclusion that if there was any such limit, it was at the age of sixteen.[2] When evening schools were being started the question of age limitation again arose. The solicitor was once more consulted. This was in 1872, and the Code of that year defined the maximum age of scholars both in day and evening schools as 18. It still remained doubtful whether the new regulation was merely a bar to the earning of the grant, or a more general prohibition of expenditure upon the education of adults who were over the specified age. The solicitor, therefore, advised the Board that if it educated persons above the age of 18, without charging a fee which covered the whole cost of their education, it was liable to have the cost disallowed by the Local Government Board.[3] Acting upon this advice the Board resolved that, without incurring any expense in the matter, it would grant the use of its schoolrooms to properly constituted committees for the purpose of carrying on evening schools for persons over 18 years of age.[4]

The Committee on the Scheme of Education was not less sanguine in its hope of introducing a liberal curriculum into evening schools than it had been in regard to the day schools; but in the case of the former a more complete disappointment was in store for them. "Evening schools," said the Committee, "are of great importance, partly as a means for providing elementary education for those who, for various reasons, fail to

---

[1] Education Department Report, 1870-1, p. cix.
[2] Board Minutes, vol. i. p. 189.
[3] *Ibid.* vol. ii. p. 657.
[4] *Ibid.* vol. iii. p. 1.

obtain sufficient instruction in elementary day schools, and partly because it is easy to connect with such schools special classes in which a higher kind of instruction than that contemplated by Standard VI.[1] can be given to the more intelligent and elder scholars. In this manner the advantages of further instruction may be secured by those scholars who are unable or unwilling to go into secondary schools, but who are both able and willing to pay for instruction of a more advanced kind than that given in primary schools."[2]

The Committee, therefore, advised, and the Board resolved, that the curriculum for evening schools for young persons under the age of 18 should be of the same character as that which had been adopted for the day schools, and the managers of evening schools were advised to adapt the instruction given to the requirements of the localities in which the schools were situated. It was further resolved that science and art classes should be established, if possible, in connection with the Science and Art Department.

The early relations between the School Board and the Science and Art Department are interesting in view of the hostile attitude which that Department has recently assumed in relation to the Board's work. In November, 1871, the Department asked the School Board to co-operate with it in organising the conduct of its examinations and in appointing local secretaries for the several school divisions of London.[3] Such a request would not have been made unless the Science and Art Department were willing, if not eager, to establish a connection between itself and the schools under the Board. To this the Board replied that its hands were so full of its own special work that it was unable to accept the Department's invitation, but that if it were renewed next year the Board would be ready to consider the invitation afresh.[4] In September, 1873, the Board resolved that permanent schools might be used for Science and Art Evening Classes provided that all expenses were met without any demand upon the funds of the Board, and that they did not interfere with any ordinary evening classes which it might be considered desirable to establish.[5]

This resolution was passed under the influence of the enforced prudence which immediately precedes a triennial election. It seems evident from the report of the Committee on the Scheme of Education that so restricted a co-operation with the Science and Art Department was not originally contemplated. It is not a little curious that in 1872-3 the Department should have wooed the Board in vain, and that of late years, when the Board made the advances, the Department should have proved so coy.

In the first enthusiasm of the moment the Board instructed the School Management Committee to consider and report upon the desirability of opening evening schools during the winter of 1871-2.[6] The result was that the Committee, in December, 1871, directed the Sub-Committee for the Instruction of Managers to urge managers to establish evening schools wherever practicable, at as early a date as possible.[7] The

---

[1] Then the highest Standard.
[2] Board Minutes, vol. i. p. 159.
[3] *Ibid.* vol. i. p. 358.
[4] *Ibid.* vol. ii. pp. 42, 50.

[5] *Ibid.* vol. iii. pp. 937, 947.
[6] *Ibid.* vol. i. p. 330.
[7] *Ibid.* vol. ii. p. 17.

notice was a short one, and managers were fully employed in the re-organisation of the day schools. Very few evening schools were opened during that winter. In December, 1872, a return of the number of evening schools already opened was laid before the Board. That return cannot now be found, but it evidently showed that very little had been done to establish evening schools, for in January, 1873, the Board requested the School Management Committee to consider and report whether more evening schools could not with advantage be opened.[1] The Committee replied with a somewhat ambiguous declaration that they would be prepared to consider any application for the establishment of such schools which was properly recommended by a duly constituted body of managers.[2] In the pressure of other work evening schools were evidently being crushed out of consideration.

In September, 1873, the Board formulated a scheme for the conduct of evening schools. The only important portion of it was the declaration that no evening school should be opened unless at least 40 names were entered on the register, or continued if the average attendance of the previous month fell below 20.[3] This resolution gave the final blow to the first attempt to establish evening schools under the School Board for London, and to the liberal curriculum which had been formulated for them by the Scheme of Education Committee. The plan which had originally been proposed was somewhat ahead of the requirements of the time. To bring it to fruition, and to attract pupils to the schools, a long period of nursing was essential. The evening schools required to be forced into popularity. To refuse to establish such a school because 40 scholars could not be at once enrolled, and to insist upon closing such a school because the average attendance fell in any one month below 20 was to deny the scheme a chance of success. The attendance at an evening school must of necessity be irregular. The scholars attend it after a long day's labour, and many of them, under pressure, are compelled to work overtime at their callings. It is no evidence of waning interest in their evening studies if they sometimes, or even frequently, fail to attend at the evening class.

Under such uncongenial influences evening schools had no chance of springing into healthy existence. Their end came in a somewhat unexpected manner. In January, 1875, the Board directed the School Management Committee to reconsider the method of remunerating the teachers in evening schools.[4] The Committee did not report until the end of June. They then declared that the Board desired that children subject to the bye-laws should make their attendances at day schools, and that evening schools should not be specially created to meet the case of half-timers. They therefore recommended that the resolutions of the Board for establishing evening schools should be rescinded; that no such schools should be carried on directly by the Board; but that the use of the Board's schools should be granted for evening classes to voluntary agencies at a small charge for rent.[5] These recommendations were adopted by the Board, apparently without challenge or debate.

---

[1] Board Minutes, vol. iii. p. 98.
[2] *Ibid.* vol. iii. p. 168.
[3] These numbers were raised to 100 and 50 respectively in August, 1874, but the resolution was rescinded in the following September.
[4] Board Minutes, vol. v. p. 225.
[5] *Ibid.* p. 892.

The reason for the Board's action is difficult to explain. The recommendation to discontinue evening classes was outside the limits of the reference which the Board had sent down to the School Management Committee. The alleged reason can hardly be taken as explaining the real motive; for the existing bye-laws of the Board precluded a half-timer from making his necessary attendances after six o'clock in the afternoon.[1] The Press appears to have taken no notice of a resolution which, although it passed through the Board without discussion, was one of considerable educational importance. The only probable explanation of the Board's action is that the evening classes had not proved successful; that the Board was, at the time, incurring very severe criticism on account of its alleged lavish expenditure, and that, therefore, it was resolved to destroy, with as little publicity as possible, a branch of the work which was costly without being popular. The work of the Board in connection with evening schools was not revived until 1882.

CHAPTER V.

COMPULSION.

On no subject in connection with education has public opinion so entirely changed during the last sixty years as on that of compulsory attendance at school. Lord Brougham, when he introduced his Education Bill into the House of Lords in 1837, stated accurately, if somewhat magniloquently, the current opinion upon the question. "There ought to be," he declared, "in no time and in no country, whatever might be the constitution of the country and the state of society, any positive and direct compulsion as to the education of the people. Those who advocated such a course," he said, "forgot that there was a line over which the law-giver ought not to pass, and beyond which he forfeited all claim to support by the violation of some of the most sacred principles—a violation of individual liberty—a system intolerable for the citizens of a free state . . . only fit for a country where, liberty being little known, slavery was the more bearable."[2]

Lord Brougham's "most sacred principles" have for many years been violated out of all recognition, without reducing the people of this country to the state of demoralisation which the speaker foretold. But change of opinion was of very gradual growth, and was obstructed by formidable obstacles. The opposition arose from two classes who imagined that they were interested in preventing the application of compulsion. One class was the parents of the children, who persuaded themselves that the wages of their offspring were essential to their comfort. In the fifties and the sixties child labour was in great demand, and the terrible cruelties to which the children were subjected were frequently exposed by the late Lord Shaftesbury, both in and out of Parliament. That

---

[1] Board Minutes, vol. iii. p. 1180; vol. iv. p. 81.   [2] Hansard, vol. xxxix. p. 415.

the cry of the parent against deprivation of the earnings of his child was largely fictitious was proved by statistics. The Census of 1851 showed that of the total number of boys and girls between 3 and 15 who were not attending school, only 16 per cent. of the boys and 9 per cent. of the girls were absent on account of employment.[1] The alleged necessary employment of the children was evidently to a large extent a cloak for the apathy of the parent.

The other class which opposed compulsory education was the manufacturers and the mine-owners. These offered a strenuous opposition to compulsory education, as they had offered to all the proposals for the amelioration of the condition of the workers which were contained in the various Factory Acts which were brought before Parliament. Their cry was that the commercial prosperity of the country would be imperilled if the children were compelled to attend school, instead of labouring in the mine or at the loom.

Such were the obstacles which educationists, convinced that no vital improvement in educational efficiency could be effected without the application of some form of compulsion, had to surmount. The process of overcoming them was slow. The earlier remedies proposed were in the nature of indirect compulsion. It was suggested that a child who had not passed a certain standard should be ineligible for apprenticeship to a trade, or incapable of acquiring the franchise.[2] It is doubtful whether such a proposal, if adopted, would have achieved its object. It was in the nature of a postponed punishment inflicted upon the child. The real offenders, the parent and the employer, remained untouched. The parent, greedy of the wages which his child could earn, would care little for the fact that the small labourer would be eventually precluded from apprenticeship, and less that on attaining his majority, he would be unable to acquire the franchise.

A more reasonable proposal was that, having regard to the fact that a very small proportion of the absentees were employed in remunerative labour, compulsion should be enforced only against those who were not actually so employed, and that employment should be treated in all cases as a reasonable excuse for non-attendance at school.[3]

The one man who saw clearly that compulsion was inevitable was Matthew Arnold. So early as 1853, while discussing the causes of scanty attendance at school, he said : " I am far from imagining that a lower school fee, or even a free admission, would induce the poor universally to send their children to school. It is not the high payments alone which deter them ; all I say is, as to the general question of the education of the masses, that they deter them in many cases. But it is my firm conviction that education will never, any more than vaccination, become universal in this country until it is made compulsory." [4]

Matthew Arnold continued to advocate this view until it was adopted by the Legislature. In 1867, three years before the passing of the Education Act, he wrote

[1] Education Department Report, 1854-5, p. 303.
[2] *Ibid.* 1850-1, p. 448. *See also* Lord Norton's Bill of 1860, *ante* p. 20.
[3] *Ibid.* 1850-1, p. 68.
[4] " Reports on Elementary Schools," p. 26.

the following instructive passage: "Throughout my district I find the idea of compulsory education becoming a familiar idea with those who are interested in schools. I imagine that with the newly-awakened sense of our shortcomings in popular education . . . the difficult thing would not be to pass a law making education compulsory; the difficult thing would be to work such a law after we had got it. In Prussia, which is so often quoted, education is not flourishing because it is compulsory, it is compulsory because it is flourishing. Because people there really prize instruction and culture, and prefer them to other things; therefore they have no difficulty in imposing on themselves the rule to get instruction and culture. In this country people prefer to them politics, station, business, money-making, pleasure, and many other things; and till we cease to prefer these things, a law which gives instruction the power to interfere with them, though a sudden impulse may make us establish it, cannot be relied on to hold its ground and to work effectively. When instruction is valued in this country as it is in Germany, it may be made obligatory here; meanwhile, the best thing the friends of instruction can do is to foment as much as they can the national sense of its value. The persevering extension of provisions for the schooling of all children employed in any kind of labour is probably the best and most practicable way of making education obligatory that we can at present take."[1]

The foregoing quotation throws a clear light on the state of public opinion in respect to compulsory education just before passing of the the Education Act of 1870, and in a large measure explains the somewhat complicated provisions of that Act for enforcing compulsion. Educationists as a body had become convinced that universal compulsion was not only necessary, but desirable. The public, more especially that portion of it which would be subject to the new law, were not openly hostile to it, but they were so apathetic upon the question of education and so little convinced of its value, that the attempt to enforce compulsion with any lack of gentleness and consideration would probably have roused a hostility which would have proved fatal to the experiment. Moreover, it was evident that compulsion would provoke more opposition in some parts of the country than in others. Child labour was most employed in the north of England and in the purely agricultural districts, and there, consequently, the strain on the forbearance of parents and employers would be the greatest.

Having regard to all these facts the prudent plan was adopted of leaving the School Boards which were to be formed under the Act to settle whether compulsion should be enforced or not. This course left the locality free to decide its own fate in the matter. If it contained a majority averse from compulsion, it was within its power to elect a Board pledged not to adopt the permissive clauses of the Act.

The Act provides that School Boards may, with the consent of the Education Department, frame bye-laws for the purpose of enforcing attendance at school. When the bye-laws have been passed they must, after certain delays, be submitted to the Education Department for approval. Before giving that approval the Education Department may cause any inquiry they may think requisite in the district for which

---

[1] "Reports on Elementary Schools," p. 125.

the bye-laws have been framed. When all these steps have been taken the bye-laws are sanctioned by the Queen in Council, and thereby acquire the force of law.[1] Any proposed alteration of the bye-laws, before it can be enforced, must undergo the same processes.

The scope of the bye-laws that a School Board was entitled to frame under the Act of 1870 was as follows: The bye-laws might require the parents of children of such age as the Board might fix, not being less than five years and more than thirteen years of age, to attend school unless there were some reasonable excuse for non-attendance. The "reasonable excuses" recognised by the Act were three in number: (1) That the child was under efficient instruction in some other manner; (2) That the child was prevented from attending school by sickness or any unavoidable cause; (3) That there was no public elementary school open which the child could attend within such distance, not exceeding three miles, measured according to the nearest road from the residence of the child, as the bye-laws might prescribe. The bye-laws might also determine the time during which children were to attend school, provided that they did not prevent the withdrawal of the child from religious instruction, or compel its attendance on any day exclusively set apart for religious observance by the religious body to which the parent belonged, and were not contrary to the provisions of any Act regulating the education of children employed in labour. They might also provide for the remission or payment of the whole or any part of the fees of any child whose parent was unable through poverty to pay the same,[2] and might impose penalties for breach of the bye-laws not exceeding such sum as, with the costs, would amount to five shillings[3] for each offence. The bye-laws were also to provide for the total or partial exemption of any child between the ages of 10 and 13 from the necessity of attending school if one of H.M. Inspectors certified that the child had reached a standard of education specified in the bye-law for that purpose.[4]

It will be observed that even if a locality decided to adopt compulsion, a large amount of flexibility in the application of the law was possible. No compulsion could be applied to a child under 5 or over 13 years of age, but any School Board might adopt a less restricted period for compulsion; might even, if it saw fit, adopt bye-laws formally and render them ineffective by reducing the age of compulsory education to a minimum. School Boards might also raise or depress the efficiency of the education in their districts by fixing a high or low standard as the qualification for total or partial exemption from attendance at school. Legislation which permitted such variations in its application cannot be described as heroic; it is characterised rather by timorousness, but it reflected the nicely balanced opinion of the times. It enabled localities which

[1] By a Bill now before Parliament it is proposed that the sanction of the newly constituted Board of Education shall be substituted for that of the Queen in Council.

[2] The power of School Boards to pay school fees of children was repealed by the Elementary Education Act of 1876, s. 10, and any bye-laws authorising such payments to that extent became inoperative. The first London School Board, after prolonged and somewhat heated debate, decided to pay the fees of scholars in Voluntary schools in cases of parents who were unable by poverty to pay the same. The discussion has no longer any practical interest, and it has not been referred to in the text.

[3] It is proposed by a Bill now before Parliament to raise the maximum fine to 20s.

[4] 33 & 34 Vict. c. 75 s. 74.

were averse from the principle of compulsion to apply it experimentally and in homœopathic doses. Any legislation which outran the average opinion of the public could only have resulted in disaster to the cause of education. It was legislation which had been effected in mindfulness of Matthew Arnold's warning that there was no difficulty in passing a law for making education obligatory, but great difficulty in enforcing it.

It was this difficulty which the School Board for London had to solve. It does not appear that it was ever doubted that the Board would eventually adopt compulsion, but the methods of enforcing it were the subject of prolonged consideration. So early as February 8th, 1871, a motion was proposed to frame at once a bye-law compelling children between 5 and 13 to attend school unless a reasonable excuse were forthcoming. This crude and ill-considered method of proceeding was met by an amendment affirming the necessity of enforcing attendance at school, under conditions which were to be the subject of further consideration. At the same time, the question of compulsion under section 74 of the Act was referred to a committee of the Board.[1]

It was not until the end of June, 1871, that the Committee presented to the Board a draft of the proposed bye-laws, together with a scheme for enforcing them. The Committee had proceeded with extreme caution in their difficult task, "under a strong sense of the responsibility devolved upon them by the Board, and with a conviction that the compulsory clauses of the Act form one of its most important features, as marking a new epoch in the history of National Education in England, and as affording the only means of making that education universal."[2] They took a considerable amount of evidence upon the actual operation of compulsion abroad, and its probable operation in London, and they came to the conclusion that "although the compulsory clauses are the true expression of a decided public opinion, this opinion has been gradually formed and pronounced with some hesitation." It should, therefore, "be carried out, especially at first, with as much gentleness and consideration for the circumstances and feelings of the parents as is consistent with its effective operation."

The bye-laws, as originally submitted, were nine in number, preceded by an elaborate recital of the statutory powers under which they were framed. The first bye-law contained definitions, only one of which was of importance. The word "school" was defined as "a public elementary school, or any other school at which efficient elementary education is given." There was a large body of opinion averse from thus limiting the meaning of the word. Many thought that the success of compulsion would be best assured by allowing attendance at any school, for a time at least, to reckon as a compliance with the bye-laws. The recommendation of the Committee was, however, adopted by the Board.[3]

---

[1] Board Minutes, vol. i. p. 54.

[2] *Ibid.* p 172.

[3] Seven members of the Committee signed a minority report dissenting from the restricted definition of a "school." The weight of the opposition will be shown by naming them. They were Lord Lawrence, Lord Sandon, Mr. W. H. Smith, Mr. E. N. Buxton, Miss Emily Davies, Mr. A. Lafone, and Mr. C. Few. Their dissent ran thus: "We are of opinion that the compulsory *regular* attendance of all children at school is more likely to be introduced with the willing acquiescence

The second bye-law was the all-important operative clause. It provided that the age of compulsion should extend over the whole period permitted by the Act— namely, from 5 to 13 years. The proposal gave rise to a considerable amount of discussion, and two amendments were moved, unsuccessfully, to reduce the period. The first aimed at making the commencing age 7 instead of 5, the second at reducing the period of compulsion to the ages of from 6 to 12.[1] The object of the movers of both these amendments was the same. Neither of them desired to curtail the period of education merely for the sake of curtailing it. Both of them feared that, by attempting too much, the Board was about to imperil the success of compulsion. The remarks of the mover of the second amendment,[2] speaking upon the first, disclose the basis of the opposition. "He foresaw that, as soon as direct compulsion was commenced, the greatest difficulties would be at the beginning and at the end of the school age. It would be difficult to compel children of 5 or 6 in all cases to go to school, and it would also be extremely difficult, and in many cases, a great hardship, if they compelled children to go to school up to 13. Statistics showed that at present parents sent their children voluntarily to school between the ages of 6 and 11, and if the Board attempted to raise that standard by two additional years feelings of irritation among the working classes would probably be aroused."[3]

When these amendments had been defeated a more specious attack was delivered against the efficient working of this bye-law by an attempt to postpone its operation. It was proposed to preface the words of the bye-law by the following qualification: "When and as soon as it shall be certified by the Education Department that suitable and efficient accommodation has been provided in the district of the Board."

The effect of adopting this amendment would have been to throw back upon the Government the performance of a duty which the Government had cast upon the Board; but the reasons for moving it could be effectively stated. The Board had recently compiled statistics which showed that there were more than 100,000 children of school age in London for whom no school places were provided. It was unjust and absurd, therefore, for the Board to pass a bye-law which compelled the parents of such children to send them to school, and imposed penalties for failure to send them. If the Board had been led away by such an argument the enforcement of compulsion would have been postponed for many a year. The Board took the more reasonable view that it was its duty to adopt the compulsory clauses of the Act, and to take precautions that no injustice was inflicted

of parents if complete freedom of choice is left to them as to the schools to which they may send their children, and that that selection will generally be made with a view to obtain the best and most suitable education, in their judgment, for their children, in return for the sacrifices which the law calls upon them to make. We think it, therefore, wiser to be content at present with securing the *regular* attendance of the children of London at *some* school—a change of enormous magnitude in the habits of the people of the metropolis—and to reserve to ourselves the power of applying hereafter to the Education Department for an alteration in our bye-laws if we find, after experience, that the schools to which the children are sent in any considerable proportion have not become such as, in the opinion of the Board, have suitable accommodation and afford efficient instruction." —Board Minutes, vol. i. p. 175.

[1] This amendment was moved in two parts.
[2] Canon Cromwell.
[3] *School Board Chronicle*, vol. i. p. 327.

in putting them into operation. The amendment was, after discussion, withdrawn, and the bye-law was adopted in its original form.

The third proposed bye-law, providing that "the school may be selected by the parent of the child," was clearly superfluous, and was withdrawn after a very short discussion. The fourth declared that the time during which a child was required to attend school was the whole time that the school was open for instruction, being not less than 25 hours per week, with a saving clause to protect withdrawals from religious instruction, as provided by the Act.

The fifth proposed bye-law, which dealt with the questions of the standard of total exemption and of half-timers, involved more important considerations. The Act, it will be remembered, permitted the Board to fix the standards to be passed by a child not less than 10 years of age who desired to claim total or partial exemption. The decision of the Board in this respect was a critical one. Had it decided to fix upon a low standard, any hope of efficiency in elementary education would have been defeated. The temptation to fix a low standard was doubtless considerable. The argument that such a course would facilitate the acceptance of compulsion was weighty. The Committee proposed Standard V. for total exemption, and for partial exemption it fixed no standard,[1] but provided that the exemption could only be claimed if the child were proved to be "beneficially and necessarily" employed. Such child was required to attend school for at least ten hours in every week in which the school was open, provided that no attendance might count in excess of three hours at any one time, or five hours on any one day, or on Sundays.[2] Attempts were made unsuccessfully to abolish total exemption altogether, and to reduce the standard of total exemption to the fourth. The bye-law was ultimately adopted practically in the terms recommended by the Committee.[3] Another bye-law, not included in the recommendations of the Committee, was introduced by the Board, declaring that nothing in the bye-laws inconsistent with the provisions of the Factory Acts was to be held to prevail as against those provisions. The next bye-law incorporated the reasonable excuses for non-attendance at school set out in the Education Act. The distance of the child's home from the nearest school which was to operate as a reasonable excuse was fixed at one mile.

The eighth bye-law, which provided for the payment or remission of the fees of children whose parents, by reason of poverty, were unable to pay the same, gave rise to more discussion than all the other bye-laws put together. It was debated at no less than six sittings of the Board, held between October 26th and November 2nd, 1871. The opposition was concentrated upon the provision for the payment of fees in denominational schools. Many members were opposed on principle to the application of public money for payment of fees in schools which were not under public control. Eventually the bye-law was withdrawn, and an independent resolution was adopted, which declared that for the succeeding twelve months remission or payment of fees should be made

[1] Standard IV. was fixed in 1879.
[3] *Ibid.* vol. i. pp. 325, 326.

[2] "Or after six o'clock" was subsequently added.—Board Minutes, vol. ii. p. 1,180.

"exceptionally, on proof of urgent temporary need, each case being dealt with on its own merits, without prejudice to the principles involved on either side, it being understood that such remission or payment of fees is not to be considered as made in respect of any instruction in religious subjects."[1]   This resolution, intentionally made temporary in its operation, in order to reconcile opponents to the proposal, was never called in question. It was acted upon by the Board until the end of 1876, when the power of the Board to pay the fees of children in Voluntary schools ceased, under the provisions of the Elementary Education Act of that year.

The last bye-law incorporated the statutory provision for a penalty of five shillings, including costs, for any neglect or violation of the bye-laws.   When all the bye-laws had been agreed to, the lengthy preamble, reciting the statutory powers under which they were made, was struck out.   The revised bye-laws were sanctioned by an Order in Council dated December 21st, 1871.[2]

The Board then proceeded to consider the machinery by which the bye-laws should be enforced.   There were two courses open to it.   It was within its power to carry out the system of compulsion by means of a paid staff, entirely under the central control of the Board, or by the formation of local committees, composed partly of members of the Board, and partly of other persons interested in the work of education and willing to give their time to it.   The Committee proposed the latter alternative, and the Board eventually adopted it, after debating and rejecting an amendment which proposed the former.   There can be no doubt that the Board, in arriving at this decision, very greatly promoted the effective administration of the compulsory law.   If compulsion had been enforced by means of a purely official staff, the work might have been done effectively, but it would have been done in a spirit of mechanical routine which would not have tended to ensure the acquiescence of those who were most nearly affected by it.   To enlist the aid of persons dwelling in the district controlled by the local committee, with knowledge of the life and needs of the locality, with tact to deal not only with the perversity and unreasonableness of indifferent parents, but also with the difficulties of those who were really oppressed by the operation of the new law, was a far more certain method of ensuring success for the experiment.

The Board, therefore, resolved that a committee should be formed for each of the ten divisions of the Metropolis, consisting of the members for that division, and of such other persons, being inhabitants or ratepayers of that division, as the Board should appoint, upon the recommendation of the divisional members.   These divisional committees were empowered to sub-divide their divisions and to form sub-committees for each sub-division.   Every divisional member was a member *ex officio* of each sub-divisional committee, and each sub-divisional committee was empowered to exercise all the powers conferred upon the divisional committee.

Upon these bodies was conferred the power to enforce the bye-laws in the district under their control.   They were instructed so to divide their districts that each section should be of such size and population as to be manageable by one official, who was to be

---

[1] Board Minutes, vol. i. p. 324.   [2] *Ibid.* vol. ii. p. 51.

called a " Visitor " : to nominate Visitors for appointment by the Board, and to direct and control their operations. Each divisional committee was empowered to appoint a clerk, who was to act as Superintendent of the Visitors.

After a few months' experience it was found that the plan of delegating perfectly independent action to the sub-divisional committees had not proved altogether satisfactory. The decentralisation had, in fact, been carried too far, and there was a lack of harmony and co-ordination between the various bodies. It was at first proposed that the sub-divisional committees should be dissolved, but the less stringent course was adopted of causing these smaller committees to report their action to the divisional committees, and the latter committees were instructed to report to the Board, on every quarter day, upon their proceedings under the bye-laws in enforcing compulsion ; on the operations of the Visitors and on the attendances at the various schools in the division.[1] The sub-divisional committees thenceforth only dealt with absenteeism in the earlier stages. When prosecution became necessary the burden of recommending it devolved upon the divisional committee.

The duty of a Visitor within his district was to see that all the children of school age attended school with regularity, unless there were some reasonable excuse for non-attendance. For this purpose he was to keep a schedule of the names and addresses of all such children, showing the names of the children who are expected to attend school ; the schools at which they were expected to attend ; the names of children who are alleged to be receiving efficient instruction in some other manner ; and the names of children not attending school, together with the alleged excuse for non-attendance. The absence from school for one whole day or two half-days in any week, without reasonable excuse, of any child who was legally bound to attend, or frequent irregularity, was to be deemed a breach of the bye-laws. The Visitor was to report any such breach to the divisional committee, and also, to the proper authority, any breaches of the Workshops Acts.

The procedure adopted for dealing with absentees was designed to temper the application of compulsion with the extremest leniency. Every method of persuasion to induce the parent to send the child to school was adopted, and only when persuasion failed was the law to be called into action. When an infringement of the bye-laws was reported, a printed notice was served upon the parent of the absentee requiring him to cause the child to attend school for whole or half-time, as the case might require. The parent was further informed that if he could give a reasonable excuse for the child's non-attendances he might attend on a certain day and hour before the divisional committee, when his excuse would be considered. The parent was warned that if he failed to comply with the notice without reasonable excuse, he was liable to be summoned before a magistrate and fined.[2]

---

[1] Board Minutes, vol. ii. p. 472.

[2] This preliminary notice was called " Notice A," and it has retained the name. In the form of notice now in use the invitation to explain excuses is omitted. The subsequent notice is called " Notice B." There are at present two forms of " Notice A," the first for cases of absenteeism solely, the second for cases of absenteeism on account of irregularities which might eventually lead to the child's committal to an industrial school.

If this appeal to the good sense of the parent failed to produce the desired result, a second notice was served, calling attention to the fact that the absence of the child from school was a breach of the bye-laws, and requiring the parent to attend before the divisional sub-committee to show cause why he should not be summoned before a magistrate. If the parent appeared in answer to this application, the committee endeavoured, by persuasion, to induce him to comply with the law; and only after all these efforts had proved fruitless was a prosecution allowed to take place.[1]

It is necessary to state shortly the alterations in the law relating to compulsion which have been effected since 1870. By the Elementary Education Act of 1873, in any proceeding for an offence against the bye-laws the Court may, instead of inflicting a penalty, make an order that the child shall attend school, and that only on failure to comply with this attendance order the penalty shall be payable.[2]

The Elementary Education Act of 1876 declared that it was the duty of the parent of every child to cause the child to receive elementary education in reading, writing, and arithmetic, subject to penalties for neglect.[3] It also forbade, under a penalty of not exceeding forty shillings, the full time employment of any child[4] under the age of 10 years, or who, being of the age of 10 years and upwards, has not obtained a certificate of proficiency in reading, writing, and elementary arithmetic in any standard not lower than the fourth, or, in the alternative, had made not less than 250 attendances after 5 years of age at not more than two schools during each year for five years, whether consecutive or not.[5] It also forbade the half-time employment of any child who, being upwards of 10 years of age, had not passed the half-time standard or was not attending school half-time in accordance with the education clauses of the Factory Acts. These provisions were made applicable to children between the ages of 5 and 14.[6] The age of 10, not only for the purposes of this Act, but for total and partial exemption under bye-laws, was raised to 11 by the Elementary Education Act of 1893,[7] and by the Elementary Education Act, 1899, it was further raised to 12.[8] But the Act of 1899 provided that a child might obtain partial exemption on attaining the age of 12 if he had made 300 attendances in not more than two schools during each year for five years, whether consecutive or not. Previous to the passing of this Act, such a child could only have obtained partial exemption on passing Standard V. The Act, therefore, has, to this extent, rendered the law of compulsion less stringent in London.

The Board in 1879 fixed the standard of half-time exemption at the fourth, and raised that of whole time exemption to the sixth. In 1898 the Standards of

[1] At the present time the committee have power to issue, if they see fit, even another form (B2) before resorting to prosecution. Under sec. 38 of the Elementary Education Act, 1876, no prosecution can be commenced unless under the direction of two members of the Board. This is a further safeguard against hasty action.
[2] 36 & 37 Vict. c. 86 s. 24.
[3] 39 & 40 Vict c. 79 s. 4.
[4] Except in cases where there is not a school within two miles of the child's residence which it can attend, or during holidays or out of school hours, and in certain other cases in agricultural districts.—*Ibid.* s. 9.
[5] *Ibid.* s. 5 and sched. i.—The standards and periods of attendance were temporarily modified for the years 1877-80 to bring the qualifications gradually up to the standard of the Act. The attendance clauses only applied to full-time exemption.
[6] *Ibid.* s. 48.
[7] 56 & 57 Vict. c. 51 s. 2.
[8] 62 & 63 Vict. c. 13 s 1.

K

half-time and whole-time exemption were again raised to the fifth and the seventh respectively.

At the present time the law relating to exemption from attendance at school stands thus :—

Age.	Half-time exemption.	Full time exemption.
Under 12	None	None.
12—13	(1) On passing Standard V. .. .. (2) Making 300 attendances for 5 years.	On passing Standard VII.
13—14	(1) On passing Standard V. .. .. (2) To a child attending school half time under the Factory and Workshop Act.[1]	(1) On passing Standard V. (2) Making 250 attendances for 5 years.[2]
14—16	No blind or deaf child is entit'ed to half-time exemption.	All children over 14 are exempt with the exception of the blind and deaf, who are required to attend school until 16.

The gradual raising of the compulsory age, and of the standards for total and partial exemption, proves that the great experiment of 1870 has been brought to a successful issue. Compulsion in education has been accepted by the public as an integral part of the educational system, and it is enforced with surprisingly little friction. It is only to the small minority of shiftless and indifferent parents that compulsion has to be applied, but in so enormous a population as that of London even a small minority is represented by a considerable number of individuals, and the machinery for the enforcement of compulsion is necessarily complicated and costly. The total annual expenditure upon this branch of the Board's work, which benefits Voluntary no less than Board schools, is nearly £50,000. There are at present ten divisional offices,[3] with a clerical staff of 65 persons. There are 318 visitors; eleven of whom, one for each division, are attached to no particular district, but are engaged in hunting up the children who are found loitering, begging, and otherwise leading a vagrant life. Thirteen of the visitors supply the places of ordinary visitors who from any cause are absent from duty.

The chief obstacle to the efficient working of the bye-laws has been found, not so much in the streets and the homes of the people, as in the police-courts which are charged with the duty of enforcing the law. In the earlier days of the Board this obstacle was greater

[1] The Factory and Workshop Act, 1878 (41 Vict. c. 16 s. 26), provides that when a child of the age of 13 years has obtained from a person authorised by the Education Department a certificate of having attained a standard of proficiency in reading, writing, and arithmetic, or such standard of previous due attendance at a certified efficient school or day industrial school, as may be from time to time fixed by a Secretary of State with the consent of the Education Department, that child shall be deemed capable of half-time employment. The standards fixed are the Fifth Standard for proficiency, and 250 attendances for 5 years.

[2] By a Bill now before Parliament it is proposed to raise the qualification to 350 attendances. The same Bill proposes to make it permissible to raise the maximum age for compulsion under the bye-laws to 14.

[3] The City and Westminster Divisions have a joint divisional office.

than it is at present, but it has by no means disappeared. Many of the magistrates who occupied the bench in 1870 were hostile to the Education Act, and took the narrowest view of the duties imposed upon them by its provisions. In some courts it was almost impossible to obtain a conviction. This class of opposition has almost died out, but another difficulty remains. It was not, perhaps, the highest wisdom to enact that summonses under the Education Acts should be heard in the police-courts. These courts, which deal with the manifold petty offences which are continually committed in a great city, are overburdened with work. The breach of the law which the parent has to answer is not an offence in the same category as the charges of drunkenness, theft, and assault which go to make up the sordid atmosphere of a police-court. It is true that, in most cases, a special time is set apart for hearing the School Board summonses; but this only mitigates the evil.

The overpressure of work has compelled the courts in many instances to decline to hear more than a specified number of summonses issued by the Board, a number far smaller than that which ought to be heard if the law is to be administered efficiently. The knowledge that there is a fair chance of escape from appearance before the court encourages the negligent parent in his defiance of the law. If the divisional committees were enabled to bring every inexcusable case of a breach of the law to a hearing with swiftness and certainty, the average attendance in the schools of London would be very greatly improved.[1]

The Board has for many years been conscious, not only of the unsuitability of the police-court as the machine for enforcing compulsion, but also of the unnecessary impediment to educational efficiency which was caused by the restriction in the number of summonses that could be heard. In 1890 it approached the Home Office with a proposal that a special magistrate should be appointed to hear all School Board cases, travelling from one district to another as occasion might require, and holding his sittings in buildings other than the police-courts. Such a scheme would promote not only efficiency, but uniformity in administration. A Departmental Committee of the Home Office considered the proposal, but it did not recommend its adoption. The Royal Commission in 1888 also reported against the proposal.[2] In 1898 the Board again went by deputation to the Home Office and explained the continued difficulty which was experienced owing to the insufficiency of the facilities for hearing summonses. The matter was again referred to a Departmental Committee, which has not, up to the present, made any recommendation. Experience does not warrant the hope that the Home Office will render any effective assistance towards the removal of this most serious hindrance to the efficiency of our system of elementary education.

Another obstacle in the way of efficiency is the too common practice of employing children in paid labour out of school hours. In cases of extreme poverty such employment is necessary, and, indeed, inevitable. The child's small earnings form a

[1] It is legal for Justices to hear and determine these cases, and in some districts of London they have done this with satisfactory results. The practical difficulty is that there is no legal provision for the payment of the court expenses of Justices sitting in this behalf.
[2] Final Report, p. 212

part of the family income which cannot be spared. The Legislature rightly recognised this necessity when, in the Act of 1876, it exempted from the operation of the employment clauses all employment of a child during school holidays and the hours during which the school was not open. But the clause of the Act which creates the exemption stipulates that such employment shall not "interfere with the efficient elementary instruction of such child," and that the child must obtain instruction by regular attendance for full time at a certified efficient school, or in some other equally efficient manner.[1]

The employment of children out of school hours has been carried to such a length as to be a breach of these conditions. The offenders are chiefly small tradesmen, who overwork and underpay the children whom necessity drives into their hard service. The hours of employment are so long that reasonable recreation, and even a reasonable period of rest, are often denied to the overtaxed worker. In 1899 the Board obtained a return from 112 schools of the number of children who thus worked for over 19 hours per week. The results of that return have been summarised thus:—

Hours per Week.	No. of Children.
19—29	1,143
30—39	729
40 and over.[2]	285

Of these children, 309 were employed in house and domestic work at an average payment of ½d. an hour; 719 were employed in newspaper and milk delivery at an average payment of 1d. an hour; 1,056 were employed in shop and factory work at an average payment of 1d. an hour; and 69 in unclassified occupations at an average payment of 1½d. an hour.

Such employment inevitably "interferes with the efficient elementary instruction" of the child who undertakes it. One headmaster reported: "The boys assisting in the delivery of milk are up, as a rule, by 5 o'clock, and present themselves late at school. As a consequence, they are more asleep than awake during the afternoon session. Those engaged in newspaper selling are out in the street until a very late hour."

When children come to school in such a condition the merciful schoolmaster lets them sleep on. They are absolutely unfitted, by previous exertion, for the work of the school. The Board has not, as yet, attempted to obtain a conviction in any such case against the employer for a breach of the provisions of the Elementary Education Act of 1876, but this will probably be done before long, and then a stop will perhaps be put to the overworking of children which almost amounts to brutality. The difficulty in dealing with such cases lies in the absence of any definite test of the interference of the employment with the education of the child. But it will be admitted that it is possible to fix a time limit beyond which the employment of a child out of school hours is unreasonable and injurious. It would not be just to forbid entirely the employment of a child liable to attend school, nor would public opinion support such a proposal. But if

---

[1] 39 & 40 Vict. c. 79 s. 9, sub-sec. 2.

[2] Some children have been employed for 68 hours per week. This, together with the school hours, would make about 16 hours' work per day, leaving 8 for rest and recreation.

it were enacted that no child of school age should be employed for more than a fixed number of hours a day, and not before 6 a.m. or after 8 p.m., it would be a boon to many a poor child whose life is made miserable by excessive labour. So long ago as 1878, casual employment in Scotland was absolutely forbidden for children under 10 years of age, and also, after nine o'clock at night between April 1st and October 1st, and after seven o'clock at night for the rest of the year, for children between 10 and 14, who had not earned a certificate of exemption from attendance at school.[1] By a Bill now before Parliament it is proposed to raise the minimum age from 10 to 12, and to penalise the employer who contravenes the Act. Scotland has always been treated in educational matters as "the most favoured nation" by the Imperial Parliament. It is difficult to understand why English children should be deprived of the boon which such protection confers.

The question arises, how far has the work of the Board in compelling the children to come into school proved successful? The diagram on the next page shows the percentage of average attendance in Board and in Voluntary schools for each year from 1871 to 1899. The percentage in Board schools for 1871 must be ignored, because the Board only possessed, at that date, transferred schools with a total accommodation of about 1,100 places. In the period under consideration, therefore, the percentage of average attendance has risen from a minimum of 65·8 to a maximum of 82·1. Before condemning the latter figure as an unsatisfactory result of thirty years of effort, it is necessary to consider the conditions under which it is determined. The percentage of average attendance represents the relation of the average attendance to the average number of children whose names are entered upon the rolls of the schools. It will, perhaps, be more clearly illustrated by a simple example. A certain school has a roll of 100 children. The school is opened ten times in one week. The maximum of possible attendances is, therefore, 1,000. If each child attended every time the school was opened, the average attendance would be 100÷10, or 100 per cent. But the actual attendances made during the week are as follows :—

50 children attend 10 times, making 500 attendances.
30   „   „   9   „   „   270   „
10   „   „   5   „   „   50   „
10· are altogether absent   ...   ...   —
                                         ─────
            Total   820   „

The average attendance of the school is therefore 82, and, in this simple case, it will be seen that the percentage of the average attendance upon the average roll is also 82·00.

In order that an absolutely accurate figure might be secured, it would be necessary that, on the very day when a child permanently ceased to attend a school, its name should be struck off the roll of that school. But this is an impossibility. By a regulation of the Education Department, no child's name may be removed from a register until after a continuous absence of four weeks, and then only if the Visitor, after inquiry, can

---

[1] 41 & 42 Vict. c. 78 s. 6.

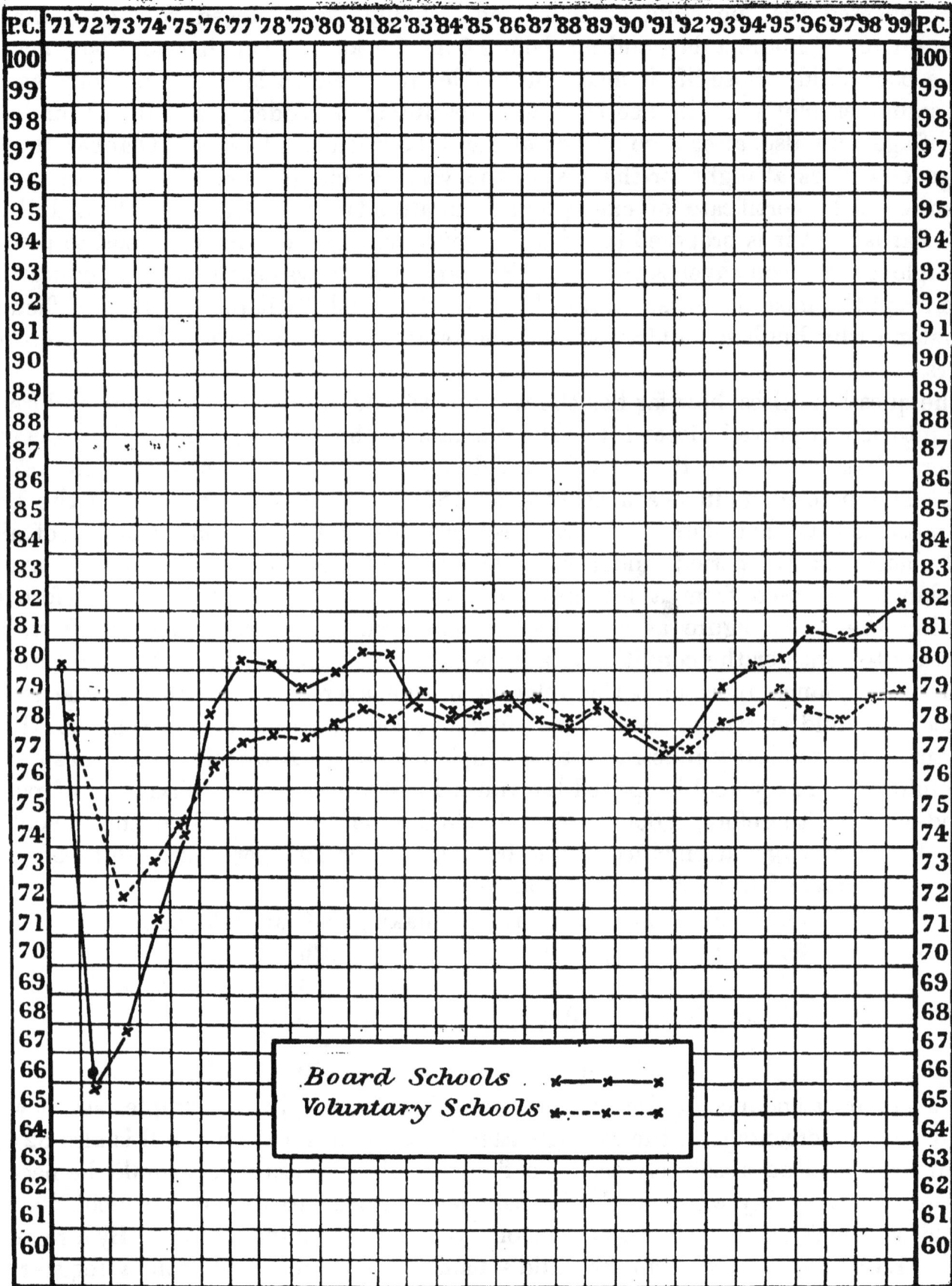

DIAGRAM II.

Showing percentage of average attendance in London Board and Voluntary Schools from 1871 to 1899.

obtain no information in regard to it.[1] In many parts of London the population is extremely migratory; families shift from one locality to another with great frequency. It is evident, therefore, that in a great many schools the roll must be inflated with names of children who could not possibly attend the school, and may be attending school in another part of London.

The percentage of average attendance is calculated upon the whole of the children upon the rolls. A large number of these children are infants under the age of 7 years, whose attendances are of necessity irregular. Infantile illnesses or inclement weather cause many unavoidable absences. There are, moreover, upon the rolls of efficient schools in London nearly 76,000 children between the ages of three and five years who cannot be compelled to attend school and whose irregularity in attendance seriously affects the averages. If the attendance of standard and non-standard children are taken separately the depressing effect of the irregularity of infants becomes evident. The average attendance of standard children in Board schools is 84·0 and in Voluntary schools 81·6; while that for non-standard children is only 77·6 in Board schools and 74·5 in Voluntary schools.

When all these circumstances are taken into consideration, it cannot be said that the efforts of the Board to induce the children to come to school with regularity have not been attended with considerable success. In the senior departments of schools which are attended by children of the better class it is not uncommon for the percentage of average attendance to vary between 92 and 95 per cent.; but no imaginable effort can be expected to raise the schools attended by the poorest children to such a standard of excellence. Increased regularity will for the future be but of slow growth, and it will result not so much from the enforcement of the compulsory law as from the insistence of a new generation of parents that their children shall receive the educational benefits from which they themselves have profited. But even as the case stands at present, it is probable that if the percentage of attendance in all the Secondary and High Schools of London could be accurately calculated, it would show no better results than those now obtained in the public elementary schools.[2]

The School Board for London is not, however, satisfied with the present rate of attendance. "The improvement," it says, "cannot be considered as other than only moderately satisfactory. The present percentage of attendance falls far short of the point which . . . might be reached"; and it proceeds to point out that the present percentage of regularity for the whole of the public elementary schools of London (81·2) "involves nearly a whole day's absence every week of five school days for every child upon the rolls."[3] This method of illustrating the results has not been happily chosen. Even the careful reader might conclude from the foregoing statement

---

[1] Board Minutes, vol. xlvii. p. 237.—This rule only came into force in 1898. Before that date, from 1885 onwards, the rule was that no child's name could be removed from the register, except in case of death, unless it had been ascertained that the child had left the school or neighbourhood.

[2] This is written in the light of ten years' experience as hon. director of a High School in a London suburb, which was attended by children of parents in very comfortable circumstances.
[3] Report on School Attendance, 1899, p. iii.

that every child on the rolls was absent from school for about two half days in every week. The fallacy of the conclusion will be apparent if reference be made to the hypothetical case of a small school of 100 children given above.[1] In that case, out of a possible 1,000 attendances, only 820 were actually made. There was, therefore, a deficit of 180 attendances during the week. If this deficit be distributed equally over the roll of the school, it would show a deficit of 1·8, or "nearly two half days" for each child. But a reference to the actual attendances made will show that this statement would be false as regards eighty of the children; that is, of 80·0 per cent. of the roll, all of whom had made better attendances.

In order to ascertain more definitely the actual state of attendance, the Board has recently prepared and issued a return, showing the attendances of children during the quarter ended December 31st, 1898, and distinguishing the numbers which made 10, 10 to 9, 9 to 8, &c., attendances respectively. The figures are further analysed to show the relative attendances in boys', girls', mixed, and infants' departments. Limiting the consideration to the children who were on the school roll of Board schools for the whole of the quarter,[2] the return reveals some not uninteresting facts. It proves that the boys make better attendances than the

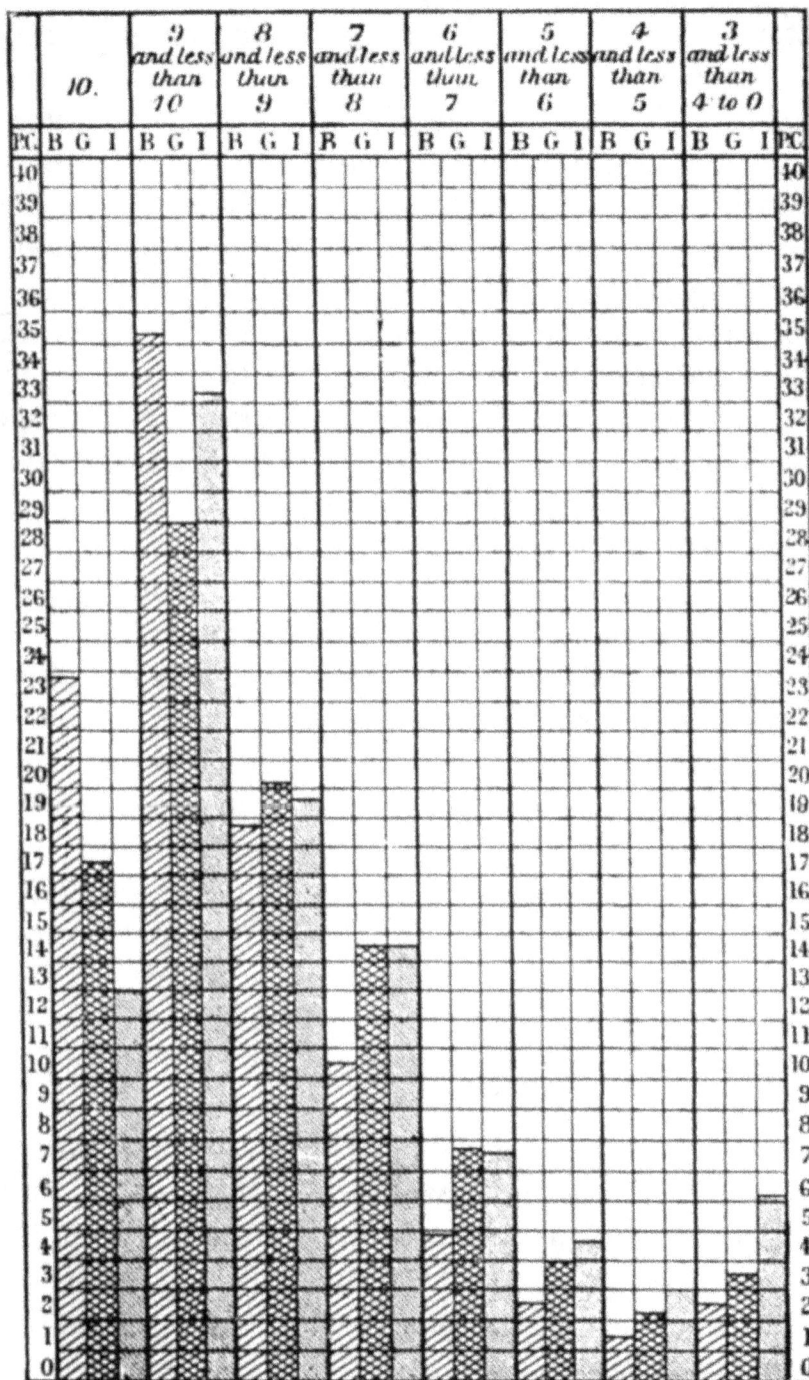

DIAGRAM III.
Showing the relative regularity of attendances :
(Boys, Girls, and Infants).

---

[2] The return gives separately the attendances of children who were not on the school roll for the whole of the quarter. This return is comparatively valueless. Any one of the children may have been on the roll of another school for the rest of the quarter, and it must also include children who first began to attend school in that quarter. There is

girls. This is due to the greater usefulness of the latter in the domestic economy. Of the boys, 23·9 made complete attendances for the quarter, as against 17·5 of the girls and 13·0 of the infants. In the case of children who made 9 or less than 10 attendances, it is somewhat remarkable to find that, although the boys retain their reputation for regularity with a percentage of 35·3, the infants overtop the girls with a percentage of 33·5, as compared with 2··9. In the class of those who make 8, or less than 9, attendances, the percentages approach more nearly an equality, being 18·8 for boys, 21·0 for girls, and 19·8 for infants.

The diagram on the opposite page represents graphically the results obtained by this return.[1] It cannot be considered unsatisfactory that more than half the total roll (50·7) should make perfect, or almost perfect, attendances, having regard to the many hindrances to regular attendance. These arise from the impossibility that infants should not often fail, from circumstances beyond control, to attend school; the need for occasional help in the household from the girls; the squalor and destitution of many of the homes from which the children come; and the unavoidable absences on account of illness, not only of the children actually suffering, but also of the children living in homes where there is infection.

CHAPTER VI.

INDUSTRIAL SCHOOLS.

Having described the powers and duties of the School Board in respect to the enforcement of attendance at school, it now becomes necessary to consider certain ancillary powers which have been conferred upon it to enable it to deal with those children who, on account of the evil influences by which they are surrounded, are in immediate danger of becoming crimnals, or, by persistent truancy from school, are likely to incur that danger.

The Industrial Schools Act,[2] which was passed four years before the Elementary Education Act, provided machinery for dealing with this class of children. It improved and rendered permanent two Acts of an experimental and temporary character which had been passed in 1861 and 1862.[3] Before 1861 efforts, not wholly successful, had been made to punish juvenile offenders with somewhat less harshness than could be the case under

---

a corresponding table for Voluntary schools, but it is based upon incomplete returns. It shows that regularity of attendance is less satisfactory in Voluntary schools than in Board schools.

[1] The mixed schools have been omitted in order to simplify the diagram. It is worth noting, however, that the percentage of attendance is better in mixed schools than the mean between boys' and girls' departments. For instance, the percentage of those who made 9 or less than 10 attendances in mixed schools was 35·1, very nearly equivalent to the same grade of boys, while the girls' percentage was only 28·9.

[2] 29 & 30 Vict. c. 118.

[3] 24 & 25 Vict. cc. 113, 132 (Scotland), continued by 25 & 26 Vict. c. 10.

the ordinary criminal law as applied to adults.[1] An illustration of the want of success of this legislation in 1845 is afforded by a report to the Education Department by one of H.M. Inspectors. "One consequence of the want of education," he said, "whether we consider it as a want of knowledge or of training, is admitted to be a frightful increase of depravity among pauper children. At the late Middlesex sessions it was stated by Mr. Serjeant Adams that no fewer than 500 children between 7 and 12 years old had been summarily convicted by the magistrate within a comparatively short period as reputed thieves. All the magistrates could do was to send those children to prison for six weeks or two months, and when the poor creatures came out again, they were compelled to follow their former pursuits, because they were without any other means of obtaining subsistence."[2]

In 1866 the whole machinery for dealing with juvenile offenders was reconsidered. The Reformatory Schools Act,[3] which dealt with children under 16 years of age who had actually committed crime, was passed, together with the Industrial Schools Act, which aimed at the rescue of children who were on the borderland of crime, but who had not yet committed any actual offence, and of offenders under 12 years of age.

Industrial Schools are placed under the control and inspection of the Home Department. They are conducted by bodies of managers, under a certificate from the Home Secretary, and the Treasury makes a grant towards the maintenance of the children detained in them. Guardians of the Poor may also contribute towards cases sent by them, and prison authorities may contract with the managers for the maintenance of any children sent to the school by the magistrates of their district.

The classes of children liable to be sent to Industrial Schools are as follows :—

1. Children under 14 :—

    (1) Found begging in the streets, whether under pretext of offering goods for sale or otherwise.

    (2) Found wandering and having no settled place of abode or visible means of subsistence.

    (3) Found destitute, either being an orphan or having a surviving parent who is undergoing imprisonment.

    (4) Found frequenting the company of reputed thieves.

    (5) Children whose parents or guardians represent to the court that they are unable to control the child and that they desire the child to be sent to an Industrial School.

    (6) Refractory children in workhouses, &c.

2. Children under 12 :—

    Charged with an offence punishable by imprisonment or a less punishment; but not previously convicted of a felony.

---

[1] 1 & 2 Vict. c. 82 ; 17 & 18 Vict. c. 86 ; 18 & 19 Vict. c. 87 ; 19 & 20 Vict. c. 109 ; 20 & 21 Vict. c. 55.

[2] Education Department Report, 1845, Vol. I., p. 155.

[3] 29 & 30 Vict. c. 117.

To these classes of children, rendered liable to be sent to Industrial Schools under the Act of 1866, certain other classes have been added since 1870.

1. Children under 14, of a woman convicted of crime, against whom a previous conviction is proved, who have no visible means of subsistence or are not under proper guardianship.[1]

2. Children who have not attended school in compliance with a school attendance order, if the parent, in the first case of non-compliance, fails to appear, or appearing, satisfies the court that he has used all reasonable efforts to force the child to attend school: in subsequent cases of non-compliance, without any conditions.[2]

3. Children living with common or reputed prostitutes or in a house frequented by such, or frequenting the company of prostitutes.[3]

A child coming under any of the foregoing categories can be brought before a Court of Summary Jurisdiction, and ordered to be sent to an Industrial School for the time specified in the order. No detention may extend beyond the date when the child attains 16 years of age; but the managers of the school are empowered to license out the child after a period of eighteen months' detention to any respectable person willing to take charge of him. The licence lasts for three months, but it is renewable. It can be revoked if the child misconducts himself.

It was essential that School Boards should possess power to deal with children who were subject to the provisions of the Act of 1866, and accordingly the Education Act of 1870 conferred upon them the right to contribute money to an Industrial School identical with that given to prison authorities.[4] School Boards were also empowered, with the consent of the Education Department, to establish and maintain certified Industrial Schools of their own; but such schools, if so established, were to be under the jurisdiction of the Home Office and not of the Education Department.[5] In 1876, however, it was enacted that the consent of the Home Secretary, and not of the Education Department, should be required.[6] Officers might also be appointed to enforce the provisions of the Act of 1866.[7]

In January, 1871, the Board instructed a Special Committee to consider the propriety of putting into operation the powers which had been conferred upon it in relation to Industrial Schools.[8] That Committee reported in the following March. They recommended that the Board should at once exercise the power to aid existing Industrial Schools and to increase the number of such schools under voluntary management. If, after such efforts had been made, it appeared that the supply of places was inadequate, the Board might then consider the propriety of maintaining Industrial Schools of its own. These recommendations were adopted by the Board, and officers were appointed to bring Industrial School cases before the magistrates.[9] The children

---

[1] 34 & 35 Vict. c. 112.
[2] 39 & 40 Vict. c. 79 s. 12.
[3] 43 & 44 Vict. c. 15.
[4] 33 & 34 Vict. c. 75 s. 27.
[5] *Ibid.* s. 28

[6] 39 & 40 Vict. c. 79, s. 15.
[7] *Ibid.* s. 36.
[8] Board Minutes, vol. i. p. 41.
[9] *Ibid.* pp. 115, 132.

ordered to be sent to Industrial Schools were to be placed in institutions in or near London, and agreements were to be entered into between the Board and the managers of those schools. The agreement provided that the managers should, on the first day of every month, inform the Board of the number of vacant places existing in their school, and that they undertook to receive that number of children, or any smaller number, that should be sent to them at the instance of the Board within the month. The Board undertook to pay the managers such a weekly sum for each child as, with the Government contribution, would make up a sum of seven shillings a week, and a further sum of £3 for every child which should be placed by the managers in a situation to the satisfaction of the Board. The Board reserved the right to appoint an Inspector to visit and examine the children.[1]

It soon appeared, however, that existing Industrial Schools were unable to provide sufficient vacant places to meet the Board's requirements, and the Sub-Committee on Industrial Schools were instructed to draw up plans for supplying the deficiency, and to report their opinion on the best scheme.[2]

This Sub-Committee reported that all the Industrial Schools in and around London were practically full, and that there was no hope of obtaining vacancies in them for children with whom the Board desired to deal. They therefore suggested four courses which might be adopted by the Board.

1. Sending children to certified Industrial Schools in the country.
2. Establishing schools under the control of the Board.
3. Making grants to enable voluntary managers to build or enlarge schools.
4. Encouraging more frequent licensing out of children.

The Sub-Committee did not see their way to recommend the adoption of either of the first two alternatives. They considered that most country schools were so far from London that the use of them would be expensive and the proper inspection of them difficult. An Industrial School under the control of the Board, they thought, lacked " an essential element of success, the benevolent interest of local voluntary managers." They advised that the power conferred upon the Board to contribute to certified Industrial Schools should be fully employed to increase the number of such institutions, and that the Board should not attempt to establish Industrial Schools of its own until this method had been tried and found wanting. They also advised that the accommodation of existing Industrial Schools should be made more available by the adoption of a more liberal system of licensing out.

The Sub-Committee, therefore, recommended that the Board should contribute a sum not exceeding £10 for each vacancy placed at their disposal by the establishment of a new school or the enlargement of existing schools.[3] The Board adopted this

---

[1] Board Minutes, p. 256.
[2] *Ibid.* p. 355. The Industrial Schools Department was at that time managed by a Sub-Committee of the School Management Committee. It did not become an independent Committee until March, 1872.

[3] Board Minutes, vol. ii. p. 23. A further recommendation to pay a grant for vacancies caused by licences-out seems never to have been put in practice. It was subsequently arranged that the Board's grant of £10 per school place should be repaid if the school should be discontinued, at the

proposal. It also resolved, notwithstanding the Sub-Committee's recommendation, to enter into agreements with Industrial Schools in various parts of the country for the reception of London children.[1]

It was within the contemplation of the Board to establish Day Industrial Schools for the education of children who could not be brought within the category of those who could be committed to Industrial Schools, but were, nevertheless, so poor and ill-cared for that they were unable to attend school, even when the fees were remitted, without further assistance. But it was found that the Board could not legally establish Day Industrial Schools, a power which was not conferred upon School Boards until 1876.[2]

Notwithstanding all the efforts of the Board to avail itself of Industrial School accommodation provided by voluntary agencies, that accommodation proved quite inadequate to meet its needs. In August, 1873, the Industrial Schools Committee were directed to report whether the time had not come for the Board to establish Industrial Schools of its own. The subject was subsequently considered by the Board in committee, and the immediate establishment of an Industrial School was recommended.[3] An amendment to this proposal, defining the accommodation of the new school as for 100 boys, was carried,[4] with an instruction to the Industrial Schools Committee to acquire suitable buildings on lease, and to apply to the Home Secretary for a certificate. Application was made to the Education Department for authority to establish an Industrial School,[5] but this authority was not granted until after the second School Board for London had been elected.

The Elementary Education Act of 1876 permitted School Boards to discriminate between children who were sent to Industrial Schools in the matter of licensing out. The Industrial Schools Act of 1866 only permitted such licensing out after eighteen months of detention. The Act of 1876 provided that the managers of Industrial Schools might license out children sent to them upon the complaint of School Boards at any time after the expiration of one month from the time of entering the school; the licence being conditional upon the child attending an efficient day school regularly and being liable to revocation if the condition was not faithfully observed.[6]

This provision enabled School Boards to establish special Truant Schools for children whose sole offence was failure to comply with an order to attend school. It was manifestly undesirable that such children should be detained for any length of time in an Industrial School, or that they should be herded with children whose antecedents were of a more doubtful character. The truant is therefore committed to the Truant School for the regular statutory term; but he is licensed out after a detention which lasts on the average about three months. He then resumes his ordinary school life, with the knowledge that if he relapses into his former habits of truancy, he will quickly find

rate of 75, 50, and 25 per cent. if the discontinuance took place at the end of three, seven, and ten years respectively from the making of the grant. In 1898, the Board agreed to make a larger grant than £10 per school place under certain conditions.
[1] Board Minutes, p. 43.
[2] Ibid. p. 350. 39 & 40 Vict. c. 79 s. 16.
[3] Ibid. vol. iii. p. 1049.
[4] Ibid. p. 1086.
[5] Ibid. vol. iii. p. 1177.
[6] 39 & 40 Vict. c. 79 s. 14

himself within the walls of a Truant School once more, without the interposition of any of the delays involved in the appearance before a magistrate and committal.

Subsequent legislation has extended the powers of managers of Industrial Schools for promoting the welfare of children committed to their keeping. In 1891 it was enacted that if any child detained in, or licensed out from, an Industrial School conducted himself well, the managers might, with his consent, apprentice him to, or place him in any trade or calling, or cause him to emigrate, although his term of detention might not have expired. In cases of emigrants, or of children who have not been detained for twelve months, the consent of the Home Secretary is necessary.[1]

In 1894 an Act was passed extending the period during which managers of an Industrial School may exercise supervision over children committed to their care on any charges other than those founded on the Education Acts. Any child sent to an Industrial School after the passing of the Act remains under the supervision of the managers until he attains the age of 18. The powers of licensing out and of revoking licences are extended to such children under certain restrictions. The retention of the child at the Industrial School on revocation may not extend beyond a period of three months; after the expiration of that time the child must again be placed out on licence. The revocation must not be made unless the managers are of opinion that the recall is necessary for the protection of the child, and the recall and the reasons for it must be notified to the Home Secretary.[2]

The Board has, at the present time, six Industrial Schools under its own management, and it has agreements with 62 Industrial Schools under other management. To 18 of these latter schools the Board has made building grants, which secure a total of 1,205 places for the Board's use. The Board's Industrial Schools afford accommodation for 1,090 children.

The school at Brentwood in Essex was the first Industrial School established by the Board under the resolutions passed in 1873 by the first School Board. It was subsequently re-named the "Davenport-Hill Boys' Home," after a well-known lady, for many years a member of the Board, who took a keen interest in its welfare. The school accommodated 100 boys. The building was not originally designed for the purposes of an Industrial School, and lately it has proved faulty in regard to sanitation. The inmates were, therefore, temporarily removed to Margate, and the Board decided that the school at Brentwood should be abandoned and a new school built upon a more healthy site. It was proposed to use the school buildings temporarily as a Truant School, but this the Home Office has declined to permit.

In addition to the ordinary school instruction the boys were taught gardening, tailoring and shoemaking. Cricket and sports were encouraged with success, but there was no gymnasium. In view of the large number of very young children who were committed to this school, a teacher of kindergarten was recently appointed; but

---

[1] 54 & 55 Vict. c. 2, s. 3. An extension of powers contained in sec. 28 of the Industrial Schools Act.   [2] 57 & 58 Vict. c. 33.

owing to the closing of the building, and the removal of the children to Margate, this experiment had to be abandoned.

It is hardly to be expected that, having regard to the early life and surroundings of children committed to Industrial Schools, their physical development should be altogether satisfactory. It is somewhat remarkable to find, therefore, that, in spite of the fact that the Davenport-Hill School did not possess all the most modern appliances which are necessary for a complete physical education, a considerable improvement in the physique of the boys was effected. H.M. Inspector of the Home Office in his last report previous to the closing of the school, said: "The boys on inspection day left a most favourable impression. Boys with the appearance of being better cared for, of manners more pleasant, more frank and easy, would be hard to find anywhere. There is a higher proportion of youngsters than is to be generally found in Industrial Schools, but they are receiving special attention. I only hope that the older boys, who are not in size below the average in these schools, will not be in any way sacrificed. They ought to have the advantages of a sound gymnastic training such as is given in both the London County Council's schools. The lads turned out of Brentwood should be as fine muscular specimens as those from any schools." [1]

The second Industrial School established by the Board was the training ship "Shaftesbury." In March, 1877, the Industrial Schools Committee reported to the Board a continuance of the deficiency of school places in Industrial Schools and that special difficulty had been experienced in getting boys on board training ships in consequence of there being no training ships in the Thames able to receive School Board cases, and the ships at the outports being occupied by children sent from particular localities. They therefore recommended that the Board should apply to the Admiralty for the loan of a vessel capable of accommodating 500 boys, and should ask the Home Secretary to certify the same for an Industrial School when it was acquired. [2] The Board adopted the report; the Home Office sanctioned the proposal and advised that a tender should also be acquired for the practical training of the boys in seamanship, but the Admiralty, after some correspondence, finally declined to lend the Board a ship. [3] The Board, therefore, entered into negotiations with the Peninsular and Oriental Company for the purchase of a ship, and the "Nubia" was acquired for £7,000 and fitted up as a training ship. A tender was also purchased in accordance with the advice of the Home Office. The new training ship was re-christened the "Shaftesbury," in recognition of the services which the seventh Earl of Shaftesbury had rendered to the outcast children of London. The ship when completed was stationed off Grays in Essex. It was certified by the Home Office in 1878 for the reception of 350 boys. The number was raised, in 1881, to 500, but it has since been reduced to 400.

The training on board the ship is mainly designed to produce seamen. Instruction in seamanship is given in four classes, commencing with the most elementary subjects, and working up to a standard of knowledge which enables a lad to take service on board

[1] Industrial Schools Committee's Annual Report, 1899, p. 17.

[2] Board Minutes, vol. vii. p. 408.
[3] *Ibid.* p. 1166.

a ship. The tender "Themis," a topsail schooner of 145 tons, is used for the purpose of giving practical instruction. Every summer she makes cruises down the Thames and along the South Coast with a crew of 3 officers and 30 boys. A selected number of the boys are also taught gun and rifle drill, to fit them to enter the Navy; and physical exercises receive particular attention. There is a full military band of 45 performers, and many of these boys find their way, after they leave the ship, into regimental bands. On shore there is a large covered bath, where swimming is taught, and also a playing field.

In addition to seamanship, boys are instructed in shoemaking, tailoring, sail-making, and cooking. Senior boys assist the ship's carpenter in carrying out the painting and small repairs of the ship, tender, and boats.

In regard to elementary education, the boys are treated as half-timers, and the instruction includes reading, writing, arithmetic, and, as far as practicable, without interfering with the main object of the training given on board the ship, in elementary English, history, geography, science, object lessons, and vocal music.

The object in sending a boy to the "Shaftesbury" being to give him a training which shall fit him for sea service, the aim of the Board is, at the end of his period of detention to find him employment in the calling for which he has been trained. To this end the cases which are to be sent to the "Shaftesbury" are selected with considerable care. Boys of inferior physique, or who have been guilty of serious offences, are never sent to the ship. The faults for which they are committed are largely the result of their environment, such as persistent truancy, not being under control, found wandering and begging. These are faults which, when corrected by the wholesome discipline of the "Shaftesbury," should not be allowed to leave a blemish upon the character of the lad who leaves the ship to make his way in the world. Unfortunately, these facts are not properly understood by the Naval authorities, who appear to imagine that a permanent taint affects the child who has been committed to an Industrial School. The Board has always found the greatest difficulty in obtaining berths for "Shaftesbury" boys in the Royal Navy, although of late years some improvement is observable in this respect.

Greater success has attended the efforts of the Board to secure berths for the boys in the Mercantile Marine. For this purpose it has appointed an agent at the port of Cardiff. Unfortunately, but a small proportion of those originally shipped remain in the service. This is due to the fact that the boys are only shipped for the voyage, and not apprenticed for a stated period. In 1898 the Board urged upon the Home Secretary the necessity of taking some steps to enable boys from Industrial Training Ships to be apprenticed. By a Statute passed in the same year provision was made for the payment of bonuses to the owners of British ships which have for one year carried boys between the ages of 15 and 19, provided that such boys shall have enrolled themselves in the Royal Naval Reserve. It was anticipated that this enactment would have facilitated the employment of "Shaftesbury" boys in the Mercantile Marine; but, up to the present time, it does not appear to have produced any appreciable effect.

In order to facilitate further the employment of boys in the Mercantile Marine, and to encourage them to remain in the service, the Board has established a Home at Cardiff, under the superintendence of its agent there. This Home has been certified as a branch of the "Shaftesbury." Boys desiring to go to sea can therefore be sent to the Home while berths are being sought for them, without passing out of the custody of the Board. Boys returning from a voyage to Cardiff can make use of the Home while further employment is being sought for them. These returned boys make a payment towards their maintenance while on shore, and arrangements are made to enable them to deposit a portion of their wages with the agent for safe keeping.

The following statement shows how the boys leaving the "Shaftesbury" were disposed of on licence or discharged during the year ended March 25th, 1899:—

To the Royal Navy...	25
To the Merchant Service ...	57
To Army Bands ...	18
To employment on shore ...	63
Returned to friends ...	24
Transferred to another school ...	1
Discharged to workhouse ...	1

The third purely Industrial School under the management of the Board is the Gordon House Girls' Home at Isleworth. This school was certified in 1897 for the reception of 50 girls. The industrial training is designed to fit the girls for domestic service, and consists in needlework, cookery, laundry-work, and domestic economy. It has been decided to provide a cottage in the grounds to accommodate 15 additional children.

The Board has under its control two schools for the reception of truants who, under the Education Act, 1876, can be licensed out after a very short detention on condition that they make regular attendance at a public elementary school. The Truant School at Upton House, Homerton, was certified in 1878 for 60 boys. In 1885 the house was practically rebuilt to accommodate 100 boys, and in 1888 it was enlarged to accommodate 40 more boys. A further enlargement of 10 school places is in course of erection. The Highbury Truant School was certified in 1891 for 150 boys, and the number of school places has subsequently been increased, first to 175 and then to 200.

The educational and industrial training given in these schools is similar to that given in an ordinary Industrial School, but the aim of the Truant School is to provide temporary rather than permanent discipline. The child is only detained until it appears probable that its habits of truancy are cured.

The success with which the aim of such a school is realised can only be tested by results. The returns of the Upton House Truant School show that 4,614 boys passed through the school between 1878 and 1898. Of this number 2,624 were licensed out and the licences were never revoked, 1,095 were re-admitted once, 502 twice, 234 three times, and 124 four or more times. It appears, therefore, that in about 57·0 per cent. of the cases a first detention effects a permanent cure, and a second detention has the same result in 23·0 per cent. of the cases. A second or further revocation of the licence

L

indicates incorrigible truancy, and, so far as these cases are concerned, the system may be regarded as a failure. But a result showing at least 80·0 per cent. of cures cannot be deemed unsatisfactory. The average length of the first detention is 89 days, of the second detention 113 days, and of the third 117 days.[1]

The Board did not exercise its power to establish Day Industrial Schools until 1895 In that year it opened a Day Industrial School in Goldsmith Street, Drury Lane, for the reception of 200 boys and girls. It is primarily designed for truant and neglected children, and children who are beyond the control of their parents. The hours of detention authorised by the Home Office are from 8 a.m. to 6 p.m., but the doors of the school are opened at 6 a.m. The children on presenting themselves are made clean and tidy, and three meals are provided during the course of the day. In the evening they return to their homes and to the adverse influences which have surrounded their young lives; but it is said that this is not so detrimental to the discipline of the school as might be supposed, "unconsciously and quietly many a child has acted as a missionary and has been the instrument of improving a dirty and desolate home."[2]

It may be thought that a day school would hardly prove efficacious in dealing with cases of truancy, but in practice it produces good results. The attraction of three wholesome meals daily has no little effect in curbing the vagrant tendency. During the first few days of detention the children have sometimes to be sent for, but after a time the habit of attending is induced and the children present themselves voluntarily. The percentage of attendance upon the roll for 1898 was 92·2, and this, when compared with 82·1, the average attendance for all the Board's day schools, speaks well for the influence which the institution exerts. During that year only one boy was sent to an ordinary Industrial School on account of non-attendance.

The following graphic and pathetic picture has been given of the class of children who attend this school: "Many of the children on admission are a rickety lot, of whom any savage nation would be ashamed, and whom an ancient Greek would probably have weeded out by some summary process of selection. . . . They are pale, flaccid, and headachy, symptoms accompanied by sores at the angles of the mouth and nose, and at the junction of the ears with the head. Their food is well prepared . . . but, . . . they are dainty, wanting in appetite, and sometimes even averse to food. Of the 116 children admitted within the year, 47 were below the average height,[3] 86 below the average weight, and 79 below the average chest measurement. Only a minority, in fact, were really healthy and perfectly formed children."

Such is the London street arab. It is not to be expected that the purely educational results should be great when such very raw material has to be dealt with. The

---

[1] Truants for whom there is no room at Upton House or Highbury are sent to the Lichfield Truant School.

[2] Governor's Report, Industrial Schools Committee's Report, 1899, p. 39.

[3] This in itself (40·5 per cent.) does not appear extraordinary. A larger number might have been expected.

[4] Governor's Report : *u.s.*

education of the children previous to entry has usually been neglected and extraordinary success is unattainable. The main object of the training is to induce self-restraint, self-respect, and self-reliance.

In addition to the ordinary subjects of instruction the girls are taught cookery, laundry-work, and domestic economy, and the boys, shoemaking and carpentry. All are taught practical drawing.

As in the case of the ordinary Truant School, the main test of the success of a Day Industrial School is the paucity of re-commitments. In the year 1898 the number of children licensed out to attend ordinary day schools was 65, and at the date of the report it had not been necessary to withdraw a single licence on account of irregularity of attendance.

The school authorities endeavour to keep in touch with the children after the term of detention has expired, and to find employment for them, and keep them employed. "Taken as a whole," the Governor reports, "our ex-scholars seem to be doing very well in the world. . . . Of the 91 children discharged during the past year, 85, we know, are in situations at the present time; and of this number 54 are in the same situations as they went to on leaving the school."[1]

In view of the continued insufficiency in the supply of places for truants, the Board in 1895 resolved to establish an additional Industrial School; and it was subsequently decided that the new school should be used for incorrigible truants, these being defined as children who have been re-committed to a Truant School for the fourth time. These are to be retained in the school for the remaining period of detention, that is, up to the age of 14. Great difficulty was experienced in finding a suitable building, and the Board has now decided to erect a school at Hither Green.

The Board is also, in conjunction with the Brighton School Board, erecting a new Industrial School at Portslade, near Brighton, for the accommodation of 120 boys. Half the school places will be at the disposal of the London Board, and a Joint Committee has been appointed to manage the school.

The establishment of a second Day Industrial School in the East End of London has also been resolved upon, and the Education Department and the Home Office have sanctioned the use, for that purpose, of the Elementary School in Brunswick Road, Poplar, which is being discontinued as an ordinary day school. The establishment of a third Day Industrial School in Whitechapel has also been authorised.

The person legally liable to maintain a child who is committed to an Industrial School under the Act of 1866 is bound, if able to do so, to contribute towards the maintenance of the child a sum not exceeding five shillings a week; but this contribution can only be enforced by the issue of a summons before a magistrate, on the complaint of H.M. Inspector of Industrial Schools, after the child has been committed to a school.[2] Full compliance with the law, therefore, involves two proceedings in court: first, the application for the committal of the child, and second, the application for a

---

[1] Governor's Report: *u.s.* p. 41.   [2] 29 & 30 Vict. c. 118, ss. 39, 40.

maintenance order. This is not the practice in regard to children committed to Day Industrial Schools under the Education Act of 1876, which empowers the court making the order for detention to make at the same time the order for maintenance.[1] The complicated procedure under the Industrial Schools Act is rendered more difficult from the fact that the burden of proving the ability of the parents to pay lies upon the applicant for maintenance.

For several years the School Board has proposed legislation upon this subject. In 1898 the Industrial Schools Committee drafted a Bill providing : (1) That the court which hears an application for the committal of a child to an Industrial School may at the same time make the order for maintenance. (2) That the applicant for maintenance should not be compelled to prove means, but that, if the parent alleged inability to pay, the burden of proof should lie upon him. (3) That a parent who has been guilty of cruelty to, or neglect, or desertion of the child proposed to be committed should be punishable by fine or imprisonment. In the same Session the Government introduced a Bill called "The Youthful Offenders Bill," which incorporated the first proposal of the Industrial Schools Committee, and also the third, without the alternative punishment of imprisonment. The Bill passed the House of Lords, but the Session ended before it had passed the House of Commons. The Board will promote a Bill similar to that recommended by it in 1898 in the present Session of Parliament.

The cost of maintaining children in Industrial Schools is necessarily large, and during recent years it has been growing heavier, owing to increasing demands of the Home Office authorities for improved accommodation and appliances. The average net expenditure per child in the Board's Industrial Schools during the year ended Lady Day, 1899, was £23 9s. 9¼d. The Treasury contributions amounted to only £7 13s. 4¾d. per child. The remainder of the cost has to be defrayed out of the rates. The London and other large School Boards have petitioned the Home Secretary for increased grants to Industrial Schools, but the petition has not as yet met with any response.

CHAPTER VII.

Finance.

The income of the School Board for London was, until 1891, derived from three main sources : (1) Government Grants, (2) the children's fees, and (3) the rates. When the Board in 1891 accepted the provisions of the Free Education Act, and established free day schools, the income from fees ceased, except as to the small amount received from pupils in Evening Continuation Schools. When in 1898 the Board freed the Evening Continuation Schools, the income from fees ceased entirely.[2]

---

[1] 39 & 40 Vict. c. 79, s. 16, sub-sec. (3).
[2] Except in respect to arrears, which were not fully cleared off until 1900.

The most important Government Grants are—(1) education grant for day schools, (2) grants for schools for blind, deaf, and defective children, (3) education grant for Evening Continuation Schools, (4) fee grant, (5) grant from the Science and Art Department, and (6) grants from the Home Office for Industrial Schools. The main income of the Board under this head is derived from the grant of the Education Department for day schools. The amount of this grant depends upon the provisions of the Code of the Education Department for the time being.[1]

The School Board in 1871 hoped that its day schools would be able to earn in grant between 6s. and 7s. per scholar, but this expectation proved too sanguine. The low average attendance in the earlier years of the Board's work very greatly reduced the grant. In the year ending March 25th, 1874, the grant only averaged 5s. 4d. per scholar. From that date it rose rapidly. In 1880 it averaged 14s. 3d., in 1890 19s., and in 1899 £1 per scholar. The gross sums earned by the Board were nearly £10,000 in 1874, a little more than £131,000 in 1880, £328,000 in 1890, and £440,000 in 1899. To these sums must be added the amount of grant which is received from the Education Department on account of evening schools. This has risen during the last ten years from £2,800 to over £16,000 per annum.

The grant next in importance is the fee grant paid under the provisions of the Elementary Education Act of 1891, replacing the income previously derived from the children's fees. The amounts received under the latter head were considerable, but for some years previous to the passing of the Act, they had been decreasing, notwithstanding the growing numbers of children in the schools. Thus in 1889, with an average attendance of 342,000 children, the Board received £124,000 in fees, and in 1891, with an average attendance of nearly 348,000 children, the amount of the fees had sunk to about £117,000. This was equivalent to a loss of sixpence a head upon the average.[2] The gradual decrease in the amount received on account of fees was due partly to the impossibility of establishing a perfectly equitable scheme of remission capable of application throughout the whole of London; partly to the difficulty of enforcing payment by parents who failed to send the fee. Some Divisional Committees exercised the power of remission sparingly, others with liberality. Parents who were refused remission in one locality were granted it when they removed to another. Those who, after refusal, continued to neglect payment were not long in discovering that the chances of escape from being compelled to pay were not unpromising. There can be no doubt that remission, which was granted charily during the earlier years of the Board, was subsequently allowed with much greater liberality.

The provisions of the Elementary Education Act, 1891,[3] are optional. The payment of the fee grant in lieu of fees is only made to managers of schools who are willing to accept the grant. Managers can elect to continue charging fees, but if the Education Department is satisfied that there is not in any district sufficient free school accommoda-

---

[1] For an account of the chief changes in the method of making this grant since 1871, see post p. 160 *et seq.*

[2] The loss between 1880 and 1891 was 1s. 9d. per child.

[3] 54 & 55 Vict. c. 56.

tion for children for whom such accommodation is required, it may direct such accommodation to be supplied in the same manner as if a deficiency of school places had been ascertained under the Act of 1870.[1]

This provision by its terms gives to parents a statutory right to free education for their children, but in so cumbrous a fashion that in many cases it is unavailable. Manifestly a small minority of persons desiring free education in a district served by a fee-charging school has no chance of securing the statutory right, for the Education Department would decline to be " satisfied," after inquiry, that it ought to put its powers into operation.

Any body of managers accepting the fee grant in lieu of fees receives a sum of ten shillings per annum for each child between the ages of three and fifteen in average attendance. But the receipt of the fee grant only abolishes the fee in its totality in schools in which the average fee was not in excess of ten shillings per child for the school year last ended before January 1st, 1891. In schools where the average fee exceeded ten shillings, a reduced fee may be charged, so long as the average rate of fees does not exceed for any school year, the amount of that excess.[2] By these confused and confusing arrangements it is possible that a school may be receiving the grant in lieu of fees and also charging a fee which gives the parents of children attending the school the right to demand free education—a right which, it has just been pointed out, they would have no reasonable hope of enforcing.

To the School Board for London the Free Education Act came as a godsend. It authorised the substitution of a permanent grant for the dwindling sum which the Board had hitherto received in school pence. Many members of the Board were opposed on principle to the abolition of fees. Some held that the grant of absolutely free education sapped the sense of responsibility in the parents; an argument which, if valid, should have prevented the payment of any part of the cost of education out of public funds. Others, more reasonably, held that it was inexpedient to sacrifice voluntarily so large a sum as £117,000 per annum, which was then available for educational purposes without any drain on public resources. The Board, however, resolved to adopt the provisions of the Act on July 9th, 1891, before it had come into operation, and even before the Bill had become law.[3] The resolution thus hurriedly passed included evening as well as day schools within the scope of its operation, although the fee grant was not payable on account of attendances at evening schools. About a month later the resolution was suspended, so far as evening schools were concerned, for six months. This suspension was continued until 1898, when evening schools were entirely freed. The loss of income involved in this change was between £5,000 and £6,000.

The financial gain to the Board from the adoption of the Act was great. The average income from fees was, in 1890, seven shillings per child. The average income from the fee grant in 1899 was nine shillings and eightpence per child. The total income

---

[1] 33 & 34 Vict. c. 75, ss. 9, 10.

[2] Under sec. 4 the Department is authorised to sanction the payment of an augmented fee in certain specified conditions.

[3] Board Minutes, vol. xxxv. p. 463. The Act came into operation on September 1st, 1891.

from fees had been steadily falling: the income from fee grant as steadily rose.[1] The income of £117,000 from fees in 1891 was represented in 1899 by an income of more than £211,000 from fee grants. The difference represents a rate of about three farthings in the £ on the rateable value of London.

The grant next in importance is that received from the Science and Art Department. This grant, which amounted to only £100 in 1874, had risen to about £5,240 in 1880. In 1898 it had increased to £30,630; but in 1899, owing to the transfer of the duty of making grants for drawing and manual training from that Department to the Education Department, the grant fell to £9,300. There are also small sums earned from the Science and Art Department by the Evening Continuation Schools and by Pupil Teachers' Schools.

Two other sets of grants are receivable from the Education Department. (1) The Grant for the Education of the Blind and Deaf under the Act of 1893.[2] This grant in 1899 amounted to about £4,000. (2) The Grant for the Education of Defective and Epileptic Children under the Act of 1899.[3]

There are thus five separate and distinguishable grants received on account of education in Day and Evening Continuation Schools. A sixth is received from the Home Office on account of Industrial Schools. This in 1899 amounted to rather more than £6,000.[4]

The sums derived from all these sources of income constitute the nucleus of the "School Fund." An estimate of the probable annual income from those sources and of the probable annual expenditure of the Board is made, and the deficiency is the sum which has to be paid out of rates.[5]

The Board have no power, in the first instance, to levy the rate.[6] That duty is imposed by the Elementary Education Act of 1870 upon the various Rating Authorities of London. The Rating Authorities were in 1871, and at present are, the Vestries and District Boards, together with the Commissioners of Sewers for the City of London and certain extra-parochial bodies, such as the Inns of Court and Chancery, as established by the Metropolis Management Act, 1855. When the London Government Act, 1899, comes into force, the Vestries and District Councils will disappear, and the Board's precepts will be issued to the new Metropolitan Councils which have been created by that Act.

The precept is in the nature of a demand note issued to the Rating Authority, requiring the latter within a given time to pay the sum named therein to the Board's Treasurers.[7] The sum thus demanded is ascertained by dividing the difference the Board's estimates of income and of expenditure amongst all the Rating Authorities

---

[1] Until 1898. There was a slight decrease in 1899; but this was due to the accident that the payments for a smaller number of schools fell within the financial year.

[2] 56 & 57 Vict. c. 42.

[3] 62 & 63 Vict. c. 32. No grant has as yet been made under this Act.

[4] Sundry small sources of income, such as rents for letting of buildings, interest, payments under the Agricultural Rates Act, 1896, sales of needlework, &c., are not enumerated in the text.

[5] 33 & 34 Vict. c. 75, ss. 53, 54.

[6] It can levy a rate within the district of any Rating Authority if that authority makes default in payment of the Board's precept.

[7] The Bank of England.

in proportion to their respective rateable values. The first Board attempted to fix the rate per £ that should be levied. It desired to raise a sum of £40,000 to make good the deficiency in the School Fund, and it resolved to issue a precept at the rate of ½d. in the £[1] for the whole of London. This plan would have proved unworkable, even if it were legal.[2] It would have been impossible to obtain, with any certainty, a specified sum by fixing a rate for the whole area. The number of empty houses and of failures to pay the rates would have varied very considerably in different districts. Thus, while in no district could more than ½d. in the £ have been obtained, in some the amount would have been considerably less. The Board was, therefore, compelled to cancel its first resolution, and to apportion the sum of £40,000 between the various Rating Authorities.[3] The rateable value of London was at that time about £20,000,000, and the rate worked out at ·48d. in the £. The Rating Authority, when it receives the Board's precept, has to levy the sum required by the necessary rate within its area. Since 1888 the Board's precepts have been issued half-yearly.

The amount demanded by the precepts has grown from £40,000 in 1871 to £1,872,000 in 1899, and the average rate from ·48d. to 12·37d. in the same years. The increase would have been much greater had it not been for the surprising growth in the rateable value of London. New buildings are constantly being erected on vacant land, and once in every five years all property is re-valued, with the result that rateable values are constantly increasing. The rateable value of London in 1899 was £36,333,000.

The Board is empowered to borrow money, with the consent of the Education Department, for the purpose of purchasing land and erecting buildings. The repayment of loans thus incurred, with interest, may be spread over a period of not more than fifty years.[4] The money is borrowed on the security of the School Fund and of the Rate, and can be obtained either from the Public Works Loan Commissioners or from the London County Council.[5] The rule of the Education Department is that not more than £10 per school place shall be borrowed for the erection of schools, but certain extras are allowed which considerably increase this amount in most cases. If the allowance of the Education Department is exceeded the difference must be paid, not out of loan, but out of the Maintenance Account. The total of the sums borrowed from time to time has amounted to £12,439,161, of which £2,615,257 had been repaid at the 25th March, 1899.

The Board has hitherto generally extended the repayment of loans over the full period of fifty years. This reduces the amounts of the annual instalments to a minimum, but, on the other hand, increases the total sums paid to a maximum. The Board has recently decided to reduce the period for repayment to forty years. Although the expense for the first ten years will be greater, the ultimate saving will be considerable.

---

[1] Board Minutes, vol. i. p. 104.

[2] The Education Act, 1870, provides that "the School Board may serve their precept upon the Rating Authority requiring such authority *to pay the amount specified therein out of the local rate*" (sec. 54).

[3] Board Minutes, vol. i. pp. 141, 155.

[4] 33 & 34 Vict. c. 75, s. 57.

[5] Succeeding to the powers of the Metropolitan Board of Works.

The saving effected by this resolution in the discharge of a loan of £500,000 at 3¼ per cent. will be rather more than £80,000.[1]

The foregoing description of the Board's sources of income must of necessity prove bewildering. It is not possible to give a coherent account of a system of finance which is, to a large extent, the result, not of any well-considered and orderly scheme, but of accidental emergencies. This is not the fault of the School Board; it is the result of the system of Government Grant. Most of the grants which have been enumerated have had a political rather than an administrative origin. The Education Grant itself was a political makeshift, devised in the hope that a Government subsidy might render Government interference with education unnecessary. When the experiment failed and the Legislature was forced to intervene, the makeshift had to be continued in order to deal equitably with schools that had been fostered under the grant system, but were not to be placed under municipal control. The grant has been too often the plaything of political parties, and the cause of education has suffered from the game. The grant system having thus become firmly rooted, every new educational development has been aided by a new grant until the present chaos has been reached. In no department of Government is there greater need of the able administrator, who will brush aside the complicated technicalities and absurdities of the present system of Government aid, and will evolve a simple and orderly method which will be intelligible, just, and an encouragement to educational efficiency. A small attempt has been made in this direction by the Code of 1900 and the Minute on Higher Elementary Schools. It remains to be seen whether this effort produces increased efficiency, as well as increased simplicity.

The details of the Board's expenditure are, to a great extent, discussed in other sections of this report. A bare enumeration of the amounts expended upon the

[1] The following figures show how this result is arrived at :—

Payments of Interest and Principal.	40 years at 3¼ per cent.	50 years at 3¼ per cent.
	£	£
First payment—		
Interest : First half-yearly payment	8,125	8,125
Principal : Half-yearly payment	6,250	5,000
Total	14,375	13,125
Ten years—		
Interest : Total of first 20 payments	143,203·125	147,062·5
Principal : Do.	125,000	100,000
Total	268,203·125	247,062·5
Full Term—		
Interest : Total of 80 payments	329,062·5	—
Do. : Total of 100 payments	—	410,312·5
Principal	500,000	500,000
Total	829,062·5	910,312·5

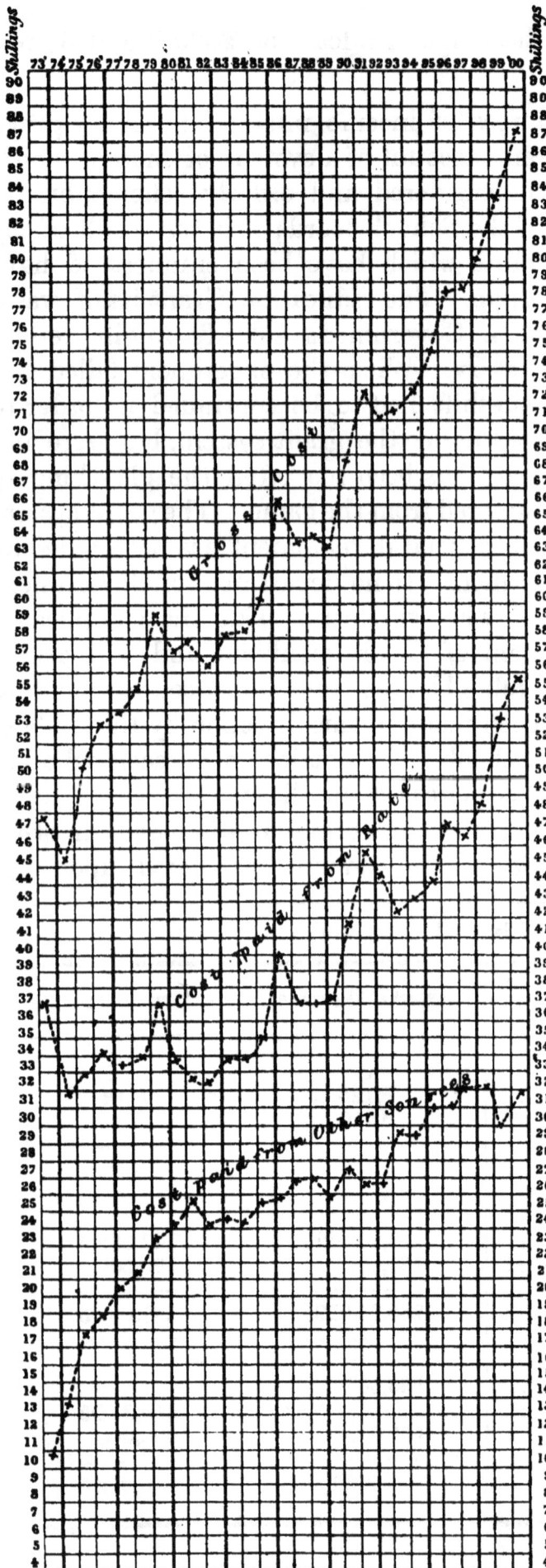

DIAGRAM IV.

various branches of the Board's work would be neither interesting nor instructive. The vital fact in the Board's finance —namely, the cost per child in day schools —has been illustrated graphically in the accompanying diagrams. The fourth diagram shows the growth of the gross and net cost per child. The gross cost is the total cost; the net cost is so much of the cost as is paid out of the rates. The difference of amount between the gross and the net cost is, practically, the State contribution in the form of grant towards the education of the children of London. It will be noted that during the first twelve years, although the gross cost increased, there was no increase in the charge upon the rates, owing to the great increase in the Government Grant. After 1885, however, both the gross and the net cost increase or decrease simultaneously. It will be noted, also, that the upward tendency is by no means persistent; it is broken by four checks or pauses—in 1879, 1886, 1891, and 1896. At each successive check the downward tendency before the rebound becomes less distinct, until, in the last case, it is not perceptible. In the first two cases the checks occurred at the end of the seventh year, in the second two at the end of the fifth. The cause of this pulsation is difficult to explain. If the growth of expenditure depended upon the varying policies of different Boards, tending towards either diffuse or frugal expenditure, it might be expected that the pulsations would recur at the end of three years or of a multiple of three years. But this is not the case. It is only possible, therefore, to draw the negative conclusion that methods of administration affect very slightly the growth of expenditure.

The fifth diagram shows the percentage of the cost per child paid from rate and from other sources respectively, to the gross cost. This diagram brings out clearly

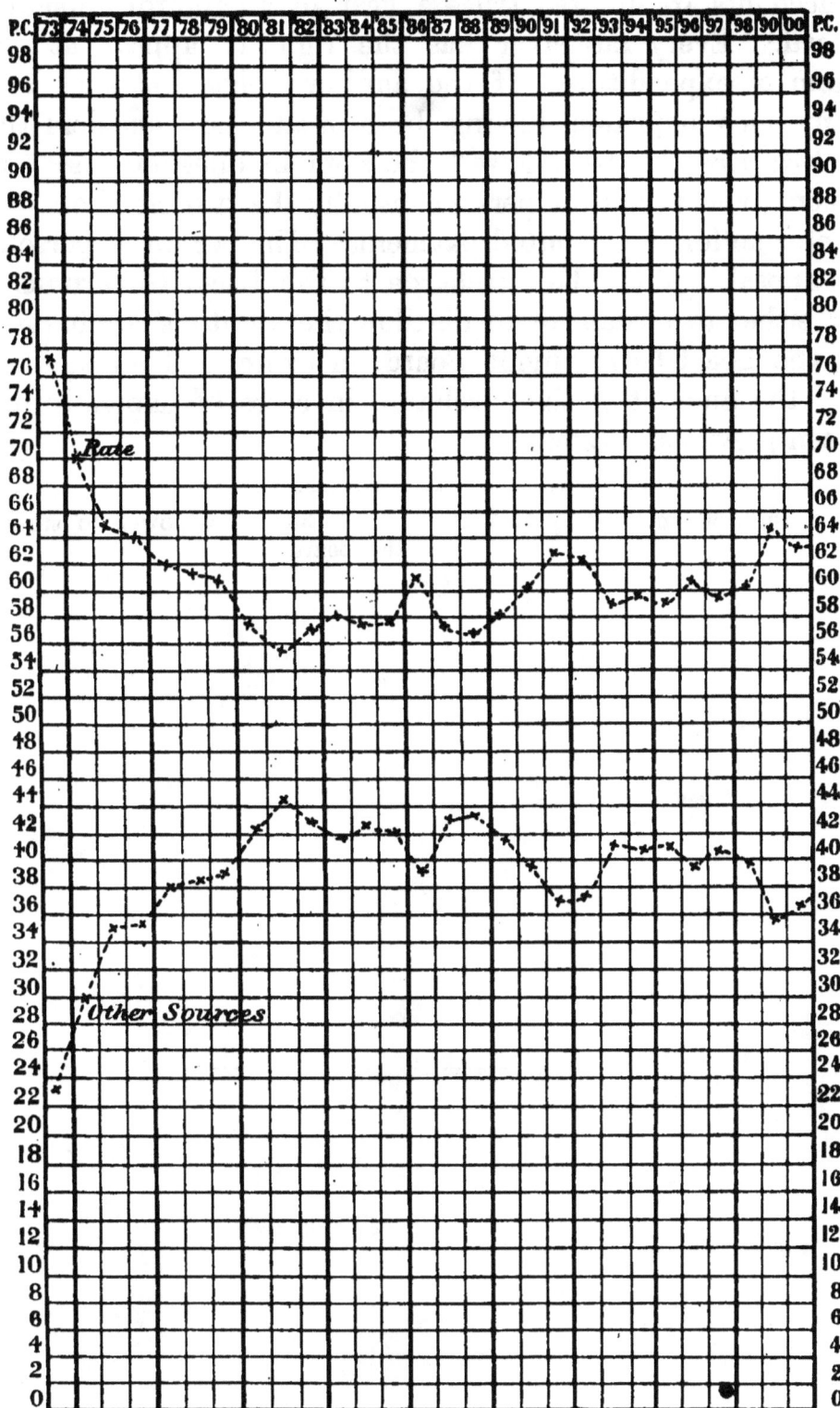

DIAGRAM V.

the fact that the total increase in the gross cost per child until 1881 was paid by the State, to the exoneration of the rate. Since that date the fluctuations have been somewhat violent, but, on the whole, the tendency has been to cast the increase of expenditure upon the rate.

The Board's accounts are audited twice a year by an auditor appointed by the Local Government Board.[1] Every ratepayer has the right to appear at the audit and to object to any item of expenditure. If the auditor holds that such objection is valid, or if, without any such objection having been made, he considers that any item of expenditure is *ultra vires*, he "disallows" the item in question and "surcharges" the amount of it upon some person or persons, usually the two members of the Board who have signed the cheque for the disputed payment.[2] The person or persons so surcharged have a right to appeal against the surcharge to the Local Government Board. That Board has power either to sustain or to disallow the auditor's surcharge. If the former course is taken, the Local Government Board, in exercise of an equitable jurisdiction, usually "remits" the amount of the surcharge in cases of expenditure the legality of which has not been previously tested.

---

[1] 33 & 34 Vict. c. 75, s. 60 amended by 42 Vict. c. 6, s. 11.

[2] But he has power to surcharge an officer of the Board.

PART III.

—

CURRICULUM AND SCHOOL LIFE.

PART III.

CURRICULUM AND SCHOOL LIFE.

CHAPTER I.

EDUCATIONAL PROGRESS.

IN the preceding section an attempt has been made to describe the problems which presented themselves to the School Board for solution, and the manner in which the first School Board dealt with those problems. In all those departments of the work which are supplemental or assistant to the main object of imparting education the story has been completed, in order that this, the concluding section, may be devoted entirely to a consideration of the advances which have been made in our system and methods of education, and the present condition of education.

When it is remembered that these advances have been made within the comparatively short period of thirty years, it will be seen that the rate of progress has been more rapid than could reasonably have been predicted. The "ideal" curriculum laid down by the first School Board has already been described, and a few facts relating to the actual condition of education in 1870-73 have been set forth, to show how vast and deep was the chasm which separated the real from the ideal. It has been shown that in 1873 the only subjects taught in the schools of the Board, with very few exceptions, were the three obligatory subjects—reading, writing, and arithmetic—and singing, drawing, needlework, and physical exercises. The conditions under which the schools were conducted rendered hopeless any more ambitious scheme. Sir Charles Reed, in his annual statement for 1874, said: "Of the school work and its results I do not propose to say one word. It is too soon altogether for us to speak upon the question. Tens of thousands of the children in our schools are, I regret to say, grossly ignorant and utterly uninstructed, and the only thing we can do is to look to their cleanliness and give them habits of order and promote their regularity of attendance, and then leave the question of results, quite certain that with good schools and most efficient teachers, all schools being now full, the results are sure to follow."[1]

At the time when these words were written, more than half the children in Board schools (52·0 per cent.) were below Standard I. With such conditions the teaching of anything beyond the mere rudiments was impossible; and some years elapsed before any marked success attended even the teaching of the rudiments. The ground had to be prepared, the dirty faces cleaned, discipline and orderliness inculcated, before any further progress could be made.

Before attempting to form an estimate of that progress it is necessary to obtain some

---

[1] *School Board Chronicle*, October 3rd, 1874, p. 320.

idea of the changes which have been effected in the Code of the Education Department in relation to the grants to day schools, for upon the results of that Code the statistics in a great measure depend. The Code is issued annually, and it has rarely been issued without more or less revision. Indeed, no one can read through the various Codes in historical sequence without being impressed with the evidence of a feverish desire on the part of the Education Department to be constantly effecting changes, often but of slight importance, which must have proved bewildering to the managers of schools. In the following examination of the changes which have been effected in the Code in regard to grants to schools between 1871 and 1900 these small details have been ignored, and the main features only have been described.

The tendency of the Codes has been a gradual abandonment of the policy of payment as the result mainly of examination, in favour of payment as the result of inspection; thus reverting to the system which was abandoned by the Revised Code of 1862. In this process there are four definite stages, marked by the Codes of 1871, 1882, 1890, and 1900.

The scheme of grants contained in the Code of 1871 did not differ in principle from that of the Codes which had preceded it. It allowed, for every school which had been open 400 times during the year, a grant of 6s. per scholar in average attendance;[1] and further, for every scholar under 7 years of age a sum of 8s. if such scholars were taught as a class of a school; or 10s. if they were taught as a separate department. For scholars over 7 years of age the further grant depended upon examination—4s. per child was paid for each pass in reading, in writing, and in arithmetic. Furthermore, a sum of 3s. per child in Standards IV., V., and VI. was paid for each pass in not more than two specific subjects.

This scheme was continued in its main outline until 1882; but in 1875 two important subsidiary alterations were introduced, both of which indicated an impending change of policy. The most notable of these was the introduction of " class subjects," which were defined as grammar, history, elementary geography, and plain needlework, for children above 7 years of age. A grant of 4s. per scholar over 7 years of age in average attendance was paid if *the classes* passed a creditable examination in any two of the above-named subjects. The grant for passes in the elementary subjects was reduced from 4s. to 3s., and the grant for class subjects was also reduced to 2s. if 20 per cent. of the children examined in elementary subjects were not in or above Standard IV.[2]

The other change was in respect to the fixed grant on average attendance. The original grant of 6s. was reduced to 4s., an extra 1s. was paid if singing formed part of the ordinary instruction of the school,[3] and a further 1s. was paid if the Inspector reported that the discipline and organisation were satisfactory.[4]

---

[1] The average attendance for any period is found by dividing the total number of attendances made during that period by the number of times that the school has met during such period.

[2] The grant for class subjects was altered in 1878 to 2s. or 4s. for one or two class subjects, subject to a reduction to 1s. or 2s. The percentages of passes in elementary subjects in the upper standards necessary to avoid a reduction of the class subjects grant was frequently varied. In 1876 it was reduced to 10 per cent. In 1879 it was raised to 15 per cent., and in 1880 to 20 per cent.

[3] This reduction, unless singing was taught, was first made in 1874.

[4] An explanatory note stated the terms under which the discipline and organisation grant would

This preliminary attempt to award the grant upon some higher consideration than mechanical success in passing examinations was more fully developed in 1882. The Code for that year introduced revolutionary changes. The new grant for infant schools was 9s. if the scholars were taught as a separate department, in a room properly constructed and furnished for the instruction of infants, or as a class under a separate teacher; but if these conditions were not fulfilled, it was reduced to 7s. A further grant, called the "Merit Grant," was offered, amounting to 2s., 4s., or 6s., if the Inspector reported the school to be "fair," "good," or "excellent." In determining the class to which the school belonged the Inspector was to have regard to the provision made for suitable instruction in elementary subjects, for simple lessons on objects and on the phenomena of nature and of common life, and for appropriate and varied occupations. Further grants were given of 1s. for needlework and for singing, the grant for singing being reduced to 6d. if the scholars were taught by ear.

For older scholars a fixed grant of 4s. 6d. was allowed, together with a merit grant of 1s., 2s., or 3s., if the Inspector reported the school as "fair," "good," or "excellent" in respect of organisation and discipline, the intelligence employed in instruction, and the general quality of the work, especially in the elementary subjects.[1] The grants for singing and for needlework were the same as those allowed for infant schools. The grant for elementary subjects was fixed at the rate of 1d. for every unit of the percentage of passes at the examination. The grant for class subjects was 1s. or 2s. for each subject, according as the Inspector's report upon the examination was "fair" or "good." Not more than two class subjects could be taken, of which one must be English.[2] No change was made in the grants for specific subjects, but a grant of 4s. a head, not dependent on average attendance, was allowed for any girl in the fourth or higher standards who attended not less than 40 hours in the school year at a cookery class of not more than 24 scholars.[3]

The Code of 1882, therefore, was remarkable, not only for the great stride it made

---

[1] be paid. "The Inspector will be instructed not to interfere with any method of organisation adopted in a training college under inspection if it is satisfactorily carried out in the school. To meet the requirements respecting discipline, the managers and teachers will be expected to satisfy the Inspector that all reasonable care is taken, in the ordinary management of the school, to bring up the children in habits of punctuality, of good manners and language, of cleanliness and neatness, and also to impress upon the children the importance of cheerful obedience to duty, of consideration and respect for others, and of honour and truthfulness in word and act."— Education Department Report, 1875-6, p. cxlvi. This note was, with slight variations, incorporated in subsequent Codes as the ground of awarding the "Excellent" Merit Grant 1882-89 and the Discipline and Organisation Grant, 1890-99.

[1] The explanations quoted in the preceding Note were repeated in the Code of 1883, and in that of 1884 with the following addition : "The Inspector will also satisfy himself that the teacher has neither withheld scholars improperly from examination, nor unduly pressed those who are dull or delicate in preparation for it at any part of the year, and that in classifying them for instruction regard has been paid to their health, their age, and their mental capacity, as well as to their due progress in learning."

[2] Elementary science was added as a class subject. Drawing was added in 1885 and withdrawn in 1887. English ceased to be obligatory as a class subject in 1891. Three class subjects were permitted to be taken by the Code of 1885; this permission was withdrawn in the following year.

[3] "And spent not less than 20 hours in work in cooking with her own hands"—added in 1885.

M

in the recognition of the fact that discipline and mental and moral training were factors in education to be considered as well as the merely mechanical results of instruction, but because it for the first time officially recognised the teaching of one branch of manual instruction. Cookery had previously been taught with considerable success by the London School Board and other Boards in the country; but this very necessary branch of education had been persistently ignored by the Education Department. The cookery grant of 1882 was the first official attempt to support the good work that was being done, and the recognition of other branches of manual training followed slowly and timorously.[1]

The principles of the Code of 1882 remained in force, with unimportant variations, until 1890, and the scheme of grants for infant schools remained unaltered until 1900. In 1890 an important change was made in the method of making the grant to schools for older scholars. The Code of 1882 created three categories of merit; the Code of 1890 created, in effect, four. It provided for a principal grant and a grant for discipline and organisation. There was a higher and a lower grant in each class. The principal grant was 12s. or 14s. The higher principal grant could not be received unless the Inspector reported favourably on the accuracy of knowledge and general intelligence of the scholars in the elementary subjects and that recitation was taught satisfactorily. The discipline and organisation grant was 1s. or 1s. 6d., dependent upon the recommendation of the Inspector.[2]

Thus a school might earn—

1. The higher principal + the higher discipline and organisation grant:
2. The higher principal + the lower discipline and organisation grant:
3. The lower principal + the higher discipline and organisation grant:
4. The lower principal + the lower discipline and organisation grant:

giving four grades of merit. Interpreted in the terms of the Code of 1882—Class 1 represented the " excellent " schools; Classes 2 and 3 the " good " schools, and Class 4 the " fair " schools.

The grant for elementary subjects upon the result of examination was abolished. The grants for needlework, singing, and for class subjects remained unaltered. The grant for specific subjects was reduced to 2s. or 3s. The sum awarded was made upon the report of the Inspector, and not upon the results of examination. Thus the system of payment by results, which had been inaugurated in 1862, disappeared.

The changes in the Code between 1890 and 1900 were but slight. Some of them have already been referred to.[3] The only other alteration worthy of record is the

---

[1] A grant of 2s. for laundrywork was given in 1890 ; a grant for dairywork in 1893. Domestic economy was made a class subject for girls in 1894. A grant for cottage gardening was added in 1895, and a grant of 6s. or 7s. per child was allowed for manual instruction in 1898 ; but a grant for this subject had been made by the Science and Art Department since 1891. Manual instruction and drawing were transferred from the Science and Art Department to the Education Department in 1898.

[2] Under conditions mentioned *ante*, Notes, p.161.

[3] In 1895, the following addition was made: " The higher grant for discipline and organisation will not be paid to any school in which provision has not been made in the approved time table for instruction in Swedish and other drill, or in suitable physical exercises ; but children employed in labour and attending school half-time and children for whom such instruction is unsuitable may be exempted."

change which was made in the administration of the grant for specific subjects in 1897. Instead of the 2s. or 3s. grant just mentioned, a grant of 1s. or 6d. was paid for each completed 24 hours of instruction given to any scholar in specific subjects, provided that a minimum of 40 hours of instruction had been given. The Department decided upon the Inspector's report whether the higher or the lower grant should be paid.

When payment upon the results of examination had been abolished it was evident that sooner or later the system of administering the Government Grant must be simplified, and the complicated system of payment for class and specific subjects superseded. Educationists had for some time been advocating such a reform, and in the present year it has been effected.

If simplicity were the only object to be desired it has certainly been achieved.[1] The grant for infants' schools is now 17s. or 16s., and the grant for schools for older scholars is 22s. or 21s. per child. The Inspector is instructed to recommend the higher grant in every case unless he is unable to report favourably upon the school. The only other grants retained are those for cookery, laundry-work, dairy-work, cottage gardening, and manual instruction. A new grant is introduced for " household management," which is to include cookery, laundry work, and practical housewifery, for girls in or above Standard V.; but schools claiming this grant cannot also claim the cookery, laundry-work, or dairy work-grants.

It will be seen that simplicity is not the only characteristic of the new Code. The whole attitude of the Department towards education has been changed. The key-note of the Codes of 1882 and 1890 was an incentive to progress by the offer of a premium upon excellence. The present Code makes the slightest possible distinction between good and bad, and it declares that, as a rule, all schools are to be assessed as good. The older Codes incited school managers to strive to rise, the present Code merely warns them not to fall too far. When the apathy of the smaller School Boards and of many managers of Voluntary schools in respect to educational progress is considered, the possible results of this Code are such as to cause some misgiving.

But the Code must be read in connection with a Minute of the Department—now metamorphosed, under the Education Act of 1899, into the Board of Education—for the establishment of higher elementary schools. By virtue of this Minute the following grants can be earned by higher elementary schools :—

1.—PRINCIPAL GRANT.

	Higher Scale.	Lower Scale.
1st Year	27/-	25/-
2nd „	35/-	33/-
3rd „	47/-	40/-
4th „	65/-	55/-

[1] The distinction between obligatory and class subjects has disappeared, and a "course of instruction," including English, arithmetic, drawing (for boys), needlework (for girls); lessons on geography, history, and common things ; singing and physical exercises, is substituted. One or more of these subjects may be omitted, and one or more of the subjects hitherto known as specifics may be added, provided H.M. Inspector deems the omission or the substitution desirable.

2.—GRANT FOR PRACTICAL WORK.

					Higher Scale.	Lower Scale.
1st Year	...	...	...	...	8/-	6/-
2nd „	...	...	...	...	12/-	10/-
3rd „	...	...	...	...	18/-	15/-
4th „	...	...	...	...	25/-	18/-

The payment of the higher grant depends upon the report and recommendation of the Inspector, having regard to the suitability of the instruction to the circumstances of the neighbourhood, the thoroughness and intelligence with which the instruction is given, the sufficiency and suitability of the staff,[1] and the discipline and organisation. The school course is to extend over a period of four years.

Somewhat stringent limitations are placed upon the right of the child to attend a higher elementary school. It cannot be admitted at all unless it has attended for at least two years at a public elementary school, and has been certified by an Inspector of the Board of Education to be qualified to profit by the instruction offered in the higher elementary school. When a child has succeeded in obtaining this certificate, his right to remain in the school, or to be promoted from one year's course to another, is still made dependent upon a favourable certificate from H.M. Inspector. This deposition of the teacher and manager from the exercise of discretion in this respect, in favour of the officer of a centralised Department, is not one of the least startling changes which the Minute has effected. Another limitation is that a child may not be recognised for grant-earning purposes after it has attained the age of 15 years, and no child may remain in a higher elementary school beyond the close of the school year in which it attains that age.[2] This is a disability which has not hitherto been imposed upon scholars in public elementary schools.[3]

It is not clear from the terms of the Minute whether a higher elementary school may be a department of a public elementary school, or whether it must be a distinct organisation conducted in a separate building.[4] If the latter be the intention, it can

[1] There must be a teacher for every 40 scholars in their 1st and 2nd year and for every 30 scholars in their 3rd or 4th year.

[2] The school year is fixed to commence on August 1st. If therefore a boy were 15 on that day he could continue to attend school for a year. If, by ill fortune he had chanced to be born one day earlier, he would be disqualified for attendance at school for the coming year. The exercise of a slight amount of ingenuity might surely have avoided such an absurdity.

[3] The disqualification for grant earning has hitherto been fixed by the attainments rather than by the age of the scholar. Former Codes provided that no attendance of any scholar who had *passed* in the three elementary subjects of Standard VII., and was upwards of 14 years of age, should be recognised,

As, since 1891, no child has ever *passed* in those subjects, the child remained a grant earner so long as it attended school. The present code substitutes for the word "passed" the words "been under instruction for more than one year." This considerably limits the grant-earning power of older children. There is a clause in a Government Bill now before Parliament which, if it becomes law, will limit the payment of the fee grant in a similar manner.

[4] The introductory words of the Minute, "A public elementary school may be recognised by the Board of Education as a higher elementary school," seem to favour the latter construction, but it is impossible to predict what interpretation the Board of Education will put upon its own statements,

hardly be doubtful that the new scheme of higher elementary education will be a boon to a few but a disadvantage to the many. The grant-earning power of the older children in public elementary schools has been considerably curtailed by the Code of 1900. There is no inducement for managers to encourage the attendance of such children in the public elementary school. There is, on the other hand, every inducement to obtain their transfer to a higher elementary school, where bountiful grants are to be earned.

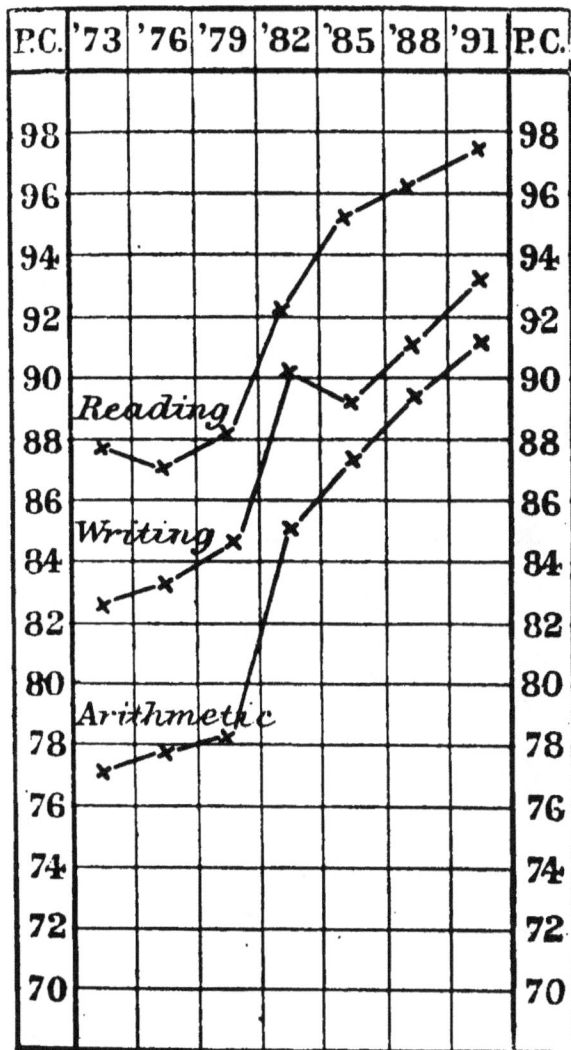

DIAGRAM VI.

But a child, in order to obtain the full benefit of the higher elementary school, must enter it at the latest at 11 years of age. For the clever child, who is legally exempt from attendance at school, whose parents desire that he should continue his education for a short period, there is no provision. It will be shown hereafter that this tendency to remain in school for slightly longer periods has been increasing of late years. It is a tendency which the new Code, in conjunction with the Minute on higher elementary schools, will in all probability check.

This somewhat lengthy excursus upon the provisions of the Codes, so far as they relate to the grants to day schools, has been necessary in order to define the sources from which the following statistics are obtained. It is somewhat dangerous to attempt to test educational progress statistically. At the best, only one side of it can be so tested, and many of the highest and most valuable aspects of education prove elusive to the statistician. But, within certain limits, statistical returns may be used with advantage. The accompanying diagram shows the percentage of passes for Government Grant in the three obligatory subjects from 1873, triennially, until 1891, when the individual examination of children by H.M. Inspectors was abandoned. The percentage was calculated upon the total number of children present at the examination and absent from it without excuse, so that in no event could the percentage ever have reached 100·00. The striking fact disclosed by this diagram is that for nine years no improvement worth naming was visible in the teaching of the obligatory subjects. The increase in the percentage of passes in each subject is minute. The interpretation of this phenomenon is, that it took about nine years to clear the schools of the uneducated, undisciplined children who came under the compulsory law, upon whom the teacher was able to produce but little impression. When this class of child disappeared from the schools and its place was taken by younger children who had undergone the preliminary discipline of the infant school, the results of examination showed a rapid improvement.

Another equally definite test of improvement is the proportionate grouping of children according to standards. The seventh diagram shows, for triennial periods from 1873 to 1897, and for 1899, the percentages of children in and below Standard III., and in and above Standard IV. respectively. In 1873 no less than 97·8 per cent. of the children were below Standard IV. In 1899 only 60·8 per cent. were so classed. In 1873 there were six standards; only 2·2 per cent. of the children were in the three upper standards. The rate of improvement in this respect may be measured

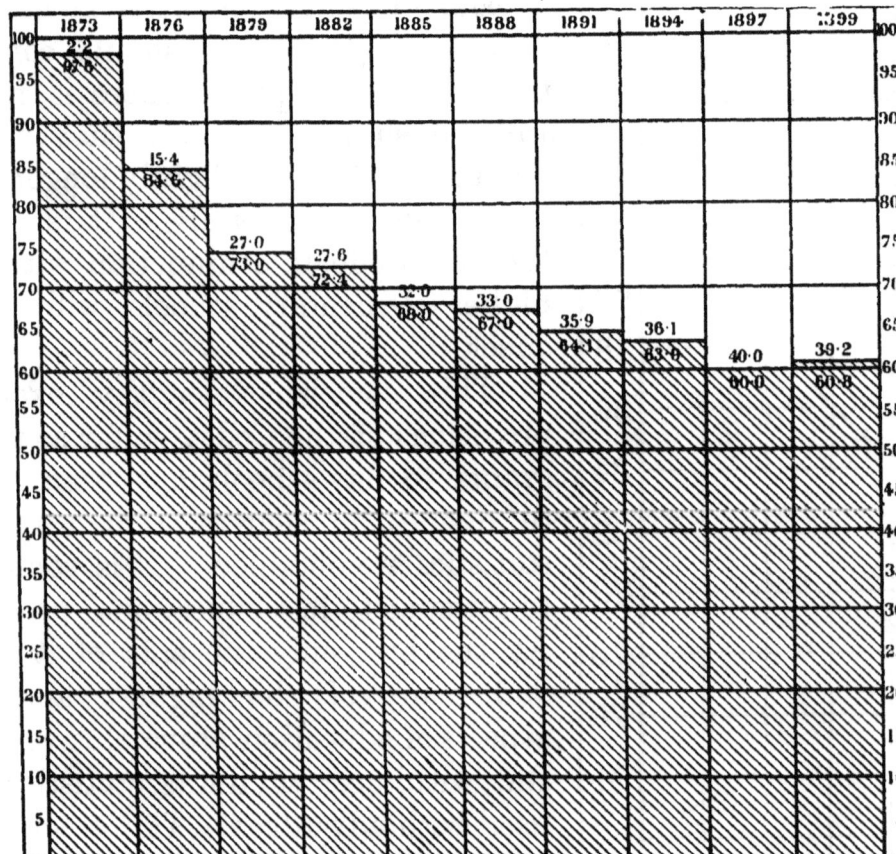

DIAGRAM VII.

by the fact that in 1899 there were 4·6 per cent. children in the VIIth and ex-VIIth Standards; more than double the percentage of children in the IVth, Vth, and VIth Standards in 1873. It would appear as if the proportion of children in and below the IIIrd Standard to that of the children above the IIIrd Standard has now reached a normal balance, and that the relation of the two sections is roughly as six is to four.

The eighth diagram shows the percentage of children in each standard from the year 1889 to 1898. It shows that the percentages of the children in the fourth and lower standards have decreased and the percentages of children in standards above the fourth have increased. It will be noted that the increase of the proportion of children in the upper standards is far more perceptible in the latter than in the earlier years comprised in the diagram. Indeed, during the first three years, 1889, 1890 and 1891, there is practically no change. It would appear, therefore, that improvement in this respect dated from the year 1892 or thereabouts.

But this evidence is too slight a foundation for the conclusion that the year 1892 marks any definite epoch in the history of education in London, unless it can be supported by similar evidence, drawn from other sources, which points to the same conclusion. There are other statistical methods of testing the rate of educational improvement which must therefore be considered.

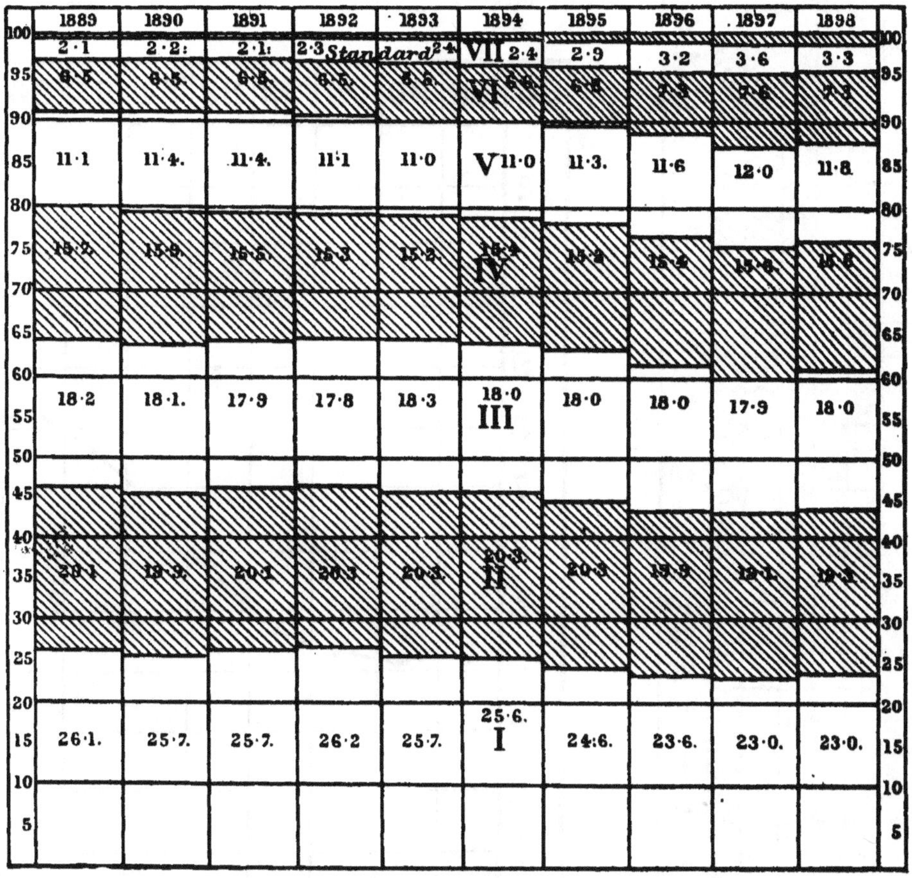

Standard	1889	1890	1891	1892	1893	1894	1895	1896	1897	1898
VII	2·1	2·2	2·1	2·3	2·4	2·4	2·9	3·2	3·6	3·3
VI	6·5	6·5	6·6	6·5	6·6	6·6	6·6	7·3	7·6	7·7
V	11·1	11·4	11·4	11·1	11·0	11·0	11·3	11·6	12·0	11·8
IV	16·2	15·9	16·5	16·3	15·2	15·2	15·3	15·4	15·6	15·6
III	18·2	18·1	17·9	17·8	18·3	18·0	18·0	18·0	17·9	18·0
II	20·1	19·9	20·1	20·9	20·9	20·3	20·3	19·9	19·1	19·3
I	26·1	25·7	25·7	26·2	25·7	25·6	24·6	23·6	23·0	23·0

DIAGRAM VIII.

One of these methods is afforded by the class subjects taught in the senior departments of the Board's schools. The Education Department allowed grant for two class subjects only, in any one department, but it was open to the Board to teach more class subjects if it deemed it expedient. If it can be shown, therefore, that from any given date the percentage of departments teaching more than two class subjects had increased, that date would be marked with some definiteness as the point at which a considerable educational improvement had begun to manifest itself.

The ninth diagram shows the percentage of departments teaching one, two, three, and four class subjects respectively in every year from 1889 onwards. The percentage of departments taking only one class subject is represented by the black at the base of the columns. The percentage of departments taking two class subjects is represented by the stippled area. The double and single hatching represent the percentage of departments taking three and four class subjects respectively.

A glance at this diagram will show that it supports in a very striking manner the surmise which was suggested by the diagram displaying the growth of the percentage of children in the upper standards. For three years—1889, 1890, and 1891—the per-

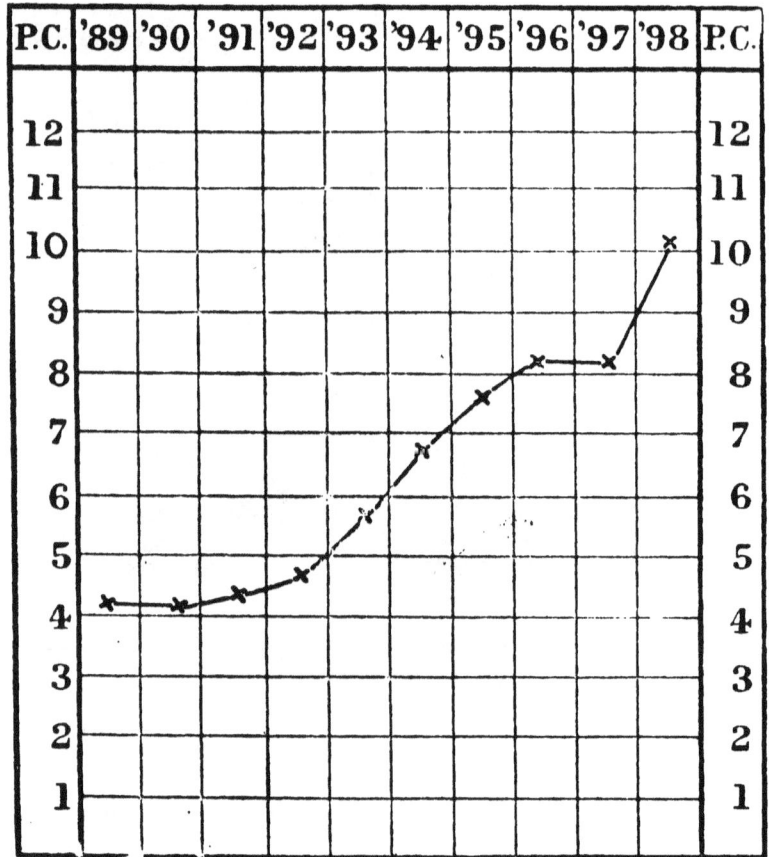

DIAGRAM X.

centages of departments taking one, two, and three class subjects remain unaltered. In 1892 a sudden change commences. Not only does the percentage of departments taking three class subjects rapidly increase, but a percentage of departments taking four class subjects insinuates itself for the first time into the diagram. From 1892 onwards the number of departments taking three or four class subjects increases with remarkable rapidity. In 1891, 94 per

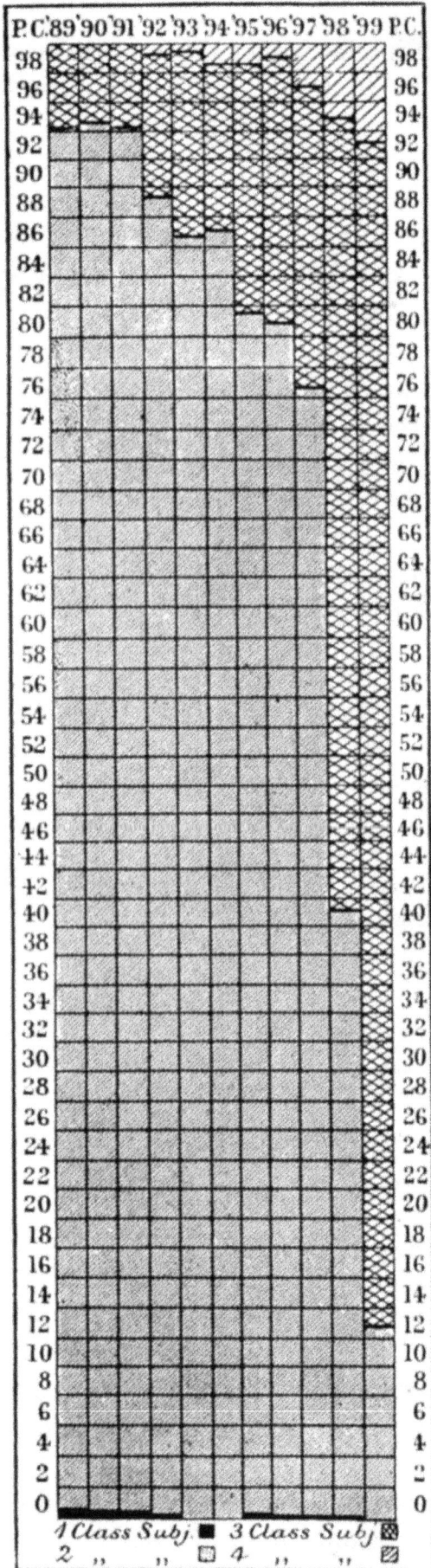

Diagram IX. ; *howing the percentages of departments taking one, two, three, and four class subjects, respectively.*

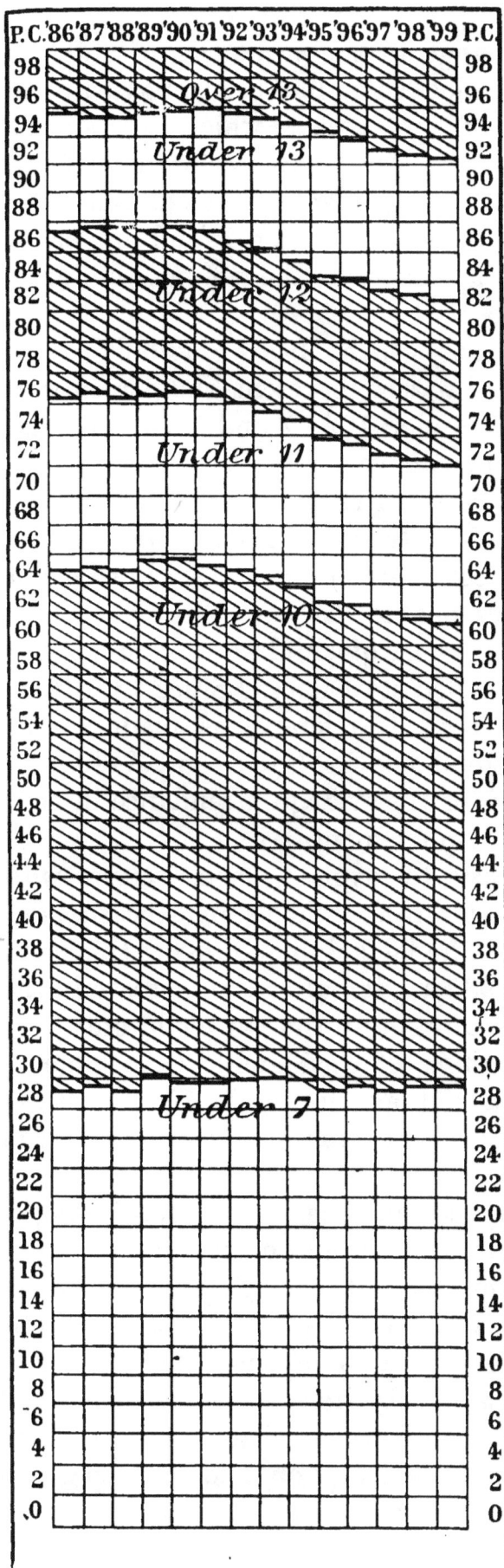

Diagram XI.; showing percentages of children in school according to age.

cent. took two class subjects or less. In 1899 more than 85 per cent. took three class subjects or more.

A similar indication is afforded by the tenth diagram, which illustrates the percentage of passes in specific subjects to the total school roll from 1889 to 1898. It will be seen that the percentage remains practically

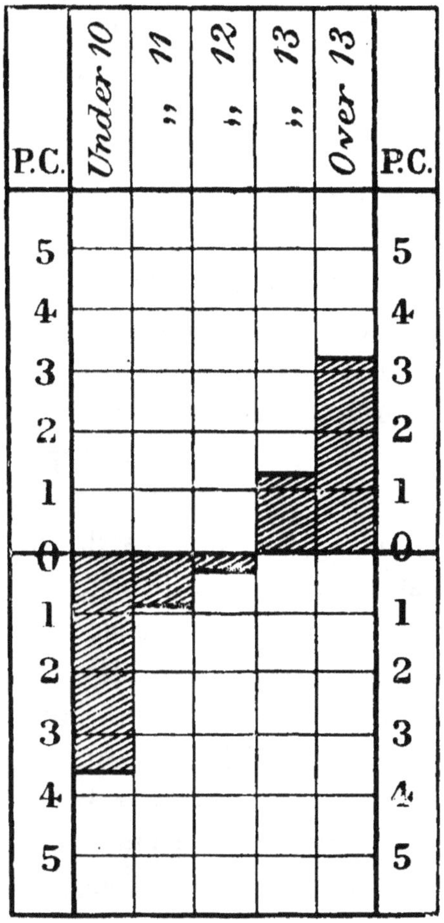

DIAGRAM XII.

stationary until 1892, when it becomes progressive.[1]

The eleventh diagram affords another confirmatory test. It represents the percentages of the ages of the children in the schools. It is possible to carry back this diagram to the year 1886. It will be observed that in 1891 and

---

[1] The percentage for 1899 cannot be given, as the grant for specific subjects was partly paid on a new basis—hours of study, not presentations.

the five preceding years there was no appreciable change in the proportion of children of the various ages, and that throughout the whole period there has been practically no change in the proportion of children under 7 years of age, a class which corresponds roughly with the non-standard children. The latter, therefore, may be eliminated from the diagram without affecting the result. Since 1891 the percentage of children over 12 years of age has increased, and the percentage of children over 7 and under 12 years of age has decreased; the decrease being most apparent in the younger children, and the increase most apparent in the elder children.

The twelfth diagram shows the displacement which has gradually been effected since 1886. The columns below the thick line at zero represent the percentages of decrease in the number of children aged 9 and under 10, 10 and under 11, and 11 and under 12 years of age respectively; the columns above the line at zero represent the percentage of increase in the number of children between 12 and 13, and over 13.

It will be seen, therefore, that three very definite changes in the conditions of elementary education, all making for improvement, commenced to operate in or about the year 1891. Up to that date, so far as statistics enable us to test the facts, the number of class subjects taken in the schools, the number of children taking specific subjects, and the relative ages of the children, all remained stationary. Since 1891 there has been continuous progression under all three heads. If reference is made to the diagram representing the percentage of average attendance in Board and Voluntary schools,[1] it will be seen that 1891 was also the year when the average attendance in both classes of schools began to show definite and regular improvement.

These results are significant, but it is not easy to explain their causes with absolute certainty. The increase in the ages of children in schools may be thought to be due to the raising of the age for exemption, but the facts do not support this view. The age of exemption was raised from 10 to 11 in 1893,[2] a year after the increase in the percentages of elder children commenced: and this alteration in the law could only very indirectly have conduced to the increase in the teaching of class and specific subjects. It is, moreover, a curious fact that the raising of the age of exemption in 1893 does not appear in any way to have increased the percentage of children between 10 and 11 in the schools.

Again, it may be alleged that the Free Education Act, and the consequent freeing of the schools, in 1891, was the cause of the revolution which began to make itself felt in 1891-2. But this explanation will hardly account for all the phenomena under consideration. The freeing of the schools appealed to the neglectful and apathetic parents rather than to those who were eager for the education of their children. The abolition of the fee might encourage these to send their children to school earlier and thus increase the percentage of children under 7, but it would hardly induce them to allow a child to remain in school who was entitled to exemption and was capable of earning wages. The Free Education Act cannot therefore be held to account either

---

[1] See *ante*, p. 134.　　[2] See *ante*, p. 129.

for the increase in the number of the elder children or for the improvement in the teaching of class and specific subjects.

The causes of the change which has been demonstrated to have taken place are probably more social in their character. The change itself is the result of forces which have been continuous in their operation, and have slowly but steadily acquired momentum. The statistics which have just been considered appear to point to the existence of three fairly well defined periods in the Board's work. The first, which comprised the first nine years of the Board's operations, was devoted to preparing the rough ground, and inducing system and order. The soil was rank and unpropitious. Little visible progress was made, even in the teaching of such rudiments as reading, writing, and arithmetic. The possibility of teaching any other subjects successfully, except in a few especially favoured schools, must therefore have been remote. In the second period, which lasted until 1891, more satisfactory results were achieved. The teaching of the obligatory subjects improved, and other subjects of instruction were gradually introduced, but they for a time, like the rudiments in the preceding period, made little headway. The third period opens with 1891-2. In it is apparent, not only a rapid development of the higher instruction, but also an improved attendance at school and a tendency to prolong the period of school life which cannot be attributed to the operation of law.

The causes which have contributed towards the latter development are three in number. The children at present in school are undoubtedly of greater mental receptivity than their forerunners, and are, on that account, capable of a wider range of instruction. If this were not the case, the introduction of a larger number of subjects would tend to diminish the efficiency of the schools, but this, tested by the only available means, has not, as will be shown immediately, been the case. They are, to a large extent, the children of parents who have had experience of the advantages of education, and are desirous that their offspring should profit more completely in a similar manner. A large number of these parents are willing to forego the possible wages that their children might earn, in order to leave them a longer time in the school. There can be little doubt that, as time passes, these influences will be cumulative in their operation; that the average intellect of the school child will grow greater, and the appreciation by the parent of the school influence will become more intense. The development which commenced in 1891-2 will surely continue under the operation of these natural causes, unless it is artificially checked, either by the adoption of a false ideal of education, or by unwise Governmental interference with a healthy natural growth.

These two causes, the increased capacity of the pupil, and the increased appreciation of education by the parent, have mainly brought about the results which have been described. But there has doubtless been a third cause, due, not so much to the efficiency of elementary education as to the inefficiency of that branch of secondary education which should appeal to the class of the community which is just above the level of that which would naturally make use of the public elementary school. So long as the public elementary school was in the stage of struggling to impart the rudiments of knowledge to uneducated, undisciplined children, it in no way appealed to that class of persons. But after a time, well designed school buildings, extensive playgrounds, well-appointed school furniture and apparatus, an expanding curriculum, and an improved tone and moral in the school, not to mention a rising rate, caused the lower middle class to look with envy upon the new institution which they had hitherto regarded with contempt, if not with disgust, and to compare it favourably with the ill-equipped, badly-staffed, and usually inefficient schools to which "respectability" condemned them to send their children. If secondary education had been organised and rendered efficient these people would not, in all probability, have overcome their aversion from the Board school, but in the absence of any such organisation, that aversion has to a great extent disappeared, and it cannot be doubted that of late years a large number of their children have been drifting into the schools of the Board. Such children would be of a good standard of intelligence; such parents would press for a liberal curriculum, and would keep their children longer at school than the majority of their poorer neighbours.

It may be objected, however, that these deductions are based upon statistics merely, and that from statistics anything can be proved. It will be well, therefore, to turn to another and totally different source of information in order to test the inferences which have been derived from statistics. The annual reports of H.M. Inspectors, published by the Education Department, provide such a test. In them we possess a record of the observations of clear sighted specialists who were well qualified to gauge progress as well as failure. It will be seen that the following quotations from these reports fully confirm the inferences that have been derived from statistics.

Mr. Alderson, in his report for 1873 upon the Division of Marylebone, one of the most prosperous districts of London, said:—

" It would be premature at present to attempt to estimate the efficiency of Board schools, or to institute any comparison between them and the Voluntary schools of the district. In their present stage they are far from realising or even attempting the comprehensive scheme of instruction which was promulgated by the late Board, which included, if I remember, history, geography, grammar, and social economy.[1] In the examinations hitherto held in them comparatively few scholars have been presented, and those mostly in the two lowest standards . . . Of one class of Board schools I can already speak in terms of great satisfaction. I refer to those cases in which Board schools have succeeded to Ragged schools, and are engaged in evolving order out of the chaos of those well intended institutions. Children of the very poorest and most neglected class, for whom previous voluntary effort had failed to provide any education worthy of the name, have been brought for the first time under the influence of skilfully organised teaching, with results already visibly beneficial, and full of promise for the future."[2]

Such was the modest summary of the operations of the first School Board. It amounted to this, that they had brought in the waifs and strays, and had subjected them to educational influences, but the result of these influences was not yet fully apparent. In 1877, the same Inspector, reporting upon the same district, gave a different picture.

---

[1] And many other subjects. See *ante*, p. 93.   [2] Education Department Report, 1873-4, p. 35.

" Of the school work in Board schools," he said, " a marked feature, due of course to their superior teaching power, is superior *nicety*. A first standard prepared by a certificated teacher is very different from a first standard prepared by a raw monitor ; but then an equally marked feature in Board school instruction in its present stage is its *limited range*. It will be a surprise to many who have credited the London School Board with an over-ambitious programme to learn that *elementary school work nicely executed* is at present the characteristic ' note ' of their operations in Marylebone. . . . The best proof of the comparative backwardness of Board school instruction is furnished by contrasting the percentage of scholars presented above the third standard in the Board schools, with the same in the Voluntary schools of the district. In Voluntary schools 30 per cent., or nearly one-third, were so presented ; in Board schools only 16 per cent., or about one sixth." [1]

This passage fully confirms the conclusion, already derived from statistics, that the first decade of the Board's work was occupied in perfecting the teaching of the rudiments, and that, for the time, no broader curriculum could be or was attempted. The next quotation, from a report by Mr. Fitch[2] on the Hackney Division for the following year, is significant of the change which was coming over the Board schools. It marks not only the improvement of the rougher children who were coerced into school, but also the advent of the child of parents of a somewhat superior class, attracted by the greater efficiency of the Board schools.

" The vigilance of the School Board officers has swept into the schools a large number of children, hitherto much neglected, who would a few years ago have been found in very irregular attendance at a Ragged school. These, however, form in nearly all cases so small a minority, and so soon succumb to the general habits of order and cleanliness which pervade the schools, that they cease to be distinguished in any marked way from the rest, and I hear of no complaints on the part of parents of well-conducted children of any evil arising from the association. On the other hand, some of the Board schools are attended by a considerable number of scholars of a higher social rank, who formerly would not have been found in elementary schools at all, but would have been paying a guinea a quarter in some little private establishment, dignified by the name of ' academy ' or ' seminary.' The parents of these children, clerks and shop-keepers for the most part, would not have been unwilling to pay higher fees, but they have discovered the inefficiency of the private schools, and now that the Board schools, with their imposing buildings, their municipal character, and their skilled teachers, are accessible to all classes, it is quite intelligible that such parents should not feel precluded from using them by the fact that the fee is only 2d. or 3d. a week. Herein the lower middle-classes appear to me to evince a true instinct, for the Board school is undoubtedly giving the best education within their reach." [3]

One more extract must be added, from a report for the year 1880, which indicates

---

[1] Education Department Report, 1877-8, p. 401.
[2] Now Sir Joshua Fitch.
[3] Education Department Report, 1878-9, p. 550.

very clearly that the rough preparatory work of the first decade had been completed, and that the ground was prepared for the initiation of higher efforts.

"I must now conclude," said Mr. Bailey, reporting on the Hackney schools, "but I can hardly do so without testifying to the immeasurable benefit which the School Board has conferred upon the East of London. Clergymen have told me that they hardly know their own parishes, so great has been the change for the better. The Board has covered the ground with schools, and the schools are filled with children. This, however, is but the first step. The schools at present are all on a level, each competing against the others as if they were so many separate Voluntary schools, instead of being, as they are, under one central authority. We may look forward to a time (may it not be far distant!) when the Board will organise their great aggregation of schools, grading them according to the different needs of the people, and bringing them into connection with the higher schools, so as to form the whole into one system capable of giving suitable education to every class of the vast population of London." [1]

This aspiration was not to be realised for some years, and it was probably, at the time, premature; but the fact that an experienced Inspector considered that the moment had arrived when a grading of schools might be attempted with advantage proves that the period during which the whole energy of the teacher was expended upon mere rudiments had passed away, and that the scholars were becoming capable of receiving a more liberal education.

That the aspiration was for the time being premature could be proved by numerous quotations from Inspectors' reports at about this period, showing that, although the teaching of the obligatory subjects was rapidly improving, the teaching of class subjects was by no means satisfactory. Mr. Stokes, in his report upon the Southwark Division for 1881, said: "The examination of class subjects affords unsatisfactory results. Nor can this failure excite surprise. The instruction of children in masses cannot but be superficial and unsound, and the preparation for an examination which allows half the examined to fail without diminution of grant is not likely to be so careful and thorough as one which inflicts a loss of money for every individual defect in learning. . . . Certain it is that in many schools seeking grants for specific subjects the upper classes are very ill-informed in their grammar, geography, and history." [2]

The want of success may have resulted in some part from negligent teaching, but it was doubtless due, to a considerable extent, to a lack of the capacity of assimilation by the pupils. The successful study of English, geography, and history requires facility in the application of the rudiments which have already been acquired. At this period the children were successful in the obligatory subjects, but had not acquired facility in applying them to other studies. They had obtained the tools of education, but they had not, as yet, learned to use them with any skill. This fact was aptly illustrated by Mr. Alderson in his report on the Marylebone district in 1881. He was commenting upon the inability of the average school child to express his thoughts clearly in writing. In the examination on English in a certain school, the boys were asked to describe, in a

---

[1] **Education Department Report,** 1880-1, p. 238.   [2] *Ibid.* 1881-2, p. 445.

letter, the day of examination. "My young friend," said Mr. Alderson, commenting on one of these letters, "commences thus: 'The Expecter came in soon after nine.' I thank him for that title. I certainly am an 'expecter' to the extent of expecting that a boy who passes in writing, passes in spelling, passes in grammar, should be able to fuse and blend those several accomplishments in a decently-expressed letter. But this, it would seem, is usually to expect too much. He is equal to the separate tests, but the composite test floors him."[1]

In the year 1885 a report was for the first time presented upon the "Metropolitan Division," which included London and certain outlying districts. The report was drawn up by the Chief Inspector, but it was very largely compounded of extracts from the reports of Assistant Inspectors. Educational questions were in consequence dealt with in greater detail and by a larger number of observers. There seems to have been a very general consensus of opinion among the Assistant Inspectors that the teaching of class subjects was unsatisfactory.[2] One of them said: "In class subjects I have nothing new to report. The practice of taking two class subjects is far too prevalent, but I am loth to check it so long as there are no other terms on which geography is to be taught."[3] It was stated, moreover, that the attempt made in recent years to force the teaching of specific subjects had failed, and that it had been to a great extent discontinued. Similar evidence was forthcoming in 1887. "My impression is," said one of the Assistant Inspectors, "that these [class subjects] are rarely mastered, and that we are at present driven to accept a somewhat low standard of attainment. . . . The great size of the classes with which teachers usually have to deal in schools under the School Board for London makes it almost impossible to give that individual attention to particular children which is possible where classes are limited to a moderate number of scholars."[4]

In 1889, although the Inspectors still found much to criticise, they sounded on the whole a more cheerful note. "I am glad to report much general progress," one of them said. "Grammar, which was perhaps the worst taught of all subjects, has come to be one of the best. . . . Geography is taught fairly well in the larger and better schools." "English, geography and needlework as class subjects," said another, "are taught in almost every school, and well taught." The same praise was not, however, awarded to the specific subjects, the teaching of which was condemned as superficial and unsatisfactory, just as the teaching of class subjects was similarly condemned a few years previously.[5]

The years 1891-2 are the dates fixed by the statistics which have been examined in the foregoing pages as those of the commencement of a rapid expansion of curriculum and improvement in efficiency. It is significant, therefore, to find that in the report of the former year all complaints of superficiality of teaching and of unsatisfactory results entirely disappear. Praise takes the place of

[1] Education Department Report, p. 179.
[2] Ibid. 1885-6, pp. 303, 304.
[3] Ibid. The two class subjects almost universally taken were English and geography for boys, and English and needlework for girls.
[4] Ibid. 1887-8, p. 235.
[5] Ibid. 1889-90, pp. 367-369.

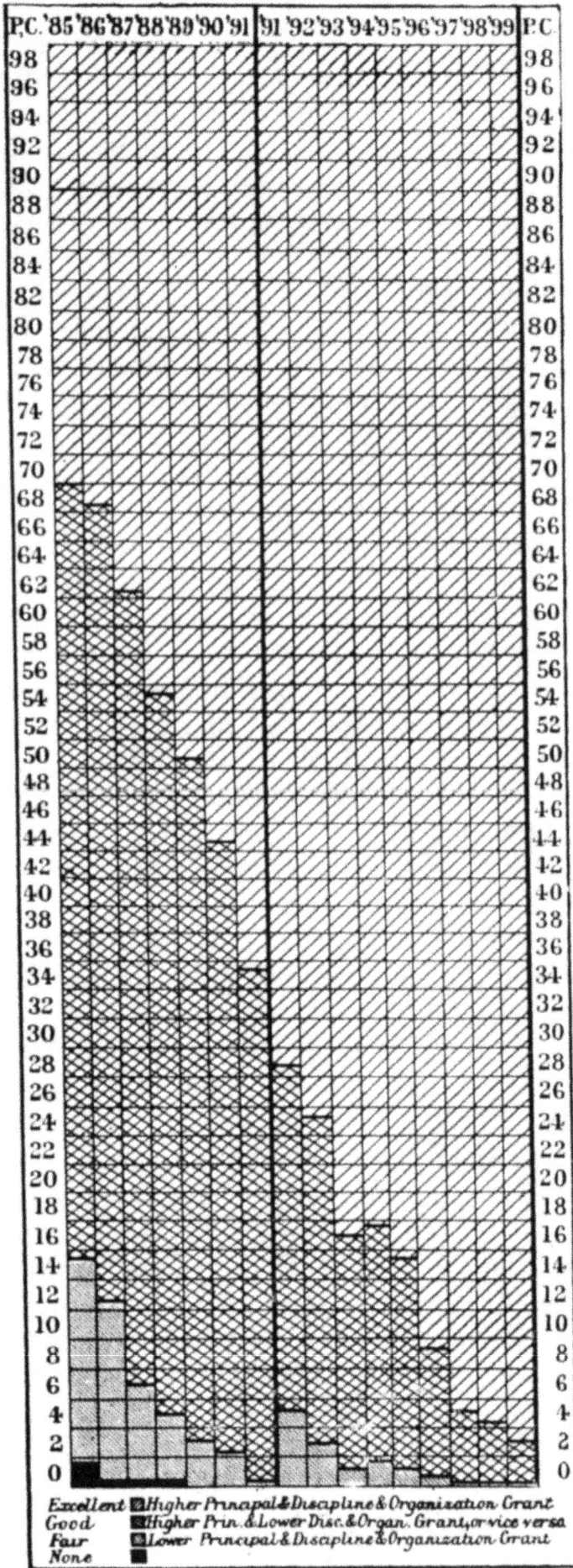

Excellent ▨ Higher Principal & Discipline & Organization Grant
Good ▨ Higher Prin. & Lower Disc. & Organ. Grant, or vice versa
Fair ▨ Lower Principal & Discipline & Organization Grant
None ■

DIAGRAM XIII.

blame. The Rev. T. W. Sharpe, the chief Inspector, after enumerating the possible subjects of instruction—obligatory, class, and specific—said: "The large proportion of full grants obtained in London schools, both Board and Voluntary, shows conclusively that the full number of subjects described above is, as a rule, taught with great intelligence and success. The highest grant for elementary subjects cannot be paid in schools for older scholars unless 'a high degree of accuracy and intelligence' has been reached in regard to all elementary subjects (a similarly high standard is required in the class and specific subjects)."[1]

Two years later Mr. Sharpe made a more definite declaration, which, although it contained some criticism, indicates with sufficient clearness the rapidity with which the wave of progress was advancing. "The teaching of most of the ordinary school subjects," he said, "manifests a steady improvement, both in the methods employed and in the greater freedom and comfort with which the schools are conducted. The subjects in which least success is obtained are expressive reading and simple composition; arithmetic also varies greatly in different schools with the intelligence of the methods; singing varies, especially in the matter of ear-training; there are marked differences in the cleanliness of the needlework; object lessons are not always sufficiently illustrated; history does not occupy its proper position in the first classes. But with these exceptions, the rest of the work has steadily improved; the scholars show greater power in mastering the substance of the reading book, the writing is better formed in character;

[1] Education Department Report, 1891-2, p. 424.

the neatness of the arithmetic leaves little to be desired ; geography is almost everywhere well taught ; the cause of English grammar has gained by its abandonment in schools where it was disliked ;[1] elementary science is steadily gaining ground ; the singing is generally very sweet ; cookery and laundry-work are spreading everywhere ; the choice of poetry for recitation has widened, and, as a general result of the work, scholars who will benefit by Evening Continuation Schools are multiplying daily."[2] This accumulation of evidence may cease here. Subsequent reports only emphasise and confirm the conclusions expressed in the last quotation.

Having thus drawn from the reports of H.M. Inspectors the proof that the inferences which have been made from statistics are reliable, it may be well to conclude this section with the statistical evidence which these Inspectors have themselves created of their opinion upon the growing efficiency of the schools. Under the Codes of 1882 and 1890 it was incumbent upon the Inspectors to assess the schools according to their respective merits. Taking the higher principal and higher discipline and organisation grant of 1890 as equivalent to the "excellent" of 1882, and the lower principal and lower discipline and organisation grant as equivalent to "fair," and the other combinations as equivalent to "good," a common basis of comparison of the Inspectors' assessments is provided. The thirteenth diagram shows the results from 1885, the first year in which exhaustive results under the new system are obtainable, until 1899. The column for 1891 is duplicated because, in that year, a portion of the schools were inspected under the old system. In 1885 only 30 per cent. of the schools received the excellent merit grant. In 1899, 97 per cent. of the schools received the higher principal and higher discipline and organisation grant.

CHAPTER II.

THE ORDINARY DAY SCHOOL.

By S. E. Bray.

It is impossible to travel any distance over the Metropolitan area without noticing lofty, commodious school-houses built of greyish yellow and red brick, which are suggestive of the purpose for which they were raised. Most of the buildings erected in the earlier days of the Board's existence do not, perhaps, speak with the same certainty of language to a stranger as those which have sprung up within more recent years ; but all have the educational atmosphere about them that tells of the early training of youth. Perhaps the neighbourhood in which these structures are situated, as well as their architectural simplicity and solidity, help one to come to this conclusion. There is a municipal air, an official precision, a scholastic tone, and a simple dignity about them which is the more pronounced in certain cases by reason of the squalor and manifest poverty of their

[1] English ceased to be a compulsory class subject in 1891.

[2] Education Department Report, 1893-4, p. 109.

surroundings. These are the Board schools, in which more than half of the **primary** education of London is being carried on. Most of them stand away from the **great** channels of traffic, where the population is dense; but some front the main **roads, or** stand back a little way from them, while a few others lie on the outskirts of the **great** city. Most of these buildings are one pile consisting of three storeys, corresponding to the three departments, each supervised by its own head teacher, into which the majority of schools are divided. The infants occupy the basement, while the other two floors are utilised separately by the boys and girls.

In some cases there are two piles of buildings, especially where a Junior Mixed department exists, and special centres have been raised for instruction in woodwork, cookery, laundrywork, and similar subjects needing a special equipment and a separate existence.

The current decade has been one of experiments. Junior Mixed departments, therefore, where boys and girls in Standards I. and II., or I. to III., receive instruction, and Senior Mixed departments for children in higher standards than those named, have been established here and there, the former usually supervised by a mistress, with assistants of her own sex, and the latter by a master under corresponding conditions. These departures from the earlier programme of the Board have worked satisfactorily, and will in all probability be encouraged in the future.

The classes in the schools are graded by the standards recognised by the Education Department, now called the Board of Education. These are seven in number, Standard I. being the lowest and Standard VII. the highest, each with its particular educational requirements in the rudimentary, class, and certain other optional subjects. Again, pupils above Standard IV. may, in addition to these, take up more advanced work in what are called specific subjects—such as modern languages, Latin, elementary science— for which additional grant was, until the present year, paid by the Education Department.

It is no longer necessary, as it formerly was, to conform to these rigid standards, although in many respects they are valuable delimitations by which to gauge the progress of the pupil; but if a teacher desires to retain them he has a wide choice for their application. He may elect to place a child in Standard I. for arithmetic, in Standard IV. for writing, and in Standard VI. for reading, whereas in the rigid days of old, the child must have been taught and examined in the same standard for all subjects.

The ancient landmarks of scholastic advancement are now practically gone. The teacher has a perfect freedom of classification of his scholars; he can exercise any original talent he may possess in method and organisation, provided it is reasonable and not an outrage on accepted notions of the conditions of educational progress. The strong teacher has taken full advantage of this liberty, and has given his pupils most of the benefits to be derived from a change which certainly makes for an ideally sound education.

It is almost axiomatic to say that a really good school presupposes a strong head teacher, and that the efficiency of all schools is directly proportionate to the capabilities of their instructors. By "strong" is meant strong chiefly in the impress of his or her own individuality, in judgment of character, in quick apprehension of a scholar's natural ability on one side and of his weakness on the other. The head teacher with these powers can marshal the forces under his command with but little waste of strength, and produce the best educational results. But all head teachers are unfortunately, not strong, and thus it is that, given the same conditions, one school differs so widely from another in tone, in discipline, in method, and in efficiency. The old system of scholars' promotion from standard to standard, based on individual examination by H.M. Inspector, had a definite tendency to support the weak head teacher, and to level efficiency in the schools. The present system of inspection, which mostly prevails—in lieu of examination at the Inspector's option, and with due notice—has thrown the full weight of responsibility for the efficiency of the school upon the head teacher.

These differences are noted, not because the London schools are exceptional in this respect, but rather because, in a statement dealing with them, it is desirable to call attention to the grades of educational efficiency which must necessarily exist, so long as individual head teachers differ so widely. No institution, perhaps, is so readily impressionable as a school; and hence it is that the character of its chief, to those who have observant eyes, is visible in almost every part of it. But this great gulf between one school and another is getting narrower every year. It was mainly the result of causes to which allusion has already been made,[1] and are rapidly disappearing.

Since 1870 the training of teachers has undergone a great change, and a fairly high standard of knowledge and culture is now attained by them. Graduates of British Universities can, at the present time, be counted by the score in the Board's service, whilst hundreds of others, by home reading and diligent study, are raising their value as exponents of the teacher's art. The gulf, therefore, is gradually closing up, for the class teachers as well as the head have their influence in the life of a school.

But, in addition to the head, there is another factor, though a comparatively small one, which determines the character of a school, so far as its tone, curriculum, and general efficiency are concerned. It is the district in which the school is situated. In some neighbourhoods the lads attend school ragged and shoeless; their appearance is symbolical of their homes. In others, though keenly touched with poverty, there is a determined struggle to hide and resist it, which is manifest in the garments and bearing of the children. In yet other localities the boys and girls represent contentment and a careful competence; but the girls everywhere, on account of their white or pink washing aprons, and other patches of colour distributed about their garments, have a more cleanly and smarter appearance than the boys.

Though it may be said generally that the children representing a particular class of parents attend one school and those of another class another, yet it often happens that a school will draw its children from two or more districts, each differing from the other in degrees of prosperity. In such cases there is a happy admixture of boys with boys

---

[1] *Ante,* pp. 84, 105.

and of girls with girls which calls forth sympathy and self-denial, and the helpful hand of the well-to-do child is often extended to its poorer friend.

One of the greatest external difficulties with which the Board has to contend is in dealing with underfed and hungry children. This condition is only too apparent in some neighbourhoods. Sickly complexions, pinched faces, emaciated limbs, and other outward signs of the need of regular and proper nourishment, are often too apparent. A hungry child is necessarily unfit to receive all the benefits to be derived from attendance at school, but the Board has no power to expend money to feed it. The Board has, however, more than once, inquired into the question of underfeeding and its results, and it has offered facilities to voluntary agencies for the provision of meals for underfed school children. In the winter months these agencies are at work, providing breakfasts and dinners for those whose parents through actual poverty are unable to do so. These meals are needed and provided only in the schools in districts where poverty is rife, and in these only to such scholars as are selected by local committees, assisted by the head teacher and his staff.

Irregularity of attendance at school, a question which has already been dealt with,[1] is a formidable foe to efficiency. It retards the work of the school, it discourages the teacher, and it is a grave injustice to those scholars who are regular and industrious. More stringent measures should be taken, and a severer penalty enforced, against those parents who wilfully neglect to send their children regularly to school.

The Board have for many years offered prizes, certificates, and medals as an inducement to punctual and regular attendance. Any scholar who does not fail more than ten times to make punctual attendance at school for a whole year receives a prize. A medal is awarded to the scholar who has not failed to be punctual every time the school was open during the same period. In the latter case two days' absence is allowed, provided due notice is given to the head teacher. Certificates for good attendance are given quarterly.

There are three different years associated with every school—viz., the calendar year, for purposes of certificates of attendance for exemption; the school year, for purposes of finance and requisitions of stock; and the educational year, beginning on July 1st and ending June 30th, at the commencement of which most of the great changes in organisation and promotion of scholars are made.

Corporal punishment is rarely administered in the presence of those not immediately connected with the school. The instrument of punishment is a cane, about two feet long, which is supplied by the Board. Every case of corporal punishment that is inflicted by the head teacher or his staff must be recorded in a book kept for that purpose, with date, name of the child, nature of the offence, the amount and kind of chastisement, together with the name of the teacher who inflicts it. The head teacher is primarily responsible for all punishments; but he may, by a *written* declaration, delegate his authority to any of his assistants whom he may consider fit to exercise it. Revocation of this authority must also be in writing. Pupil teachers are not allowed, under any

[1] See *ante*, p. 133.

circumstances, to administer this kind of punishment. The head teacher, morever, is directed to exercise a strict supervision over it, and to initial every recorded case. The turbulent spirits of the boys bring down upon them most of this form of retribution. The girls, as a rule, receive but little chastisement, and among the infants it is extremely rare. But even among the boys corporal punishment is not frequently administered. This form of punishment is only one of the sanctions of the school's laws. It is necessary for the teacher to exercise a wise discretion in its administration.

Once a year the head teachers of the various departments which constitute one school hold a conference to consider the proper correlation of the school work. These conferences have only recently been established, but there is already some evidence of their practical value.

In most schools the standards of the Education Code are retained, and each assistant teacher is told off at the commencement of the educational year to take charge of a class representing one of these standards. This class he retains, as a rule, for the twelve months, until a fresh organisation is arranged and a new educational year begins. The teacher, in this case, gives instruction in all the subjects which the children in his class are called upon to learn. This system has many advantages, but it is certain that it cannot be defended on the highest educational grounds. In some few schools, therefore, the plan has been adopted of specialising each teacher's work so that it may not be confined to a particular class or standard, but distributed over a considerable part or the whole of the school, in order to deal with a subject or subjects which he is peculiarly well fitted to teach. For the purpose of securing the best available instruction, this is undoubtedly the better plan, but it necessarily requires an augmented school staff. The question, therefore, is really a financial one of serious import.

The amount of staff allowed for a school is mainly determined by the average attendance of the previous school year. This rule, however, is rather a guide than an absolute measure of the staff allowed; in other words, it has purposely been made elastic in order that schools may be dealt with according to individual needs as affected by local circumstances, peculiarities of constitution, or any other permanent or transient conditions which require special consideration. Another factor in determining the number of the staff is the maximum number of scholars that may be apportioned to each teacher. The Board's "Code of Regulations for the Guidance of Managers and Teachers" states the rules for staffing thus :—

"In fixing the staff of a school, the head teacher is counted for thirty scholars in average attendance, except in 'combined' departments; each assistant teacher recognised by the Board of Education as 'certificated,' for sixty; each 'assistant teacher' for forty-five; and each pupil teacher in the second or third year of apprenticeship for twenty scholars in average attendance. Probationers, candidates, and pupil teachers in the first year of apprenticeship are not reckoned on the staff.

"As a general rule, in determining the staff needed in a school, the average attendance of a class under a single teacher in Standards I., II., or III. shall not exceed sixty; in Standards IV. and V. shall not exceed fifty; and in Standards above V. shall not exceed forty.   The School Management Committee shall have power to modify the staff, taking into consideration the average roll, the number of children in the respective classes, the capacity of the rooms, and the other circumstances of the school."

The Code of the Education Department controls all schools receiving grants from the Government.   The following subjects of instruction have hitherto received official recognition :—

> (a) *Obligatory subjects* (*i.e.*, "elementary subjects ")—
>> Reading, writing, arithmetic, needlework (for girls), drawing (for boys in schools for older scholars).
>> One of the "class subjects" mentioned in (*b.*) (i.), which must be taught by means of object lessons in Standards I., II., and III.
> (b) *Optional subjects*—
>> (i.) Taken by classes throughout the school (*i.e.*, "class subjects ") [1]—
>>> Singing, recitation, drawing (for girls in schools for older scholars and for boys in infant schools and classes), English, or Welsh (in Wales), or French (in the Channel Islands), geography, elementary science, history, suitable occupations (for Standards I., II., and III.), needlework (for girls), optional as a *class* subject; domestic economy (for girls).
>> (ii.) Taken by individual children in the upper classes of the school (*i.e.*, "specific subjects ") [1]—
>>> Algebra, Euclid, mensuration, mechanics, chemistry, physics, elementary physics and chemistry, animal physiology, hygiene, botany, principles of agriculture, horticulture, navigation, Latin, French, Welsh (for scholars in schools in Wales), German, book-keeping, shorthand, according to some system recognised by the Department; domestic economy (for girls), domestic science.
>> (iii.) Cookery, laundry work, dairy work (for girls), cottage gardening, manual instruction (for boys).

Any subject other than those mentioned in (*b*) (ii.), may, if sanctioned by the Department, be taken as a specific subject, provided that a graduated scheme for teaching it be submitted to, and approved by, H.M. Inspector.

Instruction may be given in other secular subjects approved by the Department, and in religious subjects, but no grant is made in respect of any such instruction. [2]

A noticeable fact in the ordinary schools of the Board is the paucity of scholars in the highest standards, especially towards the close of the educational year.   There are two reasons for this; one, the early age at which most of the scholars leave school, either through necessity, or because of the parental impression that their children's education

---

[1] Only two of these could earn grant.   By the Code for 1890, the grants for class and specific subjects were abolished, and a block grant substituted.   See *ante*, p. 163.

[2] **Elementary Education Act**, 1870, s. 97.

is completed at 13 years of age ; the other, the contributory character of the ordinary school to the Higher Grade school. This latter arrangement, an excellent one from the broadest educational standpoint, is encouraged by the Board, and, under the new Minute of the Board of Education on Higher Elementary schools, will be still further extended.[1]

Certain ordinary schools are officially named as being theoretically contributory to a Higher Grade school, but whether the contribution in upper standard scholars is to be made at the close of the educational year, depends mostly on the head teacher of the ordinary school, the managers, or the caprice of the parents and their children. The Board Inspector sometimes insists on the transference, and then it is, of course, carried out. But there is not at present any inflexible rule on this point.

In order to encourage scholars to remain longer in school, the Board has determined to award merit certificates to those scholars working in Standard VII., provided they pass an examination arranged annually for this purpose. The Board has further resolved that for the present it will not arrange any examination of its own for an "Honour" Certificate, but the head teachers are encouraged to send in scholars for such examinations as the Oxford and Cambridge Locals, Science and Art, London Chamber of Commerce, and such other examinations as may be, from time to time, approved by the Board, and that it will grant "Honour" Certificates to scholars passing satisfactorily any of these examinations. The "Honour" Certificate is to be open only to those scholars who have either obtained the "Merit" Certificate at least one year before, or who have completed a two years' course higher than Standard VII.

The visitor to a London Board school a little before nine o'clock in the morning, entering the brick-walled, spacious, asphalted playground allotted to the boys, would find most of them engaged in some form of amusement, and many darting about with such rapidity of movement that he could not help reflecting, considering the crowd of lads there, and the singular scarcity of accident, that a special providence intervenes for their protection. Some few are standing about in groups with expectant demeanour, for it is nearly time for assembly, and the head master may blow his whistle at any moment as the signal for the various classes to fall into their allotted places, and the assistant teachers will suddenly appear as though they had sprung out of the ground. The whistle is blown and the lads run at once to their assigned positions, except a few perhaps, who reluctantly leave their games, and some lethargic ones who never respond to any call with alacrity. The classes fall in two deep, with an assistant master in charge of each ; they go through one or two simple evolutions in military drill, and then march through the playground in double file, ascend the staircase, and enter their respective classrooms in the same order.

On the stroke of nine the classroom doors are closed and the first act of registration is performed, each scholar present receiving opposite his name a mark in red ink to indicate a punctual attendance. This accomplished, the Lord's Prayer is repeated, a few other preliminaries to the morning's work done, and the late-comers are admitted. The lesson in Scripture then begins, which, of course, is graded according to the attainments

---

[1] See *ante*, p. 163.

of the classes, and must be dealt with on broad lines, without reference to sectarian views or matters of interpretation. There must be no doctrine, no dogma, no criticism on creeds; but only a simple lesson on biblical facts and Christian religion and morality, drawn from the storied beauties and eternal truths of the Bible itself.

This instruction in the Scriptures is carried for about a half an hour every morning, and ceases at 9.45, when the second act of registration begins by placing against each late-comer's name a mark or stroke in black ink, and by indicating at the foot of the register in one total the number of red and black marks recorded. The register being closed, the secular work of the school commences. This secular instruction must, by the rules laid down in the Code of the Education Department, cover a period of two hours at least, in each school session of the senior boys' and girls' departments, and one and a half hours in the case of the infants. On consulting the time-table, hung in the hall or some other conspicuous position, which apportions the hours of the day among the various subjects of instruction, and which must be submitted to, and approved by, H.M. Inspector—though the head teacher is free, subject to this limitation, to arrange it in his own way, and to choose the subjects he thinks most suitable for the district—one finds that arithmetic is being taught in one class, English grammar in another, geography in a third, elementary science in a fourth, and so on. These various lessons last for three quarters of an hour, which brings the time to 10.30 a.m. Work is then stopped and the whole school is marched into the playground, class by class, for ten minutes' recreation. On returning to their places in the usual order, each class receives instruction in another subject till 11.20, when another subject supplants the previous one till the clock announces mid-day. The school is then dismissed in the same orderly fashion as it entered the building.

It is noticed that some lads, when leaving, have in their hands a printed notice. These are notifications of absence of other scholars, which will be duly delivered to the parents concerned in case such absence should be without their knowledge. Other lads remain in the classrooms, detained for a short time as a punishment for idleness, or for some offence against discipline. The Board discourages this form of punishment, and has placed two limitations to it: the detention must not exceed half-an-hour's duration, and the scholar may not, during detention, be made to do any scholastic work.

While the scholars are away at their homes, the visitor can look round the building and see what the interior is like. Its most conspicuous feature is the hall, with its wood-blocked floor, its distempered walls, ornamented by pictures of many kinds: engravings, etchings, photographs, and tastefully executed coloured prints of flowers and country scenes. There is also the Honour Board, with its white letters telling of successes achieved by individual scholars of the school. In various recesses there are cabinets and cases containing specimens utilised for object teaching, and a glazed cupboard, the repository of the scientific apparatus that works such wonders for youthful eyes. At one end of the hall is a slightly raised platform, upon which stands the head master's desk.

Some of the classrooms open out of the hall, while others open into a wide tiled corridor, on one side of which is the cloakroom with its multitude of enamelled iron pegs. One classroom is much the same as another, each accommodating about sixty pupils, each, too, being a miniature reproduction of the hall, except that about one-third of the floor is terraced and that the largest portion of it is occupied by transverse rows of dual desks, with a passage between them. Upon the slightly-raised terraces of wood most of the desks stand, rising one above the other towards that part of the wall which faces the teacher when giving his lessons. In the open space is the teacher's table, or a demonstration bench, fitted with drawers and appliances for simple scientific experiments. On the walls are more pictures similar to those already mentioned, together with maps and diagrams. A large, fixed, framed slate faces the scholars, whereon the teacher illustrates his lessons. In a recess stands a varnished cupboard of pitch pine, containing all the requisites for class instruction. In a loftier part of the building is an art room, with sunlight burners, adjustable desks for individual pupils, models, casts of fruit and conventional flowers, conveniences for clay modelling, and all the other usual appliances for efficient instruction in drawing. In some schools there is also a spacious workshop in which forty of the older scholars may, at one time, learn the elements of woodwork and be taught the use and manipulation of all ordinary tools.

After this brief survey, the visitor descends the stone staircase, the sides of which gleam with the light of glazed white brick, and re-enters the playground. Most of the boys have returned, and a restless mass of young humanity is before his eyes, making a terrible din—the unmistakable sounds of hundreds of lads bent on active pleasure. It is twenty minutes to two and the first notes of the school bell warn the lads already there that only a few more minutes of play remain, and summon others lagging at home, or idling in the streets. Ten minutes later, the bell again rings out, the master's whistle is blown, and assembly takes place in the same way as in the morning. The classrooms are reached and again the first and second acts of registration are performed at 2 and 2.15 p.m. respectively; but in the meantime the lessons have commenced. The afternoon's work is much the same as the morning's; divided into three secular lessons of about forty minutes' duration, with a recreation interval coming between; except that, as a rule, the more difficult subjects, such as arithmetic and grammar, are taken in the morning, and the easier ones in the afternoon, as, for example, drawing, writing, composition, and singing. The boys and girls of the senior departments are dismissed at 4.30 p.m., and the infants half an hour earlier.

Although there is no rule forbidding home lessons, yet these are rarely given unless it be to scholars in the higher classes, and even then there are no sanctions by which they may be enforced. The Board, indeed, distinctly forbids punishment of any kind for failure to perform home tasks that may be imposed by the teachers. In schools, however, situated in the best districts, home lessons are generally well done, without causing those manifest inconveniences to the family which must arise when home accommodation is more limited.

As the morning's work is much like the afternoon's, so is one day very much the same as another in a week's school life, although the lessons rarely follow exactly the same order, and certain subjects are only taught once or twice from Monday morning to Friday afternoon. But those subjects that are rudimentary, as reading, writing, and arithmetic, recur, of course, with persistent regularity. Friday afternoon is made, in the bulk of the schools, the most attractive session of the week, because the attendance on that occasion shows a decided tendency to fall off. Teachers, therefore, in order to check this tendency, often read and expound to their classes some pretty stories culled from the works of distinguished writers, or show them some of the minute wonders revealed by the microscope, or take them on an imaginary journey through city, field, and forest, as illustrated by the optical lantern, or tear a page from history and give it the touch of life by the same means.

We return once more to the hall of the boys' department, where there is a piece of furniture that has been overlooked. It is the library cupboard, wherein are seen about a hundred volumes waiting their turn for usefulness. The books which it contains can be borrowed and taken away by the scholar, and are exchanged at regular intervals. Many of their neighbours have gone for a holiday and are spending it in one or other of the elder scholar's homes. "Quentin Durward" is languishing after "Waverley," who is away; "David Copperfield" is looking in vain for the "Old Curiosity Shop"; "Silas Marner" misses the "Mill on the Floss"; "Rienzi" and the "Last Days of Pompeii" are supporting each other in their weariness of waiting; and Tennyson is not pleased in his loneliness. Most of them display garments that are the worse for wear, and some are so shabbily attired that the tailor's art must be practised on them before they will be permitted to have their week's or fortnight's change.

It would be impossible within the limits of the present chapter to describe minutely all the subjects of instruction and to illustrate the graduated courses and methods. Graded courses have been drawn up by the Board's specialists in many subjects, and the Education Department have, in their Code, graduated schemes for most of the subjects of instruction named therein; but teachers may draw up their own courses in numerous subjects and teach on the lines so indicated, provided such courses have been submitted to, and approved by, H.M. Inspector. The Board of Education has recently drawn up a series of schemes of instruction applicable to different classes and grades of schools, under the provisions of the Code of 1900.

All scholars in the upper standards must have an acquaintance with the metric system, and those who take elementary science in its practical form have to apply this system in all their weights and measures.

The system of free-arm drawing has recently been introduced into the schools. Each child in the lower standards draws on a millboard with soft white or coloured chalk, which he holds at arm's length. It is often surprising to find with what facility the children draw in this way, and what happy touches they sometimes give. As a means of improving the free-hand drawing which comes at a later stage in their progress, it will, no doubt, be of value.[1]

---

[1] See *post*, p. 216.

It may be said generally of the teaching, that though theory does, and must always play an important part, yet practical methods nearly everywhere prevail, and realities are introduced whenever it is possible. Any object that is fairly accessible and portable is obtained by the really keen teacher. Teaching by practical illustration is encouraged by the Board.

The school is at various times suddenly and unexpectedly called upon to go through its fire drill. The head master takes from his desk a handbell, which he rings till its sound has penetrated to every part of the building. Immediately quick words of command are heard in the classrooms; all doors fly open, each guarded by its own janitor; the classes emerge into the hall and corridor in quick time, and one by one, without haste, but yet with speed, descend the staircase into the playground. This is an interruption to the ordinary work of the school; so, while the scholars are below, the teacher's class book, which each assistant must have, is shown. In this the head master records the results of his examinations in each subject, held four times a year, and also any criticisms which he may desire to make. This book also contains a general record of work done by the assistant in his own class, posted up in this respect by himself.

The Log Book, kept by the head master, is a record of all important school events. In it may be read such entries as the following, under various dates:—

1. Standard VI. visited the South Kensington Museum in the afternoon.
2. Standard V. had a field excursion to study botany.
3. All schools closed to-day by order, on account of the Annual Drill Display held at the Albert Hall.
4. T. Smith, H. Jones, and J. Brown each obtained the Junior County Scholarship, valued at £10 a year for two years.
5. In accordance with the Board's order to test the eyes of the children annually, in the month of July, the recognised tests were put into operation, and the children classified accordingly.

Swimming has not been mentioned as part of the school curriculum. This, however, is recognised in the summer months, both by the Education Department and the Board. As only one bath belongs to the Board, municipal and private baths have to be used. About 12,000 children belonging to the Board's day schools annually learn to swim; that is, roughly, one-third of those actually under instruction in that subject.

The girls' department is usually, as regards structure, a reproduction of the boys'. The rudimentary and class subjects are also much the same in both places. The girls however, take up other work specially suitable to their sex, such as needlework, domestic economy, cookery, and laundry.

From this department one descends another flight of steps to the infants', where the two sexes work together. It is a pretty sight to see them go through their musical drill, and to observe how thoroughly they enjoy it. Many visitors remark on the deliciously soft voices among the older children and praise their singing, which for time and sweetness of tone cannot be surpassed by the boys and girls in the senior departments.

Distributed over the department are to be found, in addition to pictures, excellent models of animals and sometimes globes of goldfish supplied by the teachers themselves.[1]

No mention has hitherto been made of schools which have been recognised by the Board as "Schools of Special Difficulty"; that is, schools in which the pupils represent the lowest stratum of London life. These, on account of the extreme poverty or neglect of parents, and the almost complete absence of home training for the children, present serious obstacles to progress. Teachers receive a higher remuneration for working in these schools, the time-tables of which are usually made out on the basis of half-hour lessons, and show a comparatively narrow range of instruction. It is in those schools that most of the few half-timers in London are to be found: boys and girls who are endeavouring to solve the problem of attending effectively at school and at some factory or workshop during the same day.

Reference has been already made to beneficent voluntary agencies that exist outside the school; but no mention has been made of two associations which have done, and are doing, admirable work in their own way. One of these societies, "The Children's Country Holidays Fund," sends sickly and delicate scholars into the country for a fortnight in the summer time at quite a nominal charge; a charge, indeed, so small that it does little more than pay the return railway fare. Another, called "The Happy Evenings Association," organises and supervises amusements in the Board's buildings during the winter months for the children's entertainment. There are besides horticultural societies to which many of the scholars belong; football leagues, cricket clubs, and other institutions whose special function is amusement and physical development.

In conclusion, attention must be called to the ladder that the Board has helped to make and raise, by which, with a co-ordinated system of scholarships, an industrious and clever child may pass from the elementary to the secondary school, and thence to the University. This has been accomplished many times, with the happiest results. The Board has no power to grant money for scholarships, but generous benefactors have at various times founded scholarships and placed them at the Board's disposal. There are sixteen permanent scholarships, most of which are open to all children attending public elementary schools in London. Some, however, are limited to certain districts or schools, or to certain classes of children. In addition to these permanent scholarships, terminable scholarships have frequently been placed at the disposal of the Board by City companies and other public institutions. The scholarships vary in value from £8 to £50 a year.

---

[1] For further information see the next chapter, on Method in Infant Schools.

CHAPTER III.

ON METHOD IN INFANT SCHOOLS.

By Miss Phillips, *Superintendent of Method.*

The greatest difficulty in the way of establishing suitable method in infants' schools has arisen from the wrong conception that formerly obtained as to the function of the infants' school, which was regarded as a senior school in miniature, governed by methods of discipline and work suitable only to older scholars. The strenuous, unrelieved application to studies unsuitable to mere babies from 3 to 6 years of age, carried on under conditions of unsympathetic formality, could not produce anything more than a mechanical expertness and a superficial appearance of knowledge. The teachers in the senior schools were obliged to be contented if children received from the infants' departments were able to perform the more mechanical part of the work of Standard I., and little regard was paid to the absence of qualities of infinite importance.

But many influences which are gradually widening and liberalising elementary education are leading to a more humane conception of the place of an infants' school in the educational scheme. Among these influences the Kindergarten system has been one of the most important, and is surely, if slowly, revolutionising all preparatory education in spite of most unwise and most injudicious applications and conceptions of the system, which have necessarily brought it, in some places, into disrepute.

Teachers in the senior schools now prize the alert mental attitude and developed intelligence, the habits of work and self-control, of cheerful obedience and courtesy, which mark children sent up from infants' schools. Probably these children are able to do the mechanical work once solely demanded as well as, or better than formerly; but if this does not happen to be the case, the wiser senior teachers know the more mechanical requirements for Standards I. and II. can be speedily mastered by children who have been taught to work, and see, and think.

Early childhood is a preparation for the next stage of later childhood, and we must consider the basis of subjects and discipline which will be required in school and life after the sixth year. But a good result will not be produced in a later stage if the present stage be not lived through fully, freely and thoroughly; and the children developed freely and happily in mind and body by habits of self-control, obedience, and industry; in reality and not in appearance only. The infants' department is intended to give that training and instruction which the baby children, in other circumstances, would receive from the care of an intelligent, cultivated, educated mother, who could give a very large part of her time to her children. The little ones must live through their stage of early childhood in an atmostphere of affection, of cheerfulness, of reasonable freedom, and of constant and joyous activity.

This is the atmosphere of many of our infant schools.

The work in infants' schools resolves itself into the following :—

1. The child's physical frame has to be protected and developed.

2. The little child has to acquire a knowledge of facts in the external world, and a power of expression in language.

3. The hand has to be developed in general dexterity and flexibility—in fineness and delicacy of touch—in accordance with the child's innate tool-using, creative, and productive instincts.

4. The child's moral and social instincts have to be developed and trained.

The proper carrying out of this training constitutes what is known as "Kindergarten."

From the above considerations as to the function of an infants' school it will be seen that one of the most important subjects must be the nature, or object lessons; whether we regard them from the more strictly Pestalozzian side as exercises in sense, impressions, and language, or whether we take a slightly different view and consider them as including the collection and co-ordination of facts in relation to future science work.

Great progress is being made in rendering these lessons more really educative, and the teachers do not rest satisfied with hearing the children repeat the observations of others, but lead them to touch and see for themselves and co-ordinate and register their own observations.

The best opportunity for this real and true work comes in the lessons upon plants. Our little children grow plants in the Kindergarten, watch the development of the leaf-buds, of the flowers, and of trees. They make frequent visits with their teachers to open spaces in and round London, and even in areas of the densest population there are squares and open playgrounds where trees can be seen. Everything is being done to lead the children to care for and admire and reverence all beautiful living things, and the flowers and leaves are not brought forward by the teachers as isolated objects, but as parts, and necessary parts, of the tree or plant they belong to, fulfilling their part in the development and well-being of the whole.

The Kindergarten infant teacher does not lead the children to wrest mere un-related facts of structure from a destructive examination of the plants. The plants are not pulled to pieces, but it is suggested that they are beautiful things, living their lives in accordance with the law and order of their kind. It must not be imagined that quite little children are insensible to such ideas. Children can be taught to understand harmony in the relationship of their lives to the larger world about them, and it is through the recognition and development of this dim feeling of community and their innate love of order, that we get ultimately real discipline in the school, when children are obedient, orderly, and industrious because their relation to the community in which they live demands that they should be so.

Observation of actual leaves or flowers is rendered more thorough and exact by "free" drawing and by modelling. Each child makes a drawing on unlined paper or on a substitute for a blackboard, and the drawing is coloured with chalk or paint. The child records what he himself sees, not what the teacher tells him he can see. Perhaps in the succeeding lesson a clay model is made of the same subject.

The real use and intention of a group of Kindergarten occupations are found in this method of giving the child suitable material with which he can express some idea, or freely imitate what he has seen in nature.

Lessons on animals offer more difficulties. There is a general and most proper feeling that no animal should be brought into the school to be subjected to discomfort or fear. It is no lesson for little children to be accustomed early in life to obtain pleasure, or to wrest an advantage in knowledge from the sufferings of helpless animals. In some schools suitable animals are domesticated and lead very happy lives, and are the means of much valuable training for the children mentally and morally. But if real animals are difficult to deal with, we do very well with excellent pictures, and the teachers' blackboard drawings. Animals selected for these lessons are generally those familiar to the children—sparrows, pigeons, dogs, horses, &c. Pictures, stories, games, and visits to the Zoological Gardens make the children's notions of other animals as real as possible. If a strict Herbartian would condemn such lessons as those upon camels, elephants, &c., a part of our answer would be an appeal to him to note the delight of these six-year-old children in the play of fancy round what is so wonderful and strange and far off.

In some schools, principally in connection with language teaching, stories are gradually taking a very important place. Teachers of little children know how difficult it is to lead them to connected, sustained narration or work. We have the means of doing this with our stories, selected with great care, told in simple graphic language, and re-told by the children. In one school in particular the little girls have gained considerable facility in giving connected, simple versions of the stories. It is unnecessary to speak of the other functions of this work as a foundation for future literature lessons, but everywhere in the Board schools such work is on the increase, and teachers much enjoy their freedom of selection, and exercise and improve their own literary taste in bringing forward beautiful stories and little poems.

Painting, modelling, and free-drawing are here again used by the children to illustrate their ideas, and the strange, crude results are not only interesting to the teacher because they give a real insight into the working of the child's mind and so influence the teaching, but are of immediate use in the next drawing lesson, when the child's hasty and partial observation can be corrected.

Kindergarten games, when not elaborate, mechanical, over-rehearsed entertainments, are very valuable as a means of expression of ideas in action. Originality and spontaneity are encouraged, and children are exercised in self-reliance, presence of mind, in unselfishness and courtesy, and in habits of attention and order. Besides these advantages we must not omit that of suitable and varied physical exercise, though it is not intended that the games should partake of the nature of regular gymnastics. More regular exercises in rehearsed rhythmical movements, leading up to later drill lessons, are also given.

The occupations of painting, drawing, and modelling have been mentioned as of special value in all the above work, in stimulating real observation, in correcting hasty observation, and in deepening and registering observation. But there are other "gifts" and "occupations" being used in the schools for other purposes, and only slightly less important.

Little children's sense of form (formal) and number must have special systematic training; and balance, proportion, relative size, and sequence in the things observed and constructed must not be neglected. Admirable materials for systematic training are found in the gifts (cubes and sticks), and in the more systematised occupations, such as paper-folding, paper-cutting, chequered drawing, and sewing. Chequered drawing and Kindergarten sewing are admirably used by many teachers towards a result of excellence in the older scholar's needlework, which must depend not only on lightness and dexterity in hand adjustment, but also on the idea of uniformity of size and distance, and in the regularity of the stitches.

An enormous amount of time and effort was formerly wasted in infants' schools through teaching reading in an isolated way. Symbols, which were symbolical of nothing to the children, were forced upon them long before their power of seeing was sufficiently developed to allow them to note the slight differences in form between one letter and another. Now we are beginning to understand that ideas precede language, and language precedes its expression in written or printed characters. In our best infants' schools the old drudgery of alphabet learning and dreary, sing-song spelling of words are disappearing, and each teacher makes for herself some bright interesting combination of "Look and Say," and Phonic method.

For instance, the teacher of a class of children of six years of age looks through her reading book when preparing for the week's work, and chooses certain lessons, say one on a farmyard, one on a swan, a duck, or the spring. On Monday morning she tells, to the children's great delight, the story of "The Ugly Duckling," and the object lessons, the reading and writing lessons all grow out of this. The children form certain ideas and there is the human impulse to express these ideas, and means of graphic expression are given in the "occupations," with action in the games, and verbal expression in oral composition, and in reading and writing. Mechanical difficulties are minimised because the attention is fixed on the ideas; and many of our teachers make their own reading sheets, which are recapitulations of the chief points of some favourite story or object lesson, and are freely illustrated by the children.

Songs and recitations help distinct articulation. The effect of the whole training by means of Kindergarten apparatus is to help eyes to see and hands to execute. The children are full of pleasure, keenly interested and zealous, and in our best infants' schools dulness is unknown.

The infants' teacher, even more particularly than the senior school teacher, must be not merely an artisan, but an artist. She has to exercise much insight into child nature, and note human attributes as they are manifested in extreme youth; she has to select most closely and narrowly from the mass of a subject that which will most effectually serve her purpose for training and developing the mind. She has to present matter so selected with force, variety, vivacity, and absolute simplicity, and guide her children in relating, co-ordinating, and expressing their own observations. The whole secret of method in infants' schools consists in understanding how to stimulate and guide the children's own activity in the acquisition of knowledge and, in an atmosphere of reasonable freedom and of cheerful kindness, in fostering those qualities which shall lay the foundation for a future good citizenship.

CHAPTER IV.

HIGHER GRADE SCHOOLS.

By F. G. Landon, *Inspector to the London School Board.*

In the early days of the London School Board the conditions of school life rarely allowed more educational work to be effectively covered than was included in the six standards of elementary education as defined in the Code of Education.

The Education Code divided the work of elementary schools above the level of infant schools into six portions, which were supposed to contain a syllabus of work suited to the study of an average scholar for a year, and these separate courses were called standards. Subsequently a seventh standard was added, carrying the range somewhat further and about equal to another year's work.

With improved methods and appliances and some improvement in regularity of attendance, which is still to our regret far from satisfactory, nearly all our schools began to extend their course of work so as to cover the seventh or highest standard of the Code; but it rarely happened that a school could prepare and retain a sufficient number of pupils to form a separate class of scholars in Standard VII., and in the vast majority of cases these Standard VII. children were taught as best could be managed by the teacher of Standard VI., and in very many schools in poor neighbourhoods, where home necessities or parental indifference kept the duration of school life at its minimum point, the first class included children in the three Standards V., VI., and VII., all under one teacher.

The disadvantage of such heterogeneous classes was manifest, and an endeavour was made in May, 1887, to provide facilities for gathering together in central schools the children in the upper standards of those schools which could not provide separate classification for all the standards.

The following resolution was passed :—

"That, subject to the sanction of the Education Department being given to the general principle, the instruction of children in Standards V., VI., and VII. may, with the consent of the School Management Committee, be given in one school only in each group of schools."

In June following the Education Department gave the necessary sanction stating "that their Lordships highly approved the general principle of the proposal."

It was referred to the divisional members of the Board for the various districts of the Metropolis to suggest central schools, and more than forty schools were selected for this purpose. Efforts were made to foster the higher work in these central schools by limiting the size of the upper classes, by a more liberal supply of scientific and other apparatus, and by adding, where possible, special laboratories, chemical or physical.

It cannot be said that this movement has altogether succeeded in effecting its main purpose, though it has to some extent minimised the evils of faulty classification. It has, however, been productive of much good, and has paved the way to further developments.

As a rule, no compulsion was exercised as to the removal of small upper standards to these central schools. The scholars were informed of the central schools near their homes, and it was left to their parents to take action as to the transfer of their children.

There were several difficulties which stood in the way of the success of this plan of transferring upper standard children to central schools.

The school years ended at various dates in the different schools. The termination of the school years used to be arranged so as to fall about equally at the end of each month of the year in order to facilitate the examination of the schools by Her Majesty's Inspectors; and so a child might be transferred at the end of a year's course from one school to another school in the middle of its courses of study. When inspection was substituted for detailed examination, the London School Board took advantage of the change and arranged for the educational year for all their schools to commence on July 1st and terminate on June 30th following. This change has proved in all respects highly advantageous; but other difficulties remained.

The teachers of the schools from which the children were to be removed generally disliked the idea of losing what they regarded as the cream of their school, and objected to appearing in the eyes of their scholars and the scholars' parents as belonging to an inferior rank of schools. This gave rise to a passive opposition which did much to check the transfers. A further objection to compulsorily removing the upper standards of a school arises from its effect in weakening, if not destroying, all *esprit de corps* in the school so treated. It is highly desirable to foster this spirit, which binds together the scholars and their teachers, so that all may feel a pride in their school and its successes, and this feeling can largely be developed outside the school walls by means of cricket and other athletic sports, to which so many of our teachers give much time in no grudging spirit.

Lastly, in the case of fully half the schools selected for higher standards, their very success prevented them from being available for the purpose intended. They are so attractive to parents who can appreciate the advantages they supply, that, to secure places in them, children are entered into the lower standards, and even to the infants' departments, from a wide area, and consequently no openings are left for entry into the upper standards. In schools such as these, not only can separate classes be arranged for all the classes up to and including the VIIth, but enough children remain after they have attained Standard VII. to form a separate class still more advanced, and for these a more liberal programme of work can be attempted.

The success of these schools has shown that where fully efficient arrangements are made for carrying on the studies of children in the upper standards, there are parents who are willing to keep their children at school to benefit by the teaching, and many of the scholars remain till they are 15 or 16 years of age. The efficiency of these schools has been proved by their success in preparing scholars for pupil-teacherships, in securing passes in the Junior Cambridge Examination, in gaining County Council and other Scholarships, and in being approved by the London County Council's Technical Board as suitable schools for the attendance of their junior scholars.

Five boys' departments have so developed as to be able to be constituted as to their upper boys into organised science schools. These are:—Montem Street, in the Finsbury Division; Blackheath Road and Bloomfield Road, in the Greenwich Division; Burghley Road, in the Marylebone Division; and Thomas Street, in the Tower Hamlets Division.

These science schools have attempted with a good measure of success the somewhat stringent course of scientific work, in all cases accompanied by experimental work, which has been laid down by the Science and Art Department, and, although the greater part of the work is devoted to science, a satisfactory literary course is followed as well as some manual occupation. One of these schools, Bloomfield Road, having 140 pupils in the science section of the school, secured last year a grant of £450 14s. for science, being at the rate of £3 4s. 5d. per boy, a strong proof of the thoroughness and success of the instruction imparted.

It will be seen from what has been stated that two problems as to higher standard work remain to be solved.

There is first awaiting complete solution the original problem of providing for separate classes, each with a separate teacher for all the different standards of work.

There is secondly, the problem of providing for all children of superior intelligence and industry, whose school life can be extended to the age of 15 or 16, opportunities of adequately profiting by their special advantages, and going through a course of studies extending beyond the limits of Standard VII.

We have seen how many difficulties lie in the way of securing the first object without introducing disadvantages that may outbalance the advantage secured.

In these cases there is no need to aim at an advanced curriculum, but provision should be made for separate classes up to Standard VII. This may be secured by uniting two ordinary schools lying close together; and combining their upper standards from both boys' and girls' departments, if these are separate departments. This union might begin with Standards V. or VI. according to circumstances. We should thus have four small groups in these upper standards united together to make one fair-sized class, for which a separate teacher could be afforded. This arrangement need not interfere necessarily with the organisation of the lower parts of the schools; but every effort should be made to unite the various departments into one organic whole, so as to secure a proper *esprit de corps*.

The second problem can only be solved by providing Higher Grade schools, so that all scholars, who from superior mental power and the longer duration of school life can cover a more liberal curriculum than the work of the seven standards which is suited to the average child.

Many of our existing schools can fitly provide such a course; but as has been already pointed out, they are only able to provide for the children coming up from the lower classes of their own school, whereas all children fit to take advantage of Higher Grade schools should have the opportunity of doing so.

This proves the necessity of building schools specially adapted for this purpose, and the London School Board has already fixed upon sites for four such schools, and it is hoped that as time goes on many more will follow.

Higher Grade schools have been evolved slowly out of the necessities of the case, and we have been gradually feeling our way to the best type of school for this purpose. They were not specifically recognised till the issue of the Minute of the Board of Education in Higher Elementary schools, to which reference has been made in an earlier chapter.[1] The Minute provides that they shall be separate schools, beginning with Standard V. and providing a four years' course of instruction. Special time-tables have to be prepared, and schemes of work covering the four years' course submitted to the Board of Education.

In preparing the schemes of work for the four years' course, it will be very important to bear in mind the relation that exists between the school curriculum on one hand and the duration of school life on the other. The highest class of schools, apart from the universities, provide a scheme suitable for those whose education will be prolonged till they are 19 or 20 years of age. Secondary schools provide for those who leave school about two years earlier, and Higher Grade elementary schools should supply a curriculum suited to those who will leave school at 15 or 16; but where the schools are separate and specially provided for Higher Grade scholars, and admitting only *picked* scholars of 11 or 12 years of age, they may fitly cover a broader area of studies than an ordinary school for children of that age.

It is important that every scholar should follow to the end the course of study of the kind of school he attends. A boy who went to a first-grade school, such as Rugby for example, and left at 14, would be worse educated than a boy who left an elementary school at that age. So a child leaving its own school at 11 or 12, and going to a Higher Grade school, but only staying a year or so there, had better have remained at its former school, where the scheme of work was more suited to its time at school. It would be well, therefore, to secure from the parents before admission a statement of their intention to keep their child at school till the end of its course.

Admission to these schools should be granted as a scholarship to the best scholars of the ordinary schools, and as each of these latter schools would supply but few scholars, their school life would not be seriously affected, and it would be regarded as an honour to the school when one of the scholars gained such a distinction.

At present there are 44 schools which are regarded as Higher Grade, and it will be seen from the table at the end of this chapter, which gives the numbers in the various standards taken from the last report of the School Management Committee, that there is

---

[1] *See Ante,* p. 163.

no difficulty in any of these schools in providing separate teachers for all standards up to and including Standard VII. In 37 departments 30 children or upwards are above Standard VII., and so can have a separate classification for an advanced course of work.

These schools develop their higher work in different directions, so as to suit the wants of the neighbourhood in which they are placed. The three chief directions in which this higher work runs may be classed as scientific, literary, and commercial. Each of these three branches has some recognition in every case, though the stress of work may, and does, vary considerably. In the literary direction some language besides English is taught in every Higher Grade school. French is generally chosen, though German and Latin are also taken in some cases.

It will be seen from the table that some schools, such as Mansford Street, have been organised so that the upper department contains no scholars below Standard V., and in this respect they satisfy the latest demand of the Board of Education. Steps are being taken to bring the other Higher Grade schools into line with this requirement, but undoubtedly the best form of Higher Grade school to meet future wants will be those specially built for the higher standards only, suitably placed amidst the ordinary schools. The principle of selection of the brightest scholars from all the elementary schools can in this way only be fully carried out.

		STANDARDS.								Percentage above St. IV.
		I.	II.	III.	IV.	V.	VI.	VII.	Ex-VII	
Chelsea—										
Ashburnham	B.	34	123	97	106	72	44	10	7	27
	G.	32	148	107	98	51	48	17	15	25
Beethoven-street ...	B.	...	68	66	63	66	52	21	35	47
	G.	...	67	72	71	68	68	20	39	48
Kilburn lane	B.	39	49	67	128	118	59	55	35	48
	G.	71	113	71	75	104	52	38	21	39
*Sherbrooke-road ...	B.	...	60	58	61	49	44	48	73	54
	G.	...	128	67	65	58	45	38	67	42
William-street ...	B.	...	144	74	65	46	65	37	25	38
	G.	...	71	100	73	66	113	41	39	51
Finsbury—										
Duncombe-road	B.	72	72	94	94	59	45	25	15	30
	G.	66	82	117	111	73	42	34	...	28
Hugh Myddelton ...	B.	60	126	130	134	70	64	77	20	34
	G.	80	140	131	119	100	58	26	4	29
Montem-street	B.	48	115	58	104	54	75	...	62	37
	G.	80	125	70	97	53	44	55	47	35
Oldfield-road	B.	69	73	106	67	69	58	39	37	39
	G.	92	71	112	65	67	53	27	52	37
Upper Hornsey	B.	61	102	68	60	74	31	23	...	30
	G.	39	84	87	65	58	51	35	...	34

* This department has at least half its scholars in the higher standards.

		I.	II.	III.	IV.	V.	VI.	VII.	Ex-VII.	Percentage above St. IV.
								STANDARDS.		
Greenwich—										
Ancona-road	B.	...	67	66	65	57	53	40	31	48
*	G.	...	...	100	70	68	57	51	41	56
*Blackheath-road ...	B.	...	72	67	50	51	49	36	63	51
	G.	21	63	61	67	60	48	42	38	47
*Bloomfield-road ...	B.	...	...	51	109	68	66	83	36	61
*	G.	...	...	50	112	103	68	60	57	64
*Mantle-road	B.	...	12	54	72	57	56	39	40	58
*	G.	...	...	65	71	51	46	36	22	53
Monson-road	B.	72	75	67	60	59	45	30	30	37
	G.	68	66	63	68	63	56	49	40	44
Hackney—										
*†Mansford-street ...	B.	...	...	...	...	86	53	31	28	100
*	G.	...	...	...	...	86	40	19	17	100
*†Millfields-road... ...	B.	...	...	..	...	63	39	30	30	100
*	G.	...	...	...	...	65	48	39	34	100
Napier-street	B.	60	71	75	103	54	35	21	4	27
	G.	71	110	70	66	54	49	26	2	29
Queen's-road	B.	71	71	73	68	51	44	27	15	33
	G.	60	79	120	68	55	42	20	19	29
St. John's-road	B.	77	76	137	69	47	35	32	23	28
	G.	41	97	126	73	61	49	27	15	31
Wilton-road	B.	20	63	132	102	111	38	43	6	39
	G.	19	100	49	119	53	58	69	41	43
East Lambeth—										
Bellenden-road	B.	27	47	67	66	62	55	39	19	46
	G.	...	70	70	62	58	48	41	28	47
Beresford-street	B.	...	64	72	57	61	51	17	24	47
	G.	...	92	67	90	65	44	24	3	35
Colls-road	B.	63	67	65	67	52	39	27	16	34
	G.	37	65	112	63	53	37	26	18	33
Goodrich-road	B.	23	138	72	67	63	50	103	35	48
	G.	76	76	136	138	59	48	37	23	38
Mina-road	B.	40	64	60	84	54	32	67	19	41
	G.	71	108	74	65	61	41	30	6	30
West Lambeth—										
*Crawford-street ...	B.	...	68	76	36	62	38	65	58	55
*	G.	...	74	69	35	66	29	65	75	57
*Hackford-road	B.	...	68	70	70	63	53	65	34	50
	G.	...	73	99	63	56	43	36	33	41
Haselrigge-road	B.	...	60	111	113	64	57	66	45	45
	G.	...	72	131	65	118	38	67	24	48

* These departments have at least half their scholars in the higher standards.

† These schools have all the standards (boys' and girls') *above* Standard IV. in a senior mixed department, and all the rest in a junior mixed department.

		I.	II.	III.	IV.	V.	VI.	VII.	Ex-VII.	Percentage above St. IV.
						STANDARDS.				
West Lambeth—cont.										
*Honeywell-road	B.	...	72	73	68	113	88	31	9	53
	G.	...	82	75	119	107	48	25	19	42
South Lambeth-road	B.	...	...	113	143	64	46	35	21	39
	G.	...	48	120	72	80	56	34	26	45
Surrey-lane	B.	63	116	62	66	113	50	...	20	37
	G.	...	136	132	68	111	52	17	11	36
Marylebone—										
*Burghley-road	B.	...	...	...	129	107	99	42	109	73
*‡	G.	..	...	...	...	182	138	71	73	100
*‡Fleet-road	B.	...	...	...	120	127	67	69	48	72
*	G.	...	...	...	75	128	102	65	65	83
*‡Medburn-street	B.	...	...	...	...	106	79	...	89	100
	G.	...	...	...	...	76	105	61	78	100
Southwark—										
Keeton's-road	B.	...	92	114	57	145	55	27	19	48
	G.	...	123	74	66	106	77	38	34	50
*Monnow-road	B.	56	117	70	114	63	55	39	23	33
	G.	69	96	116	106	78	60	33	19	33
Rotherhithe New-road	B.	57	67	71	64	52	21	40	18	34
	G.	70	74	64	71	58	41	34	10	34
West square	B.	...	72	101	66	111	54	35	17	48
	G.	...	118	106	70	59	60	30	22	37
Tower Hamlets—										
Glengall-road	B.	73	80	83	74	88	79	33	3	40
	G.	...	110	67	98	92	40	31	20	40
Malmesbury-road	B.	...	68	62	102	52	44	25	...	34
	G.	...	...	140	71	108	38	27	...	45
Portman-place	B.	...	...	103	116	56	59	38	5	42
	G.	...	...	110	124	123	48	17	12	46
*Rutland-street	B.	...	...	53	55	48	40	67	16	61
*	G.	...	...	20	49	97	43	69	21	77
Thomas-street	B.	68	94	109	61	54	97	...	71	40
*	G.	63	89	86	112	96	87	105	57	50

* These departments have at least half their scholars in the higher standards.

‡ In Burghley-road girls' the standards above IV. are in an upper girls' department, and the other standards in a lower girls' department. In Fleet-road all above Standard III. are in a senior mixed department, and the other standards in a junior mixed department. In Medburn-street all above Standard IV. are in a senior mixed department, and the other standards in a junior mixed department.

CHAPTER V.

THE TRAINING OF TEACHERS.

(i.) THE PUPIL TEACHERS' SCHOOL.

By J. NICKAL, *Inspector to the London School Board.*

The education of young persons who desire to become teachers in elementary schools has received special attention from the School Board for London, and the improvements which is has effected on the system formerly general have been very widely adopted by other educational bodies.　Such young persons are designated " pupil teachers " from the fact that, although engaged in the actual duty of teaching children, they are themselves pupils, both as regards their general education and their technical training.[1]　Beginning formerly at the age of 13, usually at the close of a course in the elementary school, such boys and girls were apprenticed for five years.　They were expected to teach five or six hours per day for five days in the week ; they had a right to instruction from the head teacher of their school for, on the average, an hour a day; and they were obliged, in preparation for their daily lessons and with a view to an examination at the end of the year, to study privately in the evening.[2]　The objections to these arrangements are apparent.　Much could be said both against the practice of entrusting in any degree the education of children to teachers necessarily so immature, and much also against the overpressure which must ensue where study is to be taken up at the end of a hard day's work.　The quality of the instruction given by the head teacher to the pupil teachers necessarily varied according to his ability and the amount of interest taken in the task. When it was satisfactory as to quantity it was rarely of uniform merit, as the same head teacher could, indeed, scarcely be expected to teach all the subjects of the pupil teachers' curriculum in the very best manner.　In addition to multiplicity of subjects, he had also the difficulty of dealing simultaneously with several students in various stages of their career.　The defenders of the system sought support in its economy, and in the fact that it did produce large numbers of teachers, skilful in the manipulation of large classes, and of considerable ability in imparting that species of elementary knowledge which can be gauged by a direct test in reading, writing, and arithmetic.

The London School Board at first adopted the method of training pupil teachers which was universal in the country.　But in 1881 the experiment was made of collecting them for the purpose of instruction into central classes.　These centres were spread over London in such fashion as to be most readily accessible to the pupil teachers at work in the schools surrounding them.　The instruction was given in the evening and on Saturday morning, and the pupil teachers were still required to teach all day in the schools.　The chief advantages gained by the new plan were that each subject of the

---

[1] " A pupil teacher is a boy or girl engaged by the managers of a public elementary day school on condition of teaching during school hours under the superintendence of the principal teacher, and receiving suitable instruction."—The Day School Code, 1900.

[2] See *ante*, p. 87.

curriculum could now be taught by teachers more specially conversant with it, and that pupils of the same standing could be grouped together. Their technical training as teachers was still entrusted to the heads of the schools to which they were attached as members of the staff.

This first change in the pupil teacher system was good so far as it went, but it was still felt that too great a strain was put on the powers and energies of the students. The undesirability of taking them from home in the evening, and the difficulty of securing sufficient time for private study, were further objections. In 1885 a considerable measure of relief, together with a provision for better opportunities of study, was given to the pupil teachers by new arrangements of the School Board. It was then determined that they should be taught in the daytime, and that the amount of actual teaching work which they were expected to perform in the schools should be diminished. In order to carry out these purposes the pupil teachers were distributed into two sections, a junior and a senior division; the former being withdrawn from the schools for the purposes of instruction during five half days weekly, and the latter during three and four half days in alternate weeks. Suggestions were still made that the evening private study of the students might by its amount become detrimental to health, and the rule was finally laid down that it should on the average not exceed three hours on any evening, or twelve hours in the week.

The evening classes had been held in ordinary schools, but appropriate buildings were now gradually erected for the instruction of pupil teachers only. These were provided with suitable classrooms, with halls for assembly and examination purposes, and with science laboratories and art rooms. The teaching staff of the new institutions was now entirely and solely occupied in the work of educating the pupil teachers, instead of, as in the old evening classes, being chosen for the most part from the body of teachers at work in the ordinary schools in the daytime. It became thus possible to secure a staff more highly qualified in general, and specialised in certain directions, as for instance, in language, in art, and in science. But the removal of the pupil teachers on certain half-days from the classes of children to which they were attached as actual teachers might seem to introduce a difficulty in the organisation of the ordinary schools. This was obviated by appointing the pupil teachers in pairs, a senior with a junior, and arranging that the latter should be present at school when the former should be at the central classes for instruction.

Yet another step further to lessen the strain of work and study was taken in 1896, when it was determined that in addition to the half holiday on Saturday afternoon, the pupil teachers should be released from school on one other half day in each week. And a final improvement in this respect was effected in 1898 when the seniors as well as the juniors became teachers for half their time only. It is only necessary to mention further in connection with this subject that a probationary period to the whole course, which amounts generally to a year, was formerly spent half at the schools, and half at the central classes; but is now passed, with the exception of a few weeks at the beginning, entirely at the latter.

Though it cannot be claimed that the earliest part of the training of elementary teachers, called pupil teachership, is even now quite satisfactory, yet the steps which have been detailed have been decidedly in the direction of improvement, and the credit of leading the way belongs to the London School Board.

To carry out this training the Board has, as aforesaid, erected ten special schools. Not all the centres are, however, housed in this way; two are yet in temporary premises. Steps are being taken to provide for the latter.

The buildings are not on a uniform plan, but, providing, as they do in essential matters, similar accommodation, a description of the Hackney Pupil Teacher Centre may be given as a specimen. This is built over lower storeys occupied by an ordinary school, and consists of two floors, comprising a hall (for assembly, examination purposes, social gatherings, &c.), five classrooms, with accommodation, if necessary, for 50 students each, a needlework room, two art rooms, a chemical laboratory, and three teachers' rooms.[1] One classroom is provided with a demonstration table.

The centre is attended by 241 pupil teachers and students in the probationary stage, distributed as follows :—

				Boys.			Girls.
Probationers	...	...	...	4	...	...	26
Candidates	...	...	...	8	...	...	40
First year	...	...	...	7	...	...	52
Second year	...	...	...	11	...	...	49
Third year	...	...	...	7	...	...	37

The students of the same standing form more than one class, sub-divisions being made according to ability and progress. The average number taught together is about thirty, though smaller classes occur for some subjects—*e.g.*, mathematics, in which the boys have a separate course.

The teaching staff comprises a head teacher, eight assistant teachers (two of whom are women), and three visiting teachers. Two of the latter are art teachers, and the third conducts the physical exercises of the girl students.

The pupil teachers and probationers attending this centre come from schools situated in North-East London, chiefly in the Hackney Division, but also from a few in the Finsbury and Tower Hamlets Divisions. The centre has been so placed as to be easily accessible by omnibus, tramcar, and rail, and many of the students are able to walk from their schools and homes. The students from a few schools in the suburbs which are at long distances from the nearest centres are allowed travelling expenses. The choice of centre is left in the first instance to the probationers or their parents, to be decided according to convenience; but, being made, no change is permitted without leave.

There are twelve such centres throughout the whole of London, one attended by girl students only, the rest being mixed. The total number of students is 2,887 (456 boys,

---

[1] A physical laboratory, a gymnasium, and a   are desiderata. The first two exist at some centres. dining-room for those unable to go home at noon,

2,431 girls). The nett cost per head calculated on the average attendance for the year ending March 25th, 1899, was £4 3s. 7¾d. The yearly salary of the head teachers is £350-£400 (men), and £260-£300 (women); of assistant teachers £150-£200 (men), and £130-£165 (women). Books are for the most part bought by the students, but are sold to them through the agency of the Board at cost price. Stationery is chiefly provided by the Board. Each centre has a reference library and a museum, the latter chiefly illustrative of natural history. In addition to the fittings of the chemical laboratory. such apparatus as is necessary for the teaching of physical science is supplied.

The students are largely drawn from the elementary schools, and are of the social status so implied. It is the duty of the local managers of the schools (since with them rests the right of nominating pupil teachers to the Board for appointment) to ascertain by inquiry or otherwise that they are from suitable homes, their circumstances being such as to guarantee that they will be able to devote proper attention to their studies, and to proceed at the proper time to the training college. An increasing number of pupil teachers have, however, had the advantage of education in secondary schools, either as children of parents who are able to pay for such education, or as holders of scholarships from elementary schools. They are allowed, under certain conditions, to enter the work at a more advanced age, and to complete their apprenticeship in a shorter period. The introduction of such students is an advantage, as there has been some danger of making the training of teachers too narrow and the type too uniform. This is guarded against also by the regulation that the principal teacher shall be a person of university qualification, and that the staff shall include one or more persons who have had some training or experience in places of secondary education.[1]

In ordinary cases the Board prescribes the passing of an entrance examination for probationers. They are examined in arithmetic (the ordinary rules and processes, including practice, proportion, vulgar and decimal fractions, averages, percentages, and stock), English grammar and composition, handwriting, outline of the geography of the world, outlines of English history. A paper to test general intelligence is set, and girls are required to take an examination in needlework. In addition each applicant may be examined in one of the following subjects at choice :—Latin, French, German, algebra, mechanics, physics, animal physiology, botany, or domestic economy. They are also required to read with fluency, ease, and just expression. A limit of marks is fixed, failure to obtain which involves rejection.

Boys and girls who have obtained a defined measure of success at the County Council examinations for scholarships may be excused the entrance examination; those who have passed certain local examinations of the Universities of Oxford and Cambridge are eligible for a shortened engagement.

Having passed the entrance examination (or its equivalent), and being certified medically as fit, the applicants are eligible to be selected by the local managers of schools that have vacancies for probationers. They are chosen after conferring with the

---

[1] Revised Instructions issued to H.M. Inspectors, 1900, p. 42.

head teacher, and it is the duty of the managers to depute one of their number to visit the homes of the probationers to see whether the surroundings are in every way likely to conduce to their physical and moral well-being.

At the end of their probationary year the students may be presented for approval to H.M. Inspectors, and become known as candidates. Only at the close of another year, and after successfully passing an examination, are they recognised as pupil teachers and apprenticed.

During their engagement they receive pay as follows :—

	Boys, per week.		Girls, per week.
Probationers	nil.	... ...	nil.
Candidates	5s.	... ...	3s.
1st year pupil teachers ...	5s.	... ...	3s.
2nd year pupil teachers ...	12s.	... ...	8s.
3rd year pupil teachers ...	14s.	... ...	8s.

The commencement of the first year and the close of each year of pupil teachership is marked by an examination; that for the last year [1] being preliminary to entrance into a training college or to recognition as an assistant teacher. The examinations are held by H.M. Inspector, and are on lines laid down by the Government Code. They comprise English (grammar, composition, reading, and recitation), English history, geography, arithmetic, euclid and algebra, elementary science (physiography), music (theoretical and practical), teaching, drawing, needlework (for girls), and Latin or French.

Some of these subjects are left optional by the Code, but are all taken up in the Board's central schools, where the best students are further encouraged to prepare themselves for the Matriculation Examination of the London University with a considerable degree of success. In science and art also the centre teaching has not been limited by the bare requirements of the Government syllabus.

As, however, the final examination for pupil teachers is that for admission into training colleges, it necessarily determines in great measure the curriculum of the central schools. A sketch of the requirements for the present year is therefore given. The students are expected to read with precision, ease, and just expression from one of Scott's novels, or from Macaulay's " Essay on Frederick the Great "; to repeat from memory 100 lines of Shakespeare or Milton with clearness and force, and show knowledge of meanings and allusions; to write legibly, and to set copies in large and small hand. In Theory of Teaching they are to be acquainted with the method of drawing up notes of lessons, and with the methods of teaching any subject taught in elementary schools (Infants' School Method and Discipline are also included for those engaged in such schools). In practical teaching they are to be able to give a lesson on any subject taught in elementary schools, and to answer questions as to the mode of giving any such lessons. Their knowledge of geography must comprise the outlines of the geography of the world, with special

---

[1] Commonly called the Queen's Scholarship Examination.

reference to India and to the chief British Colonies and dependencies; and candidates are advised to practise the drawing of sketch maps. The outlines of English history, from the Norman Conquest to 1870, are required, and special reference is made to the expansion of the British Empire from 1558 to 1858. Candidates must be prepared to write a short essay on a given subject, and their knowledge of English language and literature must extend to parsing and analysis of sentences, elementary etymology, and a general outline of the history of the English language; they must also have specially studied, and have a general knowledge of the style and subject of Pope's " Essay on Man," Epistle IV., or Shakespeare's " Julius Cæsar." In arithmetic the principles and practice are to be studied, including the measurements of rectangular areas and solids; women have alternative questions in algebra, not extending beyond simple equations of one unknown, with problems leading thereto; men are to take algebra to quadratic equations of one unknown, with problems; ratio, proportion, variation, arithmetical progression; and Euclid, Books I. and II., with simple geometrical exercises. Elementary science must include elementary physics, chemistry, and astronomy; candidates being expected to have an experimental knowledge of chemistry and physics, and to be trained to notice and record the positions of the various heavenly bodies. Six foreign languages are named in the Code for two of which, but not more than two, credit may be obtained. The pupil teachers of the Board usually take Latin and French. The examination papers on these contain passages for translation into English from Pliny's Letters, Book I. 1 to 12, and Coppée's " Le Trésor"; also grammatical questions, easy passages for translation from English into Latin and French, and easy pieces for translation into English from books not prescribed. Candidates are also tested in drawing (freehand and geometrical) and in music (theoretical and practical). Women candidates have a further examination in domestic economy and needlework, the former comprising a knowledge of food, its functions and preparations, clothing and washing, hygiene of the dwelling, rules for preserving health, the management of the sick room, and thrift. Finally, credit may be obtained for marks received at an examination for certificates granted by certain of the universities after an attendance at not less than twenty-four lectures in language, geography, or history. The Board has arranged and paid for several courses of lectures of this kind on behalf of its students, given by university lecturers.

The curriculum thus sketched varies in part from year to year, chiefly in respect of the books prescribed for reading and the Latin and French authors chosen. It will be seen that, taken as a whole, it is sufficient very fully to occupy the time of the students during apprenticeship. Their progress in each subject is recorded quarter by quarter in journals, of which each student has one. The same book contains a record of the practice and criticism lessons which they give at the schools, with the head teacher's remarks. A general report is also entered each quarter, summarising their progress in their studies and in teaching, and recording the character of their conduct, regularity, and attention to duty. This book is laid before the local managers at each of their meetings, and serves, if occasion may arise, as a full account of the pupil teacher's career.

In addition to this continuous record the yearly examinations held by H.M. Inspectors, which have been mentioned above, serve as a test of the student's progress. In the Instructions to Inspectors, the following directions indicate the method and spirit in which the officers of the Board of Education are to test and supervise the training of these young people :—

"Pupil teachers are required to perform exercises in reading and recitation, and to give evidence of their practical skill in teaching. The collective examinations include papers in the compulsory subjects of English language (including grammar and composition), geography, history, arithmetic, euclid and algebra for boys, and needlework for girls, and in the optional subjects of physiography and theory of music. A foreign language may be taken as an optional subject. No papers will be set in foreign languages, but you should encourage their study where circumstances allow, and test the efficiency of the instruction when given, by hearing lessons in central classes, and by examining the pupil teachers' exercises and note-books.

"Penmanship, spelling, and method of teaching are no longer treated as separate subjects, not because they are unimportant, but because proficiency in them may be ascertained by a better method. Accordingly, you will require pupil teachers to set copies on the blackboard at your visits to the schools, and you should insist on a plain, legible, and not too ornate style of handwriting in their examination papers and exercise books. Spelling is a matter of habit and care, and you should expect correct spelling throughout the work and not merely in dictation exercises. Questions on the theory of teaching are somewhat premature for such young persons, but the papers set on other subjects will be framed with a view of ascertaining whether the pupil teacher has that clear grasp of principles and method which is a condition of good teaching.

"You should endeavour to ascertain how far the pupil teacher's course, considered as an apprenticeship in the art of teaching, has served its purpose. With this view, you will generally hear the pupil teachers teach and question their classes on the days of inspection. In the third year the pupil teacher should prepare at regular intervals, and enter in a book, the notes of lessons, of which you will select one in order that it may be given in your presence. You should also point out the usefulness of criticism lessons or model lessons given in the presence of the pupil teachers. If by the end of the second year the pupil teacher proves to be seriously deficient, either in the habit of application or in aptitude for teaching, a special report should be made on the case, as it is most undesirable to encourage apprentices to remain in a calling for which they are not fitted. Managers and teachers should pay increased attention to the pupil teachers during the last year of their engagement, and obtain for them, whenever possible, special assistance in connection with any subjects in which the examinations of the previous years have shown them to be deficient. The practice of gathering the pupil teachers together, not only for the purpose of hearing their reading and recitation, but also in order to go over their papers with them, and to point out their merits and defects, may usefully be adopted whenever circumstances allow."

The results of the Queen's Scholarship Examination, which closes the pupil teacher's career, allow a comparison to be made between the students trained in the schools of the London Board and those of the rest of England. This is exhibited in the following table, which gives the results for the current year :—

	MEN.				WOMEN.	
Passed in	All England, excluding London Board.	Students from London Board Schools.			All England, excluding London Board.	Students from London Board Schools.
1st Class	463=16·5 p.c.	67=67 p.c.	...	...	1748=19·8 p.c.	319=82·9 p.c.
2nd Class	870=31 „	28=28 „	...	...	2854=32·4 „	60=15·6 „
3rd Class	1123=40·1 „	5= 5 „	...	...	2576=29·2 „	6= 1·5 „
Failed ...	358=12·4 „	0= 0 „	...	...	1645=18·6 „	0= 0 „
	2804	100	...	...	8823	385

The list of successful candidates is published in the order of merit. Of the first hundred names, thirty-nine are those of students from the Board schools.

In conclusion, it must be mentioned that the London Pupil Teachers' Association was founded some years ago, under distinguished patronage, for the promotion of the physical training and intellectual culture of the members. This association has two divisions, for the boys and girls respectively. Athletic fêtes, swimming tournaments, lawn tennis tournaments, are held periodically. Debating societies, reading clubs, chess clubs, &c., have been organised. Visits to places of historical interest, to picture galleries, studios, &c., are arranged. Picnics, country excursions, visits to the universities, take place from time to time. Each centre has it own cricket, football, lawn tennis, and swimming clubs. Each has also its own select choir for musical practice, and very successful concerts are given in the winter. Social gatherings are occasionally held for the students and their friends. *Esprit de corps* is promoted by the formation of old students' clubs, and distinguished honours achieved by members of the centres are recorded on "honour boards" displayed in the halls.

The general direction and control of the pupil teachers is vested in the School Management Committee of the Board, and the details are regulated by the Sub-Committee on Pupil Teachers.

(ii.) TRAINING CLASSES FOR TEACHERS.

By W. T. GOODE, M.A., *Organising Superintendent of Instruction of Ex-Pupil Teachers.*

One of the most recent developments of the Board's work is the institution of classes for the purpose of training teachers for the Government certificate. For some time a difficulty has been experienced by those who wish to enter the ranks of the teaching profession, in obtaining an adequate training in the principles and practice of teaching.

The number of places vacant each year in the residential training colleges is much smaller than the number of candidates wishing to enter, and although, since 1889, training classes for externs have been attached to the University Colleges of the country, there still remains every year a considerable number of would-be teachers for whom no opportunity is afforded of being trained.

In their case the usual practice has been to enter a primary school as an assistant teacher, and after a year's experience, to present themselves for the first certificate examination; following this after another year's interval with the second or final examination for the Teacher's Certificate.

These intervals, of one year each, are the irreducible minimum laid down by the Board of Education, but as may be easily imagined, the double strain of teaching and study causes the majority of these teachers to make the intervals much longer.

In 1898, the London School Board determined to do something towards providing the opportunities of training for some at least of the teachers of London, to whom otherwise they would be entirely lacking.

A special scheme was drawn up under which this, the first experiment of the kind made by a School Board, has been carried out.

The teachers selected are required to produce evidence of having passed the Queen's Scholarship Examination, or an equivalent, just as if they were entering a training college; and after favourable report by the Board's medical officer, and approval by the Board of their general ability as teachers and students, they are appointed as assistant teachers in the Board's schools. Here they are held responsible for only small classes of thirty in average attendance. The week is equally divided between teaching and study—two days and a half being spent in school, and a similar time in classes where these student-teachers are prepared for the examinations for the Teacher's Certificate.

Rooms have been specially prepared in one of the schools in the centre of London, and a special staff of teachers appointed, the whole of the arrangements being under the care of the superintendent.

Formal instruction in the subjects of the examinations is given, but care is taken to make the courses as much a practical training as possible.

Thus, every week, two of the students are chosen to prepare and give lessons before the other students and the superintendent, the lessons being followed by criticism. An ordinary day school, which is held in the same building in which the students' classes are taught, affords ample opportunities of practising in this way.

In addition to this, the students are specially placed under the care of the head teachers of their respective schools, to be watched and directed. Work of a special kind is arranged for them where possible, and they are under the constant supervision of the superintendent, receiving advice and criticism on their work and the methods they adopt.

In this way it is hoped to give many of the advantages of a college course, with a much greater amount of practical experience than any training college course will allow.

The length of the course is ordinarily three years; but any unusually able students may be permitted to complete the examination course in two years, on special recommendation by the superintendent of the classes.

During the whole of the time that teachers remain as students in these classes they are paid a salary of £30 per annum if women, and £35 per annum if men, besides receiving free instruction in all the subjects necessary for the Governmental examinations for the Teacher's Certificate.

Although the scheme has not yet passed beyond the experimental stage, sixty students are receiving this training at the hands of the Board. A small number have already passed the examination at the end of the first year, but the month of July of this year (1900) will see the first really crucial test of the success of this new departure in the work of the Board, for then more than half of this number of students will present themselves for examination.

CHAPTER VI.

SPECIAL SUBJECTS OF INSTRUCTION.

(i.) SCIENCE.

By W. H. GRIEVE, *Science Demonstrator.*

In writing upon instruction in the above subject, one naturally asks the question, whence is its origin and what changes has it undergone since its first inception? To answer this question it is necessary to go back to December 18th, 1884, when the London School Board passed the following resolution: "That the peripatetic plan of teaching mechanics be tried in some district or districts of London." To give effect to this resolution a small committee was appointed. A word of explanation is necessary as to what is meant by the teaching of Mechanics. In drawing up a series of science courses that might be taught experimentally to children, it was thought by the Education Department that Matter and its properties, the various forces acting upon Matter, and the recognised mechanical contrivances invented by man for saving time and labour, generally known as the mechanical powers, should comprise a course extending over a period of three years, and should be known by the name of "Mechanics." Accordingly, on this plan, teaching was commenced on June 1st, 1885, in twenty schools of the Hackney and Tower Hamlets Divisions.

Since then, subjects, other than Mechanics, have been introduced, and science in all its branches has been continually added, until in every school under the London School Board, in some form or another, it forms a part of the regular curriculum.

The science taught at the present time may be conveniently classified under one or other of three different headings.

First.—The work done in the Schools of Science, which are four in number.

At Blackheath Road, Greenwich (School of Science), 25,957 attendances, of an hour's duration each, were recorded last year in science, of which 2,469 attendances were made by girls in studying hygiene and physiology.

P

At Bloomfield-road, Plumstead (School of Science), 39,292 attendances were made, of which 7,787 were by girls.

At Medburn-street, St. Pancras (School of Science), 32,154 attendances were registered, with 146 names on the roll.

At Thomas-street, Limehouse (School of Science), 18,536 attendances were recorded, with 167 on the roll.

The payments for attendances in these day science classes, by the Science and Art Department, vary from 1d. to 3d. per lesson of one hour's duration for an elementary stage of a science subject, and from 2d. to 8d. per hour for an advanced stage. When practical work is done in a laboratory reported upon as properly equipped, 1½d. to 4½d. for each attendance of one and a-half hours' duration is given for the elementary stage, and 3d. to 8d. for the advanced stage.

Secondly.—The work performed in the science classes, registered by the Science and Art Department. Apart from the four Schools of Science, there are working in connection with the Science and Art Department no less than forty-five schools, which are distributed among the nine divisions of London as follows :—Chelsea has 6 schools ; Finsbury, 4 schools ; Greenwich, 4 schools ; Hackney, 4 schools ; East Lambeth, 8 schools ; West Lambeth, 9 schools ; Marylebone, 3 schools ; Southwark, 4 schools ; and the Tower Hamlets, 3 schools.

The total number of hours bestowed during the year in giving instruction in science to these classes, amounted to the grand total of 295,250. The subjects taken vary in popularity, if we may judge from the number of schools taking them. Thus, chemistry claimed the attention of 23 schools ; mathematics, 22 schools ; hygiene, 15 schools ; magnetism, 11 schools ; physiology, 10 schools ; botany, 9 schools ; physiography, 8 schools ; and sound, light, and heat, 2 schools.

In making a summary of the whole work done in the forty-five schools, we find that 5,058 presentations were made in the elementary stages of the various sciences, and 498 in the advanced stages. The number of individual students on the Science and Art Register, and not on the Register of the Education Department, was 2,941, whilst the number of individual students presented for examination was 1,881. Many of the scholars in these classes and from other schools entered their names as candidates for scholarships which had been placed at the disposal of the Board. Of that number, 21 boys selected physiology as their science subject, 6 preferred elementary science, 22 took mechanics, and 12 sat in chemistry for the intermediate examination. The girls, however, preferred to take domestic economy in 54 cases, physiology in 17 cases, and botany in 3, for their science subjects.

Thirdly.—The taking of science, under Schedule IV. of the Education Code, as a specific subject, or, under Schedule II., as a class subject. In the former case the total number of children examined was 51,626 ; in the latter it amounted to 56,083.

Until very recently little attention has been paid to the teaching of science experimentally in the girls' departments of our schools. To render the subject as interesting as possible, it was proposed as an experiment that lectures on domestic economy, or some kindred subject, should be delivered in some of the girls' schools; and from a circular sent out it was found that 250 head mistresses were desirous of having such a course delivered. In these lectures experiments were shown with the air-pump, the barometer, the balloon, upon the making of oxygen and hydrogen gases, upon the theory of combustion, on ventilation, &c., &c. These lectures having proved a success, it has naturally secured that more time and attention should be paid to science.

The most important epoch in the development of science teaching must now be described. Upon this it is desirable to speak more fully, as it relates to science *as now taught* in the schools. For many years it had been a subject of frequent discussion and inquiry at the meetings of the British Association, how far the science teaching, as carried on in the elementary schools of the country, was productive of lasting good to the children. It was contended by some that too much was being done for the child, that the effect of a mere demonstration lesson in science, however interesting and showy, soon passed away, and in some cases left but a dim outline of the phenomenon it was intended to explain. Why not put the child in the position of an investigator and let him try to find out for himself some truth by direct experiment? Such were the proposals which led the British Association in 1887, when holding their meeting at York, to appoint a Committee for the purpose of reporting upon the various methods of instruction adopted in elementary schools. Upon that Committee the London School Board was represented. In the following year reports were presented to the Association, in which were included suggestions for the carrying out of a course of elementary instruction in physical science, upon what is known as the "Heuristic" method. Briefly summed up, this method may be described as—

1. The teaching of scientific methods as a value to intellectual training.
2. To make the scholars think for themselves, and thus to form habits of exactness.
3. To enable the scholars to acquire information direct from their own experiments.

This, then, is the problem which the Board has set itself to solve; to see how far such a method of instruction in science is possible to be carried out. Notwithstanding numerous obstacles which have beset its pathway, a fair measure of success has attended the experiment. In the year ending Lady Day, 1894, the number of registered scholars in "practical science" was 45; whereas in 1899, at the same period, the number was 1,039. It has always been felt that to carry on this kind of work successfully, the teachers of the schools should have some previous training, and that rooms should be set apart from ordinary school purposes for the children to work in. The Board has recognised this by the sanction which it has given to the establishment of pedagogical science classes for teachers, and also by approving the plans for the adaptation of certain rooms in some of the schools for the purpose of the work.

This science teaching, which is being gradually introduced into the schools, both in the boys' and girls' departments, is known by the name of "Experimental Science." Huxley, when addressing a large audience at Manchester, is reported to have said: "That the education which precedes that of the workshop should be devoted to the cultivation of the intelligence, and especially to the imbuing of the mind with a broad and clear view of the laws of that natural world with the components of which the handicraftsman will have to deal."

By way of beginning, measurements are performed by the children—viz., linear, superficial and cubical, preferably in the metric system, using very simple objects that fall within the reach of most children. It must be admitted that those who enjoy such advantages would afterwards enter upon practical life with a distinct and ineffaceable experience of scientific methods. They would observe, measure, and reason in a different way for the future.

Next they are taught the use of the balance and the art of weighing correctly. A splendid course of exercises can here be introduced, dealing with the relative densities of solids and liquids. For girls this knowledge is useful when testing the purity of many liquids used in the household, and for boys in the detection of the alloying of metals. The course proceeds to deal with the general effects of heat upon matter. The girl here obtains, from very simple experiments, a correct idea of the principles of ventilation, the construction and use of clinical and household thermometers; and the boy can learn at what period of the frost his father's water-pipe bursts.

The girls then study the difference between conduction, convection, and radiation of heat. From a simple experiment, which they themselves perform, they can tell you why a cotton fabric is to be preferred to a woollen one in the summer; why the water in the boiler behind the kitchener rises to the cistern in the bath room; or whether water boils more quickly in a kettle covered with soot than in one new and polished. The boy can explain why ice is packed in flannel or felt in summer, and why it is necessary, when descending into mines, that the safety-lamp should be surrounded by a gauze of close mesh.

Boys and girls are then encouraged to take up the questions of evaporation, of distillation, and of filtration, as a means whereby liquids may be separated from any impurities which they contain. Where possible, daily readings are taken of the weight of a bag of sea-weed, previously moistened with water, so as to ascertain the loss in weight by evaporation. Opportunities are afforded of explaining such instruments as the hygrometer, and its use in preparing weather charts. The girls, at the same time, can be taught to observe the most favourable condition of the atmosphere as regards moisture, for drying and airing clothes. They are next instructed in the question of the composition and weight of the air, bringing in the use of the barometer as a means for measuring the heights of mountains, for observing the distance of a balloon from the earth, and likewise in foretelling the weather for the next twenty-four hours.

Latent heat and specific heat are then touched upon. In the former case, we have a good practical example in the machine for making ice-creams; and, in the latter, of the railway foot-warmer, which is filled with hot-water, owing to the high specific heat of water. The children are shown that the latent heat of ice is very great as compared with that of other substances, which is a matter of the greatest importance. If snow and ice were immediately converted into water at 0°C, with little or no absorption of heat, the sudden melting of the snow on the hills and mountains would expose the inhabitants of the villages below them to the most terrible floods and inundations.

Tyndall, in his popular work upon " Heat as a Mode of Motion," says that the vast influence which the ocean must exert as a moderator of climate here suggests itself. The heat of summer is stored up in the ocean, and s'owly given out during the winter. This is one cause of the absence of extremes in an island climate. Simple experiments upon these two points are set the children to work. As an example of latent heat, some small pieces of ice are placed in a beaker of water and well stirred up with a thermometer, whilst the beaker is gently heated. They are asked to describe fully the changes of temperature that occur both before and after the ice has melted. For specific heat, they are given cylinders of lead, iron, and copper of the same weight. These cylinders are suspended by threads in boiling water for a certain time and afterwards transferred to three separate vessels, containing water of the same weight and temperature. The children thus learn which metal has raised the temperature of the water the most; from which result the fact is patent that whilst the metals were subjected to the same heating process, one had a greater capacity for storing away heat than the other two; and when a suitable opportunity presented itself, it raised the temperature of the water to the greatest extent.

Water is next dealt with, its sources, its uses, and its composition. The difference between hard and soft water: the action of its hardness on soap: the measurement of the hardness of water. Many are the experiments which can be set to children upon the subject of water: to mention one only, upon its analysis, where a gentle current of steam is allowed to pass over iron filings, which are being heated in an iron tube. The gas evolved is collected and tested to show its identity with hydrogen; at the same time, the iron filings are weighed before and after heating, to show increase in weight.

The burning of animal, vegetable, and mineral substances in air, the rusting of metals, the preparation and examination of the active part of air, are also dealt with. The action of acids upon metals, and the study of the gases evolved also claim attention. A brief research on chalk, the properties of chalk and lime, a comparative study of the action of acids upon chalk, lime, and marble, bring the course to a close.

(ii.) Drawing.

By A. W. F. Langman, *Drawing Instructor.*

The growth of drawing in the schools of the London School Board has been gradual but at the same time progressive.

In the early days of the Board the drawing taught in the schools, consisted of three branches—viz., freehand, geometry, and model—and these were examined by the Science and Art Department in the month of March; the examination throughout the whole of London taking place on the same day.

In some of the schools the older scholars, those in Standards VI. and VII., were taught model drawing, whilst those in Standards IV. and V. were taught geometry, and the remainder of the children, Standards I., II., and III., freehand.

The results at the beginning were somewhat poor, principally because the teachers had very large classes and a very limited choice of a graduated set of freehand copies to work from. In other schools freehand was the only drawing attempted. This was absolutely wrong, as model drawing is more important, more useful, and at the same time if properly applied would lead to the children taking a deeper interest in the subject.

A stimulus was given to the drawing under the Board some fifteen years ago by the Science and Art Department issuing a new graduated syllabus, and making drawing compulsory in all boys' schools. It was examined by an Inspector from the Science and Art Department, South Kensington, by means of annual examinations, taking place the month previous to the ending of the school year. In the two lowest standards, I. and II., the awards were made by the visiting Inspector. The other standards worked papers in his presence, which were sent to South Kensington and assessed there.

The syllabus upon which the work of Standards I. and II. was based consisted of figures made up of straight lines and drawn by means of rulers. Occasionally set-squares were used. These forms were reproduced by freehand, and a few questions upon the definitions of lines and figures were asked by the Inspector. In the next standard, III., curved figures were introduced as freehand examples. The ruler work consisted of enlarging combinations of squares, rectangles, and frets, printed on cards. In Standard IV. scale drawing began. The children were taught to draw on squared paper, or from examples to be worked on plain paper, usually to a scale of one inch to a foot. A few questions were also set upon the drawing of scales. The construction, however, was seldom thoroughly explained, and compasses and set-squares very rarely used. The freehand tests were more complicated than in Standard III., more difficult, and not interesting. In the next three standards, V., VI., and VII., one-third of the time allotted to drawing was supposed to be devoted to model drawing, an admirable subject for training observation. Unfortunately, on account of the excessive amount of finish expected, only a few models were practised instead of a number of common objects based on these models.

Freehand in the upper standards consisted of examples more difficult and varied in type. Much of the work turned out was neat, wiry and stiff. Plane geometry formed part of the curriculum in Standard V., and compasses were unfortunately used for the first time in mechanical drawing. This subject was not taken in girls' schools above Standard V. In boys' departments solid geometry was taken in Standards VI. and VII. In Standard VII. shading from casts or models was occasionally taken.

The weak points were inaccurate scale drawing, and rulers used in the place of set-squares; stiff freehand lacking in growth and tangential curvature; poor methods of drawing models and wrong application of parallel perspective.

Again slight alterations were introduced into the Government Code, and an alternative syllabus was added for those schools who might like to make a rapid forward movement. The alternative syllabus depended too much upon specialists being attached to the staff of every school, or else the work in some of its sections was apt to become loose and lacking disciplinary training.

Several arrangements of this type of syllabus have been made, and an excellent one, introduced by one of the two Drawing Instructors, has many points of improvement in it. It is, however, necessary that there should be a more elementary syllabus, showing an advance on the present Code, especially in the lower standards.

As there are a larger number of elementary teachers who have gone beyond the requirements for the "D," or the ordinary school teacher's certificate, there is some chance of a general forward movement in drawing and its teaching in the ordinary schools. The introduction of elementary botany and science into the curriculum of the schools has also given an impulse to drawing for its general educational value in assisting word descriptions of form and apparatus.

The technical training which most children require has led the Education Department to slightly modify the geometrical and ruler drawing syllabus as suggested by one of the Board's officials. A further development has also been made by the continuation of scale drawing from Standard IV. to VII., and an attempt made to prepare the boys in their drawing for the wood-work centres under the Organiser of Manual Training.

It was thought that the work of the schools as a whole would be better if some inspection and instruction were carried out, similar to that in vogue in the Birmingham and other large Boards, and which had been tried for a time by the London School Board and then dropped. One Drawing Instructor was appointed to devote the whole of his time in supervising the drawing taught in the schools of the Board. Later on, London was divided into two districts and a second Drawing Instructor appointed. The first thing to attempt was to make the work of the second drawing syllabus more thorough, and to improve methods. This task the teachers made all the easier by welcoming anybody who had the requisite knowledge and sympathy.

There was in the early time of the Board an annual exhibition of drawings from the different schools, but the exhibits were selected from the better work shown at local exhibitions. Some of the work was good and of quite an elementary character; being mostly freehand from the flat and model outline. Some attempts had been made to make the work more interesting by colouring freehand examples, and the introduction of coloured paper, although it produced for a time hard outlines of poor ornament feebly coloured, yet it had its effect in breaking through the monotonously bare outline work, and helped to show the way to better things. The annual exhibitions gave opportunities of finding out the general tendency of the work, and afforded some idea, although a limited one, of some of the principal weaknesses. Exhibitions are for other purposes than those usually understood by the teachers. They are not merely for the purpose of exhibiting prize works, but rather for the dissemination of methods and types of work which, from time to time, seem best to adopt. Unfortunately, they do not represent as much as they should the bulk of the work taught in the ordinary Board school. The dangerous element of these exhibitions is the anxiety of each school to get more and more rewards for the sake of increasing the prize list. These exhibitions and the work being done at a very small number of schools, together with a lack of some kind of general progress, brought about the appointment of more highly qualified art teachers.

After a few years the Board established two art classes, one at Monnow Road, Bermondsey, the other at Medburn Street, St. Pancras, where scholars who showed some taste and ability to draw were sent and taught by a specially qualified art teacher. The art classes and centres commenced by working more thoroughly the shading and model drawing prescribed for the upper standards by the Education Department. The demand for technical education had also forced handwork to the front, and as drawing and modelling are essential elements in the training of the hand and eye, more attention was paid to this subject.

This idea has grown and there are now under the Board about eighty classes of this type, where some very good work is being done in the way of giving the children a liking for the subject and also a means of studying the beautiful.

The bulk of the drawing in the elementary schools under the School Board for London has hitherto been taken on the lines of the Code syllabus of the Education Department. The introduction of an alternative syllabus and the substitution of inspection instead of an annual examination has given the teachers of drawing an opportunity for introducing other sections of art work.

These sections are to give greater variety and interest in the drawing, and are also intended to bring about the education in form, other than that expressed by a mere outline. The sections referred to are free-arm drawing, brush work, elementary design, clay modelling, nature drawing by means of shading and painting. The development of this work is bound to be gradual, as the teachers, having had to work under different conditions, and who have to instruct in a number of other subjects, cannot be expected to be fully equal to new requirements.

It has been felt that the work in some of the infant schools was more in accordance with a child's natural bent. The brush work and modelling in clay from natural objects, and attempts to bring out the scholars' imagination in these schools, have been somewhat checked in the senior departments by the drawing of straight-lined objects in outline for two or three years. The work in the lower standards has consequently seemed dry and uninteresting. It has been thought advisable to introduce free-arm drawing by means of coloured chalks, or any soft pointed substance upon washable millboards, or toned paper. The child is thus taught to judge his work at arms' length, and should be the better able to estimate proportion. The masses are represented by broad lines, thus defining the solid or block forms and not merely the silhouette or boundary line.

It has been found that stumping has resulted in wasted time and cleaned up hard outlines, and has been discarded in favour of the freer method of work with a soft point.

The power of expressing an edge, and also the broad effect of a mass, is thereby increased. The use of squared paper is restricted to its proper sphere, viz., that of mechanically enlarging a map or plan.

Brush work by means of blobs or blots executed on squares has also been given up, because it led to endless repetition of mechanical and meaningless forms. · Brush work is very interesting, as giving greater freedom and power over mass forms, and creates a taste for colour. It may, however, become mere flourishing, and it requires to be used on a constructional basis. The constructions should be framed upon the principles of simple ornamental analysis.

It is also necessary gradually to discipline the children to a more exact rendering of natural objects. The representation of a plant from nature by means of the brush, pencil, charcoal, chalk, or modelling in clay, forms an interesting field for both teacher and pupil, and its value extends far beyond that of art alone. The stock of information is increased, and the memory is also considerably strengthened. The examples chosen should neither be very large nor complicated. Some valuable work has been done in this direction by several schools, in which a plant has been dissected with regard to its ornamental details and then arranged to fill a given space.

An interesting section carried out in several of the schools is that of stencilling, the design for which has been drawn from letters, figures, and conventionalised sprigs of leaves, flowers, and fruits. The stencils have been cut and used by the pupils themselves.

Several schemes of modelling in clay or plasticine are being tried in the upper standards, V.-VII. There are many examples of excellent technical art teaching, both in washes, brush, and decorative work, which have been produced by scholars in various schools of the Board.

The art classes are of two kinds at present, one in which picked children from different schools attend at one centre, and another which is filled partly by selected children in the same school at which the specialist attends. As there is a natural limit imposed upon these classes, both by age and the capacity of the child, there will be no interference with other institutions.

(iii.) SINGING.

By A. L. COWLEY, *Singing Instructor.*

Music in elementary schools is one of the educational developments of the latter half of the nineteenth century. In the early years of the century vocal music was not considered to be among the necessary subjects of the education of the common people, and there are teachers and officers still in the service of the Board who, as boys, found no teaching of music in their school curriculum, and whose school days were passed, year after year, without even the singing of a hymn or school song.

In 1840 Wilhem's method of teaching singing was adapted to English use by John Hullah, and issued by authority of the Committee of Council on Education. A prefatory minute commenced with the following statement : " The information derived from the Inspectors of schools and from various other sources had made the Committee of Council acquainted with the fact that vocal music has been successfully cultivated in comparatively few of the elementary schools of Great Britain."

This method of Wilhem's, commonly known as the "fixed *do*" method, being introduced with State authority, and aided by influential friends of education and aristocratic patronage, was for a time very popular. It served to awaken interest in the subject, and afforded a further proof of the statement in the Minute already referred to, that " there is sufficient evidence that the natural genius of the people would reward a careful cultivation," but after more than thirty years of officially undisputed possession of the schools and training colleges, it practically died out in the schools, and the condition of school music might still be described in the words previously quoted : " Vocal music has been successfully cultivated in comparatively few of the elementary schools of Great Britain," and " the children acquire no power of further self-instruction, and little or no desire to know more of music."

During this period a method based upon the old fundamental principle of key-relationship, known as the Tonic Sol-fa method, had made much progress in Sunday-schools and evening classes, and, without any official recognition, had found its way into some of the day schools. In 1869 the Committee of Council recognised this method as having been adopted on a sufficient scale to justify official sanction, and intimated that " the Tonic Sol-fa method and notation would therefore be accepted upon the same terms as should from time to time be applicable to the ordinary method and notation both in training colleges and schools."

The condition of music in elementary schools at this period may be judged from the fact that previous to the recognition of the Tonic Sol-fa method only one school out of all those under inspection had obtained a grant for music as a specific subject, and in the year ending March, 1871, the number of schools obtaining the grant had only risen to 43.

From this brief retrospect it will be seen that when the School Board for London, commenced its work vocal music had received but scant attention in elementary schools throughout the country, and very little progress had been made with the subject.

One of the earliest steps taken by the School Board for London having reference to the teaching of singing appears in a report on books and apparatus brought up at a meeting of the Board held early in 1872, which said :

" Your Committee have also considered the question of the system of music teaching which would be best for adoption in Board schools. The Tonic Sol-fa system appears to possess great advantages in simplicity, and in the facilities which it offers for teaching children in a short time. Your Committee would therefore recommend that managers be advised to adopt the Tonic Sol-fa system of teaching vocal music."

After discussion, the recommendation of the Committee was adopted, and it should be noticed that the resolution simply *advises* the adoption of the method which, at the time, was thought to be the best. The policy of the School Board for London in this matter has always been to place the responsibility as to methods of work on the head teachers. So long as satisfactory results were achieved, the teachers have always been free to adopt whatever system they thought best.

At the meeting of the Board, held on June 26th, 1872, Mr. Macgregor brought up a report of the School Management Committee, which said:

"The Board on June 12th resolved that an officer be appointed to examine and report and generally to promote the teaching of singing in Board Schools. The School Management Committee have received applications from several candidates for the above post. After careful consideration, they recommend the appointment of Mr. Evans as singing instructor. It is to be understood that Mr. Evans will only be expected to give his services to the Board during the daytime."

In moving the adoption of the report Mr. Macgregor said:

"In regard to the singing, the Board had agreed to teach the Tonic Sol-fa system, but that was not to prevent the old system from being taught. The instructor now appointed, who was one of the best men in London, would be expected to be impartial as between the two systems, being, in fact, strictly undenominational and unsectarian in his notes."

The following extracts from the Music Instructor's first report are of interest as showing the backward condition of the singing at this time and the unpromising material to be dealt with :—

"I have now visited all the schools—most of them twice and many three times. In seventeen schools I found singing was not taught at all. Three of the teachers could not teach it; and most of the others had only just opened their schools.

"In seventy-eight schools the children were only taught to sing a few hymns or school songs by ear. Five schools had just begun teaching by the Tonic Sol-fa method. In one the children were being well taught to sing by notes on that method, and had made good progress. The Tonic Sol-fa method is the only one used in any of the schools where the children are taught to sing by notes. The singing generally is fearfully coarse and noisy, the boys especially singing with all the force they can command. Certainly, in many schools the material to be cultivated is very raw indeed, and much time and labour will be required to get anything like good singing."

The report goes on to set forth plans for future work, and it is worthy of note that from the first the teaching of music has been done, not by visiting teachers, as in Scotland and other places, but by the regular staff of teachers.

In the early years of the Board's work one of the chief hindrances was the fact that, owing to the subject having been much neglected in the training colleges, very few of the teachers could teach singing properly. Classes for teachers were consequently a prominent feature of the work, and these classes were well attended and very successful.

In the light of the present enormous extent of the School Board's work, it is interesting to find it on record that at first the Music Instructor was able to visit every school once in six weeks. At the present time it would take six or more instructors to visit every school once in six months.

In 1873 the Board adopted three certificates of proficiency for teachers, pupil teachers, and scholars respectively, corresponding with those of the Tonic Sol-fa College, but bearing the seal of the Board and the signature of the music instructor. These are not at present in use, but the Board now recognises the certificates of the Tonic Sol-fa College and any equivalent certificates of other public bodies.

In 1876 the first performance of music by the Board's scholars and teachers at the Crystal Palace took place. The occasion was the presentation of Scripture prizes to 4,000 of the scholars, the Right Hon. W. E. Foster, M.P., being in the chair. Four hymns were sung by the whole body of prize winners, after which six school songs and two anthems were rendered by a selected choir of certificated voices. Compared with the present time this was truly the day of small things, but it marked a real and considerable advance, and the *Tonic Sol-fa Reporter* spoke of it as ' a grand meeting," and, referring to the singing of the hymns, said : " Verily there is a marvellous change coming over the tone and spirit of school singing."

In 1877, on a similar occasion, the select choir included 610 boys and 700 girls. Lord Sandon, who distributed the prizes, said he was delighted with the sweetness and purity of the voices, and that he had never enjoyed school singing so much before.

These Crystal Palace concerts have been continued, at first annually and afterwards triennially, to the present time. The particulars of one or two of the recent festivals will serve to show the great advance which has been made in the musical attainments of the Board's scholars. In the festival of 1896 nearly 5,000 scholars, selected from 257 departments of the Board schools, took part. A noteworthy feature of this concert was the addition—for the first time—of orchestral accompaniment to several of the pieces. These were played by about 250 pupils from the Board schools. The band was constituted as follows :—

1st Violins	...	...	... 83	Bassoon	... ...	1
2nd ,,	...	...	... 50	Cornets	... ...	17
3rd ,,	...	...	... 40	Horns	... ...	6
Violas	...	...	... 11	Baritones	... ...	4
'Cellos	...	...	... 9	Euphoniums	... ...	2
Double Basses		...	... 5	Trombones ...	... ...	6
Piccolos	...	...	... 4	Bombardons ...	... ...	4
Clarinets	...	...	... 11	Timpani, Side Drums, &c. ...		4

The 'cello and double bass players and a few of the violinists were teachers, but all the others were scholars. The clarinets and brass instruments were played by boys from the Board's Industrial Schools.

Last year (1899) the number of singers and players was about the same. The programme of three-part music, most of it specially arranged for the occasion, for 1st and 2nd soprano and contralto voices, was as follows :—

HYMN ...	... ...	" Above the Clear Blue Sky "	... *W. H. Harper.*
HYMN ...	... ...	" Thy Precious Word " ...	... *A. L. Cowley.*
PART SONG ...	...	..." Morning Prayer " ...	... *Mendelssohn.*

Semi-Chorus and Chorus	"I Waited for the Lord" ("Lobgesang")	*Mendelssohn.*
Glee	..."Strike the Lyre"	*T. Cooke.*
Chorus	..."Sailors' Chorus"	*L. O. Emerson.*
Part Song	..."Old Tubal Cain" ...	*C. A. E. Harris.*
Choral March	"Hail! Fatherland" ("Tannhäuser")	*Wagner.*
Canon...	"The Skylark's Song"... ...	*Mendelssohn.*
Choral Song... ...	"The Death of Nelson" ...	*J. Braham.*
Folk Song ...	"All through the Night" ("Ar hyd e nos") ...	*Welsh Air.*
„	..."Farewell to Erin" ("The Cruiskeen Lawn") ...	*Irish Air.*
„	"Auld Lang Syne"	*Scottish Air.*
National Anthem ...	"God Save the Queen"	

The *Musical Herald* report of the concert said: "The concert touched a very high mark indeed," and the *School Music Review* said: "The choir was, we believe, the best constituted children's choir that has ever sung at the Crystal Palace. The tone was really beautiful, the balance almost perfect, the intonation excellent, and the attack firm and prompt."

In 1889, a Vocal Music Competition by choirs from any of the public elementary schools of London was established. The Challenge Medallion, to be competed for annually, was presented by four gentlemen who were anxious to promote efficiency in musical instruction.

These competitions aroused considerable interest and proved very effective in raising the standard of singing in the best schools, and setting before the teachers as a whole a high ideal of school song. They were conducted as follows:—

By means of preliminary competitions held in the several districts from which entries had been received, six choirs were selected for the final competition, at which the adjudicators were Sir John Stainer, Mus. Doc., and W. G. McNaught, Esq., Mus. Doc.

Each choir had to sing:—

I. A prepared test piece (glee, madrigal, or part song).
II. A sight-singing test, specially composed for the occasion.
III. A piece of its own selection.

Correctness of time and tune, quality of tone, pronunciation of words, preservation of pitch, and expression were the points on which the adjudication was based. All the music was in three parts for soprano, mezzo-soprano, and contralto, and was sung without accompaniment.

On the last two occasions the competition was followed by a short demonstration of school musical work, including action songs by infant school choirs, instrumental performances by school bands, and ear tests, and sight-singing from both Tonic Sol-fa and Staff notations by the united choirs.

In 1898 the competitive element of these occasions was eliminated and a vocal music display was held. The programme included the following items:—

Five school choirs each sang two pieces (part-songs or glees).

Two action songs by an infant class.

Instrumental selections by a school band.

A costume recital of selections from an operetta by a school choir.

These were conducted by teachers of the schools taking part, and the united choirs under the direction of the Board's Superintendent of Music, rendered a hymn, an anthem, two part-songs, a sight test from the Tonic Sol-fa notation, composed for the occasion by Sir John Stainer, Mus.Doc., a sight test from the staff notation, composed for the occasion by E. H. Turpin, Esq., Mus.Doc., and an ear test composed for the occasion by W. G. McNaught, Esq., Mus Doc.

Sir John Stainer and Dr. McNaught, who had been requested to attend, made the following report :—

"The choral performances were marked by great thoroughness of preparation, and were generally excellent in every way. In previous years the greatest fault in the singing of the various choirs was a tendency to get flat. Although this fault was not entirely eradicated in to-day's demonstration, we are glad to record that the singing generally was distinguished by good intonation. As to the highly important matter of voice production, we are glad to observe that all the choirs had given attention to the matter. In some cases the singing was surprisingly good in every particular—in artistic execution, beautiful tone and blend, and unity of attack. The pieces sung by the united choirs were also prepared with great pains. The sight-singing and exhibition of ear training were remarkable evidences not only of the natural capacity of the children, but of the skill of their enthusiastic teachers. We are glad to remark that a school band played some selections. It is very desirable to offer every possible encouragement to the formation of school bands of the orchestral type. We should like to add that the performance to-day gives clear evidence of the excellent musical work being carried out by the School Board. We are gratified to find that much of the music being studied is calculated to improve the taste of the children as well as to cultivate their practical skill."

(iv.) Manual Instruction in Wood and Metal.

By S. Barter, *Organiser and Instructor in Manual Training.*

Manual instruction is the designation of the training in woodwork and metal-work instituted in 1891, but really the term covers kindergarten and clay modelling, and, in its widest application, drawing. The restricted application has, however, been very generally adhered to throughout the country for the sake of convenience, and although it cannot be regarded as entirely descriptive, a better name seems unfortunately unobtainable.

Probably in every age thinking men have seen the close connection between the most universal, if humblest, of man's distinctive faculties—the power to make and use tools—and his highest achievements, and there have never been wanting advocates of educational training of faculties through the use of tools. Still, it appears to be generally admitted that all modern experiments took their origin in the work of Pestalozzi and Frœbel at the beginning of the century now closing. In this work England has never taken a pioneer part, and if we can now regard with satisfaction our own later efforts, we must not forget the debt due to Leipsic, Paris, Philadelphia, and Naas.

Drawing of the ordinary routine kinds—freehand and model usually—has long held a place in our school system. Kindergarten and clay modelling were the earliest adopted of the newer forms of hand and eye training which involved the shaping of tangible substances. Lastly, wood work and metal work were taken up. It is with these that we are immediately concerned, but the connection with the more elementary branches must no more be omitted, than the ultimate ends of all the kindred subjects can be overlooked.

The natural faculties of observation, accuracy, and deftness of finger—hand and eye training—are alike the main objects, but the group of subjects included in hand and eye training have been found, even by their less enthusiastic advocates, and even opponents, to be not without effect in connection with the more abstract subjects of the school course. Arithmetic is distinctly benefited by the new subjects, and while too much stress is no doubt laid by some writers on the development of morals by means of manual training, it is not too much to hope that self-reliance, resource, and the power of personal judgment are increased by the new departure in education.

Probably the earliest important step in this country towards the adoption of manual training—*i.e.*, the higher branches, wood work and metal work—was taken in 1887. At that time the Code of the Education Department made no provision for the subject, and the Board was unable to devote any money to the work. The City and Guilds of London Institute and the Drapers' Company generously came forward with funds, and a Joint Committee, appointed by the London School Board and the City and Guilds of London Institute, was formed, and classes attended by boys from elementary schools were established at several centres in London. The instruction was largely carried out on the lines indicated by the City and Guilds of London Institute. It was disciplinary, consisting entirely of carpenters' joints and exercises in wood work, and the drawing connected with them. The Joint Committee encouraged experiment in the most generous spirit, and the work was carefully kept in a living, active condition, while many ideas were tried and adopted, modified or abandoned.

From the first a somewhat new departure was taken. The association of drawing with the bench work was early realised as a means of giving life and reality to both, and operating beneficially on the teaching both of drawing and tool operations. Incidentally, it gave the opportunity to the boys of acquiring in a natural easy way, some knowledge of dimension, measurement, and the use of scales.

Experience led to the introduction of simple models with gratifying results. Boys love to make some definite object of utility, or of beauty, and this wish was found to be a potent lever to procure from them attention, thought, and care.

From these earlier experiences the present scheme of manual training as taught in our schools was gradually formulated. It now consists chiefly of models, with disciplinary exercises interspersed. The models are carefully graded and arranged so as to constantly stimulate the faculties of the child, each model containing a repetition of some previous tool manipulation, and presenting some new difficulty, adequate, but not too great for the pupil to overcome.

In 1891 the work was beginning to pass from the experimental stage, and the Science and Art Department offered a grant for the subject   But it was regarded as a special subject till the Education Department, in 1898, placed it under its own administration.   From that time it has been regarded as an ordinary subject of the school course.   The general attitude of the departments concerned towards manual instruction has been distinguished by the freedom which they have allowed to teachers and managers, in their various circulars and instructions on the subject, down to this year.   This action has been extremely fortunate for the natural growth of a new subject on lines suited to the special needs of our people.

The important change made by the Education Department when the transfer from South Kensington to Whitehall took place was to substitute inspection for examination. This change was equally gratifying to those engaged in the work and beneficial to the subject itself.   Nothing taught in school is so easily judged by an expert while the work is in progress.   He has the opportunity of rapidly and effectively testing every child at work and gaining a knowledge of the teacher's method, which, after all, is, or should be, aimed at in the ordinary examination by a set test.

The classes first organised by the School Board for London in several disused rooms of the schools were conducted from 3.30 to 5.30 p.m. by the staff of the school.

The question of training teachers for the work had already secured attention, and some had been trained either at Naas or in the classes of the Joint Committee ; but opportunities were now afforded to others to take one or more courses of Swedish Slöyd.   Sufficient skill in tool manipulation was practically unattainable in short courses in the Slöyd Seminarium, and selected teachers were now allowed to pass through a further course in the classes of the Joint Committee.

The work done in the first classes of the Board did not compare favourably with that of the classes on the centre system conducted by the Joint Committee.   This failure was largely due to the difficulties the teachers had to contend with.   The boys were weary after the mental work of the school, and little opportunity was afforded the teacher for preparing a suitable course of instruction.   The Board, therefore, determined upon the " centre " system, which has worked decidedly better.   Each boy has one lesson weekly, either an ordinary morning or afternoon, so that each centre has ten distinct classes from contributory schools in the immediate neighbourhood.

Difficulties still existed in procuring as instructors teachers with manual skill or skilled artisans who could teach.   These difficulties are not entirely surmounted now ; but the Board has trained and employed both classes of teachers without prejudice.   It was fortunately found that a considerable number of artisans who secured appointments were already more or less qualified as teachers.

It was decided in 1891 to commence instruction in Swedish Slöyd at Flora Gardens (later transferred to Brackenbury Road), Goodson Road, and Berners Street.

At the two last-named, Slöyd, as Naas Slöyd is usually understood, has been completely abandoned, whilst at Brackenbury Road considerable modification has been made in the work. The failure of Slöyd at two schools, and the necessary modifications at the third, are directly attributable to (1) The endeavour on the part of the teachers to take the Swedish course without modification; and (2) the use of the "knife," which is only a tool of approximation, requiring prolonged practice before any degree of skill can be attained, and giving inaccurate results with consequent disappointment and loss of interest—the unsatisfactory work at early stages having noticeable results in the inaccuracy of all subsequent tool operations; (3) To the excessive use of glass paper, which destroys in the pupils the habits of precision and self-reliance so vital in all training in hand dexterity; (4) the ineffective association of drawing with the work. Remembering that the Swedish Slöyd course was not constituted with this object in view, we cannot be surprised at the almost complete failure of the models to afford good opportunities for drawing lessons. This is the gravest defect of the Slöyd course.

Still, although the Swedish course is weak in drawing and in other important respects, it has made a great impression upon the general lines of manual instruction in London. The steady maintenance of educational ideals, and the complete severance from the too common idea that manual instruction is simply the commencement of training of workmen, are the most valuable portions of the Swedish scheme.

In the choice of material in which to train children in the use of tools, wood has almost universally been found to be the most suitable, readily lending itself to modelling, besides being light and cheap.

The common wood working tools are typical of all, or nearly all, in use, even where material very different from wood is employed; and, on the whole, wood gives opportunities for the greatest variety of manipulation. It can be modelled with the greatest accuracy, and the work may be associated with good drawing lessons.

It is almost impossible to over-estimate the value of drawing as a means of education, and nowhere does its value become more real than in the manual training room. Drawing, taught from flat copies or from models, is more or less an abstract subject, which only appeals to such pupils as have already an apt appreciation of form, and quite fails to captivate the attention of the majority.

In the manual training room the keen wish of the boys to learn the practical handling of tools, and to make some simple models, is the force which is quite simply employed to make the boys understand not only the drawing, but through the more abstract drawing, their little problem at the bench. Nor does the influence end here, but gradually the value, and some of the marvellous compression of language in a mechanical working drawing, is realised, with the result that the child's reasoning is, if not strengthened, at any rate assisted, and consequently the teaching of the bench work is rendered vastly simpler.

As a training of the eye to form, drawing in the manual training room becomes a more pressing matter to the child. The sweeping curves in the surfaces of some finished model which he can admire and is about to make himself, he finds, are

Q

represented by the curves he is making in his preparatory drawing, and knowing the actual shape is to be presently created, and by himself, he can be induced to take much more interest in his drawing lesson.

(v.) COOKERY.

By MISS EMILY BRIGGS, *Superintendent of Cookery.*

Attached to the many of the London Board Schools, which are fast becoming landmarks in the Metropolis and its suburbs, may be found small school kitchens, in which elementary cookery has been taught for more than twenty years. For this purpose the most central of a group of schools is chosen, so that for the 470 contributing schools there are 168 cookery centres. The teachers for this subject are drawn from the various domestic economy training colleges or schools which are now established in Great Britain.

It has been found that the more highly educated teacher produces the best results, as she not only simplifies the science of cookery sufficiently for the mental capacity of the children, whose ages vary from 10 to 14, but her knowledge also enables her to teach thrift and economy as a principle, and not simply because her pupils are mainly of the artisan class.

The girls pass through two or three stages or courses of instruction, according to the length of their school life. Each course numbers twenty-two lessons, and each lesson is of the same duration as the usual school session.

The syllabuses of instruction commence with lessons on the cleaning and management of stoves, cleaning all requisite kitchen utensils, and comprise every simple mode of English cookery—viz., roasting, boiling, stewing, grilling, and frying; soups with meat and soup maigre; bread, cakes, and pastry; tea, coffee, and cocoa-making; cookery for invalids, with hints for the management of the sick room.

The method of teaching is mainly practical, with simple explanations of the science. The London plan is almost unique, insomuch as every lesson opens with one hour's lecture, during which the teacher demonstrates the dishes in the lesson, and her pupils, after the careful washing of hands, cleaning of nails, tying up hair, and donning neat aprons and sleeves, immediately copy the models thus given them. In other words, each child at once makes the dishes she has seen demonstrated whilst the instruction given in the lecture is fresh in her memory. This, in contradistinction to the more usual method of allowing an interim of one, two, and in some cases three weeks to elapse between the lecture and the actual practice by the pupils, has proved most effectual.

Periodic exhibitions of the work done by the pupils are held, and the exhibits have been judged and approved by some of the leading chefs in London. But perhaps the strongest proof that good work is done lies in the fact that frequent letters of thanks and appreciation are received by the teachers from the parents, testifying to the increased usefulness of the child at home. This is the more gratifying, because when the teaching of this subject was first introduced, prejudice against it was almost insuperable, and parents put every possible obstacle in the way of their children attending the classes.

Now it is so popular that in some districts, where the beneficent effects of education have developed the intelligence and discriminating powers sufficiently to rightly value the instruction, that parents endeavour to keep their girls at school to the age of 15 and 16, so that they may obtain a more advanced knowledge of cookery and other domestic subjects. If girls are taught that within the home lies a wonderful chemical laboratory, a work intellectual enough to satisfy the most ambitious, they will gradually realise, as women, how much depends on them, and the importance of their responsibilities as mothers of the generation to come.

It is interesting to note, and also a sign of the times, that this instruction is gradually being extended in some districts to boys, so that they will go forth more fully equipped, at least for the soldier's, sailor's, and colonist's life.

But perhaps the most interesting feature is the happy influence the instruction in cookery has upon the blind, deaf, and those children whose mental capacity is not equal to that of the average child. The very dullest of these are charmed to make a cake for mother, to say nothing of the stimulating effect of being able to produce the same results as their more favoured companions in full possession of all the senses.

(vi.) DOMESTIC ECONOMY OR HOUSEHOLD MANAGEMENT.

By Mrs. E. LORD, *Domestic Economy Superintendent.*

The teaching of household management in connection with the schools of the London School Board includes the elements of hygiene and physiology, and the theory and practice of cooking, laundry work, general household management, personal hygiene and home nursing.

All the work is based on scientific principles, and in practice has to be done at the lowest possible cost and with the least possible waste. The scheme is graduated, and provides both revision and examination so as to make the results really permanent.

The general plan adopted by the Board is the teaching of these subjects in specially adapted buildings called " centres." These centres are so-called because the girls from the surrounding schools attend alternately, and according to arrangement, on one half day per week, during the last three years of their recognised school career.

The most improved plan of buildings for these centres is a combination of a cookery centre, a laundry centre, and a housewifery centre, and is called a Domestic Economy school.

The housewifery centre is on the ground floor and consists of:—

		Feet.	Inches.		Feet.	Inches.
(1) A lecture room		22	0	×	16	3
(2) A bed room		16	6	×	11	0
(3) A sitting room		14	0	×	13	9
(4) A kitchen and scullery ...		22	0	×	15	6

These rooms are furnished and fitted as a model working-man's house, except that more cupboard room is provided, to allow for the larger number of working utensils —*e.g.*, brushes, &c.—required for a class of girls working.

By careful arrangement of colours the children are taught that usefulness and art may be combined, and comfortable substitutes for cheap stuffed furniture are placed before the children's eyes. All the utensils provided in these centres are those used by the artisan class. A cottage stove is fixed in the kitchen, and the children cook daily the dinners for themselves and the teachers.

On the second floor, and over the rooms indicated, there is a cookery centre and a laundry centre, fitted with all the appliances for teaching cookery and laundry effectively.

During the first part of a girl's training she works in these centres with all the aid of the various appliances, but during the third stage, in the housewifery kitchen, the work is done under the ordinary conditions of the working-man's home and with as few appliances as possible.

All the rooms are lofty and well ventilated, especially the laundry, and the building is erected apart from the ordinary school in a corner of the playground.

The cookery centre is a room 30 ft. long by 22 ft. wide, with a fixed square counter.

The teacher being in the middle is able to see the children at work, and the counter provides a large amount of space for efficient practical work. Gas stoves, and close and open ranges are provided, so that the children may become familiar with the use of the various kinds of stoves in the dwelling-houses of both the better and middle as well as the artisan class.

The children are taught the use of various utensils, and, afterwards, how to manage without them—*e.g.*, cups, spoons and other ordinary kitchen utensils are used, and at the same time practice is also given in the use of ordinary weights, measures and scales. At one end of the room a raised gallery is fixed with desks where the children sit to receive their lectures, take notes, and see the teacher demonstrate the dishes the children are afterwards to practise.

The laundry centre is a room 30 feet long and 22 feet wide. This also has a raised gallery at one end where the girls sit during the lecture and demonstration. A copper for boiling water, or boiling the clothes, is placed near a sink, and a large stove sufficient for heating thirty-six irons is placed in a recess in one corner of the room. A large zinc screen is made to cover the front of this stove, so as to prevent some of the heat radiating into the room.

The ironing tables and washing stools and tubs are all movable, and are such as are used in the artisan homes of London. No special machinery is allowed, all the washing being done by hand except the very coarse articles, which are washed on a grooved board. This prevents the destruction of the clothes so disastrous in the steam laundries. Only ordinary household appliances for drying are used, so that the children are familiar with the work as it is done in the home.

GENERAL ORGANISATION.

First Stage or First Year's Course—
> Six months' cookery, including a knowledge of the foods to be cooked.
> Six months' laundry work, including a knowledge of the clothes to be washed and ironed.

Second Stage or Second Year's Course—
> Six months' cookery, including a further knowledge of food, and the principles of cookery, with instructions for diets.

Third Stage or Third Year's Course—
> Includes marketing, preparing dinners in the housewifery centre, with the apparatus found in a working man's house and at a stated cost; also home nursing and general household management.

The following is a short *résumé* of the syllabus:—

Stage I.—Standard V.

Food and Cookery Section—Twenty-two lessons, including:—
> Cleaning of utensils and washing dishes.
> Theory of food—Milk as a perfect food.
> Cooking food—Meat: How to choose good meat.
> Roasting of beef, &c.
> Characteristics of beef, mutton, &c.
> Rules for boiling.
> Pork and bacon as articles of diet—Choice and selection.
> Fish—How to select and cook it.
> Eggs—How to test, preserve, and cook them.
> Milk—Preservation and cleanliness.
> Vegetable foods.
> Oats, porridge, biscuits.
> Roots and tubers, fruit, potatoes, &c.
> Beverages—Tea, coffee, cocoa, &c.

Stage I.—Standard V.

Clothing and Laundry Work—Twenty-two lessons, including:—
> Water—Its source: hard, soft, &c.
> Cleaning laundry utensils.
> Flannels and woollens, washing of—Their source.
> Disinfection and removing of stains.
> Processes of washing.
> Linen and cotton—Washing and ironing.
> Drying clothes—Fresh air as a disinfectant.
> Management of the fire.

Washing of printed cottons.
Silk—Washing and cleaning of.
Skins and furs—How to preserve and clean.
Directions for disinfection, &c.

Stage II.—Standard VI.

Food and Cookery—Twenty-two lessons, including :—
  Management of the fire.
  Economy of fuel.
  Kitchen ranges—How to clean.
  Principles of cookery—Flesh food.
  Boiling and steaming suitable joints, and cost.
  How to preserve flavour and nutritive properties.
  Roasting and baking suitable joints, and cost.
  Stewing as an economical way of cooking.
  Soup making.
  Economy in the kitchen.
  Dinners for a working man.
  Infants' food.
  A children's dinner.
  Diet for invalids.
  Serving and making of invalids' dishes.
  Preservation of food, &c.

Stage II.—Standard VI.

Housewifery Section—Twenty-two lessons, including :—
  Importance of cleanliness in a home.
  Firelighting, blackleading, and cleaning a grate and fire-irons.
  Lighting a room.
  Selection of a house—Situation ; general convenience ; hints on furnishing.
  The drainage of the house—Cleaning of drains.
  Water supply—Cleaning of water cisterns.
  Setting a table—Breakfast ; dinner.
  Directions for dusting.
  Ventilation of different rooms.
  How to make a bed—How to furnish a bed economically.
  Dusting a sitting-room—Polishing furniture.
  Personal cleanliness—Baths.
  Fresh air as an aid to health.
During each lesson there is practice in various kinds of housework, such as washing
dishes, laying and lighting fire, cleaning lamps, kitchen flues, sink pipes, brasses, taps,

knives, washstand, windows, setting tables, dusting rooms, making beds, sweeping carpets, tidying cupboard, cleaning floor, scullery work, &c.

Stage III.—Standard VII.

1. Housewifery Section—Twenty-two lessons, including :—
   Portioning out weekly income.
   Buying a dinner—Teacher to take class out shopping; shopping and marketing to form an important part of each lesson.
   Planning a week's dinner at a stated cost for a family of four persons.
   Strength-producing foods and their value.
   Mixed diet—Vegetarian dinner.
   Digestion in the mouth, stomach, intestines.
   Planning a week's breakfasts and teas.
   Making tea and setting table.
   Cleaning a sitting room.
   Cleaning a bedroom.
   Cleaning a kitchen.
   Clothing—Its uses, making, and mending.
   Boots and shoes, hats, cleaning of.
   Corsets and tight lacing.
   Suitable clothing for men and boys.
   Suitable clothing for women.
   Suitable clothing for infants.

During each lesson there is practice in various kinds of housework, such as cleaning rooms, dusting, bed-making, mending clothes and stockings, folding and brushing, cooking different meals, &c.

2. Home Nursing—Twenty-two lessons, including :—
   The Nurse : Qualifications, dress.
   Cleaning a bedroom
   An ideal sick-room.
   How to make up fire quietly.
   Arranging the bedroom.
   Ventilation of the sick-room.
   Changing sheets.
   How to prevent bed-sores.
   Common ailments and their remedies.
   Infant complaints.
   Infectious diseases—Isolation and general treatment.
   Preservation of health—Personal cleanliness.
   Exercise and recreation.
   Temperance.

Thrift—Savings banks, building societies, clubs.

Warmth and light.

Ventilation, &c.

The plan of each lesson is:—

(*a*) An intelligent explanation of the food to be cooked and the principles underlying the cooking of the food.

(*b*) A demonstration by the teacher showing how the principles taught are applied to the cooking of the actual food.

(*c*) Practice by the class individually to test and to confirm the lesson given by the teacher.

(*d*) Short notes to be written at the end of the lesson on the work done.

This method as applied to cookery is entirely new, the general method adopted in cookery schools in England being simply a demonstration by the teacher and the children practising the dishes shown the week following. It will be readily seen, however, that by taking the demonstration and practice at the same lesson, and taking one principle at a time, the children are able to retain and assimilate the knowledge imparted, and by practising the dishes immediately after the demonstration are much more likely to retain what they have learnt.

Another improvement in the teaching of cookery is the explanation of the principles underlying the teaching of cookery, and a general knowledge of the food to be cooked. It is of little use putting recipes into the heads of those who know nothing of their composition, nutritive value, and their suitability for the requirements of the human body. Under this amalgamated scheme, now to be generally adopted in the centres of the London School Board, all this is taught.

It might be argued that the mother is the proper person to teach such a subject to her daughter, and that such teaching would seriously interfere with other more important studies. It must, however, be admitted that with the compulsory attendance of children at school there is little opportunity, and the vast majority of mothers are unable to teach domestic science, as they know little of it themselves. With regard to the interference with other studies, the Commission appointed to inquire into practical and manual instruction in Irish schools state in their report: "It has contributed greatly to stimulate the intelligence of pupils, to increase their interest in school work, and to make school life generally brighter and more pleasant. No loss was observed to the literary side of school studies in any school, In some cases the literary studies were positively improved."

The number of girls who are taking this amalgamated scheme of instruction under the London School Board may be roughly calculated as at four to five thousand, and this is in addition to the girls who attend the teaching of cookery and laundry work apart from the amalgamated scheme. It must, however, be readily recognised that a continued and graduated course cannot but be of greater value than any number of fragmentary lessons on the subject. The chief aim is to lay the basis of sound teaching in the principles which underlie the laws of health; to stimulate the intelligence of the pupils and to increase their interest in school work, and to improve the general health and condition of the homes of the working-classes. Any attempt at making the teaching in elementary schools degenerate into merely skilled handwork, and training for cooks, laundresses, &c., is deprecated under this scheme. At the same time, the practical results have been such as to convince the most confirmed sceptic of the natural capability of the children to understand this work.

What, then, should be the results of this work? To quote the remarks of the medical officer at the recent Sanitary Congress :—

"I am convinced that domestic science, if efficiently taught, will have a far reaching influence on the health and well-being of the population. The full fruit of such teaching will, however, ripen but slowly. Its effects will be felt gradually, and in proportion to the extent to which it will find its way in practice into the homes of the people and to the efficiency with which it will be carried out there. It will tend to guide the men and women of the future to husband their means, and to use them in a manner which will be beneficial to themselves and to others. They will have clearer ideas as to how to guard against many discomforts, misfortunes, and diseases to which their progenitors in their ignorance are now a prey. As a result they will have greater home comfort, and will live happier lives. They will reach to a higher standard of health and attain to a longer duration of life. They will be stronger both in body and mind, and have greater capacity for work. In the aggregate the nation will be enormously strengthened to work out its destiny in the ages to come."

(vii.) NEEDLEWORK.

By Miss S. LOCH, *Examiner in Needlework.*

It will, perhaps, be best to preface this chapter on Needlework in the London Board schools by tracing to its commencement the history of the system now in vogue for teaching this subject. It cannot be denied that at one time, in our large towns in England, and also, I fear, in country districts, the women of the working classes were sadly deficient in the knowledge of how to cut out, fix, and make up ordinary articles of underwear ; how to knit (at any rate in the South of England—in the North the knowledge of knitting never seems to have died out), and even how to properly mend their own or their husbands' and children's clothes. One of the first public efforts to improve this state of things was the publication, about fifty years ago, of a clever little manual on needlework, by Lady E. Finch, called "The Sampler," designed specially to improve the teaching of this subject in schools, and so to train up in more thrifty ways the wives and mothers of the succeeding generation. At this time no settled syllabus for all primary schools had been prescribed, and this book proved most useful in introducing into the schools the idea of teaching plain needlework on a regular system. The plan it advocated was introduced into many schools in town and country, and also into some of the training schools for teachers, with much success.

In due time the Education Department found it necessary to add a needlework schedule to the Code of Education in use throughout the country. This schedule was compulsory in all Primary schools, but allowed a choice to be made between earning one shilling or two shillings per head in the girls' departments, dependent upon the subject being taught as part of the ordinary curriculum of the school, when one shilling per head was claimed, or on its being taken as a class subject, when the cutting-out requirements were greater, and the two shillings per head could be earned.[1] The same efficiency of work was, however, required from all, and a Needlework Directress was appointed by the Government to oversee and regulate all matters appertaining (both as regards methods and results) to the needlework, knitting, and cutting-out in Primary schools and training schools for teachers, the male Government Inspectors continuing to see the work in their annual visits to the schools. The needlework of the pupil teachers is also under this lady's control. Some little time, however, before the appointment of the Directress of Needlework, the London School Board had found it necessary to appoint a lady to act as needlework examiner in their schools, to inspect and arrange the work in its various details. As time went on the rapid growth of the schools under the London School Board rendered it imperative to appoint more examiners, whose duty it was to see that the instruction given to the children was imparted on proper educational lines, and that the results attained to the standard of efficiency required by the Education Department.

At the present time the staff in connection with this subject consists of :—

1. Two women needlework examiners, who divide the area of London between them as regards inspection.
2. An examiner of needlework requisitions, under whom also work a staff of women to whom reference will be made later.
3. Three women needlework stocktakers, who take stock annually of all the material which is sent into the schools from the Board's Store.

The Store has a department set apart entirely for needlework goods, and on the receipt of the requisition forms (which are filled in by the head teachers and duly checked and overlooked by the examiner of requisitions) the goods are sent out to the schools in due course. As the schools under the London School Board count by their hundreds, and there is an immense amount of work connected with checking and supervising the requisitions and also in issuing the articles required, it will readily be understood that arrangements have to be made for the issue of these requisitions to be spread over the year. Each head teacher is responsible in money or kind for the goods sent in. The materials, which are chosen by the needlework examiners, are issued to the schools at cost price, and after being made into garments are sold, also at cost price, at the end of the year's work (after the Government Inspectors have paid their visit) to the children and their parents. No profit is allowed to be made on any of the articles made in the schools under the School Board for London. It may be

---

[1] The New Code for 1900 has abolished this sliding scale for the Needlework Grant, and has incorporated it with the Block Grant earned by the schools.

interesting here to note that for the financial year ending March 25th, 1899, £4,985 0s. 5d. worth of materials was issued to the schools, and the amount received for the sale of needlework garments during the same year was £3,307. It will be understood that a certain amount of floating stock is left in the schools at the end of the financial year. Given below is the number of yards, &c., of those materials most in use in the schools which have been issued during the year :—

Calicoes, &c., ... 198,431½ yards
Flannels, &c. ... ... 18,235 yards
Yarns ... ... 7,811¾ lbs.

Besides the ordinary garments which are made in the schools and sold afterwards to those desiring to buy them, the children make annually several thousand garments, &c., for use in the various Industrial Schools, and the laundry, cookery, and housewifery centres under the Board. These articles include, galatea shirts, flannel vests, nightshirts, knitted socks and stockings, overalls, pinafores, sleeves, and caps, and miniature garments for washing and ironing in the laundry centres.

During the last year 12,941 of these articles were made. As great uniformity is required for these garments, they are not cut out by the children in the schools, but are prepared by the staff of women mentioned previously, who work under the direction of the examiner of the needlework requisitions. These women also prepare the material which is issued in the form of practice and test pieces to the schools for purposes of instruction. During the year ending March 25th, 1900, 61,917½ yards were used in this department of the work, 240 dozen pieces of tape (18-yard pieces), and 1,965 lbs. in weight of stocking web. The number of test pieces issued during the year was 1,591,980.

To the first needlework examiner appointed by the London School Board is mainly due the introduction into English schools and training colleges for teachers of what is termed the "simultaneous system" of teaching needlework and cutting-out. The necessity of adopting some system by which needlework could be taught otherwise than individually was imperative owing to the large number of children forming the school classes. The instruction begins by means of what is called "drill" in the infant schools which, as the name implies, means performing to the word of command the various actions necessary to the formation of a stitch both in needlework and knitting. There are also drills for threading needles, putting on thimbles and holding the work in the proper position in the hand. These latter drills are taken in the baby classes (where the children are generally 4 years of age) and the needles used are called "baby threaders" and have no points. These drills are, as a rule, interspersed by little songs which illustrate the actions required—hemming, sewing and knitting, are all taught on this method in the infant schools, and are sometimes also introduced into the upper schools, when the children are specially backward, or have not been through the curriculum of the infant schools before joining the older children. The object of the instruction in needlework and knitting in the infant schools is primarily the training of hand and eye and not the production of finished work; the occasional adaptation of what the children have learnt to some useful and pretty article has done much to interest them in their needlework and knitting lessons. The advantages of teaching needlework by drill are obvious to those who have tried both the individual and collective method of teaching; but it may be well to particularise here what those advantages are found to be. They are briefly :—

1. The power of dealing with large classes of children, whom it would take far longer to teach individually.
2. Time is thus economised.
3. Discipline is improved.
4. Accuracy is ensured.
5. A wholesome competition, one with the other, is engendered.

The drill lessons given to the children vary in length from twenty minutes in the baby class to one hour in the older classes.

The progressive character of the teaching is continued in the upper schools, where the ages of the children range from 7 to 14 or 15 years. The children are divided into classes as they sit for other subjects, and work by the progressive syllabus drawn up by the Education Department. The time given to the subject has varied, up to the present, from three to four hours weekly, but a new rule has just been issued by the Board limiting the time to three hours weekly. It would not be possible to get very much done in this time unless the best and quickest methods of teaching were adopted. A brief explanation of the method of simultaneous teaching may be useful. The teacher, standing before her class, shows the formation of the stitches on a large demonstration frame, which is a frame with white tape stretched down and across it, so as to form squares of about an inch. These pieces of tape are meant to represent the magnified threads of the material on which the children are working. The teacher works upon this frame with a large bone needle and thick cord, and also draws diagrams on a chequered blackboard to illustrate her lesson. Cutting-out is taught simultaneously in the same way on the chequered blackboard, the lines of which correspond with the sectional paper the children have before them, and on which they draw the pattern to scale. The pattern is then transferred full size to cutting-out paper, and from this pattern the garment is cut in material. Of late years much advance has been made in the teaching apparatus and appliances for needlework, such as large demonstration pieces of work for the teachers' use, which have been invented by one of the teachers under the Board, and a system of teaching cutting-out in paper by means of folding, which has been adapted to all garments by one of the Board's needlework examiners. Mending is a necessary part of the year's work. Dress-making, and the proper use of the sewing machine are taught in those schools where the conditions for the same are favourable, but they do not form part of the syllabus of the Education Department. Fancy work is not taught. The girls who are in training in the Board's pupil teacher centres are also most carefully instructed in needlework in its various branches, and also in methods of teaching the same, so far as the time allotted to the subject permits.

The subject of needlework in the schools is a very favourite one with the children, and its value as a factor in their after life cannot be over-estimated. The argument which is often now advanced that the universal use of the sewing machine renders so much tuition in hand sewing unnecessary is not a sound one. The superiority of the hand-made garment over the cheaper machine-made article both as regards appearance and true economy is well known to all who have really studied the subject, and the homely arts of darning and mending save many a penny in a thrifty household.

(viii.) PHYSICAL EDUCATION.

1. FOR BOYS.

By T. CHESTERTON, *Organising Teacher for Boys.*

Although the subject of physical education is of vital importance, yet for nearly twenty years subsequent to the passing of the Elementary Education Act of 1870, it did not receive from the School Board for London a fair amount of the attention which such an important subject deserved. It is true that something was done in the majority of the schools to teach military drill and extension motions from the Infantry Drill Book, but this was manifestly inadequate for the object in view. Nothing further was attempted until 1882, when the so-called Swedish system of drill was taught by a special instructor, to a number of teachers, with a view to its introduction into the schools; but, owing to the unpopularity and unsuitability of the system, the attempt to introduce it into the boys' departments was not entirely successful. In order that the physical training of the children should be conducted in a systematic and methodical manner, the Board resolved in 1889 that physical exercises should be introduced into the school curriculum. Teachers were required to qualify themselves to impart the instruction, and were allowed the option of studying either of two systems then about to be introduced—one, the so-called Swedish, the other a combined system of drill and physical exercises compiled by the present writer. The Board engaged two instructors to carry out the work, the teachers receiving their instruction at various classes organised for the purpose. The course of instruction consisted of twenty-five lessons, each of one hour's duration. This experiment continued for three years, during which time 423 teachers attended the Swedish drill classes, and 1,038 the classes for instruction in the combined system. In 1893 the Board dispensed with the services of the Swedish instructor, and appointed a second instructor to co-operate in teaching throughout the schools the combined system of drill and physical exercises.

Few subjects in the curriculum of the schools under the School Board for London enjoy a wider popularity than that of physical education. In the great majority of the schools it is taken up with the greatest enthusiasm both by scholars and teachers. With the exception of children physically unfit, the whole of the scholars, numbering over half a million, receive systematic instruction in some form or forms of physical exercise suited to their capacities, the object in view being (*a*) the provision of healthy recreation under discipline; (*b*) the promotion of all-round bodily development and growth.

The system of physical exercises now taught in boys' departments was compiled after long and careful study of the whole of the Continental systems; and the aid of an experience of twenty years in the teaching of all branches of physical culture was brought to bear upon it. Although originality is not claimed for the system, the classification and adaptation of the exercises are original. The classification is the result of a close study of the chief anatomical and physiological features of the body, and is, therefore, a scientific one. This classification has regard to the fact that each class in a school consists of a large number of children, irrespective of age, physique, or social position. Each exercise serves some physiological purpose, nothing being introduced for the mere sake of display or effect. The exercises can be performed by the scholars under ordinary circumstances, and while dressed in their usual clothing. No movement can be considered as acrobatic, while the hands and clothing of the children are never in contact with the ground. No difficult or complicated movement is found in the system, which, provided the exercises are taught in their proper order, will be found to be an eminently rational one.

The exercises are arranged as follows :—

Commencing positions of the upper and lower limbs.
Head movements.
Arms raising and swinging.
Arms bending and stretching.
Trunk movements.
Trunk and arm movements.
Leg and hip movements.
Leg, hip and arm movements.
Side lunging.
Direct lunging.
Side lunging with arm movements.
Direct lunging with arm movements.
Balance movements.
Shoulder movements.
Shoulder movements with direct lunging.
Exercises when on the march.
Marching in various formations and figure marching.

The exercises can be taught in four different ways :—

1. As free movements by word of command.
2. By the aid of dumb-bells.
3. With or without dumb-bells to musical accompaniment.
4. When two or more classes occupy the same room, one class performing the

exercises as a silent drill, without in any way interrupting the work of the others.

A limited amount of military drill is incorporated with the exercises, as an auxiliary to them. Though based on the Infantry Drill Book, this drill is somewhat modified to meet the requirements of school children, nothing being taught which is not essential to the purpose. By its use children are enabled to assemble methodically, to form classes, and to move from one point to another in an orderly manner. It teaches the children to walk with a regular step, and in a manner conducive to a good carriage. It accustoms them to orderly formations, teaches them the value of co-operation, and the necessity and advantages of discipline.

The class teachers are responsible for the instruction in physical exercises, and, in order to qualify themselves to impart the instruction, they undergo a course of twenty-four weekly lessons at various training classes conducted by the Board's organising instructors. Each lesson is of one hour's duration, and teachers, to become eligible for examination, must attend at least twenty-one times. The classes are held from 6 to 7 p.m., this hour having been found to be most convenient to those teachers engaged in the Board's Evening Continuation Schools. During this course the whole of the exercises embodied in the system are taught. In addition to the practical instruction, lectures on the theory of physical education are given during the course, particular attention being paid to the following points :—

Muscular movement.
Effects of exercise on the chest, lungs, heart, and circulation.
Air and ventilation.
Food and clothing.
Skin and its functions.
Games and swimming.
Effects of respiratory movements.
Spinal curvature.
Injurious positions assumed during school life.
Rules for conducting the lesson in physical exercises.

During the course, teachers undergoing training are visited by the Instructor at their respective schools, in order that their ability to impart instruction to the children may be tested. Any faulty method of instruction, or weakness in conducting a class, is pointed out by the Instructor, who also assists the teacher by giving a typical lesson to the class. The Instructor continues these visits until he is of opinion that the teacher is qualified to take the examinations. The examinations are held at the termination of the course, and certificates are awarded to those who satisfy the examiners. The practical examination consists in each teacher performing the various movements at the command of the Instructor, and imparting instruction to a class of teachers in the presence of the examiner. In case of failure in the practical examination, a teacher is required to undergo a modified course during the next session before being allowed to take the examination again. The theoretical examination lasts about one and a half hours, and consists in answering on paper about four questions bearing on physical culture in connection with the education of school children. In case of failure in this part of the examination, the teacher is allowed to sit for the subject on a future occasion. This examination is quite distinct from the practical one and is held by a different examiner and on different days. Marks are awarded for practice and theory independently, and certificates are only granted to those who pass in both. Should a candidate pass in one part of the subject only, success in that part is acknowledged, but the certificate is withheld until a pass is obtained in the other part. In the case of teachers possessing advanced certificates in animal physiology and hygiene, the taking of the theoretical examination is optional.

The average time allotted to physical education in the schools of the Board is one hour per week, consisting of five minutes during both morning and afternoon session, and a weekly lesson of not less than twenty minutes' duration. The scholars are taught while dressed in their ordinary clothing ; overcoats, sachels, &c., being removed before the formation of the class. A very pleasing feature in many schools is the mass drill, the whole of the classes being assembled in the playground, and performing exercises of a simple nature, so that the youngest scholars may participate in them.

In every school where ample playground space exists a great speciality is made of the methodical assembly of the scholars. The children are marched from the class-rooms and formed up in recognised positions. The chief object in view is the prevention of panic in case of emergency, though many other advantages accrue from this practice. It is extremely valuable as a means of maintaining discipline ; obedience and promptness are secured ; the tendency to roughness and noise is counteracted ; while such an assembly, if followed by a drill lesson, effects a considerable saving of time. In the majority of schools the assembly is also observed before each session, either in the playground or in the hall. This is found to be a great stimulus to punctuality, but a lesson in physical exercises is not then given, as, among other reasons, a sufficient interval has not elapsed since the children's meals, or active participation in various games.

In the Board's Truant Schools, Industrial Schools, and on board the training ship *Shaftesbury*, the physical education of the boys is carefully carried out. At these institutions systematic training is given in free movements, followed by the use of dumb-bells, wands, &c., and, in the case of the *Shaftesbury*, of portable gymnastic apparatus, such as horizontal and parallel bars, vaulting horse, &c.

Prior to 1889 the Board organised public competitions among elementary schools with a view of encouraging military drill, a banner, presented by the Society of Arts, being awarded to the school gaining the highest marks. In that year physical exercises were included in the competitions as an impetus to physical education, a banner being awarded for that subject. A fair amount of interest was at first evinced among teachers, but entries for these competitions gradually diminished, until at last it became difficult to obtain sufficient. In 1896 the competitive element was eliminated, and displays were substituted, proving far more satisfactory.

In 1898 the Board decided to supply light wooden dumb-bells and wands for the use of the elder children in the senior departments. No school is recommended for a supply of such apparatus unless the Instructor certifies that the free movements are thoroughly taught, and that such progress is made by the elder scholars as will warrant its use. A great number of schools have received supplies of dumb-bells and wands, on request of the head teacher; a clear indication that the teachers have recognised the fact that free movements alone are insufficient for the physical training of their elder scholars. In addition to the above-mentioned apparatus a few schools have received supplies of clubs, but these have only been granted on the special recommendations of the Instructor, and chiefly for display purposes.

Recently, portable gymnastic apparatus has been supplied to a few schools possessing halls, for the use of the more robust among the elder pupils. It consists of horizontal and parallel bars and climbing ropes. The above-mentioned apparatus is only supplied to schools where teachers are found capable of imparting instruction in elementary gymnastics, and is only used under the personal supervision of these teachers. Owing to the simple construction of the horizontal and parallel bars, they can be readily erected by the scholars previous to the lesson, and as readily taken down by them at its conclusion. The climbing ropes are fixed by iron clamps to the girders overhead.

A very pleasing feature in the physical education of the children attending the schools of the Board is the keen interest shown by a large number of teachers, especially of boys' departments, in the encouragement of outdoor games amongst their pupils. It is, indeed, remarkable in some schools to see with what ingenuity such games as football, rounders, cricket, &c., are carried out, in spite of the fact that in many instances the playgrounds are of limited area, and the ground in every case asphalted. A visit to the parks, open spaces, and commons in and around London, on any Saturday morning throughout the year, will convince the most casual observer that every effort is made by the teachers to foster a love of healthy outdoor sports and athletic games amongst their pupils.

During the past few years the teaching of swimming has made great strides throughout the schools, and is recognised as part of the curriculum. This branch of physical education is taken up most enthusiastically by teachers and scholars of boys' and girls' departments. Each scholar is allowed twenty lessons free of cost. The instruction is imparted by the school staff, the local baths being used for the purpose. During the past year nearly thirty thousand children received instruction in swimming, and over eight thousand were taught to swim. In connection with the swimming, instruction is also given in life-saving, and the resuscitation of the apparently drowned.

It is pleasing to observe that the erroneous idea, prevalent among many teachers some years ago, that the physical training of school children was simply an adjunct to school displays and exhibitions in order to enhance their spectacular attractiveness, has been dispelled, and that a due appreciation of its educational value now exists in the minds of the teachers

R

2. For Girls and Infants.

By Miss E. Kingston, *Organising Teacher.*

The School Board for London recognises to the fullest extent the necessity of a physical as well as a mental training for the children in its schools, and has, during the last few years, spared neither effort nor expense to make that training as thorough as possible. There is daily, in all the girls' and infants' departments of the schools, a steady, systematic physical training of a most useful, if not altogether showy kind.

In the earlier years of the Board's work little was done for the encouragement of physical exercises for girls. In 1870 the School Board appealed to the Education Department to permit the attendance of girls at drill to count as attendance at school, as was the case with the boys; but it was met with a point blank refusal. It was not until some years after that the Swedish system of physical training was introduced into the schools; but the syllabus of work was very meagre when compared with the amount and variety of the exercises which to-day are practised. The Swedish system of " free movements" forms a perfect physical training for girls and infants. It is in the progression and order of these movements that this system has its greatest strength, and experience has shown that it produces a harmonious development of every part of the body, has a healthy and strengthening effect on the nervous system, with rest and relief to the worried and overtaxed brain. The exercises follow in a certain order, are suitable to the weakest child, are progressive from the simplest and gentlest, step by step, to the strongest and most complicated ones. They are particularly adapted for use in our large schools, as no apparatus is required, and the movements can be performed in a limited space—a difficulty, unfortunately, frequently met with.

The amount of time devoted to this important branch of education has of late years been considerably increased. According to the Board's Code, "The time-tables must provide for a definite lesson once a week of not less than twenty minutes' duration, and not less than five minutes' systematic instruction in both morning and afternoon sessions."

This time is mostly adhered to in the case of infants' departments. The short daily lesson being usually given in the classrooms between 9 and 10 a.m. and 3 to 3.30 p.m., but in the girls' departments it is mostly given, when the weather permits, in the playground after the recreation interval, and consists mainly of "marching," and "running" exercises.

The weekly lessons in the girls' departments are generally of thirty minutes' duration, and are usually given in the hall, where one has been provided. The Board has recently decided that, in the Higher Grade schools, at least an hour per week shall be devoted to the physical training of the girls.

It is almost impossible to speak definitely of the progress being made in physical training in the schools. In many schools the work is carried on under the greatest difficulties, while others are surrounded by every advantage. In the latter, good progress is being made, and each year a steady improvement in the physique of the children is noticeable ; but, unfortunately, in the former class of schools, where the exercises have to be taught in the classrooms, the slovenly gait of the girls is often only too apparent.

The work in the infants' departments is necessarily of the simplest character, but is invaluable as a preparation for the training given in the upper schools. The greatest importance is attached to the frequent repetition and the correct teaching of the elementary positions, in order that the best results may accrue from the performance of the exercises. No set syllabus of work is used, but the exercises consist mostly of "arm" and "shoulder-blade" movements and "marching."

Great difficulty is experienced in the teaching of good marching, but the value of it, in its effects upon the discipline of a school, and upon the deportment of the children generally, cannot be over-estimated. In order to prevent that rigidity of the limbs which the children are wont to assume on hearing the word "march," the use of the word "walk" as a command is frequently made. It is found to convey a clearer impression to the minds of the children, and the marching becomes more natural as a consequence.

For hall or playground drill the children are arranged in files. Much time is saved in the opening and closing of files by the use of painted lines or lead grooves, which are placed upon the floors of the halls of most infants' departments. The first class children are taught how to "open and close files," in order to prepare them for the work of the upper schools.

A syllabus of exercises has recently been issued by the Board as a guide to the teachers in the arrangement of their work for the various standards throughout the school. The exercises are carefully graded, and arranged in groups, according to the general effect which they have upon different parts of the body :

1. *Preparatory movements.*—This group consists of simple movements of the arms and legs. They serve to gain general attention, a good posture of the body, and prepare the class for the lesson.

2. *Leg movements.*—These movements tend to draw the blood downward to the lower extremities, and thereby stimulate the general circulation, where it has become somewhat congested during the time the children have been sitting at lessons.

3. *Dorsal movements.*—This important group of exercises comprises : trunk bendings, forward, backward, and downward, combined with various "arm" and "shoulder-blade" movements. They are extremely valuable, in that they raise and expand the chest, and straighten the spine. By so doing they counteract the many bad postures which the children assume during school life.

4. *Arm extensions.*—Great prominence is given to this group, as they are invaluable for expanding and developing the chest, and causing deeper and more energetic respirations.

5. *Balance movements*—These quiet movements follow the vigorous arm-

stretchings, as they help to regulate the breathing and the increased action of the heart. They produce a more general muscular contraction.

6. *Shoulder-blade movements.*—These help to strengthen the muscles of the back, correct the position of the shoulder-blades, and expand the chest.

7. *Abdominal movements.*—These are very strong movements, and are mostly used by the elder children. They strengthen the abdominal muscles and stimulate digestion.

8. *Lateral bendings.*—These exercises also affect the internal organs, and act strongly on the side trunk muscles.

9. *Leaping.*—These exercises come at the end of the lesson, as they are very difficult of execution, and necessitate a general action of nearly the whole muscular system. They do much to develop the general elasticity of the body.

10. *Respiratory movements.*—The lesson is completed by one or other of these movements, which consist mostly of slow arm raisings, combined with slow leg movements, in rhythm with deep respiration.

Three or more examples of exercises are given under each of the previous headings for each of the different standards, and are used for certain periods throughout the year. When the exercises are obliged to be taught in the classrooms, and the children have to remain standing at the desks, or between the seats, where movement is limited, slight modifications are made, and many of the most valuable exercises are of necessity omitted.

In Standard I. the simple "turnings" and "facings" are taught, while in Standard II. and upwards "turnings," "numberings," "closing and opening of files and ranks," are practised regularly.

Marching and running, combined with strong leg movements; figure marching, including "company marching," "cross marching," &c., are taught to train the children in accuracy of detail, a different figure being taught in each standard. Fancy steps of various kinds are practised, and are much enjoyed by the girls. These do much towards making the children light and graceful in their movements.

The Board lays great stress upon the importance of making the children assume a good posture while sitting or standing at lessons, and it is gratifying to note a great improvement in this particular. General rules for such postures are given to the teachers during their course of instruction at the physical training classes.

Music during the performance of the exercises is not generally advocated. It has been found from experience that the chief value of the exercise and its correct execution have often been overlooked when music has been introduced; the work, in most instances, loses much, if not all, of its precision and smartness, and develops into a loose, slipshod style, which counteracts all the real benefit which should be derived from its peformance. Music is, however, very generally used with the "marching" and "fancy steps," and it has done much towards helping forward a freer and more graceful carriage of the children.

The physical training of the girls in the upper classes of the Higher Grade schools is a matter of the highest importance, and is one which has lately occupied the attention of the Board. Light, movable apparatus, such as wands and dumb-bells, are supplied for the use of such children, to supplement their " free movements."

The children are at an age when the rate of growth is great, and as a consequence they show many physical weaknesses and are inclined to fall into slipshod habits. In addition, the mental strain is greater than at any other period of school life. The time devoted to the subject of physical training should, therefore, be correspondingly greater; but until lately one short practice of twenty minutes' duration was the maximum time given. The Board's decision, " that at least an hour of systematic physical exercise must be given in such schools," will do much to secure better results.

Although the Board has lately built two or three fully-equipped gymnasia, there is great diversity of opinion with regard to the use of fixed apparatus for the training of young girls. We must not lose sight of the fact that girls of this age require very careful handling, and the least danger of strain must be avoided. Considering the size of the classes, and having regard, also, to the want of stamina of many of the children, it is impossible to give that individual care and supervision which are necessary in gymnastic work.

Skipping affords a very pleasing and beneficial form of exercise. Ropes are supplied by the Board, on the recommendation of the organising teacher, to such schools as are proficient in their general exercises.

The displays of physical exercises, given by the scholars of selected schools at the Albert Hall every other year, have done, and are doing, much to raise the standard of efficiency in the schools, and show what perfection of movement can be attained by careful and steady training. The competitive element has been abolished; but it is generally acknowledged that the display has not suffered in consequence. It is freer, more ingenious, more intelligent, more pleasing, and for variety, originality, and scope cannot easily be surpassed. Besides " free movements," displays are given in the use of wands, rings, dumb-bells, and balls, together with skipping, swimming, and life-saving drills.

According to the Board's Code, swimming is included in the term "Physical Exercise," and rapid strides have been made of late years in girls' schools in the teaching of this important art. A voluntary organisation of teachers, the London Schools Swimming Association, has done much to aid the Board in this branch of physical training. At the end of the present season alone there were 162 girls' schools affiliated to the association. Eight thousand girls received instruction in swimming, and 1,800 girls were taught to swim. Of these, 800 earned the London Schools Swimming Association certificate for swimming a distance of not less than fifty yards.

Swimming is taught during school hours by one of the ordinary staff of the school, the time spent at the baths being duly noted on the time-table. Free admission to the baths is obtained for the children by means of vouchers supplied by the Board. The children are taught the swimming drill on land before entering the water. The movements are introduced as part of their physical exercises during the winter months, and have been found a valuable aid in teaching children to overcome certain initial difficulties in the water.

At each lesson the children again practise the drill, standing in the water at the shallow end, round the sides of the bath. For the arm movements alone, they stand firmly on the bottom and incline the body on the surface of the water; for the leg practice, they are made to turn round, to support themselves by the rail round the bath, and by raising their feet from the bottom they rest upon the water.

When these separate movements have been well practised the children are encouraged by the help of the teacher or monitor (who is able to swim) to try the combined breast-stroke.

The Board issues certificates of proficiency to girls who can swim a distance of twenty yards. In order to encourage general swimming several shields and trophies have been given by private persons to the girls' schools, the winning of which depends on the percentage of Association Swimming Certificate holders in the schools. Life-saving and resuscitation of the apparently drowned are taught in many schools, and silver and bronze medals are awarded by the Life Saving Society to encourage this humane work among the children.

Fire drill has lately been made compulsory by the Board, and a card giving a few general rules to be observed in cases of fire or panic is hung in a conspicuous position in every department.

They are as follow :—

1. The fire alarm shall be given by means of the school bell.
2. Each class teacher shall see the whole class (i.) clear of the room; (ii.) clear of the building; and (iii.) as soon as possible clear of the premises.
3. During experimental fire drill children must not be taken out into the streets.
4. Where there is more than one staircase the classes which are to go down each shall be predetermined.
5. Specific rules bearing on the order in which the classes are to leave the building, or on any other special circumstances for which it may be necessary to provide, are to be hung in each classroom.
6. During school hours no exit doors leading from the school building into the playground are ever to be locked.
7. When roof playgrounds are in use, one assistant, at least, must always be in charge. On the fire alarm being given during play-time, the teacher in charge of the roof playground must secure the exit and give the signal to the children to fall into line by classes. The rest of the staff must proceed to the roof, and the classes must be conducted down, beginning with the lowest.
8. It is the duty of the caretaker when the alarm of fire is given to secure all the playground gates.

The time occupied in the simultaneous dismissal of all the departments depends upon the size of the school and the structure and arrangement of the school building. The average time is from two to three minutes, when about 1,200 children are transferred in an orderly manner from a building some three storeys high to their allotted places in the playground. The good effect on the discipline of the school cannot be over-estimated, besides the beneficial results in the prevention of panic.

All mistresses entering the service of the Board are required to qualify for its physical education certificate within three years from the date of their appointment, unless exempted by the School Management Committee on the ground of physical disability. In order to meet this requirement classes for the instruction of teachers are held annually at six different centres in London. The course consists of twenty-five lessons, given weekly, and each of an hour's duration. The syllabus of work taken is similar to that taught in the schools.

During the course of instruction the organising teacher who conducts the class gives short and incidental lectures on the chief points relating to exercise, such as :

1. Effects of exercise (local and general).
2. Respiratory movements.
3. Effects of different groups of exercises on the body.
4. Rules to be observed during and after muscular exertion.
5. Symptoms of over-exertion.
6. Effects of bad postures.
7. Good postures for standing, reading, writing, and needlework.
8. Rules for conducting a lesson in physical exercise.
9. Ventilation of rooms used for exercise.

At the end of the session the teachers are examined in "practical" work by an independent examiner, and all who fail to pass the test are required to undergo another course of instruction before presenting themselves again for examination. Besides this examination in "practical" work, each student, according to present rules, must obtain the advanced certificates in physiology and hygiene of the Science and Art Department.

Physical training forms part of the general education of the Board's pupil teachers during the five years of their apprenticeship. In some centres the instruction is given very regularly and systematically ; but the time devoted to the subject is very inadequate, being only, on an average, from thirty to sixty minutes once a fortnight.

Free movements, wand and dumb-bell drill, are mostly taught. In those centres where efficient work is done, provisional certificates are issued to the students at the end of their apprenticeship, which relieve them from attending the full course of lessons given in the training classes after they leave college. Before receiving these certificates each student is required to give a practical demonstration of her knowledge, and show that she is capable of teaching a class of young children.

The organisation of the physical training of the children of the girls', junior, and infants' departments of the Board is entrusted to **three** organising teachers, whose duties are as follows :

1. To train the teachers.
2. To visit the schools, to see that the instruction is given regularly and in a thorough manner.
3. To help the newly-appointed teachers.
4. To correct imperfect teaching.
5. To inspect the work of each class at least once a year.
6. To report to the Board on the progress and efficiency of the physical training in their schools.

The occasional visits for the purpose of inspection are paid without notice, so that by them a good general idea of the state of the work is obtained, besides affording the organising teacher an opportunity of ascertaining where to direct her future efforts in order that they may be utilised to the best advantage.

CHAPTER VII.

THE ABNORMAL CHILD.

(i.) THE BLIND.

By Miss GREENE, *Superintendent of the Instruction of Blind Children.*

The first School Board for London did not attempt to deal with the education of blind children. Until 1874 this work was left entirely in the hands of voluntary agencies. Undoubtedly the law of compulsion applied no less to blind than to sighted children but it would have been useless to drive the blind child into school if no special provision were made for its instruction.

In April, 1874, the Board determined to facilitate the elementary education of the blind. It resolved that the divisional committees should be asked to take steps to induce blind children to attend the ordinary schools, and that the "Society for Providing Home Instruction for the Blind" should be informed of the fact, in order that it might provide special instruction for these children. In 1875 the Board appointed a peripatetic teacher to instruct the blind in the ordinary schools.

Thus the work went on for five years. In 1879 the Education Department was persuaded to recognise the fact that this very benevolent and necessary work was being carried on in the schools of the Board. The Education Department then agreed to recognise the attendances of blind children at any convenient centre for special instruction, as if those attendances had been made at the schools at which the children would otherwise have presented themselves. Earlier in that year the Board had appointed the present writer to be Superintendent of the Instruction of the Blind. Later on, two assistant instructresses were appointed. Centres were organised for the instruction of blind children, furnished with the necessary books and apparatus.

In 1885 a Royal Commission was appointed to consider, among other questions, the various systems of education of the blind and the deaf as practised in England and abroad. The Commission sat for about four years, and important evidence was given before it in regard to foreign methods, more especially the Saxon (Fürsorge) system and the provision made for the blind in Paris by the "Société de Placement et de Secours."

In 1889 the Commission reported. They recommended that the education of the blind should be placed under State control instead of being left in the hands of philanthropic agencies, or the Poor Law Guardians, by whom it was sometimes under-taken as a mode of charitable relief. They also recommended that the age of compulsory instruction should be extended to 16 years.

In order to give effect to these recommendations a Statute was passed in 1893[1] which dealt with blind and deaf children. It imposed upon the "school authority" (in the case of London, the School Board) the duty of providing elementary education, including industrial training, for blind and deaf children, in some school certified as suitable by the Education Department, and, if necessary, of establishing and maintaining such a school, or contributing to such establishment and maintenance. It contained provisions for boarding out the child in a home conveniently near the certified school. In the event of the adoption of this plan the parent of the child was made liable to contribute towards the expenses incurred by the Board on the child's behalf. On failure to agree to the amount, it may be settled by a court of summary jurisdiction. The age of compulsory attendance of blind and deaf children at school was raised to 16 years, and no partial exemption was permitted. The duty is imposed upon the parent of causing a blind or deaf child to receive suitable education, and it is no excuse for non-compliance that there is no elementary school within a reasonable distance of the child's home.

This Act came into operation on January 1st, 1894. It followed in many of its provisions the precedent of the Industrial Schools Acts rather than that of the Elementary Education Acts. In April, 1895, the Education Department issued Regulations in regard to the boarding-out of blind and deaf children.[2] These Regulations enabled the school authority to nominate to the Education Department for appointment bodies of managers to control the boarding-out of children. These committees are called " Boarding-out Committees." Very stringent conditions are laid down concerning the homes in which the children are placed. Not more than two blind or two deaf children may be sent to one home, and the blind and the deaf must not be sent to the same home. The " foster parent," for such is the technical name of the person entrusted with the care of the child, must not have more than four other children resident at home. The foster parent has to sign an undertaking that he will feed and lodge the child properly and " endeavour to train the child in habits of truthfulness, obedience, personal cleanliness, and industry." A member of the boarding-out committee must visit the home at least

---

[1] 56 & 57 Vict. c. 42.   [2] *See* Owen : Education Acts, Ed. 1897, p. 636.

once a month, and yearly returns must be made to the Education Department of the number of children boarded out.

By a Minute dated April, 1894, the Education Department authorised a grant at the rate of £3 3s. per annum if the child has received efficient elementary education other than manual or industrial training, and his attainments are found to be satisfactory, regard being had to his necessary disqualifications, and a further grant at the rate of £2 2s. per annum if the child has received regular and satisfactory instruction, and has made satisfactory progress, in some course of manual instruction or industrial training approved by the Department.[1]

When the Act was passed the School Board for London had 156 blind, or partially blind, children under instruction at twenty centres. The Superintendent was assisted by six blind instructresses, for whom guides were allowed, to lead them to and from the centres. The children were taught reading and writing by means of the "Braille" system, arithmetic by means of Taylor's arithmetic boards, and geography by aid of relief maps and globes. They were inspected with the sighted scholars at the Government inspections of the ordinary day schools, and they earned the ordinary Government Grant.

In order to carry out the provisions of the Act it was necessary to reorganise the work of the Board's centres for the instruction of the blind. The Board decided to bring the children together into larger classes and thus reduce the number of centres. This the Board was enabled to do by adopting the boarding-out system in regard to some of the children, and by paying for guides and travelling expenses for others. The number of centres was reduced to eight, meeting each morning and afternoon. It was decided that, so far as was possible, the children should continue to receive part of their instruction in the ordinary day school. They are for this purpose divided into two sections—the seniors attending the ordinary school in the morning and the centre for the blind in the afternoon, the juniors attending in reverse order. The plan of teaching at the centres by means of blind teachers is continued; but a sighted helper is appointed to each centre to assist in the care of the children.

In 1894, the Board decided to place certain blind children in institutions. Most of the cases chosen for sending to such institutions were those giving promise of exceptional ability, having either considerable teaching power or special musical capacity. The Board entered into an agreement with the Royal Normal College for the Blind, Upper Norwood (which was founded in 1873, and carried on a very successful work, especially in training the blind in music), to receive certain cases for higher education. Under the will of the late Henry Gardner, a sum of £300,000 was left for the benefit of blind persons in England and Wales, four-ninths of which sum was to be applied to the education of the blind in music, or their instruction in suitable trades. Over one hundred of the scholarships awarded under this trust have been gained by children taught in the Board's classes, which have mostly been held at the Royal Normal College for the Blind. In July, 1894, the Duke of Westminster, the President

---

[1] *See Owen : Education Acts*, Ed. 1897, p. 341.

of the Royal Normal College for the Blind, suggested the transfer of that institution to the School Board for London. After protracted negotiations it was decided to carry out a scheme whereby the college was transferred to the Board, and the work for the senior students, *i.e.*, those over 16 years of age, was continued by a voluntary committee, no part of the expenditure on this section of the work being paid for out of the rates. The transfer was effected in January, 1897. The institution was worked under this dual control for over two years and a half, but on account of certain difficulties which occurred, it was thought well both by the Board and the voluntary committee that it should revert to its voluntary character. The Board was, therefore, repaid the amount expended by it upon the college, and gave up its control in September, 1899, reserving to itself the right to continue to send certain cases of blind children requiring higher or musical education to the Royal Normal College at a specified rate of payment.

The Board has decided to acquire another institution, to be entirely under its own management, in which it will educate such blind children for two or three years preceding the age of 16, with especial attention to technical training which will assist them to support themselves in after life.

The number on the roll at the day centres is now 206. The children are examined annually in the month of February by H.M. Inspectors of schools. There are six boarding-out committees. The cost per child at the Board's day centres amounts to about £12 12s per annum. In cases where children are boarded-out, or sent to institutions, the cost is considerably more, ranging from £30 to £45 per annum, but in these cases the parents are required to contribute towards the maintenance of the children according to their ability.

(ii.) The Deaf.

By William Nelson, *Superintendent of the Education of the Deaf.*

The first class for the education of the deaf under the School Board for London was opened in September, 1874, at Wilmot Street, Bethnal Green.

At the beginning there were only four or five pupils in attendance, but as it became known that special instruction was being provided for these children, the numbers steadily increased, and more centres had to be opened in different parts of the Metropolitan area.

It was just at this time that the burning question of rival educational systems for the deaf was coming to the front in England. On the one hand there was the German or oral system, the main principle of which was education through speech and lip-reading; and on the other the sign system, which advocated the use of signs, finger-spelling and written language, and did not attempt to teach speech.

At Wilmot Street the Committee of the School Board adopted what might be called a compromise between these two systems, and for the first three years an attempt was made to teach both articulate speech and finger-spelling at the same time.

This, however, did not constitute a fair trial for either system. In 1877 a pure oral school was opened as an experiment, and finally in 1880 the oral or speech system was adopted in all the centres. No change has been made since, with the exception that about twenty very backward children have been grouped together for special instruction and have been taught finger-spelling as far as possible.

The great advantage of speech and lip-reading to the deaf, if they can be taught, cannot be questioned, even if the result is in many cases somewhat laboured. It is believed, that by more carefully thought-out methods of organisation, a better and fairer trial can be given to a system, which promises so much for a section of people whose method of intercourse has shut them off so entirely, as a class, from the rest of the world. To ensure perfect success many conditions are necessary: good attendance, efficient classification, first-rate teachers, suitable and convenient centres, a sympathetic public, and appreciative parents.

Many of the difficulties which the Board encountered in its work in behalf of deaf mutes have been overcome by the provisions of the Act for the education of blind and deaf children, to which reference has already been made.[1] Those provisions apply to the deaf as well as to the blind, except that a deaf child under seven years of age cannot be compelled to attend school.

The general classification of deaf children under the School Board, for educational purposes, is being considered on the following basis:—There are (i.) about 72 per cent. of congenitally deaf children with fair mental capacity; (ii.) about 16 per cent. of backward children of low mental capacity; and (iii.) 12 per cent. who, previous to becoming deaf, had acquired a limited, but very important, power of speech.

At present these groups have representatives in each centre, without any possibility of the above classification for teaching purposes. It has been decided, however, to place the children of Group II. in cottage homes in a suburban district. The homes will have a central school, workshops, and gymnasium, and good playing fields and garden. There they will be taught by methods suited to their special needs, and particular attention will be given to physical and industrial training. This will at once be better for themselves, and for the other two more intelligent groups.

Group III., or the semi-mutes, consists of two or three children in each centre. When these are gathered together it will be possible to take advantage of the foundation of language in their possession, and to build upon it by methods more rapid and more nearly approaching those of the ordinary schools.

The teaching at the regular day centres will then be concentrated on the congenitally deaf, Group I., about three-fourths of the whole number.

The principle of linking two small centres together is being tried, one for children from 5 to about 9 years of age, and the other for older children. It is found that small isolated centres of not more than two teachers cannot do the most efficient work. The teachers' energies are too much spread out over pupils at all degrees of educational attainment.

---

[1] See *ante*, p. 249.

At Balham an infant school has been established on somewhat new and very promising lines. The idea of this school is to secure attendance when the children are not more than 5 years of age, if possible, and to take advantage of that hereditary tendency to speech which is believed by many to be in the possession of the baby deaf child for the first few years of its life, before it dies out. The hitherto dreary year of abstract articulation teaching, which had so little in it of interest to the child, is here being filled with the life and pleasure associated with a good kindergarten. For this purpose a Froebel teacher has been engaged. Natural pantomimic games, always, however, accompanied by words, are being developed, and give the most intense delight; and just as music supplies the chief æsthetic want of the blind, so drawing, particularly in colour, affects the deaf. Expression from every side is aimed at, and it promises to do much for that spontaneity of speech which is so particularly wanting. This school is working out the scheme on which will be based all the infant deaf teaching in the future under the Board.

Drawing is, however, being carefully taught at all the centres. Art handicraft probably gives the best opening in life for the deaf, and it is absolutely necessary that the instruction leading up to it should be thorough in this respect.

The training of teachers is not as satisfactory as it should be. The otherwise excellent Blind and Deaf Act of 1893 unfortunately made no provision for this. But the standard is rising, and the present demand for good training may be expected to produce the desired result shortly.

A great improvement is being made in providing the new centres with good halls, and also in making a more careful selection of neighbourhoods for the convenience of the deaf population. These children are not really so scattered as might be imagined. There may be said to be, not colonies, but distinct groups in Bethnal Green, Tower Hamlets, Bermondsey, Walworth, and Clerkenwell, and it is here that the largest centres are rising up. There are very few deaf children in the City and Westminster, and generally in the West of London they are more scattered and less easily collected together.

The general public do not realise that there are a great many more deaf than blind people. The defect of hearing does not command notice, and hence it has always been found that the deaf are generally passed by. When they are discovered they are often treated and spoken to in such an unnatural way as to make it quite impossible for them to understand.

The parents of these children invariably treat them with great affection, but one of the important duties of the teacher who desires his pupil to speak and lip-read is to seek their co-operation. Speech at school and signing at home cannot lead to good results. Generally the parent signs unconsciously and speaks at the same time, and it is often difficult to convince a mother that her child is really deaf on this account.

At the present time there are nineteen centres with a staff of sixty-three teachers and a superintendent. About one hundred children are boarded out with foster parents, conveniently for attendance at the classes. Many of these are sent to London by the school authorities of country districts who have not made provision themselves for instructing the deaf.

The attendance at the centres is, on the whole, good. It is higher than in the ordinary schools, but a day's absence in the case of a deaf child is more serious than in the case of a hearing child.

Evening continuation classes were opened in 1898, and have been well attended and popular. They supply a distinct want, and as they become better known their field of usefulness will increase, reaching, no doubt, many people who have become deaf after the ordinary school age has passed, and to whom the acquirement of lip-reading will be particularly advantageous.

The London County Council has recently awarded valuable scholarships in art to two promising deaf boys. This may be regarded as the stepping-stone to a higher field of work for the deaf, for which they have both a special liking and a particular aptitude. Last year a boy from one of the centres passed an examination of the College of Preceptors, taking exceptionally high marks in algebra, which is a most satisfactory outcome of competition in the open field, with no favour, and an indication of what can be done with the intelligent deaf.

The centres are annually examined by H.M. Inspectors; and so important has the subject become, that recently a special Inspector has been appointed to take charge of this work in all the deaf schools in England. His influence promises to be very great in breaking down many of the old barriers to progress. Already a broader spirit is being manifested in regard to the work of other schools, both Continental and British, and the future of deaf mute education is full of promise.

(iii.) THE PHYSICALLY AND MENTALLY DEFECTIVE.

By Mrs. E. M. BURGWIN, *Superintendent of Schools for Special Instruction.*

Among so vast a number of children as that which comes under the control of the London School Board, many are to be found who, on account of some physical or mental defect, are incapable of profiting from the instruction which is given in the ordinary school and need separate educational treatment. Not only can such children derive no advantage from the ordinary curriculum, but their presence in a class forms an impediment to the progress of the other scholars.

These children are chiefly cripples, epileptics, or of a low order of intelligence. The latter are not to be confounded with idiots: they belong to a class in which the mental ability, although far below normal, is capable of cultivation and improvement. If the child eventually proves incapable of benefiting from the education provided, it usually passes, with the consent of the parent, from the control of the School Board to that of the Metropolitan Asylums Board.

The difficulty caused by the presence of these children in the day schools had long been felt; but it was not until 1891 that the Board attempted to deal with it. The

Royal Commission on the Instruction of the Blind, Deaf, &c., had reported " that, with regard to the feeble-minded children, they should be separated from ordinary scholars in public elementary schools, in order that they may receive special instruction." In March, 1891, the Board considered this recommendation, and resolved " that special schools for those children who, by reason of physical and mental defect, cannot be taught in the ordinary standards or by ordinary methods, be established, and that the schools be designated ' Schools for Special Instruction.' " In July, 1892, two Special schools were opened, and the present writer was appointed Superintendent of this branch of the Board's work.

In 1898 the Board defined in greater detail the methods of dealing with this question. A Departmental Committee of the Education Department had come to the conclusion that one per cent. of the children between the ages of 7 and 14 needed special instruction. The Board accepted this estimate, but it declared that it was not expedient at once to make provision for this number of children. It was agreed that the accommodation to be provided should be considered on the basis of the needs of each locality. It was further agreed that no class should contain more than twenty scholars; that no centre should, if possible, be for fewer than two classes or more than five, but that if only one class could be formed in any locality, it should be conducted in the ordinary school building and not in a specially erected centre.

The commencement of this valuable work was not unattended with difficulties. No child was taken out of the ordinary school and sent to a centre unless it had been examined by the Board's Medical Officer and the Superintendent, and had been certified by them as requiring special treatment. But parents are often unwilling to admit the deficiency of their children, more particularly in mental cases. It was a question, too, whether the Board, although it had power to compel a child's attendance at school, was empowered to compel it to attend any particular school. It not unfrequently happened, therefore, that parents protested against the classification of their children as defectives, and demanded, as of right, that they should continue their education in the ordinary school. The cost of the education of defective children is necessarily greatly in excess of the cost of the education of the normal child. The gross cost of a defective child in the year ended March 25th, 1899, was £9 8s. 3d. But, until recently, Government did not recognise this fact, and the centres for defectives could earn no greater grant than the ordinary schools.

These difficulties have recently been overcome by the Elementary Education (Defective and Epileptic Children) Act of 1899.[1] This Act is framed upon the same principles as the Blind and Deaf Children Act, 1893, to which reference has already been made.[2] The most striking difference between the two Acts is that while the latter makes the education of the blind and deaf compulsory upon the education authority and upon the parent, the former is permissive merely. The school authority is at liberty to adopt its provisions, or not, as it sees fit, and the obligation to educate a

---

[1] 62 and 63 Vict. c. 72.   [2] See *ante*, p. 249.

defective or epileptic child between 7 and 16 years of age is only imposed upon the parent "where a special class or school is within reach of the child's residence."

The school authority (in this case the School Board) has power to ascertain (1) the number of children in its district who, without being either imbecile, on the one hand, or merely dull or backward, on the other, are, by reason of physical or mental defect, incapable of receiving proper benefit from the instruction given in the ordinary schools, and (2) the number of children who, not being idiots or imbeciles, are unfit by reason of severe epilepsy, to attend ordinary public elementary schools. A parent is given the right to present his child to the school authority for medical examination, and also can be compelled to do so under a penalty not exceeding £5. A child is not "ascertained" under the Act to be defective or epileptic until it has been so certified by a qualified medical practitioner.

The provisions for the erection and maintenance of schools, and for boarding out defective children, are similar to those in regard to the blind and deaf[1]; but epileptic children can only be dealt with in certified schools. No establishment for boarding such children may be licensed to accommodate more than fifteen children in one building, or comprise more than four such buildings.

This restriction upon the accommodation of an establishment will greatly increase expenditure upon defective children, and more especially the expenditure upon epileptics, who can be dealt with in no other way. The Board was so impressed with the importance of this question, and with other administrative difficulties which would be created by dealing with such small numbers of children, that it decided to postpone the provision of accommodation for epileptics, and it petitioned the Education Department to promote in Parliament an amending Act, excluding epileptic children from the operation of the clause. This the Department declined to do, and urged the Board to carry out the provisions of the Act. This deadlock has not as yet been brought to an end.

In February, 1899, the Education Department issued rules for the boarding out of defective children, and a Minute regulating the Government Grant for defectives and epileptics. The grant amounts to fifty shillings for each unit of average attendance, with an addition, if manual instruction is given, of thirty shillings for younger and forty shillings for elder children.

There are now under the control of the Board 53 centres, having a roll of 2,154 children, taught by 119 certificated teachers. One centre is devoted exclusively to cripples who are unable to attend the ordinary schools. As the Act empowers the Board to pay for conveyances or guides for the children to and from school, the adoption of the centre system is greatly facilitated.

The children in these special schools are often physically, as well as mentally, weak. As a rule, twenty minutes is the longest period for which they are able to work at one time. They are usually taught Scripture, reading, writing, arithmetic, singing by the

---

[1] See *ante*, p. 249.

Tonic Sol-fa method, drawing, colouring, modelling in clay, basket weaving, and needlework. Great attention is paid to physical exercises.

The concrete form of instruction is adopted in the lower classes, and the transition from this to the abstract is a tedious and most difficult process. The teacher endeavours to stimulate the dormant faculties by varied occupations which interest and give pleasure to the pupil. When once the transition from the concrete to the abstract is effected the battle is more than half won and subsequent progress is, if slow, not so painful.

The elder girls attend cookery and laundry classes on two afternoons in each week, and the elder boys receive manual instruction on one afternoon in each week.

The system of instruction attains its completest triumph when it becomes possible to return a defective child to the ordinary school. This end is not infrequently achieved. In the year ended March 25th, 1899, out of an average attendance of 1,250 no less than seventy-one children returned to the day schools.

The following quotation from a letter received from a head master of one of the Board's ordinary schools illustrates a case of perfect cure: "I have this morning sent one of the lads who came to me from the Special school a year ago to a good place in a stick factory, where the training in design which he began in the Special school and continued here will be of use to him. He is to have six shillings a week to begin with, and has prospects, as some of the hands can earn £4 per week. I am very pleased, because it shows what can be done with some of these weak lads."

But even if such a complete cure as that which is thus described cannot always be effected, the system of training often does enough for the improvement of the child's intelligence to prevent it becoming in after life a burden upon others. In many cases these children, on leaving the Special school, are able to undertake simple employments, and are thus rescued from the life of hopelessness and misery which would otherwise have been their portion.

CHAPTER VIII.

THE EVENING CONTINUATION SCHOOL.

By S. E. BRAY, *Inspector of Evening Continuation Schools.*

The Board's work in connection with evening classes, which had been dropped in 1875,[1] was resumed in September, 1882. At that time the Board had been in existence about twelve years, and thought was naturally directed towards those boys and girls who had already passed out of the day schools, beyond the range of the Education Act, and had entered upon the threshold of the labour world with the struggle for livelihood before them. The question arose, what real equipment had they for the battle? Ought not

---

[1] See *ante*, p. 119.

something to be done to enable the poorer youth of a great city to continue and extend, by payment of a small fee, the education which had been imparted in the day school? Ought not those children, whom compulsion had only partially reached, to have an opportunity to repair the defects of their early training? The Board answered these questions in the affirmative, and determined, in the spirit of its motto, *Lux Mihi Laus*, to dispense a little light in the evenings as well as during the day. Accordingly, 83 evening schools, 43 for males and 40 for females, were opened in various parts of London, with the result that over 9,000 students enrolled their names as members. The proportion of males to females was in the ratio of two to one. These evening classes, however, were not the Evening Continuation Schools of to-day. They were purely elementary in character: mere miniature reproductions of the day school, subject almost entirely to the same conditions, having standard distinctions, standard examinations by H.M. Inspector, and restrictive regulations in regard to class and specific subjects of instruction.

In the following session, 1883-84, the Board, in order to encourage the teaching of commercial subjects and of science and art, allowed, at a nominal fee, the use of the school buildings to responsible teachers and others, who might wish to carry on classes in advanced work, especially under the regulations of the Science and Art Department. These advanced classes were entirely of the private adventure order, the Board only exercising over them a slight supervision, and taking no financial responsibility. Thus the higher education in evening work was necessarily left to individual and unofficial effort, which, supported by a demand for the study of science and modern languages, particularly among the younger teachers of London, and assisted by the sessional fees of the students, and substantial grants from the Science and Art Department, made a fairly successful beginning by securing about 1,300 students. It may therefore be considered that from this period evening schools consisted of two sections— viz., the elementary classes under the direct control and management of the Board, and the advanced classes for which the Board was not directly responsible.

The succeeding session was mainly characterised, so far as the elementary classes were concerned, by an increase in the number of students, the allowance of a more liberal staff, the reduction of weekly fees, and the adoption of a low sessional fee; the awarding of prizes for the first time for regularity of attendance, the establishment of French classes, and the encouragement of a closer connection between the elementary and the advanced classes.

In 1885 the Recreative Evening Schools Association was formed. It was a voluntary union of educationists for giving an impetus to evening class enterprise by introducing into the curricula, at their own cost, such subjects of instruction of a semi-recreative character as would the more effectively appeal to those young people who, suffering from physical exhaustion after a heavy day's labour, either had no inclination for evening study, or, having such inclination, desired mental food of an easily digestible nature. The Board welcomed the co-operation of this Association, which supplied the schools with musical instruments and portable apparatus for musical drill, with lanterns and slides to illustrate instruction in geography, history, and popular science, and introduced into the school course vocal music, clay modelling, wood carving, cookery, and domestic economy. Its life was, however, a short one, for after vigorously continuing and extending its work for about ten years, the Association announced its own dissolution, partly on account of lack of funds, but mainly because its mission had been accomplished. The Board took over the Association's apparatus, and from that time more than filled the place which the Association had vacated.

During the next two sessions (1886-88), the classes, both elementary and advanced, were gradually but surely gaining in numbers, strength, and importance, until a decision of the Auditor of the Local Government Board compelled the Board to refuse admission to the elementary classes of all pupils over twenty-one years of age. Although the Board subsequently abandoned its resolution for the exclusion of adults in favour of another motion admitting them at a comparatively high fee, and, later still reverted to its original position by which adults could be admitted as students on exactly the same terms as the younger ones, yet a blow had been struck which visibly affected the classes, diminished their numbers, and retarded their growth. But the Board, a few months afterwards, made a successful attempt to counteract this depression. It appointed nine organisers, whose duty it was to supervise the classes and to advise the Board as to the best methods of obtaining a higher efficiency in the schools. These organisers, otherwise employed during the day, could only devote their evenings to this special work. In addition to this limitation of time, they were further prevented from concentrating their attention on special weaknesses of organisation and teaching by the wide field of their duties. But, nevertheless, the session of 1889-90 showed an increase of four thousand students in the elementary classes alone; instruction in the French language was taken up with renewed vigour; and, for the first time since the year of their birth, the classes displayed such vitality that, instead of closing as usual at Easter, the bulk of them were permitted to extend their courses till July. This has become a recognised practice since that time.

The Education Code of 1890 brought great changes, which were rendered possible by an Act of Parliament[1] which declared that section 3 of the Elementary Education Act (which provided that elementary education should be the principal part of the education given in elementary schools) should not apply to evening schools. The changes in regard to the evening schools were as follows:—

1. Book-keeping, German, shorthand, needlework, and laundry-work were added to the list of grant-earning subjects. Instruction in science and art, manual training, and physical exercises were recognised as part of the curriculum of the classes, though no grants were payable for them from the Education Department; and more latitude was allowed in the teaching of English, geography, elementary science, and cookery.

2. It was no longer necessary for a student to be examined in the elementary subjects (reading, writing, and arithmetic) in order to earn a grant in special subjects of instruction.

---

[1] 53 & 54 Vict. c. 22.

The first change enabled the Board to take the sole responsibility for the management of advanced classes which had been, year by year, steadily growing in importance. The second permitted a student to put his knowledge in a particular subject to the departmental test without going through the drudgery of an examination in the three elementary subjects. These changes were, in part, the cause of an increase of nearly 12,000 students in the session 1890-91, when swimming was, for the first time, specifically encouraged by the Board as a subject of instruction.

There is little of importance to record from that time until 1893, when a separate Government Code was issued for " Evening Continuation Schools," a name which the Board thenceforth adopted in lieu of " Evening Classes." This Code gave managers and teachers greater freedom in the organisation of their schools, allowed students more liberty in regard to the number, and a wider range of choice in regard to the nature of subjects which they might take up. It also recognised the attendance of adult pupils at the evening schools, substituted visits of inspection for annual examinations, and based the grants payable on the total number of hours of instruction instead of on the average attendance and the results of annual examinations.

The era of advanced work had now fully commenced. Science classes were increasing in number and were gradually growing into science schools, and commercial studies were becoming more popular every year. Workshops were being multiplied and utilised in evening education, wood-carving was receiving more encouragement, laundry-work was being taught at centres, and vocal music in mixed classes was taken up with considerable enthusiasm. This was followed in the session 1894-5 by a further extension of the centre system for instruction in history, literature, gymnastics, and citizenship, both the first and the last being illustrated by lantern slides. Specially qualified teachers were appointed for this purpose, most of whom succeeded in awakening an intelligent interest in these subjects.

From this point to the year 1898, the Board, though opening a few additional schools, was mainly content to watch the various innovations it had made, and to consolidate the evening class work. It was not till the session 1898-9 that the fees were abolished; commercial schools (for commercial subjects only) were established, and science and art classes officially consolidated into schools of that name. Further innovations which characterised this session were the teaching of ambulance and home nursing by medical practitioners; the appointment of lecturers to create and foster an appreciation of standard literature; the teaching of mechanical drawing as a stepping stone to machine drawing and building construction, and the institution of an annual competition in dramatic literature among the few classes that took a studious interest in that subject.

In order to note the advance made in the number and character of the schools in seventeen years, the following quotations from the Annual Report of the Seventeenth Session of the Evening Continuation Schools Committee is worth careful consideration:—

" During the whole session 321 schools were open in 248 buildings. Of this number 3 schools were open for adults only (*i.e.*, students over 18 years of age); 3 schools were open for instruction in a science or art subject or subjects; and 10 schools of a special character were opened for the first time :—

> "(*a*) Three schools for special instruction in commercial subjects.
>
> "(*b*) Two schools for special instruction in commercial and science and art subjects.
>
> "(*c*) Five schools for special instruction in science and art subjects.

"The total number of schools, compared with the number open in the previous session, shows an increase of 26 ordinary schools; of 2 schools for adults; of 3 schools [for instruction in science and art subjects]; and of 10 special schools.

"The total number of pupils admitted during the session was as follows :—Ordinary schools, 99,973; schools for adults, 2,295; commercial schools, 2,032; commercial and science and art schools, 1,720; science and art schools and classes, 3,101. Total 109,121 (52,552 male pupils, 41,891 female pupils, and 14,678 pupils attending mixed schools). Of this number, 23,062 were over 21 years of age (as against 7,776 last session), and 8,004 under 14 (as against 11,531 last session). The whole number, compared with that for the previous session, shows an increase of 51,535."

These facts show what a great organisation has grown from a mere germ in the course of a few years. An increase of one hundred thousand students, the number of schools almost quadrupled, centres for special work now counted by the hundred that were formerly not represented at all, specialisation of schools in regard to subjects, differentiation respecting age, the higher education in science, art, commerce, and literature acquiring a robust strength; physical culture extending, domestic subjects becoming increasingly popular—all these only tell a dull story in comparison with the general good that they have brought about, and the humanising forces that have radiated from them towards the heart of struggling London.

The evening schools are now controlled and supervised by two authorities—viz., the Board of Education, which is the central authority for the whole country, and the London School Board. The former gives grants for proficiency out of the Imperial Treasury, and by means of a Code for ordinary schools, and by rules and regulations for the due governance of science and art classes, lays down the conditions under which such grants will be paid. The Board of Education has a large Inspectorial staff, whose duty it is to visit and inspect the schools, report as to efficiency, and recommend what payments shall be made. In regard to ordinary schools, there is no individual examination of students, but in science and art schools there are annual examinations, the results of which to a considerable extent determine whether a higher or a lower grant shall be made.

The School Board appoints local committees of managers, whose duties in regard to evening schools are analogous to those undertaken by managers of day schools. The special duty of superintending the evening schools belongs to the Evening Continuation Schools Committee of the Board, assisted by six sub-Inspectors, who were appointed in 1899 to replace the nine organisers before mentioned.

The evening classes meet in the ordinary buildings of the Board, primarily designed for the accommodation of day-school children. Inconvenience has arisen in connection with evening education on account of the scholars' desks, which, being constructed for children between the ages of 7 and 14, do not quite conform to the physical proportions of those of maturer years. This difficulty has been minimised by the supply, in some cases, of special portable desks, and in others, by the introduction of a new form of dual desk, which better suits the convenience of both day and evening class pupils.

All the schools open in the middle of September, and continue, with short vacations at Christmas and Easter, until Whitsuntide. They then close for the session, unless, for some particular reason, it is desired to keep some of them open till the summer vacation, in order to continue a few special and well-attended classes on one or two evenings per week. In the following autumn they commence practically a new life. Localities change their character so often in regard to their educational requirements, that a curriculum which would be suitable for one year might be in many respects unpopular in the next. Many of the old students return, and the school readily picks up the thread of its existence, and generally pursues its usual course; but, on account of the possibilities of change arising from local circumstances, each evening school is regarded for official purposes as a new school every year.

Most of the teachers engaged in evening schools are employed in a similar capacity during the day. Though this is a gain in many respects, yet there are some disadvantages associated with the practice. Jaded energies on the part of both teachers and taught are distinctly unfavourable conditions for the acquisition of knowledge. A partial remedy for this appears to lie in the engagement of teachers who should only be permitted to work half-time in the Board's day schools.

Nearly all the schools may be said to have an intellectual, a physical, and a social side. Some, however, lack the last; and these, scarcely without a single exception, are the worst attended, the least vital, and the most colourless schools in London. The reason does not lie far away. London has not that cohesion, that dovetailing of municipal and local authority and influence, that characterises well-managed provincial towns and Continental cities. There is more individual and family isolation in London than, perhaps, in any other city in the world. Social life for the poor is practically non-existent except through the instrumentality of local philanthropists, ministers of religion, educational centres, and the various "Settlements" that have sprung up in recent years. The student therefore feels that he needs a recreative side to his existence, and he quite naturally thinks and expects that this should be developed in connection with the institution which has voluntarily undertaken the training of the other sides of his nature. Indeed, many poor hard-working factory girls openly say that some of the happiest hours of their lives have had their source in the Evening Continuation Schools of the Board. It is found that, where the social phase of the school is ignored or neglected, its tendency is to drive the not unreluctant student to seek for recreation in clubs and other places that devote their attention exclusively to it. Hence it is that in most schools a Social Committee exists, which sometimes consists mainly of the students themselves. This Committee organises entertainments in the winter months, and in the spring and summer arranges for cricket, cycling, tennis, or rambling clubs in connection with the school, according to the needs and conveniences of the district. Reading-rooms, too, supplied with newspapers and magazines by the managers and teachers, are gradually being introduced into the schools, and are apparently much appreciated by the students. All the schools are free; stationery and text-books are supplied without cost to the student. No text-books, however, may be removed from the school, but the Board encourages the pupils to purchase their own books, which it supplies at greatly reduced prices. Prizes, mostly in the form of books, have for many years been offered for regularity of attendance; but the conditions for obtaining such prizes have recently been altered and made much more stringent than they formerly were. Certificates are also given for proficiency in certain subjects, especially where such proficiency is easily tested without undergoing a written examination.

Evening school students are encouraged to submit their knowledge to the test of external examining bodies, such as the Society of Arts, the London Chamber of Commerce, and the Civil Service Commission. The number of students who submit to these tests is rapidly increasing. About twelve hundred candidates from the evening classes were examined by the Society of Arts alone during the session of 1899-1900 in French, German, Spanish, Portuguese, book-keeping, and shorthand. The certificates of this Society have a high value with English commercial firms.

Three matters of interest which affect the schools as a whole remain to be noticed— viz., Staffing, Lantern Lectures, and the Centre System. Schools are staffed on the basis of the average attendance for the first four weeks of the previous session, reckoning approximately one assistant for every twenty-five students. The staff must be reduced by one full-time assistant when the average number for each assistant falls below twenty. This does not include the head of the school, who is called the "Responsible Teacher." Provision in excess of the staff allowed by the average attendance of the previous session is made to meet an exceptional influx of students, or any persistent increase of numbers as the session advances.

All evening schools in which a systematic course of instruction in geography, history, or science is adopted are permitted to have the partial or exclusive use of a lantern for purposes of illustration. Lantern lectures on these subjects are exceedingly popular, and tend to create large classes.

The Centre System in evening schools is the outcome of the necessity for special equipment in the teaching of certain subjects, and the limited number of students who desire, or are qualified to receive, instruction in them. Kitchens of spotless cleanliness and cheery brightness, laundries fitted with modern appliances, workshops provided with benches and tools, and gymnasia have been established in certain school buildings, to which the students from the surrounding schools must go, if they desire instruction in the subjects for which these centres were built and equipped. Similar provision has recently been made for *repoussé* metal work and for engineering. In one school, situated in an iron-working district, there is an engineers' shop fitted with all appliances incident to the trade. Motive power for lathes is supplied by a steam engine, and a forge assists the students to make their own tools. These industrial centres will probably grow. As the apprentice system is decaying it is in the highest degree desirable that these workshops should be multiplied—workshops in which the theory and practice of the great industries in the district shall be taught.

Any person who is exempt from the legal obligation to attend a day school may attend an Evening Continuation School. There is no limit of age beyond this restriction. Old and young may, and do come—grey-haired men and women—to get the rudiments of knowledge, or to listen to stirring episodes of history, or stories and lessons drawn from our best literature. There is no test of nationality, for newly arrived Russians, Poles, Germans, French, Spanish, and many others of foreign extraction and birth, are to be found in the East End schools, struggling with praiseworthy zeal, and with the aid of Yiddish speaking teachers, to master the elements of the English tongue.

The ordinary evening schools, which as a rule are open for two hours on three evenings in each week, form the most substantial part of the Board's evening work. Systematised efforts have been made to secure the immediate attendance in these schools of all scholars who have left the day school. For this purpose, certain day schools are considered as contributory to certain evening schools, and the head teachers of the former are required to make a quarterly return of such pupils as are leaving school. This return is sent to the responsible teacher of the evening school, whose duty it is to put himself into communication with the scholars named. Head teachers of the day schools are exhorted to exercise their influence in the same direction.

But grave obstacles must be surmounted before the co-ordination of work between the day and evening schools can be completed. At present there is a great gap between them which the Board is endeavouring to bridge over. In London the distance between the place of labour and the home, the demands for overtime work at certain periods of the year, long hours of work persistently swallowing up the early parts of the evenings, seriously militate against both the commencement and continuity of attendance at the evening school. Difficulties, too, in the way of true co-ordination, arise from the fact that head teachers of day schools are allowed a somewhat free hand in the choice of subjects of instruction, with the inevitable consequence that most of the day schools in a particular district may be found to have made a widely different selection in the higher subjects for the more advanced pupils. This would be immaterial if an evening school existed in connection with every day school; but as this is not so, the attempt at co-ordination so far has not been altogether successful, because success is impossible under existing conditions. Another serious obstacle to individual progress lies in the practical impossibility of home study. Students as a rule do not, probably from physical exhaustion or household inconveniences, show that keen desire for strengthening their knowledge in this manner which might otherwise be expected of them.

The Adult schools are like the ordinary schools as regards curricula, only differing from them in the matter of the age of the students and the mixing of the sexes. The special schools in poor districts are few in number. They have a very limited course of a semi-recreative character, such as would be likely to attract boys and girls of the lowest class. The names of the subjects usually taken in these schools are marked with an asterisk in the list given below. The most popular subjects in these ordinary schools are as follows, their relative popularity being indicated by the order in which they are given :—

1. Shorthand.
2.* Ordinary Arithmetic.
3. Book-keeping.
4. French.
5.* Needlework (including dress-making and cutting-out).
6.* Writing and composition.
7.* Gymnastics.
8. Drill.
9* Swimming and life-saving.
10* Reading and writing (combined,.

This list takes no cognisance of geography, history, literature, or of the subjects taught at centres, such as cookery and woodwork, all of which are very acceptable to the average evening class student.

Special lecturers in English literature have been appointed to give at various central schools interesting descriptions of the works, characters, and lives of the poets, dramatists, novelists, and other standard writers, in order to create and encourage a love of English literature. Some of these lectures have been most successful in drawing large audiences. Classes of 100 students of all ages are not uncommon in this subject. Indeed, in a recent experience of a short course of six lectures, a hall has been filled with an audience exceeding three hundred. These lectures do not represent the ideal method of dealing with the subject as a serious course of study. They merely attempt to describe the chief treasures and to point out where they lie, in order that students may be encouraged to dig and discover them for themselves.

The name " Science and Art School " explains itself. All these schools are well equipped with the appliances and laboratories usually found in similar institutions. They are attended, as a rule, by older and more serious students than those who become members of the ordinary schools. In one institution alone, nearly 1,600 students have been admitted during the present session, consisting mostly of clerks, mechanics, apprentices in skilled trades, and teachers in public elementary schools. The Board has voluntarily put a slight restriction on the scope of the instruction in these schools. It has made a compact with the Technical Education Board of the London County Council, with the view of preventing overlapping, not to teach certain sciences, especially in the advanced stages, which require an exceptionally elaborate equipment for efficient instruction.

The commercial specialities of the evening schools must be briefly dealt with. The Board has set apart ten schools for commercial teaching during the evenings. These buildings are generally situated near main arteries of traffic, to secure easy access to students from other districts. They are staffed with teachers of exceptional qualifications and skill, who receive a higher rate of remuneration than is accorded to those in the ordinary schools. It may be said that the Board has only taken the second step in this new departure, but each one has been productive of most gratifying results—results which appear to show that students have gladly seized the opportunity so long deferred and so much desired.

With these schools open five evenings in the week for about three hours each evening, there is every chance of rapid progress for the really earnest student. In one of these schools during the present session 1,200 students have been admitted, and the great majority of them have shown great regularity in attendance and attention to work.

Modern languages form an important part of the curricula of these schools. It is only of quite recent years that a really rational and effective system of teaching this subject has been adopted—a system mainly based on education by the ear, and on conversational practice by the student. Many systems are still being used in the evening schools, each with its own exclusive name, but all really based on the above-mentioned method. French, German, Spanish and Portuguese are thus taught in these schools.

Some considerable changes will take place next session in the organisation of Evening Continuation Schools—changes that will probably affect more than half the schools of London. Their object is to increase the size of small schools and of small classes. It has, therefore, been decided to transform many existing schools, now used exclusively by males or females, into schools for both sexes, to be supervised by one responsible teacher; and in cases where separate departments for either sex have occupied the same building, and the neighbourhood is not considered too poor or lowly for the impending change, the classes of these separate departments, in the same subjects and grades, will be combined for purposes of instruction under certain limitations. There is no doubt that these arrangements will lead to a more economical administration. It is expected, too, that a higher efficiency will be attained, for numbers give extra energy and vivacity to the teacher, and exact more vitality and sympathy from the taught.

A more liberal staffing for the larger schools; the appointment of further special lecturers to deal with history; an increase in the number of adult and commercial schools; the help of the services of a highly qualified medical practitioner as examiner superintendent of ambulance; the decision of the Board to give an extended course in that subject and to award its own certificates for proficiency; the proposed increase in the number of physical laboratories—these changes, and many others, combined with the prospect of the establishment of a labour bureau, and the strong desire that manifestly exists for the tests of an official examining body appointed by the Board, should give a further impetus to evening class work, and place the schools on a higher plane of efficiency than they have hitherto attained.

There is one essential difference between the day and the evening school, which it is important to always bear in mind, but especially so when contrasting them from the point of view of attendance, efficiency, or the individual application of the student. With the day scholar, attendance is *compulsory*; with the evening student, it is *voluntary*. Reference has already been made to the physical exhaustion often so apparent in the face of the student as he enters the school. Is it any wonder, therefore, that many, after a short struggle, retire from their self-imposed task, and succumb to the demands of the day upon their energies? Others, with more courage and determination, fight a sterner battle, and only accept defeat when "overtime" supervenes, and the necessities for daily bread speak their commands; but return again to the struggle when the burden is uplifted. Some, made of tougher metal still, though delayed by obstacles, and intermittently prevented from attending the lectures, snatch an hour at least from every day for private study. These three classes mainly represent, in fairly equal proportions, the characters of the students attending the Board's evening schools. Some few there are who have an even, pleasant road for their onward journey, but they are not included in this classification.

The duties of teachers in Evening Continuation Schools, especially those of the responsible teacher, are anxiously arduous. Some, of course, perform these duties in a perfunctory manner, and are easily satisfied; but nothing can exceed the energy and devotion of others, who give a high tone to their schools. No labour can be too great, no time too precious, no thought too engrossing, if they only can be made to promote the success and prosperity of their school and the welfare of the students in it.

NOTE

On the Exhibit of the School Board for London at the Paris Exhibition (1900)

in illustration of Part III. of the foregoing Report.

CHAPTER II.—The Ordinary School :—

> Schemes for Teaching various Elementary Subjects (3 cards; 4 packets).
> Scheme for Teaching Reading.
> Scheme for Teaching Writing.
> Eight examples of Children's Work (in a portfolio); one in a frame.
> Map Drawing (in album).
> Album of Photographs of Types of Children and of Children at Work.

CHAPTER III.—Method in Infant Schools :—

> Photographs of Children at Work (in portfolio).

CHAPTER V.—(i.) The Pupil Teachers' School :—

> Eight Photographs of Students at Work, &c. (in portfolio).

CHAPTER VI.—Special Subjects of Instruction :—

> (i.) Science—
>> Notebooks.
>> Scheme of Teaching.
>> Selection of Apparatus.
>
> (ii.) Drawing—
>> Scheme of Free-Arm Drawing (Burrage Grove School).
>> Monochrome from Cast (Colls Road Art Centre).
>> Pencil Drawing from Nature (Montem Street School).
>> Stencils Designed and Cut by Scholars (Sherbrooke Road School).
>> Painting from Objects (Lavender Hill School).
>> Model from Nature and Design Modelled from the same (Sherbrooke Road School).

(iv.) Manual Training—

Board of Examples of Woodwork from a Complete Scheme of Instruction and Various Models; with a portfolio of drawings.

Three Examples of Wood-carving.

Four Examples of Metal-work.

(v.) Cookery—

Three Models of Pocock Street Cookery Centre.

Portfolio of Diagrams.

Photographs.

(vi.) Domestic Economy—

Case of Specimens of Laundry-work.

Photograph of a Centre, &c.

Three Syllabuses of Instruction (framed).

Two Dolls, to illustrate Method of Bandaging.

One Doll, to illustrate Suitable Clothing for Infants.

(vii.) Needlework—

Specimens of Needlework and Knitting from various Standards in Ordinary Schools, and from the Pupil Teachers' Schools.

(viii.) Physical Exercises—

(i.) Album of Photographs of Exercises for Boys' Schools.

(ii.) Album of Photographs of Exercises for Girls' and Infants' Schools.

INDEX.

A.

ABBOTT, Sir William, 8.
Aberdare, Lord, Education Bill of, 20.
Abnormal Child, The, 248.
Absence from School, Percentage of, 39; Method of dealing with, 128.
Address to the Crown, 18.
Adults, Evening Schools for, 264.
Adventure Schools, Statistics of, 42, 52, 82; why popular, 83.
Age, School, maximum, 117; for blind and deaf, 249; of compulsion, 125; of exemption, 126, 130; in Industrial Schools, 139; in Higher Elementary Schools, 164; average, of children in day schools, 169.
Agent, for books, &c., appointed, 114; for shipping boys, 144.
Agreements, with Industrial Schools, 140.
Alderson, Mr., Reports by, 80, 81, 172, 174.
Algebra, 94.
Animals, Lessons on, 191.
Annual statement by Chairman, 49 note 3.
Apparatus, School, 88; Grant for, 89; under Board, 113; proposed charge for, 115; Sub-committee on, 116.
Apprenticing Industrial School Children, 142.
Architects employed to design schools, 68.
Area allowed per child, 68.
Arithmetic, teaching of, 74, 76, 79, 80, 205; Grant for 100; progress in, 175, 176.
Arnold, Matthew, on Ventilation of Schools, 53; on unsuitable reading books, 90; on compulsion, 121, 122.
Art Classes, 216; Rooms, 185.
Attendance, Irregular, 105; at Evening Schools, 119.
—— Order, 129.
Attendances, Grants upon, 79, 160; Registration of, 183.
Audit of Board's Accounts, 156.
"Available" Places, 49.
Average Attendance, 47, 133; Grant on, 160.

B.

BAILEY, Mr., Report by, 174.
—— J. T., on School Planning, 70, 73.
Ballot, Election by, 28.
Barn, The, Model of Early School, 55.
Barton's Chantry, 7.
Bath-street Board School 70.
Bell, Dr., 13, 86.

Ben Jonson School, 64.
Bermondsey Ragged School, 54.
Bible used as Reading book, 77, 88; use of under Board, 97.
Blind, Grants for, 149, 250; Instruction of, 248; Royal Commission on, 249.
Board of Education, Proposed, 17; Created, 23; Minute of on Higher Elementary Schools, 163.
—— of Trade, Administered Science Grants, 18;
Board Schools, Special Grant for Poor, 22; Attendance in, 133.
Boarding-out Committees, 249.
Books, School, 88; Grant for, 89; Grant discontinued, 90; under Board, 113; Sub-Committee on, 114, 116; Proposed Charge for, 115; for Pupil Teachers, 203.
Borrowing Powers, 152.
Boys, Average Attendance of, 137; Teaching of Cookery to, 227; Physical Education of, 237.
Brentwood Industrial School, 142.
British Association, Influence of, on Science Teaching, 211.
British Schools, Design for, 56; Teaching in, 74, 76; Books charged for in, 89; Deficiency of Apparatus in, 90; Desks in, 91.
Brougham, Lord, On Deficiency of School Places, 4; Promotes Legislation, 16, 17; on Adventure Schools, 42, 82; on Voluntary Schools, 50; on Compulsion, 120.
Brunswick Road, Proposed Day Industrial School at, 147.
Brush Work, 216.
Buildings Adapted for Schools, 55, 56.
Butler, John, 8.
Bye-Laws, 122 et seq.; Proposed Postponement of, 125; Enforcement of, 127.

C.

CANDIDATES, 204.
Cardiff, Boys Home at, 145.
Carlton Road Board School, 70.
Carpentry taught in Industrial Schools, 144, 147.
Casual Employment of Children, 132.
Cathedral Schools, 6.
Catholic Schools before Reformation, 5; Poor-School Committee, 15; Teaching in, 78.
Census Figures, 36, 37, 121.
Census Books, Board's, 38.
Centres, For Pupil Teachers, 202; for Cookery Laundry Work, &c., 226 et seq.; for Blind, 248; for Deaf, 251; for Detectives, 254; for Evening Schools, 263.

Certificated Teachers, 87, 107.

Certificates, of Regular Attendance, 180 ; of Merit, 183 ; Honour, *ibid.* ; for Singing, 219.

Chairman, Election of, 29 ; Need not be an Elected Member, 30 ; Receives no Salary, 39 ; Annual Statement by, 49, note 3.

Chantry Commissioners (of Henry VIII.) 7 ; (of Edward VI.) 6, 7, 8.
—— Schools, 7, 8.

Child labour, 120, 122 ; out of school hours, 131, 132.

Children, and the Criminal Law, 138 ; Condition of, in day Industrial Schools, 146 ; in ordinary schools, 179 ; Underfed, 180.

Choir Schools, 6.

Church of England, Schools of, 12, 14.

Circulars "No. 86," 34 ; on Religious Instruction, 100.

City and Guilds of London Institute assists in Manual Instruction, 223.

Classrooms, evolution of, 56, 57 ; Prussian system of 63 ; accommodation of, 68, 70 ; description of, 185.

Class subjects, Grant for, 160 ; Increased teaching of, 167, 182.

Clergy, Benefit of, 6.

Cobbold-road Board School, 70, 72 ; Elevation of, frontispiece.

Code of Education Department for day schools, Revised, 20, 79, 80 ; of 1871, 32 ; scope of, 92 ; Changes in, 160 *et seq.* ; Subjects of instruction in, 182.
—— —— for Evening Continuation Schools, 260.
—— of Regulations for Managers, 110, 181.

Condemned Schools, number of, in 1871, 45.

Conditions of Employment of Children, 129.

Contributions to Industrial Schools, 140.

Commmissions of Henry VIII., 5, 8 ; of Edward VI., 5, 8 ; of Long Parliament, 11 ; Newcastle, 19 ; of 1886, 22 ; on Blind and Deaf, 249.

Committee of Council on Education, 17 ; Plans of, 55 (and see Education Department).
—— on Returns, 36, 40.
—— on Scheme of Education, 92 *et seq*, 117.
—— on Bye-laws, 124.
—— on Industrial Schools, 139.

Commonwealth, The, Education under, 10.

Competitions, Singing, 221 ; in Physical Exercises, 240.

Compton Mews British School, 55.
—— Street Board School, 68.

"Compromise," The, 99 ; Attacked, 100.

Compulsion, 32, 97, 120 *et seq.* ; How far Successful, 133.

Conference, Teachers', 181.

Congregationalists, 14.

Conscience Clause, 97.

Cook, Mr., Reports by, 75.

Cookery, 95 ; Grant for, 161 ; Teaching of, 226, 229.

Corporal Punishment, 180.

Correspondent, Duties of, 110.

Cost per Child, 154.

County Council, Proposed Control of Education by, 22 ; Power of to lend money, 152.

"Covenant," The, 12.

Cripples, Education of, 254.

Cromwell, Gregory, Education of, 5.
—— Oliver, 10.

Cumulative Vote, 28.

Curriculum, 74, 82, 91, 93, 204, 259.

Curtains dividing Classes, 53.

D.

Dames' Schools, 52, 82.

Dartmouth Road, Wesleyan School, 55.

Davenport Hill Boys' Home, 142.

Day Industrial Schools, 141 ; Condition of children in, 146 ; Proposed new, 147.

Deaf, Grants for the, 149 ; Royal Commission on, 249 ; Instruction of, 251.

Defective Children, Grant for, 149 ; Instruction of, 254.

Desks, School, 53, 56, 90 ; Grant for, 91 ; in Board Schools, 113.

Detention in school as a punishment, 184.

Diagrams, 41, 49, 134, 136, 154, 155, 165, 166, 167.

Discipline, Grant for, 161, 162.

"Discretionary" subjects of instruction, 94.

Dissenters, 12, 14, 16.

Distribution of books, 114.

Divisional Committees for enforcement of Bye-laws, 127.

Divisions, School Board, 27.

Domestic Economy, Teaching of, 227.

Drapers' Company assists manual instruction, 223.

Drawing, Grant for, 19 ; Teaching of, 70, 94, 205, 213 ; in Industrial Schools, 147 ; Free-arm, 186, 190, 216.

Drill, 93, 187 ; in Needlework, 235 ; Swedish system of, 236.

Dumb-bells, use of, 241, 245.

E.

Earnings of Children, 121.

Education, before Reformation, 5 ; of girls, 6 ; First legislation for, 8 ; During Commonwealth, 11 ; at Restoration, 12 ; after the Revolution, 12 ; by Societies, 14, 15 ; Effect of, 15 ; Government aid to, 16 ; attempted legislation on, 16-20, 22 ; Legislation on, 20, 22 (note 1), 122, 129, 137, 148, 149, 249, 255, 259 ; Progress of, 159 *et seq.*
—— Department, 18 ; Defines School Board Divisions, 27 ; Influence of, 32 ; and Board's statistics, 33 ; Statistical rule of, 36, 39, 45 ; Inquires into efficiency of schools 43 ; Powers of, 91 ; Approves Bye-laws, 122 ; Rule of, as to Removal of name from school roll, 133 ; Consent of, to Loans, necessary, 152 ; Approves Higher Grade Schools, 193 ; Directress of Needlework under, 234 ; Grant for Blind and Deaf, 250.

Efficient Schools, Number of, in 1870, 45.
Ejected Schoolmasters, 10, 12.
English, Teaching of, 161, 175, 205.
Emigrating Industrial School Children, 142.
Employment of children, 129, 132.
Endowed School Commissioners, 94.
Endowments, before Reformation, 5; during Commonwealth, 11; of Parochial Schools, 12.
Enumerators, 38.
Epileptic children, 151; Education of, 255.
"Essential" subjects of instruction, 94.
Evening Schools, 117 et seq.; Limitations on, 119; Temporary failure of, 119; Made free, 148; Instruction in, 257 et seq.
Evesham, Endowment at, 7.
Ex-Pupil Teachers, 87, 107.
Examinations, for Grant, 74, 80, 161; Abolished, 163; of Scholars, 183, 195, of Pupil Teachers, 203; in Evening Schools, 263.
Examiners in Needlework, 101, 234.
Exemption from attendance at school, 123, 126, 129, 170.
Exemptions, Table of, 130.
Exercises, Physical, 238, 243.
Exhibitions, 94.
Extravagance, Charges of, 96.

F.

FACTORY Acts, 18, 121, 128, 129.
Fee Grant, 149.
Fees, School, 51, 115, 121, 123, 127; Decreased amount received in, 149; Abolished, 150.
Finance, 33, 148 et seq.
Finch, Lady E., and Needlework, 233.
Fines for breaches of Bye-laws, 123, 127.
Fire-drill, 187, 246.
Fitch, Sir Joshua, Report by, 173.
Form "No. 74L," 40.
Forster, Rt. Hon. W. E., introduces Education Bill, 20.
Fox, J. W., Education Bill of, 18.
Franchise, Educational, 20, 121.
Free Education, 149, 170.
Freehand Drawing, 214.
Free-arm Drawing, 186, 190, 216.
French, Teaching of, 102, 205.
Fürsorge Method for Blind, 249.

G.

GALLERIES in schools, 56.
Games, School, 241.
Gardening taught in Industrial Schools, 142.
Garments, Making of, 235.
Geography, Teaching of, 74, 76, 79, 94, 102, 175.
Geometry, Teaching of, 94.
Germany, School Buildings in, 63; Compulsion in, 122.
Gibson, Mr. Milner, Education Bill of, 19.
Gifts, in Kindergarten, 192.

Girls, Early education of, 9; Average attendance of, 137; Taught Domestic Economy, 226 et seq.; Physical Education of, 242.
Girls' Industrial Schools, 145.
Goldsmith-street Day Industrial School, 146.
Gordon Home Industrial School, 145.
Government Aid, 16.
Graded Schools, Plans for, 65; Curriculum in, 93; Condition of, 102.
Grammar, Teaching of, 95, 102, 175.
Grants in Aid of Education, 16, 160; Proposed limitation of, 22; under Revised Code, 79; for Specific Subjects, 81, 160; for Class Subjects, 160; for Training Colleges, 86; for Pupil Teachers, 87; for Books, 89; for Desks, 91; for Evening Schools, 117; for Industrial Schools, 140, 148; for Day Schools, 149, 160; in Lieu of Fees, 149; from Science and Art Department, 151; for Higher Elementary Schools, 163; for Science Teaching, 195, 209; for Needlework, 234; for Blind and Deaf, 250; for Defective Children, 256.
Gray's Yard Ragged School, 54.
Guild Schools, 7.
Gymnastic Apparatus, 241.

H.

HALF-TIMERS, 119, 126, 129, 144, 188.
Halls for schools, 68, 70; Description of, 184.
Harp Alley School, 59; Teaching in, 74.
Health Sub-Committees, 112.
Henry VIII., Influence of, on Education, 5.
Highbury Truant School, 145.
Higher Elementary Schools, 153; Grant for, 163, 196.
Higher Grade Schools, 193.
Hill Street British School, 54.
History, Teaching of, 74, 76, 79, 103, 176, 205.
Hither Green, Proposed Industrial School at, 117.
Holland, School Buildings in, 56.
Home and Colonial Society, 14, 92.
Home Lessons, 185.
Home Office, Declines to appoint Magistrate for Education Cases, 131; Jurisdiction of, over Industrial Schools, 139; Grant from, 148.
Home Secretary, Deputation to, 38.
Honour Certificate, 183.
Hospital Schools, 7.
Hours of attendance at school, 126.
Household economy, 95.
Household management, Teaching of, 227.
Housewifery, 227.
Hullah, John, method of teaching singing 217
Hume, Joseph, Education Bill of, 18.
Huxley, Professor, 92, 99, 211.
Hymns in schools, 99.

I.

INCOME of Board, 148.
Incorrigible truants, 147.

Independent schoolmasters ejected, 12.
Indirect compulsion, 20, 121.
Industrial Schools, 32, 131 *et seq.* ; Classes of children liable to be sent to, 138 ; under voluntary management, 139 ; Day, 141 ; Cost of maintenance in, 148.
Inefficient schools, Number of, in 1871, 45.
Infant schools, First started, 14 ; Plans for, 65 ; Curriculum in, 93 ; Condition of, 102, 105 ; Grant for, 160, 161, 163 ; Method in, 189.
Infants, Low average attendance of, 135, 137 ; Physical education of, 242.
Inspection of schools, 74, 85 ; of Pupil Teachers' schools, 206.
Inspectors of schools, First appointment of, 12 ; of Committee of Council, 74, 85 ; inquire into efficiency of schools, 44 ; Duties of, 85 ; Appointed by Board, 101.
Instructions, Hours of, 184 : Special subjects of, 209 *et seq.*
Instructors, in Singing, 101 ; in Drawing, 215.
Iron Buildings for Temporary Schools, 61.

J.

JEWISH Voluntary Schools Association, 15.
Johnson Street School (Ben Jonson), 64.
Joint Committee on Manual Training, 223.
"Journal, Pupil Teachers'," 205.
Junior Mixed Departments, 70, 178.

K.

KINDERGARTEN, 93, 102, 142, 189, 190, 192, 253.
Knitting, 235.

L.

LABOURERS, Statute of, 8.
Lancaster, Joseph, 13, 86.
Lansdowne, Lord, 18.
Latin, Teaching of, 94, 205.
Laundrywork, 95, 227.
Lawrence, Lord, Elected First Chairman, 30.
Legislation Attempted, 16-20, 22 ; Successful, 20, 24 (note 1), 122, 129, 137, 148, 149, 249, 255, 259.
Libraries, School, 88, 186.
Licensing Out of Industrial School Children, 141, 142, 145, 147.
Lip-reading, for deaf, 252.
Loans, Repayment of, 152.
Log-book, Teachers', 111, 187.
London, Municipal expenditure of, 3 ; Rateable value of, 3, 152 ; Excluded from first education scheme of 1870, 4 ; Early schools in, 15 ; First School Board for, 29 ; Number of school places required in, 36 ; School provision in, 42 ; Efficient and inefficient schools in, 45 ; Increase of child population of, 47 ; Shifting of population in, 49, 135 ; Probable condition of in default of education, 50 ; Compulsion in, 130 ; Rating of, 151.
London Government Act, 1899, 151.
Long Parliament, and Education, 11.

M.

McNAUGHT, W. G., Report on Music, 222.
Magistrate, for hearing summonses, 131.
Maintenance, Order for, 148
———, Cost of, 148.
Managers, Local, 109 *et seq.*
Manual Training, Grant for, 162 ; under School Board, 222.
Manufacturers, Oppose compulsion, 121.
Marlborough, Duke of, Education Bill of, 20.
Mattersey, Endowment at, 8.
Mechanics, Teaching of, 209.
Medals, for punctual attendance, 180.
Melbourne, Lord, establishes Parliamentary Grant, 17.
Mensuration, Teaching of, 94.
Merchant Service, Boys trained for, 144.
Merit Certificate, 183.
Merit Grant, 161.
Method in infant schools, 189.
Metric system, 186.
Milton, Influence of, 11.
Minute, of February 20th, 1840, 55, 56, 57 ; on Higher Elementary Schools, 153, 163.
Mixed method of instruction, 56.
Modelling in clay, 191, 216.
Monitors, 14, 86, 109.
Mulcaster, on Education, 9, 10.
Municipal expenditure of London, 3.
Museum, Educational, 89.
Mutual instruction, System of, 56.

N.

NAAS, Slöyd at, 225.
National Schools, 14 ; School buildings of, 55 ; School plan of, 58 ; Curriculum in, 74 ; Lack of books in, 89 ; Desks in, 90.
Navigation, Proposal to teach, 95.
Needlework, 94 ; Examiner of, appointed, 101, 104 ; Grant for, 161 ; Teaching of, 233.
Newcastle Commission, 13, 19, 33, 51, 53, 77, 78, 83, 87, 90.
Newington Green Day School, 54.
Noel, Hon. Baptist, on Curriculum, 74.
Normal School, Proposal for, 17, 86.
Northumberland (the Protector), 5.
Norton, Lord, Proposal of, 20.
Notices to parents, 128, 129.

O.

OBJECT Lessons, 93, 94, 161.
"Obligatory" subjects, 182.
Old Castle Street Board School, 66.
"Optional" subjects, 182.
Oral method for deaf, 252.
Orchard Street School, 54.
Orchestras, School, 220.
Organisation, Grant for, 161, 162.
Organised Science Schools, 195, 209.
Overbuilding alleged, 96.

P.

PAKINGTON, Sir John, Education Bills of, 19.
Parents, Complaints of, 111 ; oppose compulsion, 120 ; may select school, 126 ; Prosecution of, 129 ; unable to control child, 138 ; liable to contribute to maintenance of child in Industrial School, 147 ; in blind, deaf, or defective boarding institution, 2.
Parliamentary Grant, 17.
Parochial Schools, 12.
Partial exemption from school attendance, 123, 126.
Partitions for classrooms, 55.
Payment of school fee by Board, 123, 127.
—— of Grants on result of examination, 160.
Peek, Mr. Francis, gives prizes for Biblical knowledge, 101.
Penalties, for breach of Bye-laws, 123, 126 ; for illegal employment of children, 129.
Physical training, 92, 143, 237.
Pictures in schools, 184.
Planning of schools, 55, 73 ; Board scheme for, 64.
Plans of schools, 58, 67, 69, 71.
Plants, Lessons on, 190.
Playgrounds, 59, 183.
Police Courts, Enforce compulsion, 131.
Portslade, Proposed Industrial School at, 147.
Prayers in schools, 99.
Precept, Board's, 151.
Presbyterian schoolmasters ejected, 12.
Priest, Duties of, before Reformation, 7, 8.
Principal Grant, 162.
Private Schools, Statistics of, 42, 52.
Privy Council, Committee of, 17 ; approves Bye-laws, 122 ; (and see " Education Department ").
Prizes, 180.
Probationers, 107, 203.
Prosecution of Parents, 128, 129.
Protestantism, Influence of, on education, 9.
Provisors, Statute of, 8.
Prussia, System of classrooms in, 63, 66 ; Compulsion in, 122.
Public Elementary Schools, Statistics of, 42, 52.
Public Works' Loan Commissioners, 152.
Punishments, 180, 184.
Pupil Teachers, 57, 107 ; Scheme for training, 86 ; Salaries of, 108, 202 ; Board's scheme for training, 200.

Q.

QUINQUENNIAL valuation, 152.

R.

RAGGED School Union, 15.
Raikes, Robert, inaugurates Sunday-schools, 13.
Railway arch used as school, 54.
Rate, Amount of, 3 ; Proposed limitation of, 23 ; Growth of, 154.
Rateable value of London, 3, 152.
Ratepayer, Right of, to object to expenditure, 156.
Rating authorities, 151.

Reading, Teaching of, 75, 78, 79, 80 ; Unsuitable books for, 90 ; Grant for, 160 ; Progress in 165, 176.
Reasonable excuses for non-attendance, 123, 126.
Reay, Lord, on unavailable school places, 49.
Recreative Evening Schools Association, 258.
Reed, Sir Charles, on Education in 1874, 159.
Reformation, Influence of, 5.
Reformatory Schools Act, 138.
Registered Teachers, 87.
Registers, School, 111, 133.
Registrar General, and educational returns, 37.
Registration, of punctual attendances, 183.
Remission of school fee, 123, 126 ; of surcharge, 156.
Report, Managers' annual, 112.
Representative Managers, Committee of, 112.
Requisitions, 114, 115 ; for needlework, 234.
Religion, Influence of, on education, 6, 14, 78.
Religious Instruction, 14, 27, 75, 92 ; Conditions of, 97 ; Withdrawal from, 123.
Religious Tract Society, 101.
Restoration, The, Legislation of, 11.
Revised Code, 20, 32, 79 ; Effect of, 80, 81.
Revocation of licence, 141, 142, 145, 147.
Revolution, The, Effect of, 12.
Robson, E. R., on School Planning, 67.
Rogers, Rev. W., 57.
Roll, The school, 133.
Royal Navy, Boys trained for, 144.
Royal Normal College for Blind, 250.
Russell, Lord John (afterwards Earl), Education Bills of, 18, 19 ; Resolutions moved by, 19, 20.

S.

ST. PAUL'S National School, 54.
St. Thomas Charterhouse Schools, 57
Salaries of teachers, 107.
Sample room, 116.
" Scandalous " schoolmasters, 10
Schedules, Visitors', 128.
Scheduling children, 38, 48.
Scholarships, 188, 254.
School, Definition of, 124 ; Parent may select, 126.
School Board for London, Creation of, 21 ; Election of first, 27 ; Election of Chairman of, 29 ; Statistical work of, 33-51 ; Miscalculation of number of children requiring accommodation by, 40, 46, 47 ; Admits miscalculation, 48 ; Classification of schools by, 45 ; Growth of accommodation under, 49 ; School buildings of, 51-73 ; Buildings transferred to, 54 ; Rules for transfers of, 59 ; Decides on immediate erection of twenty schools, 61 ; Erects school on "Prussian" system, 63 ; Scheme for school planning of, 64 ; Curriculum, first scheme of, 91 *et seq.* ; Present curriculum of, Part III., *passim*, Religious instruction under, 97 ; Secular instruction under, 1873, 102 ; Teachers under, 105 ; Managers under, 109 *et seq.* ; Books and apparatus of, 113 *et seq.* ; Evening schools under 116 *et seq* ; 257 *et seq.* ; Compulsion under, 120

et seq. ; Industrial Schools under, 157 *et seq.* ; Finance of, 148 *et seq.* ; Higher Grade Schools under, 193 ; Training of pupil teachers by, 200 ; Training of assistant teachers by, 208 ; Special subjects taught under, 209 *et seq.* ; Teaching of singing under, 217 ; Manual instruction under, 222 ; Cookery under, 226 ; Domestic economy under, 227 ; Teaching of needlework under, 233 ; Physical education under, 237 ; Training of Blind by, 248 ; of Deaf, 251 ; of Defective children, 254 ; Evening Continuation Schools under, 257 *et seq.*

School Boards, no part of original scheme of Education Act, 1870, 21 ; may establish Industrial Schools, 139.

School buildings, 31, 42, 51, 53, 196, 202.

School Fund, The, 151.

Schools, before Reformation, 16 ; after, 10-13 ; Statistics of, 42 ; Plans of, 58, 67, 69, 71 ; Modern plan of, 73 ; Curriculum of earlier, 74 ; Management of, 110 ; Truant and Industrial, 137 *et seq.* ; Ordinary Day, 177 ; "of special difficulty," 188 ; Higher Grade, 193 ; for pupil teachers, 200 ; of science, 209, 261 ; for blind, 248 ; for deaf, 251 ; for defectives, 254.

Schoolmasters, in 17th Century, 10 ; in Adventure Schools, 83 ; in Inspected Schools before 1870, 85 ; under Board, 105 ; Training of, 200 *et seq.*

Science and Art Department, 18, 94.

Science Schools, 118, 195, 210, 258.

Science teaching, in Day Schools, 76, 209 ; in Evening Schools, 261.

Scotland, Casual employment of children in, 133.

Secondary Education, Provision for, 23, 94.

Select Committees on Education, 16, 17.

Senior Mixed Departments, 70, 178.

"Shaftesbury" Training Ship, 143 ; Physical Exercises on, 240.

Shaftesbury, Earl of, 18, 82, 121, 142.

Sharpe, Mr., Reports by, 175, 176.

Shoemaking taught in Industrial Schools, 142, 147.

Shorthand, Teaching of, 95, 265.

Singing, 92 ; Instructor of appointed, 101, 104 ; Grant for, 160, 161 ; Progress of, 176 ; Teaching of, 217.

Shipping Agent at Cardiff, 144.

Sites, Great cost of, 2, 51, 57 ; Necessary steps to secure, 61.

Skipping, as a physical exercise, 245.

Slöyd, Teaching of, 225.

Smith, Right Hon. W. H., on Religious Instruction, 98.

Social Economy, Teaching of, 94.

Societé de Placement et de Secours, 249.

Societies, Educational, for Promoting Christian Knowledge, 12 ; Sunday School Union, 13 ; National, 14, 15 ; British and Foreign School, 14, 15 ; Congregational Board of Education, 14 ; Home and Colonial, 14 ; Wesleyan Educational Committee, 14 ; Ragged School Union, 15 ; Catholic Poor School Committee, 15 ; Jewish Voluntary School Association 15.

Somerset (the Protector), 5.

Southwell, Endowment at, 6.

"Special difficulty," Schools of, 188.

Special subjects of instruction, 209 *et seq.*

Specific subjects, Grant for, 81, 161, 163 ; increased teaching of, 169, 182.

Staff, School, Number of, how determined, 181.

Stainer, Sir John, Report on Music, 222.

Standards, Grouping of children in, 166, 167, 178.

Statistics, 30, 33, 38, 42, 44, 51, 60, 75, 116, 132, 165.

Statistical Committee, 36 ; Reports of (1872), 46 ; (1879) 48 ; recommend immediate erection of twenty schools, 61.

Stencilling taught, 217.

Stokes, Mr., Report by, 174.

Stocktakers (needlework), 234.

Store, 114, 116, 234.

Subdivisional Committees for enforcement of Bye-laws, 127.

Summons for non-attendance at school, 131.

Sunday-schools, 13, 97.

Supervision of Industrial School children, 142.

Surcharge, Auditors', 156.

Swedish Slöyd, 225 ; Drill, 237, 243.

Swimming, Teaching of, 187, 241, 245.

T.

TABLE of Exemptions from School Attendance, 130.

Tailoring taught in Industrial Schools, 142.

Tanner's Hill Day School, 54.

Teachers, Qualifications of, 83, 84 ; Certificated, 87 ; Registered, 87, 88 ; decline to give religious instruction, 100 ; under Board, 105 *et seq.* ; Salaries of, 107 ; in Pupil Teachers' Schools, 203 ; how selected, 111 ; Liberty of, to classify scholars, 178 ; Assistant, 181 ; of Infants, 192 ; Training of, 200 ; in Evening Continuation Schools, 267.

Teaching Staff Sub-Committee, 111.

Telegraphy, Proposal to teach, 95.

Temporary Schools, 60.

"Themis," The, tender to the "Shaftesbury," 144.

Time Table, 97, 184.

"Times," The, on first School Board election, 28, 29.

"Tonic Sol-fa," 218.

Trained Teachers, Inadequate supply of, 105.

Training Colleges, Grant to, 84 ; Proposed, under Board, 106 ; Lack of accommodation in, 106, 207 ; Substitute for, 207.

Transfer of schools, 54, 59 ; Rules for, 59 ; number of, 60.

Treasury, The, first administered grant, 16 ; Grant for Industrial Schools, 148.

Tremenheere, Mr., Report by, 74.

Treasurers of Board, 151.

Trinity, Teaching doctrine of, 100.

Truant Schools, 33, 137 *et seq.*, 145, 147.

U.

UNAVAILABLE school places, 49.

Unavoidable absences, 137.
Underfed Children, 180.
Units of classes, 65.
Upton House Truant School, 145.

V.

" Varied occupations," Grant for, 161.
Ventilation of earlier schools, 53.
Vestries, Opposition of, to Board, 95.
Vice-President of Council of Education appointed, 18 ; Office of abolished, 23.
" Visitors," School Board, 128, 133.
Voluntary agencies in connection with Schools, 112, 188.
Voluntary Schools, Proposed Rate Aid for, 21 ; Special Grant for, 22 ; Unable to overtake deficiency of school places, 50 ; Attendance in, 133.

W.

Wages of children, 121.
Wands, Use of, in physical exercises, 241, 245.
Wesleyan Educational Committee, 14.
Wilhem's method of teaching singing, 217.
Wilmington Mission Hall, 54.
Woodwork, Manual Training in, 225.
Works Committee, 59.
Workshops adapted for schools, 57.
Writing, Teaching of, 75, 79, 80 ; Grant for, 160 ; Progress in, 165.

Y.

Youthful Offenders' Bill, 148.

Z.

Zoological Gardens, Visits to, 191.